Infinite Boundaries

Habent sua fata libelli

Volume One of Early Modern German Studies

Sixteenth Century Essays & Studies, vol. 40
Raymond A. Mentzer, General Editor

Composed by Thomas Jefferson University Press
at Truman State University, Kirksville, Missouri 63501
Cover Art and Title Page by Teresa Wheeler, TSU Designer
Manufactured by Edwards Brothers, Ann Arbor, Michigan
Text is set in Stone Serif 10/13. Display type is Adobe Duc De Berry.

INFINITE
BOUNDARIES
∞

ORDER, DISORDER, *and* REORDER
in EARLY MODERN GERMAN CULTURE

edited by
MAX REINHART

VOLUME 40
SIXTEENTH CENTURY ESSAYS & STUDIES

This book has been brought to publication
with the generous support of Thomas Jefferson University Press
at Truman State University, Kirksville, Missouri
and Frühe Neuzeit Interdisziplinär

LIBRARY OF CONGRESS CATALOGING-IN-PUBLICATION DATA

Infinite boundaries : Order, disorder, and reorder in early modern German culture / edited by Max Reinhart
    p.   cm. — (Sixteenth century essays & studies : v. 40)
    Includes bibliographical references and index
    ISBN 0-940474-43-3 (alk. paper).— ISBN 0-940474-44-1 (pbk. : alk. paper)
    1. Germany—Civilization—16th century. 2. Germany—Civilization—17th century. 3. Germany—Civilization—18th century. 4. Boundaries—Social aspects—Germany—History. I. Reinhart, Max, 1946– . II. Series.
DD65.I54   1998   97–32755
                                                                  CIP

To Klaus Garber,
Director of the Institut für Kulturgeschichte der Frühen Neuzeit
(Osnabrück),
who inspired the founding of FNI

Contents

Contents

Illustrations

ix

Illustrations

Preface

To adapt T. W. Baldwin's memorable simile, this book represents the first fruition of "the egg which Frühe Neuzeit Interdisziplinär laid at the University of Georgia." Baldwin was of course speaking of the implementation at Saint Paul's school around 1512 of the Erasmian curriculum, the "egg" from which Elizabethan pedagogy, so Baldwin, was sprung.[1] As a result of the egg laid in Georgia in 1991, a society for the interdisciplinary study of early modern Germany, Frühe Neuzeit Interdisziplinär (FNI), was able to field its first international conference in April 1995 at Duke University. One hundred participants from the U.S., Canada, Sweden, the Netherlands, and Germany attended; eight disciplines were represented and forty-five papers presented, eighteen of which constitute this first FNI publication. Any further similarity with the egg that Erasmus laid is purely coincidental.

The idea for FNI was inspired by conversations between 1988 and 1990 between the editor and Klaus Garber, recent founder of an interdisciplinary group for early modern European studies at the Universität Osnabrück.[2] Several American scholars began to discuss the possibility of establishing a similar group in the U.S. dedicated to early modern German studies. On 5–6 April 1991 twelve colleagues met in Athens, Georgia, to found "Frühe Neuzeit Interdisziplinär." Brian G. Armstrong, then president of the Sixteenth Century Studies Conference, spoke on "Learned Societies and the Educational Enterprise," in which he made a strong plea on behalf of interdisciplinary research by historians. Over the next several months FNI identified three specific goals: first, develop a national network of colleagues willing to share knowledge and advice on questions relative to their respective disciplines and to explore avenues of cooperation across walls; second, pro-

[1] Thomas Whitfield Baldwin, *William Shakespeare's Small Latine and Lesse Greeke*, 2 vols. (Urbana: University of Illinois Press, 1944), 118.

[2] On 5 December 1996 that group formally became the Institut für Kulturgeschichte der Frühen Neuzeit. It is housed in the Aula des Osnabrücker Schloß.

xi

mote greater representation of early modern German studies at conferences in the U.S.; and third—a long-range goal—seek affiliation with an American library having major holdings pertinent to early modern German studies.

Response to the first two initiatives was immediate and gratifying. Within one year of its announcement FNI could claim about forty members and had become a subgroup of the Sixteenth Century Studies Conference, making it possible to organize regular sessions at the national level in early modern German studies. In the fall of 1993 FNI and Duke University began to explore the option of creating a research center in early modern German studies, with the Perkins Library's special collections at its core; the centerpiece would be the Harold Jantz Collection: ten thousand titles encompassing all aspects of German culture from the late sixteenth century to the early eighteenth century. These initial talks culminated in the 1995 conference "Infinite Boundaries: Separation and Unity in Early Modern German Lands." The event marked the first time early modern German scholars across the field's entire spectrum had convened under a single roof and theme for the purpose of challenging and being challenged by colleagues from outside their own disciplinary boundaries.

The conference organizers' aim in selecting the theme was to provoke a general rethinking about boundary formation and disruption both in the historical *Frühe Neuzeit* as well as in the reception and criticism of early modern Germany. Specific topics were posed in eight disciplinary sections: art history, cultural studies, literature, musicology, political history, religion, science and medicine, and social history. After the meeting the task of selecting the eighteen outstanding essays for publication fell to a distinguished committee of referees: Susan Karant-Nunn (Portland State University), James Van Horn Melton (Emory University), H. C. Erik Midelfort (University of Virginia), Bruce Moran (University of Nevada at Reno), Peter Parshall (Reed College), Thomas Robisheaux (Duke University), Christoph Schweitzer (University of North Carolina), Alexander Silbiger (Duke University), Blake Lee Spahr (University of California at Berkeley), and Merry E. Wiesner (University of Wisconsin at Milwaukee). This difficult assignment was further complicated by the editor's charge to aim for a balance of disciplinary weight among the papers. Inevitably, therefore, a number of excellent studies had to be excluded, though these are, as expected, already finding their way into print elsewhere. The willingness of a number of the judges to provide continued oversight and rec-ommendations for improvement beyond the selection stage has contributed immeasurably to the quality of scholarship found here.

Funding for the conference, including publication subvention, came from a number of sources. Major funding was provided by the Max Kade Foundation and by Duke's Vice Provost for Academic and International Affairs. Other substantial contributions were made by the Josiah Charles Trent Memorial Foundation; the Vice President for Research of the University of Georgia; Perkins Library; the Society for German Renaissance and Baroque Literature; and the Departments of German Studies, History, Music, and Religion at Duke.

Several other individuals deserve recognition for their contribution to the organizational success of the conference, beginning with my extraordinarily able codirector, John L. Sharpe III of the Perkins Library. The conference coordinators are also due special acknowledgment, since they are in fact the people who had responsibility for developing the ideas for the respective disciplinary sections and working collectively to guarantee the program's conceptual coherence. Tom Robisheaux's contributions, from tactical adviser to critical reader, are simply too numerous to enumerate: his fingerprints are everywhere.

A sincere word of appreciation must also go to the dedicated staff of the Sixteenth Century Journal Publishers for their expertise and concern with always "getting it right." Thanks above all to managing editor Robert V. Schnucker and associate editor Paula Presley for the impeccable integrity they have brought to every stage of the publication process.

Finally, I should like to express my deepest respect and thanks to the eighteen authors whose studies are included here. It has been both a challenge and a pleasure to edit writing of such consistently high quality and readability. Furthermore, these contributors not only demonstrate the courage to challenge reigning opinions and methods; they also recognize an obligation to communicate their message to a general scholarly audience with eloquence and clarity. I think that, as a group, these essays exemplify an important new approach among some historians: one that assembles a broad base of explanation (its horizontal dimension) even as it plumbs specialist depths (its vertical dimension).

In conclusion, I very much hope that all of the skillful and hard-working people mentioned above will find their efforts richly rewarded in the pages of this book.

Athens, Georgia

Max Reinhart
President, FNI

Introduction
Interdisciplinarity, Boundary Work, and Early Modern German Studies

Max Reinhart

> *wol regieren sey viel eine größere kunst als die gräntzen erweitern.*
> Julius Zincgref, *Apophthegmata* (1628)

> *The boundary of the field is a stake of struggles.*
> Pierre Bourdieu, "The Field of Cultural Production" (1983)

BOUNDARIES ARE AS IMPERMANENT AS THEY ARE INEVITABLE. No one knows and fears the impermanence of boundaries more than the claim jumper. Individuals, groups, institutions that have shaken, transgressed, appropriated, or otherwise risen upon the ruins of recognized boundaries labor, if in vain, to construct new and this time impregnable defenses against future assaults. Boundaries signify ownership; but ownership stirs rivalries; rivalries provoke conflicts; and conflicts change boundaries. Would it not therefore be an honorable task to neutralize the provocation of boundaries for the sake of peace? Having grown weary by the mid-sixteenth century of the struggle over religiopolitical boundaries, the Germans thought to do just that by legislating permanence to borders: in principle, *cuius regio eius religio* would absolutize borders into discrete units of sovereignty and thereby remove hostile competition. But a century of religious wars followed. A later idea was to co-opt the necessity of boundaries. By twisting the Tacitean-Lipsian doctrine of *prudentia* in the direction of "good government at home," namely, by focusing on domestic issues and ignoring border maintenance, one could perhaps eliminate the expansionist instinct, as an apothegm by the Heidelberg Calvinist Julius Wilhelm Zincgref suggests; but the subsequent sad history of Palatinate borders illustrates the fallacy in that. The fact is, one's boundaries define one's home; ignore them and someone else will be

1

happy to claim them and redefine your home, your field, your self. Besides political turf, boundaries also demarcate all other fields of human interest, whether laws, genres, morality, aesthetics, sexuality, class, race, or meaning in general. Boundaries are also as inevitable as they are impermanent.

The organizers of the first international meeting of Frühe Neuzeit Interdisziplinär in 1995 proposed to investigate the question of boundary formation and change in the early modern German lands for two reasons. First, there was immediate consensus that many prevailing views on early modern German culture had far too narrow an explanatory base, betraying what Bernd Moeller long ago had called "a reductionist dogmatism with respect to historical understanding."[1] Second, there was deep dissatisfaction over the belated entry of early modern German scholars into the arena of interdisciplinarity, which is to say, into the larger intellectual discussion about the production of knowledge. These concerns raised certain key questions: What ideological boundaries distort or inhibit our knowledge of early modern German culture? To what degree can knowledge gained from beyond the walls of specialization enhance or correct our perspectives on disciplinary objects? What are the implications of this kind of innovative knowledge for specialization and disciplinarity? How can we begin to remap knowledge gained in this way to reflect more adequately the historical complexity of early modern Germany and our own relationship to it? The problem of borders and boundaries appeared to be inherent in all of these questions. Although contributors were by no means encouraged to follow a particular methodology (the goal of FNI is not to promote any school of thought but to advance good research in early modern German studies), the topic itself as well as the conference and postconference discussions among the authors and their critical readers received inspiration from the theoretical current known as boundary work.

---

[1]"ein[e] das geschichtliche Verstehen geringschätzend[e] Dogmatik"; see Moeller, "Probleme der Reformationsgeschichtsforschung," *Zeitschrift für Kirchengeschichte* 76 (1965): 251. Moeller was of course criticizing the impoverished historical ground of theological scholarship on the Reformation. Cf. Charles C. Lemert's polemic in favor of wider rather than more specialized knowledge: "The Shallowness of Depth," *Liberal Education* 75, no. 7 (1989): 12–13.

"Boundary work" as a technical term originated in the sciences in the early 1980s as a kind of neo-Diltheyan tool for distinguishing scientific from nonscientific knowledge and has closely accompanied the rise of interdisciplinarity as an ancillary concept.[2] Julie Thompson Klein understands boundary work specifically in its function as boundary crossing and characterizes its relationship to interdisciplinarity as follows: "Two claims about knowledge appear widely today. The first claim is that knowledge is increasingly interdisciplinary.... The second and related claim is that boundary crossing has become a defining characteristic of the age."[3] Its methodological utility owes much to its dynamic topographical metaphors (e.g., joint, break, manifold; intersection, overlap, plural site; migration, remapping, trading zone) and concepts (e.g., patterns of distribution, broad socio-cultural features, shared ideologies or techniques) by contrast with the more static ones of structure. These new metaphors "allow us...to free ourselves to move around the object, and have the object move around us, in a multi-dimensional, multi-directional analysis."[4] As Jonathan Culler explains in *Framing the Sign,* the production of context qua text is itself a corollary to this idea of liberated movement about a site; context too is a product of "interpretive strategies." The sign is constituted within a frame of interpretive practice of one kind or another.[5] This frame is more or less analogous to what Pierre Bourdieu calls the field of cultural production, which is ringed by boundaries under steady attack and thus comprises a site of struggle. Two warring principles emerge from the concept of the field: the heteron-

---

[2]It seems to have been first proposed by Thomas Gieryn, "Boundary-Work and the Demarcation of Science from Non-science: Strains and Interests in Professional Ideologies of Scientists," *American Sociological Review* 48 (1983): 781–95. Interestingly, it was exactly one hundred years earlier (1883) that Wilhelm Dilthey published his monumental anatomy of the human sciences, *Einleitung in die Geisteswissenschaften.* In fairness, I should note that the concepts in boundary work derive in part from two other fields in the early 1980s: modern planning theory (see e.g., R. O. Maxon and I. Mitroff, *Challenging Strategic Planning Assumptions* [New York: Wiley, 1981]) and political border studies (e.g., *Journal of Borderlands Studies,* issued since 1986).

[3]Julie Thompson Klein, *Crossing Boundaries: Knowledge, Disciplinarities, and Interdisciplinarities* (Charlottesville: University Press of Virginia, 1996), 1. Klein's book provides an excellent resume of interdisciplinarity over the past twenty-odd years. As she frames the issue, boundary work represents the latest phase of that history.

[4]Harvey Goldman, "Innovation and Change in the Production of Knowledge," *Social Epistemology* 9, no. 3 (1995): 222.

[5]Jonathan Culler, *Framing the Sign: Criticism and Its Institutions* (Norman: University of Oklahoma Press, 1988), xiv, and passim.

omous principle (supportive of the dominant political sphere) and the autonomous principle (artistic and other relatively independent interests).[6]

Social scientists have been particularly concerned to probe the epistemological value of boundary work for producing innovative knowledge and to evaluate what boundary language can contribute to our understanding of institutional structures.[7] Sometimes identified with a new brand of theoretical pragmatism in American studies,[8] boundary work has also proved useful in program and curricular reform. Jeffrey Peck's influential model (1989), for example, which calls for a more differentiated German studies program, is rich in boundary language: the new interdisciplinary model is to be a "site or strategic location...the in-between-space where the clash of multiple subjectivities can foreground difference" by stimulating reflection on "how such a new object is constituted."[9]

All of the essays in this book seek to correct or avoid or overcome certain trammels and aporias in previous research on early modern German culture. The language of boundary work enters into the critical vocabulary of the respective authors with varying degrees of explicitness. The same may be said of the degree to which classical studies on boundary work (or other studies in related mode) are directly addressed.[10] Few if any of the contributors would characterize themselves primarily as theorists. They are all historians first,

[6]Pierre Bourdieu, "The Field of Cultural Production, or, The Economic World Reversed," trans. Richard Nice, in *The Field of Cultural Production: Essays on Art and Literature,* ed. Randal Johnson (New York: Columbia University Press, 1993), 29–73, esp. 40–43.

[7]*Social Epistemology,* a quarterly journal published by Taylor & Francis in London and New York since 1987, is devoted to the discussion of these problems. See in particular *Boundary Rhetorics and the Work of Interdisciplinarity,* special issue of *Social Epistemology* 9, no. 2 (1995).

[8]Cf. Giles Gunn, *Thinking across the American Grain: Ideology, Intellect and the New Pragmatism* (Chicago: University of Chicago Press, 1992).

[9]Jeffrey Peck, "There's No place Like Home? Remapping the Topography of German Studies," *German Quarterly* 62, no. 2 (1989): 184.

[10]The following short chronological list is highly selective and focuses only on important studies in English that I find to be particulary relevant to boundary work (as opposed to interdisciplinarity in general): Clifford Geertz, "Blurred Genres: The Refiguration of Social Thought," *American Scholar* 42, no. 2 (1980): 165–79; Norbert Elias, Herman Martins, and Richard Whitley, eds., *Scientific Establishments and Hierarchies* (Dordrecht: D. Reidel, 1984); Michel de Certeau, *The Practice of Everyday Life,* trans. Steven F. Rendall (Berkeley: University of California Press, 1984); Steve Woolgar and Dorothy Pawluch, "Ontological Gerrymandering: The Anatomy of Social Problems

which is to say simply that their findings are not made pursuant to any theoretical predetermination but surface from painstaking reading of archival and other primary sources. This is not to disparage theory that has praxis as one of its dialectical components; such theory is able to avoid blinding by the multiplicity of events and can "read" historical culture semantically.[11] This book's challenge to historical norms comes from a strong commitment to investigate questions in terms of the *Sinnkonstruktion* particular to early modern German cultural forms. This principle has been well articulated in the publications of the conference's special guest, Michael Stolleis, a historian of public law with the Max-Planck-Institut für Europäische Rechtsgeschichte in Frankfurt. His synoptic view of the evolution of public law in the empire (chapter 1), always accompanied and encouraged by ever more rarefied peaks of spiritual patriotism, frames a period from about 1500 (the humanist-driven crisis of true national self-discovery) to about 1815 (the sentimentalization of patriotism into a spiritual empire).

Several of the papers here reflect the greater attention paid by historians since the *Annales* to local, or situated, contexts, thus repre-

---

Explanations," *Social Problems* 32, no. 3 (1984): 214–27; J. L. Bintliff and C. F. Gaffney, eds., *Archaeology at the Interface: Studies in Archaeology's Relationships with History, Geography, Biology,and Physical Science* (Oxford: BAR, 1986); Joseph Buttigieg, ed., *Criticism without Boundaries: Directions and Crosscurrents in Postmodern Critical Theory* (Notre Dame, Ind.: University of Notre Dame Press, 1987); Sigma Xi, *Removing the Boundaries: Perspectives on Cross-Disciplinary Research* (New Haven: Sigma Xi, 1988); S. Leigh Star and James R. Griesmer, "Institutional Ecology, 'Translations,' and Boundary Objects," *Social Studies of Science* 19 (1988): 387–420; Tony Becher, *Academic Tribes and Territories: Intellectual Enquiry and the Cultures of Disciplines* (Milton Keynes, U.K.: Society for Research into Higher Education and Open University Press, 1989); Mattei Dogan and Robert Pahre, *Creative Marginality: Innovation at the Intersections of Social Sciences* (Boulder, Colo: Westview Press, 1990); Donald Fisher, "Boundary Work and Science: The Relation between Power and Knowledge," pp. 90–119 in *Theories of Science in Society,* ed. Susan Cozzens and Thomas Gieryn (Bloomington: Indiana University Press, 1990); Stephen Green-blatt and Giles Gunn, eds., *Redrawing the Boundaries: The Transformation of English and American Literary Studies* (New York: Modern Language Association, 1992); Julie Thompson Klein, "Blurring, Cracking, and Crossing: Permeation and the Fracturing of Discipline," *Knowledges: Historical and Critical Studies in Disciplinarity* (Charlottesville: University of Virginia Press, 1993); Linda Salter and Alison Hearn, eds., *Outside the Lines: Issues and Problems in Interdisciplinary Research* (Montreal: McGill-Queens Press, 1996); John Welchman, ed., *Rethinking Borders* (Minneapolis: University of Minnesota Press, 1996).

[11]Cf. Niklas Luhmann, *Gesellschaftsstruktur und Semantik,* 3 vols. (Frankfurt a.M.: Suhrkamp, 1993).

senting a definite shift in concern from long-term structures to a focus on events as a means of elucidating those structures. The discipline of human geography in particular has introduced a way of thinking about history in terms of boundary concepts.[12] Local contexts are more chaotic but can be more satisfying in their complexity than universalist-binary projections (e.g., official versus popular, winners versus losers). Edmund Kern argues (chapter 2) that what is needed to achieve the proper balance between the local and the universal, i.e., accounting for site-specific phenomena while providing a control on the jungle of phenomena is a "continuous migration, but not vacillation, between the two perspectives."[13] The studies by Marc Forster and David Luebke negotiate between such categories in seeking to gain a precise fix on local or regional problems. Forster (chapter 3) finds that clericalism and communalism, traditionally considered to be in opposition, in fact constituted "aspects of the dynamic between popular and official religion that created the successful Catholicism of Southwest Germany." Luebke (chapter 4) penetrates further into communalism to demonstrate, on the basis of one German village, Nöggenschwihl, that the "institution of communalism" itself struggled between competing forces: wealth and power (universal category) was in fact undermined by patriarchal dominance (local category).

In literary studies scholars have recently developed a new understanding for the liminal and interstitial relationships between genres

---

[12]Of special importance, Edward W. Soja, *Postmodern Geographies: The Reassertion of Space in Critical Social Theory* (New York: Verso, 1989); for earlier history, Michael Kearney, "Borders and Boundaries of State and Self at the End of Empire," *Journal of Historical Sociology* 4, no. 1 (1991): 52–74.

[13]I borrow the fitting image of the "jungle of phenomena" from Ludwig Huber, "Editorial," *European Journal of Education* 27, no. 3 (1992): 193–99. Kern's language in this passage resonates with that of Edward Muir, *Microhistory and the Lost Peoples of Europe*, ed. Muir and Guido Ruggiero (Baltimore: Johns Hopkins University Press, 1991) and Carlo Ginzburg, *Cheese and the Worms: The Cosmos of a Sixteenth-Century Miller*, trans. John Tedeschi and Anne Tedeschi (Baltimore: Johns Hopkins University Press, 1980). Muir credits Ginzburg with developing the microhistorical approach and concludes: "Ginzburg uses Menocchio's inquisition trials to trace the reciprocal relationships between popular and elite culture" (x). The four or five "micrological" studies (if they may be so characterized) contained in this book clearly recognize the migratory, reciprocal relationship between the local and the universal and avoid the danger of exclusively focusing on what is marginal or exotic.

and combinatory, or hybrid, types of early modern texts.[14] In his study of the comical treatment of Judas, poetologically out of place in sixteenth-century religious drama, Paul Casey (chapter 5) employs the psychoboundary term of "perversion" to describe a blurring of generic law. This blurring resulted, unexpectedly, "in a more sympathetic and, indeed, more enlightened psychological conception of Christ's betrayer." Much of the innovative knowledge currently being produced through the study of hybrid texts is taking place at the intersection of *verbum* and *pictura,* which is to say, between literature and art. Interestingly, what today is being called intertextuality, or intermediality, is conceptually cognate with the aesthetic principle underlying the Horatian dictum *ut pictura poesis,* by which seventeenth-century poets and painters sought to transcend the simple word/image opposition.[15] Friedrich Polleroß, in his study of the rhetoricity in the buildings of the Viennese Johann Bernhard Fischer von Erlach (chapter 6), extends the connection between word and painting to include architecture. The Jesuits also employed a strategy in architecture to promote religious hegemony at the turn of the seventeenth century. In Jeffrey Chipps Smith's observations on Saint Michael's Church in Munich (chapter 7), architecture is a type of text, "within a distinctly Bavarian context," by which the Jesuits established a powerful identification between the Archangel Michael and Wilhelm V, Duke of Bavaria. In a paper that is highly challenging to disciplinarity, Pia Cuneo (chapter 8) unifies the categories of nationalism, Protestantism, and economics within the frame of a sixteenth-century broadsheet, itself imbedded in the field of community, the enhancement of which constituted the broadsheet's ideological work. Scholarship that recognizes the plurality of the broadsheet's function provides us with "a broader understanding of how Protestant identity was fashioned than scholarship tending to focus exclusively on doctrinal debates."

[14]This new territory is presently being investigated in terms of intertextuality, or intermediality. For the early modern period, see esp. Wilhelm Kühlmann and Wolfgang Neuber, eds., *Intertextualität in der Frühen Neuzeit: Studien zu ihren theoretischen und praktischen Perspektiven* (Frankfurt a.M.: Peter Lang, 1994); in English, the edition by Ingeborg Hoesterey and Ulrich Weisstein, *Intertextuality: German Literature and Visual Art from the Renaissance to the Twentieth Century* (Columbia, S.C.: Camden House, 1993) is also useful.

[15]See Mieke Bal, *Reading "Rembrandt": Beyond the Word-Image Opposition* (Cambridge: Cambridge University Press, 1991).

One of the exciting developments in intermediality concerns the trading zone between literary text and musical gesture. Steven Saunders analyzes the function of *musica politica* at the court of Ferdinand III (chapter 9), where political doctrines were articulated in musical settings to promote the cultural hegemony of Catholic Hapsburgs in a time of crisis. (Compare the Jesuit use of architecture described by Jeffrey Chipps Smith.) Elsewhere in musicological scholarship the boundaries of canon formation have been permeated to let in marginalized forms and groups (e.g., non-Western tonal influences, women composers). As they are drawn into the center of the picture and as historical authorities on early modern aesthetics are reread critically, new areas of research become relevant.[16] Paul Walker's reflections on the question "What Did Burckhardt's Renaissance Sound Like?" (chapter 10) conclude that the limited vision of standard historians of the Renaissance—which owed in part to the inability, until the advent of early music recording in the later twentieth century, to hear how German Renaissance music actually sounded—helps to explain why music "finds itself something of an 'outsider' in general cultural studies of the period." In his art historical study of "Germany's Blind Renaissance" (chapter 11), Christopher Wood is similarly critical of the interpretive tradition and argues for the rehabilitation of monumental art in the German Renaissance. Wood focuses on the boundary image of the "shifting position," one of the seminal features of German art of the period, particularly characteristic of memorial artifacts. The "tactile" gaze swerves and pokes about "from side to side and back to front…from more than one point of view at the same time." Disparaged by Panofsky and Warburg as anti-optical, or gothic, this "blind" art is undergoing a new appreciation in recent criticism as protomodern.

To return to the "outsider" image invoked by Paul Walker, one may contend that boundary work, whose highly mobile metaphors enable the close observation of objects from all angles, should be uniquely suited for rethinking the category of the Other, which much trendy criticism has managed to reduce to a cliché. Hans Hillerbrand, one of the conference's two plenary speakers, places his exposition on "The 'Other' in the Age of the Reformation" (chapter 12) in terms of

[16]See among others, Katherine Bergeron and Philip Bohlman, eds., *Disciplining Music: Musicology and Its Canons* (Chicago: University of Chicago Press, 1992).

how the Other was made visible through social control. He is able thereby to turn the critical mirror back upon the viewer (or reader!) and to bring to light different kinds of the Other, not external to but inside of society. "By embracing the boundary theory of social control, this paper means to call attention not to the stranger, but to the Other, arguing that this Other is a societal construction." Kristin Zapalac's look at the real and symbolic boundaries between Christian and Jewish bread procession rituals in late medieval Regensburg (chapter 13) is a dramatic case study in the societal construction and imposition of boundaries. What began without apparent malice as the establishment of spatially defined zones of religious operation arrived in time at a tragic denouement, "when the city's pious Christian bakers refused to sell bread to the inhabitants of the *Judengasse,* an intersection that culminated in the infamous pogrom of 1519." The idea of social control receives further analysis in Jole Shackelford's paper (chapter 14)—presented in the conference section History of Science and Medicine—on the curious chemistry of an outsider cosmological theory, Paracelsianism, that appealed in equal measure to religious outsiders, i.e., dissenters, and to insiders from the ranks of Danish Lutheran orthodoxy. Were the outsider Paracelsians naturally drawn to dissent, or were they driven there? As for the orthodox insiders, their hope that Paracelsian chemical philosophy would result in the creation of a unified Christian and rational cosmological theory ultimately placed them on the outside of the victorious oligarchical state and church.

Three other essays also explore the problem of outsiders and other marginalized subjects in early modern German culture. All three provide strikingly fresh insights gained by the coupling of exhaustive archival research and intimate familiarity with current criticism. The purpose of Sigrun Haude's analysis (chapter 15) is to test existing assumptions about Anabaptist women. Her question "Were Anabaptist women radical?" is formulated to reveal the inadequacy of a simplistic yes/no, either/or response (compare Ed Kern's critique of binary projections). Evidence collected in the scrutiny of inquisitorial records (local, site-specific) suggests that existing assumptions about Anabaptist women are overstated on some counts (social radicality) and understated on others (religious radicality). Stephen Burnett's archive-based investigation of how and why Hebrew printing was regulated in Germany between 1555 and 1630 (chapter 16) proceeds from an apparent anomaly: on the one hand, Jewish blasphemies were not to be tolerated; on the other, printing of Jewish books flourished in these years. The dichotomy proves illusory, however, when one looks beyond the dogmatic–confessional horizon to two "intellectual developments" that made it possible to control a vigorous Jewish printing industry, viz., a new standard of censorship and the training of Christian Hebraists capable of delivering expert judgments. On the basis of a thorough examination of sixteenth- to eighteenth-century archival records in Augsburg and Vienna, Kathy Stuart (chapter 17) offers a multisited analysis of the figure of the city executioner. The study provides yet another fascinating example of the kaleidoscopic scrolling of meanings occasioned by contextual changes. The quintessential Outsider, the ultimate dishonorable character, the executioner, part quack, part folk hero, was also honored in his inside-out role as medical practitioner and healer.

In one of the most thought-provoking and some ways disturbing essays of the volume (chapter 18), Constantin Fasolt's meditation on the religiopolitical overlap between the fundamental concepts of sovereignty and heresy, we are reminded of the hazards of being blind to certain boundaries. Whether the result of self-interest, self-delusion, or the inevitable erasure of one boundary by another, the danger is that in renaming old realities (e.g., religion, heresy) with new terms (e.g., sovereignty), intellectuals may once again fail to recognize the past in the present and unwittingly misdiagnose what it is that ails us. "It is worth remembering," Fasolt writes, "that there once were narrow circles of medieval professionals who enjoyed a privilege of examining the boundaries of the faith precisely analogous to the privilege enjoyed by their modern successors of examining the boundaries of nature. The age of religious wars began when one of those examinations (intended to deal with indulgences, announced in Wittenberg, composed in Latin) unexpectedly caught the popular imagination. The result was the violent disintegration of a social and political order. It is a sobering thought that something like that could happen to us."

Public Law and Patriotism in the Holy Roman Empire

Michael Stolleis

As everywhere, there was in early modern Germany a local, or regional, and a central patriotism for the whole political entity. Whenever the existence of the empire was threatened, imperial patriotism arose (1521, 1600, 1635, 1689–91, and 1789–1806). Imperial patriotism and the development of national identity are parallel but not identical phenomena. The more the political energy of the empire faded, the more the "juridifaction" of the political structures took place. In the end, politics and law were nearly contradictory factors. Imperial patriotism seems also to represent an attitude of special professions: professors of public law (*Reichspublizisten*) and *consiliarii*, or judges of the imperial courts (*Reichskammergericht* and *Reichshofrat*), etc. They combined imperial patriotism and self-interest. We can therefore speak of a humanistic-intellectual and an anti-Roman Protestant imperial patriotism that counted on the *Reich* for protection. The same attitude is visible in small territories and cities, in anti-Hapsburgian imperial patriotism (1635), and in anti-revolutionary imperial patriotism for the old "gothic constitution."

FIVE YEARS AFTER THE "REUNIFICATION" OF GERMANY the subject of patriotism is once again being discussed. People from the radical right wear buttons that say "Proud to be German" and in doing so make an aggressive claim to "normal" patriotism. Others declare that Germany can now, finally, achieve a balanced degree of national sentiment. Still others declare their allegiance to "constitutional patriotism" and the values of western democracy. Lurking behind all of these debates is the shadow of the Second World War and the Holocaust. Early modern history has also left an impression on what came after it.

To speak about public law and patriotism in the period from Luther's Reformation to the end of the Holy Roman Empire in 1806 is thus also a kind of reflection about contemporary issues. Germans have problems with patriotism. Normally they are "local patriots."

11

They prefer to identify with their immediate environment, with their village or town, countryside, place of origin, linguistic or dialect community. This patriotism with roots, bound above all to a sense of dynastic succession, which the Swabians and the Saxons, the Bavarians and the Friesians, the Prussians, and other Germans from Lower Saxony, Silesia, Mark Brandenburg, East Prussia, Baden, the Allgäu, Franconia, and the Palatinate all display, could not be directly translated into patriotism for the empire. The empire was far away and was, for most people, of an unreal size. And so there was always a double patriotism, one for the homeland and another, more distanced, for the empire. In situations of conflict it was mostly the locally developed loyalty, or, if you will, the provincial patriotism that was the victor over identification with the greater entity of the empire.

This division can also be registered at the linguistic level. The word *Reichspatriotismus*, imperial patriotism, is a technical German term that originated in the eighteenth century. It was used to distinguish that patriotism having as its object the empire. The normal patriot was, in the eighteenth century, a friend of humanity who loved his city and his country and was willing to take action on their behalf. The *patria* included the community, which shared a common language or dialect and could be enveloped by a commonly experienced horizon of landscape and history. Identification with the ruling house contributed to this as well. This can be felt even today in the sixteen states of the Federal Republic of Germany, at least in those states having a strong historical tradition and on which the ruling dynasty left a noticeable mark.

The special mentalities of the older free imperial cities (e.g., Hamburg, Bremen, Lübeck/Frankfurt) or capital cities have led to an ardent (and sometimes ironically practiced) "local patriotism."

Patriotism in Germany is thus a complicated matter. This applies not only to the choice of the object of the sentiment but also to the historical methods with which it can be captured. Here we are dealing with past emotions. The historian can only decipher them when appropriate texts are available. There is certainly no lack of such texts: quite the opposite. The time from the later Middle Ages to the end of the Holy Roman Empire in 1806 produced written and printed matter in such abundance that the problem lies not in searching for suitable texts but rather in making good choices as to which texts should be treated. Particularly with reference to my field of interest, so-called *Reichspublizistik*, the scholarly study of public law, one scholar has correctly noted "that the mountain of books piled up by scholars of public law in the Holy Roman Empire in the seventeenth and the following ink-besmeared ages can hardly be said to be well researched."[1] The decisive methodological question is therefore not one of quantity but rather one of evaluation; the writers of this time who were occupied with the empire were, to a certain extent, imperial patriots by trade. They saw the empire as the vineyard in which they worked and on whose existence they depended, as one can most clearly see in 1806 as the ruins of the empire suddenly could no longer nourish the innumerable imperial jurists, privy councillors, aulic court judges and councillors, professors, lawyers, and diplomats who had been living off of it. To put it another way: sources for imperial patriotism are chock full of self-interest. It is political literature in the broadest sense of the word.

The last prefatory remark to my theme is at the same time a formulation of my first hypothesis. My impression is that "imperial patriotism" in Germany in the early modern period is an indicator of a crisis in the empire. One can, that is, observe critical peaks in the evolution of the phenomenon.

1. The first peak of imperial patriotism is to be found in the transition from the fifteenth to the sixteenth century, that is, during one of the most difficult times of all for the Holy Roman Empire, as imperial reform politics, divisions of belief, and particularistic social and confessional wars shook the empire.

2. The second peak, as I see it, begins in the middle of the Thirty Years' War, around 1635, and continues for a generation into the time of the reign of Louis XIV, which the empire, especially in the Alsace and the Palatinate, felt helpless to resist.[2]

---

[1]Bernd Roeck, "Titelkupfer reichspublizistischer Werke der Barockzeit als historische Quellen," *Archiv für Kulturgeschichte* 65 (1983): 333; cf. Roeck, *Reichssystem und Reichsherkommen: Die Diskussion um die Staatlichkeit des Reiches in der Publizistik des 17. und 18. Jahrhunderts* (Stuttgart: Franz Steiner, 1984). Unless otherwise noted, all translations are my own.

[2]For the period around 1635, see Adam Wandruszka, *Reichspatriotismus und Reichspolitik zur Zeit des Prager Friedens von 1635* (Graz and Cologne: Böhlau, 1955); for the later period, see Kurt von Raumer, *Die Zerstörung der Pfalz von 1689 im Zusammenhang der französischen Rheinpolitik* (1930; reprint, Munich and Berlin: Oldenbourg, 1982).

3. The third peak, finally, comes about at the end of the eighteenth century, as it were in a consciousness of the anachronistic character of the imperial constitution and yielding a certain "Love in the Time of Agony." The explanation for this timing is ready to hand. Those things that are newly acquired or threatened by loss are most violently loved. Enthusiasm for the empire in 1871 is an example of this; the melancholy, devoted attraction exerted by the empire between 1789 and 1806 is another. Crises generate counterenergies; and imperial patriotism at the time of the Holy Roman Empire is a political statement not to be underestimated, since it sought to compensate for the political strength and ability to act that was missing from the empire itself. Given the way the empire was constituted, it remained grave and peaceful, old-fashioned and apolitical. Let the enemy charge the gates and it would be weeks and months until particular interests could be overcome and a decision made for common action. This, moreover, could come about only when imperial patriotic energies could be mobilized.

Still, below the straw fire of imperial patriotism ignited by crisis and war situations, there was also a stable attraction about the empire, which rested less on the level of emotions than on sober political calculation. These too can be considered as part of imperial patriotism. Many of the smaller territories and small territorial lords were natural imperial patriots since, when they considered their powerful neighbors, it was only reasonable that they hold to the empire. The same can be said of the free imperial cities, whose privileges and chances for political development were tied to the empire and for whom the pressure of territorial absolutism could be difficult. And finally there was the confessional imperial patriotism of the Protestants, who held to, and had to hold to, emperor and Imperial Chamber Court in times of need and who could rely upon the empire when it was necessary to shore up the Religious Peace of Augsburg and the Peace of Westphalia.

*   *   *

The various motivations for early modern imperial patriotism have not yet all been named. If we now turn to the first blossomings of this sentiment at the close of the fifteenth and early decades of the sixteenth century, we see imperial patriotism primarily as a movement among intellectuals, springing from the spirit of humanism. The humanists developed an imperial patriotism that emphasized "national" self-discovery based on a classical source: Tacitus' *Germania*. Riding the surge of interest that began late in the fifteenth century, the *Germania* grew into a cult book of national sentiment. Particularly on the upper Rhine, in Basel, Schlettstadt, and Strasbourg, patriotism blossomed in the spirit of Tacitus, connecting, in this brief classical text, the new historical consciousness of the dominion of the emperor and empire with the ethical, brave, natural people of the North.

Conrad Celtis, Heinrich Bebel, Jakob Wimpfeling, Sebastian Brant, and Beatus Rhenanus should be mentioned in this connection—Rhenanus, above all, as the editor of the first complete works of Tacitus.[3] Ulrich von Hutten displays most clearly this mixture of enthusiasm for classical antiquity and learnedness, imperial patriotism, hopes for ecclesiastical reform, and "anti-Roman feelings." His *Arminius* (written ca. 1519) is the sum of the components of this mood, and Hermann the Cherusker is, from that point on, a sure signal that a reader is in the presence of imperial and national longings.[4]

In the imperial patriotism of the humanists of southern Germany something erupted that had been stymied in the long and ultimately unsuccessful efforts to reform the empire and the church in the fifteenth century: the hope for an emperor who, like Arminius or Barbarossa, would bring back "German freedom," unite the nation, and purify the church. Thus people in this critical time placed their hopes

---

[3]See esp. Joseph Knepper, *Nationaler Gedanke und Kaiseridee bei den elsässischen Humanisten: Ein Beitrag zur Geschichte des Deutschtums und der politischen Ideen im Reichslande* (Freiburg i. Br.: Herder, 1898); Helmut Tiedemann, "Tacitus und das Nationalbewusstsein der deutschen Humanisten am Ende des 15. und Anfang des 16. Jahrhunderts" (Ph.D. diss., University of Berlin, 1913); Paul Fritz Joachimsen, "Tacitus im deutschen Humanismus," in *Gesammelte Aufsätze*, vol. 1, ed. Notker Hammerstein (Aalen: Scientia, 1970), 275; Else-Lilly Etter, *Tacitus in der Geistesgeschichte des 16. und 17. Jahrhunderts* (Basel and Stuttgart: Habing & Lichtenhahn, 1966); and Kenneth C. Schellhase, *Tacitus in Renaissance Political Thought* (Chicago: University of Chicago Press, 1976).

[4]Klaus von See, *Deutsche Germanen-Ideologie: Vom Humanismus bis zur Gegenwart* (Frankfurt a.M.: Athenäum-Verlag, 1970); Ludwig Krapf, *Germanenmythus und Reichsideologie* (Tübingen: Niemeyer, 1978).

in the imperial reforms set into motion by Maximilian I;[5] in 1519 they placed their hopes in Emperor Charles V, that "young, noble blood" (Luther), in whom one could have confidence that he would choose the Reformation and in this way lead his whole world empire to renewed faith and doctrine.

The imperial patriotism that flared up in the early years of the century was certainly not directed at the complete empire of Charles V but rather at the Holy Roman Empire with the limiting addition "of the German Nation" (*teutscher Nation*). This limiter had become commonplace during the fifteenth century.[6] It made clear that the empire had neither the aspiration nor the possibility for European domination. The empire had, ultimately, become a spiritual phenomenon, and the patriotism directed to the empire made use of, it is true, the honorable formulations; but it was in point of fact more closely allied with a development of early modern national sentiment. In this sense the humanists cultivated a deeper feeling for their fatherland and raised Tacitus to a national author, praising German ethics and loyalty and condemning national drunkenness as vicious.[7] The humanists availed themselves of Tacitus for historical speculation and contemporized him, especially when, after the outbreak of the Reformation, the matter at hand was the antagonism between German sincerity and alleged Roman deceit.

Imperial patriotism in this confessional variant thus had a notable "anti-Roman feeling," and in its eyes the Antichrist, the great

[5]Heinz Angermeier, *Die Reichsreform 1410–1555: Die Staatsproblematik in Deutschland zwischen Mittelalter und Gegenwart* (Munich: C. H. Beck, 1984); Adolf Laufs, "Reichsreform," in *Handwörterbuch zur Deutschen Rechtsgeschichte*, vol. 4 (Berlin: Erich Schmidt, 1990), 731–39.

[6]Karl Zeumer, *Heiliges römisches Reich deutscher Nation: Eine Studie über den Reichstitel* (Weimar: Böhlau, 1910); Rudolf Smend, "Zur Geschichte der Formel 'Kaiser und Reich' in den letzten Jahrhunderten des Alten Reiches," in *Staatsrechtliche Abhandlungen*, 3d ed. (Berlin: Duncker & Humblot, 1994), 9–18; Notker Hammerstein, "Das Römische am Heiligen Römischen Reich deutscher Nation in der Lehre der Reichs-Publicisten," *Zeitschrift für Rechtsgeschichte* 100 (1983): 119–44, esp. 121–22, and "Das 'Reich' in den Vorstellungen der Zeitgenossen, in *Reichsstädte in Franken*, ed. Rainer Albert Müller (Munich: Bayrische Staatskanzlei, 1987), 44–55.

[7]On the reception of Tacitus' *Germania*, see Manfred Fuhrmann, "Einige Dokumente zur Rezeption der taciteischen 'Germania,'" *Der altsprachliche Unterricht* (1978): 39–49; on Germanic ethics, see See, *Germanen-Ideologie*, n. 5 (see n. 4 above), and Michael Stolleis, ed., epilogue, *Jus Potandi oder Zech-Recht*, 2d ed. (Frankfurt a.M.: Metzner, 1984).

Whore of Babylon, resided in Rome.[8] From this projection of every-thing negative the young and still uncertain self-esteem of the nation drew its strength—in any case, until about 1530, or so long as it appeared that the Reformation would include the whole empire. "German freedom" in this context meant primarily freedom from the Roman yoke, from the clergymen who were seen as exploiters. This demand for freedom was never directed at the emperor or the empire, though it was used against the constriction of multiple lordships at the local level, against fees, unfair taxes, the burden of servitude, and the like.

Emperor and empire remained surrounded, even in the Peasants' War of 1525, by the glory of the unreal, the distant, the untouchable. They were, to a certain extent, points of perspective for all political longings, in which here, for the first time, the mixture of the sacred with concrete desires for reform, so typical for Germany, culminated.[9]

*   *   *

A generation later the fronts had hardened. The so-called Counter-Reformation had come into action with the Council of Trent, the first index of prohibited books had appeared, and those territorial lords who had remained with the old faith pressured urban Protestants in particular, according to the motto *cuius regio eius religio*.[10]

Similarly, in the Lutheran and Reformed camps the orthodox had taken control of the reins. Once a quick expansion of the Reforma-tion could no longer be reckoned with, Protestants began, hedgehog fashion, to hunker down; they sought legal protection in terms of the Peace of Augsburg and by appeal to the Imperial Cameral Court and the Imperial Aulic Court.[11] As Martin Heckel puts it, a "militant con-fessionalization inexorably engulfed intellectual life, the general out-look of the masses, legal thought, and domestic and foreign

[8]Carl Schmitt, *Römischer Katholizismus und politische Form* (1923; reprint of the 2d ed., Stuttgart: Klett-Cotta, 1984); on Schmitt, see Klaus Kröger, *Complexio oppositorum: Über Carl Schmitt*, ed. Helmut Quaritsch (Berlin: Duncker & Humblot, 1988), 159–65.

[9]Dietmar Willoweit, "Von der alten deutschen Freiheit: Zur verfassungsgeschicht-lichen Bedeutung der Tacitus-Rezeption," in *Vom normativen Wandel des Politischen*, ed. E. V. Heyen (Berlin: Duncker & Humblot, 1984), 17–42.

[10]Martin Heckel, *Deutschland im konfessionellen Zeitalter* (Göttingen: Vandenhoeck & Ruprecht, 1983), with further bibliography.

[11]Michael Stolleis, *Reichspublizistik und Policeywissenschaft: 1600–1800*, vol. 1 of *Geschichte des öffentlichen Rechts in Deutschland* (Munich: C. H. Beck, 1988), 155.

politics."[12] Conflicts over religious and, of course, economic issues began to occur with ever greater frequency.[13] Those united by the Augsburg Confession moved visibly into a defensive posture. The more they felt themselves to be under pressure, the more they were inclined to turn confessional issues into national ones and to invest "German freedom" with a double significance.

This is clear, for example, in the Protestant opposition to the curial theses of Cardinal Roberto Bellarmino (1542–1621). In 1589 Bellarmino had renewed the ecclesiastical argument that the classical Roman Empire had been transferred first to the pope and then, under papal agency, to the German emperors.[14] To counter this argument it was asserted either that the *translatio imperii* was carried out by Charles the Great's "own power" or, following Marsilius of Padua, that the Roman people had acclaimed this transfer by popular sovereignty. Both arguments were easily united with the imperial patriotic feelings of the Protestants, but the theoreticians of early absolutism of course found the argument from imperial dominion more appealing than that from popular sovereignty, which they mistrusted.

A second, Protestant, patriotic frontline was erected against Jean Bodin for two reasons. First, the German patriots could accept neither Bodin's understanding of Charles the Great as a French emperor nor his untenable conclusion that the classical Roman Empire had been transferred to the French. Second, Bodin's thesis that the empire was an aristocracy, with the emperor *primus inter pares*, caused no little excitement, for the thesis contradicted not only the generally accepted political semantics of the empire but also dangerously weakened the emperor's protective position, which was of such great importance to the Protestants. Particularly the smaller members of the empire relied upon this protection, as they depended on the Aulic Court, dominated by the emperor, when issues were to be decided involving the interpretation of the Religious Peace of Augsburg.

In the first two decades of the seventeenth century the psychic temperature of the nation soared. The imperial constitution was blocked. In 1601 a deputation responsible for the Imperial Cameral

---

[12]Heckel, *Deutschland*, 88 (see n. 10 above).

[13]The conflicts in the earldoms of the Wetterau, in Aachen, and Magdeburg are well known, as are the "Cologne War" of 1582, the so-called Strassburg Canon Conflict, the conflict of the four monasteries ("Vierklöster"), and the conflict in Donauwörth.

[14]Werner Goez, *Translatio Imperii* (Tübingen: J. C. B. Mohr, 1958), 305–24.

Court ceased its activities. In 1608 the Imperial Diet was for the first time dissolved without a formal decision of adjournment, and the Union and the League came into being as mutually threatening military organizations. In 1613 the Imperial Diet finally collapsed. The war against the Turks (1593–1609) was an external threat; nor did domestic concerns fare any better, given the tendency to establish limited military factions and then allow artificial threats to prolong any and all negotiations.

These circumstances led to the establishment of public law and the *Reichspublizistik* so closely connected to it; this occurred moreover solely on the Protestant side.[15] Beginning in 1600 the university at Altdorf offered the first lectures and tutorials *ex iure publico*; in Jena about the same time the first systematically prepared textbook collection of public legal writings was produced; in 1607 the first chair in public law to be so named was established in Giessen. Within a few years the academic guild was of one mind that a new discipline had been created or had been reborn: the ice was broken. "Through the grace of God," wrote Johannes Limnaeus in 1629, "public law is finally getting the respect due it."[16] The methodological principle of the new discipline was that imperial constitutional law must be mined from "native" legal sources, not, that is, from Roman law, but from the fundamental laws of the empire. Just as the empire is no longer classical or Roman but limited to the German nation, so Roman law cannot set the standards for the imperial constitution. There is, according to the opinions of two experts regarding the conflict in Donauwörth, "a remarkable difference between the classical Roman and the current German emperor, and therefore the imperial constitution cannot be drawn out of Roman law, or Bartolus and Baldus; rather, much more must derive from the law common in the empire and thus resting on the old constitutions, on the Golden Bull, the imperial and royal capitals of the decisions of the Imperial Diet, and their constitutions."[17] Inherent in this soon dominant method-

---

[15]Michael Stolleis, "Reformation und öffentliches Recht in Deutschland," *Der Staat* 24 (1985): 51–74.

[16]"nunc vero singulari Dei gratia jus publicum majestati suae redditum, in dies splendorum debitum recepit." Johannes Limnaeus, *Iuris publici Imperii Romano-Germanici libri IX* (Strasbourg: Paul Ledertz, 1629), 1: dedication.

[17]"… dass ein mercklicher Underscheid, zwischen dem alten lateinischen, und jetzigen teutschen Kaysern seye, unnd dass demnach ipsa totius reipublicae Germanicae forma nicht auss den Lateinischen Rechten, oder Bartolo und Baldo …, sondern viel

ological maxim was an imperial patriotic element: the retreat from the universal positions of the Middle Ages to an ideal of national identity as manifested in a particular historically developed constitution.

This position was shared in principle by all those who wrote *Reichspublizistik*, even though deep conflicts remained as to who in the empire possessed sovereignty and where the empire belonged in the old Aristotelian catalogue of forms of governance. Thus Dietrich Reinkingk, the Lutheran representative of the "imperial" position, was as much an imperial patriot as Limnaeus, who represented the position of the imperial estates, or the professors from Giessen and Marburg, Hermann Vultejus and Gottfried Antonius respectively, who debated the same issue.[18] They were all imperial patriots in that they all hoped to overcome the constitutional crisis and to achieve a balance between emperor and empire; all likewise proved themselves to be *kaisertreu*, loyal to the emperor, with the notable exception of the scandalous Hippolithus à Lapide.[19] But even he, who was audacious enough to champion the extermination of the Hapsburgs, was in no way an enemy of the emperor; he was simply entranced by the conception of government that had been realized in England after the Glorious Revolution of 1688.

*   *   *

In 1618 war between Bohemia and the Palatinate broke out, initially tearing apart the Electoral Palatinate. It then developed via the war between Denmark and Lower Saxony (1623–27) from a limited religious war into a European struggle for power among the major com-

---

mehr auss des Reiches ublichem herkommen und dahero rhürenden alten Verfassungen, auss der Guldin Bull, Kaysern und Königlichen Capitulationen, des Reiches Abschieden und Constitutiones zunehmen." *Beständige Informatio facti & juris wie es mit dem am Keiserlichen Hof wider des H. Römischen Reichs Statt Donawerth aussgegangenen Processen/ und darauff vorgenommenen Execution/ aigentlich und im Grund der Wahrheit beschaffen seye* (s. l., 1611), 123; cf. Stolleis, *Geschichte des öffentlichen Rechts*, 1:148–49, with further bibliography (see n. 11 above).

[18]Christoph Link, "Dietrich Reinkingk," in *Staatsdenker in der frühen Neuzeit*, 3d ed., ed. Michael Stolleis (Munich: C. H. Beck, 1995), 78–99, with further bibliography; Rudolf Hoke, "Johannes Limnaeus," ibid., 100–17.

[19]Hippolithus à Lapide (= Philipp Bogislaus von Chemnitz), *Dissertatio de ratione status in Imperio nostro Romano-Germanico* (s. l. 1640); cf. Rudolf Hoke, "Hippolithus à Lapide," in *Staatsdenker*, 118–27 (see n. 18 above).

batants on German soil. What began as a Protestant patriotic mood of awakening combined political ambitions with a longing for the "German freedoms" into an unusual brew.[20] Several significant cultural events occurred in precisely these years: the founding near Weimar in 1617 of the famous intellectual sodality known as the Fruchtbringende Gesellschaft (Fruitbearing Society); the founding in Strassbourg in 1633 of the Aufrichtige Tannengesellschaft (Upright Society of the Pines); and the publication in 1624 of Martin Opitz's momentous *Buch von der Deutschen Poeterey*. In general, there took place in those years a broadly patriotic movement for purity of the German language and for reflection on the basic aspects and forms of German literature.[21]

The course of the "Great War" was decisive for the development of imperial patriotism, which had grown markedly since 1600. Once the confessional energies had exhausted themselves and European power politics were plainly in evidence, contemporaries punningly described this development as a shift from *amor religionis* to *amor regionis*, clearly recognizing the threat to the empire inherent in it. The battle of Nördlingen in the fall of 1634 proved to be the actual turning point. The emperor emerged from this battle so strengthened that he dared to establish a special peace with the strong Lutheran princes, that is, with Saxony. The Saxon elector explained his motivations for accepting this offer, beginning as follows: "The glorious, holy, and brilliant edifice of the empire was once a thing of wonder to all but its enemies, who reacted with horror and fear when they observed the unity and good harmony in which it existed." Now, however, the elector continued, because of the intervention of "foreign potentates,"

> [the empire is] pitifully deformed, miserably devastated, and destroyed...such that the healing fundamental laws and other praiseworthy, considerate ordinances, which had bound up the

---

[20]Julius Wilhelm Zincgref, *Quodlibetischer Weltkefig* (1623); on the opposite polemics of Gaspare Scioppio, see Stolleis, *Geschichte des öffentlichen Rechts*, 1:194, n. 408 (see n. 11 above).

[21]A synopsis in Christoph Stoll, *Sprachgesellschaften im Deutschland des 17. Jahrhunderts* (Munich: List, 1973). For recent developments in research on the literary sodalities, see studies esp. by Martin Bircher, Klaus Conermann, Klaus Garber, Ferdinand van Ingen, and Wilhelm Kühlmann.

empire in love and unity, peace and quiet, right and justice, are shaken and confused.[22]

The Peace of Prague, concluded in 1635 and accepted by most of the imperial estates, strengthened the position of the emperor and could have provided a balanced foundation for a new order in the empire. It tied together the traditional imperial-patriotic goal of "conserving the commonwealth of our beloved fatherland of the German nation"[23] with the rational point of view of a raison d'état for the empire (*ratio status imperii*).[24] The Prague treaty allowed the Hapsburgs to pursue their goals and in so doing to utilize the energies of imperial patriotism. In this situation the emperor was the genuine imperial patriot in the sense that he created peace and prevented the intervention of foreign powers (Sweden and France) with the ardor of a true German emperor.

The public reaction of the writers of *Reichspublizistik* to the Peace of Prague was extraordinarily lively and varied. For some the treaty represented the fervently awaited end to suffering, the hard-won compromise between the confessional camps, the triumph of "reason" in the face of opposition from the theologians. For others it was exactly the opposite, namely, a scarcely veiled victory for the Roman Catholic party and a serious threat to the empire from imperial absolutism. Thus an anonymous broadsheet from 1636 urged the "Saving of the old German Freedom from the Destructive and Dishonorable Un-peace of the Peace of Prague."[25] Both parties used imperial-patriotic arguments to support their positions, and both invoked the well-being of the "beloved fatherland," thus demonstrating once more what power imperial patriotism had already won in this early phase.

---

[22]"… das herrliche heilige und helleuchtende Reichsgebäu, welches vormals männiglich zur Verwunderung, den Feinden aber, wann es in seiner Einigkeit und gueten Harmonie sich befunden zum Schreckhen und Forcht gewesen … [ist] erbärmlich deformiert … kläglich devastiert und zerstärt, … die heilsame Grundgesetze und andere löbliche, bedachte Ordnungen, wodurch man gegeneinander in Liebe und Einigkeit, Friede und Ruhe, Recht und Gerechtigkeit verbunden, zerrüttet … und uber einen Haufen geworfen." Quoted in Wandruszka, *Reichspatriotismus*, 40–41 (see n. 2 above).

[23]"Conservation Rei publicae unsers lieben Vaterlands deutscher Nation," ibid., 42.

[24]Stolleis, *Geschichte des öffentlichen Rechts*, 1:203 (see n. 11 above).

[25]*Vindiciae secundum libertatem Germaniae contra Pacificationem Pragensem das ist: Rettung der alten Teutschen Freyheit, gegen dem schadtlichen und schändtlichen Pragerischen Friedens Unfrieden* (Stralsund, 1636).

No one could afford to ignore a patriotic argument. With increasing frequency one finds in broadsheets the concluding formula, "from a true patriot"; in others, the authors chose pseudonyms such as "Teutschfreund" (Friend of the Germans), "Friedlieb" (Lover of Peace), "Wahrmund" (True Mouth), "Teuteburg" (Folksburg), or "Sincerus" as a means of expressing German sincerity, love of peace, freedom, and fatherland.

The same picture emerges in the Baroque literature at the time of the war. Martin Opitz and Andreas Gryphius, Johann Michael Moscherosch, Georg Philipp Harsdörffer, Johann Rist, Johann Klaj, Philipp von Zesen, Daniel Casper von Lohenstein, Justus Georg Schottel, Friedrich von Logau, and others were by and large "imperial patriots" in the sense that they wished for the end to a war hostile to culture, for the preservation of the empire, and for unity between the emperor and the estates. Furthermore, with varying intensity, they were active in movements to purify the language, and they stormed against the *alamodisches Wesen* in customs, clothing, and language.[26] Thus in 1643 in Hamburg another literary sodality, the Deutschsinnige Genossenschaft (Germanophile Society) was founded; in 1644 a book by Johann Heinrich Schill appeared with the flowery title *Der Teutschen Sprache Ehren-Krantz* (The Laureate Wreath of the German Language); and also in 1647 Carl Melchior Grotnitz von Grodnow published his state textbook *Teutsch gekleideter Regiments-Rath* (Instruction Manual for German Government).[27] One could add any number of similar examples in which German patriotism was expressed, but there is no need to do so. The tendency of literature and *Reichspublizistik* to run parallel to each other, the overemphasis on imperial-patriotic elements in the confessional conflict, and the relative clarity of the writings of imperial patriots: all these characteristics are commonly recognized and are not our subject here.

A phase of exhaustion and concentration on rebuilding the territories followed the Peace of Westphalia (1648). The continued existence of the empire had been assured and the position of the imperial

---

[26]Fritz Schramm, *Schlagworte der Alamodezeit*, vol. 15 of *Zeitschrift für deutsche Wortforschung,* supplement (Strasbourg: Karl J. Trübner, 1914); Wilhelm Frenzen, "Germanienbild und Patriotismus im Zeitalter des deutschen Barocks," *Vierteljahresschrift für Literatur- und Geistesgeschichte* 15 (1937): 203–19.

[27]Johann Heinrich Schill, *Der Teutschen Sprache Ehren-Krantz* (Strasbourg, 1644; Carl Melchior Grotnitz von Grodnow, *Teutsch gekleideter Regiments-Rath* (Stettin, 1647).

estates confirmed; the territories could progress confidently into "modern states," the development on which the empire had run aground.[28]

This phase of peace in the empire did not last long, however. France soon began its attempts at expansion, first with a move against Holland (1672), then with the subjugation of ten Alsatian imperial cities and the occupation of Trier in 1673. In 1674 the empire declared war against France. This war did not run smoothly for the empire, notwithstanding the liberation of Trier in the fall of 1675. The empire was thwarted at the Peace of Nijmegen (1678–79) and threatened in the East by the Turks; Spain was all but eliminated as a power player. France exploited these conditions in demanding the (legally untenable) so-called reunion in Alsace, in Lorraine, and in the Palatinate. Trier was encircled by French territories, and in 1681 Strasbourg came under military occupation.

These events released a wave of imperial-patriotic indignation that was greater than anything seen heretofore.[29] It was now clearer even than at the Peace of Prague that the princes would have to learn to calculate public opinion into their power equations. Louis XIV was made into the archenemy of the empire. Johann Joachim Becher, for example, a mercantilist and *Projektemacher* from the Palatinate, wrote a tract anonymously in 1675 entitled *Machiavellus gallicus, that is, Transformation and Reincarnation of Machiavelli's Soul in Louis XIV, King of France.*[30] Many others wrote similar works in the heady atmosphere of the illegal occupation.[31]

This patriotism reached its peak as French troops in the so-called Palatinate War of Succession (1688–97) used scorched-earth tactics of setting fire to cities and villages and destroying fruit and wine cultiva-

---

[28]Stolleis, *Geschichte des öffentlichen Rechts*, 1:225–30 (see n. 11 above).

[29]Karl Hölscher, *Die öffentliche Meinung über den Fall Strassburgs 1681–84* (Munich: Chr. Kaiser, 1896); Raumer, *Zerstörung der Pfalz*, with further bibliography (see n. 2 above).

[30]*Machiavellus Gallicus: Das ist Verwandlung und Versetzung der Seele des Machiavelli in Ludovicum XIV. dem König von Frankreich, vorgestellet durch hundert politische frantzösische axiomata... Beschreiben durch einen Ehrlichen Teutschen* (675), 1.

[31]Otto Brunner, *Johann Joachim Bechers Entwurf einer "Oeconomia ruralis et domestica,"* Sitzungsbericht der österreichischen Akademie der Wissenschaften, 226, no. 3 (Vienna: Rohrer, 1951); Herbert Hassinger, *Johann Joachim Becher: Ein Beitrag zur Geschichte des Merkantilismus* (Vienna: Holzhausen, 1951); Michael Stolleis, *Pecunia Nervus Rerum: Zur Staatsfinanzierung in der frühen Neuzeit* (Frankfurt a.M.: Klostermann, 1983), 96.

tion, thereby making the name of their commanding officer, General Melac, a symbol of sheer evil.[32] As late as this century in the Palatinate butchers' dogs were named "Melac" in memory of this event.

In order to understand the powerful growth of imperial patriotism at the end of the seventeenth century one must couple a second, positive experience with the negative one, which had a strong nationalistic impetus. This second experience was the feeling of relief that accompanied the freeing of Vienna from the Turks in 1683. *Türkenmode* was one by-product of the success of this liberation. Another was the renewed rise of the Austrian Hapsburgs as a European superpower, accompanied by an exceptionally clever and effective form of emperor propaganda and corresponding "imperial style." The new imperial style is reflected in the reigns of Leopold I (1658–1705), Josef I (1705–11), and especially Charles VI (1711–40).[33] Thus the jurist Friedrich von Logau, a Hapsburg subject, wrote in verse in 1654:

> *Österreich.*
> Österreich heisst Osten Reich,
> denn hierauss entsteht das Licht.
> Darauff das gantze deutsche Reich
> Wesen, Wohlfahrt, Wachstum richt.[34]

> [*Austria*
> Austria means eastern empire,
> For the light comes from here.
> Upon which the whole German Empire
> Establishes its essence, welfare, growth.]

For the humanities the period 1683–1740 is often referred to as one of "imperial euphoria,"[35] and indeed the growth in Hapsburg political power is marked by a corresponding glorification of emperor and empire that was hardly imaginable in 1648. Even accounting for the

[32]Friedrich Kleyser, *Der Flugschriftenkampf gegen Ludwig XIV. zur Zeit des Pfälzischen Krieges* (1935; reprint, Vaduz: Kraus Reprint, 1965); Raumer, *Zerstörung der Pfalz* (see n. 2 above).

[33]Karl Otmar Frh. von Aretin and Notker Hammerstein, "Reich," in *Geschichtliche Grundbegriffe* (Stuttgart: Ernst Klett, 1984), 5:428.

[34]Friedrich von Logau, *Sinngedichte*, ed. Ernst-Peter Wieckenberg (Stuttgart: Philipp Reclam, 1984), 212.

[35]Von Aretin, "Reich," 5:475 (see n. 33 above).

familiar pompous indulgences of the High Baroque, which traded heavily in rhetorical hyperbole, the rising tide of the movement cannot be overlooked.

In the last years of Charles VI's reign the tide of Hapsburg success began to recede and with it the radiant aura of imperial patriotism. Between 1733 and 1735 nearly all of Italy was lost and Lorraine became French. In 1739, with the Peace of Belgrade, Austria suffered the humiliating loss of the Balkans.

The year 1740, with the change in rulers in Austria, Prussia, and Russia, clearly marks the beginning of a new period. The Austrian-Prussian dualism takes the stage and will remain until 1866. With its three Silesian Wars (1740–45), Prussia won for itself a position among the European superpowers and began finally to pursue a political line essentially independent of the empire. In those cases in which Prussian politics appeared to be friendly to the empire, as in the War of Bavarian Succession (1778–79), the so-called Potato War, or the intervention against Carl Theodor's exchange project with the founding of the Union of Princes (*Fürstenbund*) in 1785, their anti-Hapsburg, pro-Prussian patriotic motivations are unmistakable.[36] To take one example: the Union of Princes had as its goal that "the imperial, German system, which had been cautiously and painstakingly erected hundreds of years ago and protected at sacrificial cost in goods and blood,...might be preserved in its unimpeachable essence and that it might be dealt with in a way that is consonant with its constitution."[37] In fact, the motivation was far less to preserve the empire than to restrain Austria, which, once relieved of the difficulties of governing the independent-minded Hapsburgian Netherlands,

---

[36]Ernst Rudolf Huber, "Der preussische Staatspatriotismus im Zeitalter Friedrichs des Grossen," *Zeitschrift für die gesamte Staatswissenschaft* 103 (1943): 430–68; see further Anna Lübbe, "Die deutsche Verfassungsgeschichtsschreibung unter dem Einfluß der nationalsozialistischen Machtergreifung," in *Rechtsgeschichte im Nationalsozialismus*, ed. Michael Stolleis and Dieter Simon (Tübingen: J.C.B. Mohr, 1989), 63–78.

[37]"... dass das mit besonderer Sorgfalt und Mühe seit Jahrhunderten und mit so mannigfaltigen grossen Aufopferungen von Gut und Blut bisher erhaltene teutsche Reichs-System...in seinem ungekränktem Wesen beständig aufrecht erhalten, und auf eine constitutionsmässige Weise gehandhabt werden möge." "Assoziationsvertrag zwischen den Kurhöfen Sachsen, Brandenburg und Braunschweig-Lüneburg," in *Quellen zum Verfassungsorganismus des Heiligen Römischen Reiches Deutscher Nation 1495–1815*, ed. Hanns Hubert Hofmann (Darmstadt: Wissenschaftliche Buchgesellschaft, 1976), 62:315–21.

had expanded its German holdings enormously with its takeover of Bavaria.

In the decades between 1740 and 1806 the empire's ability to exist as a "third power" between Austria and Prussia was curtailed. Nevertheless, even as the empire lost in political substance it was able to preserve and even improve its legal mechanisms. Scholars of public law documented these changes with no small amount of display, interpreting and communicating them to the university community. Annual increases in the number of trials exerted a considerable burden on the Imperial Cameral Court and the Imperial Aulic Council.[38] The greater the legal intricacies and scholarliness, the less political room to maneuver. Goethe's remark about the German Empire is thus understandable: "Where the scholarly begins, the political ends."[39]

Corresponding to my initial hypothesis that "imperial patriotism" represents a special emotional identification with the empire, stimulated by crises, we note that after the middle of the eighteenth century a new variety of this sentiment began to arise.[40] It is by no means an easy task to distinguish this stream from the contemporary "national" sentiment. Along with the traditional devotion to the empire, a new "national spirit" is discernible among Germans, one that will develop in a number of directions.

First, in the search for a national context a distinctly antiparticularistic direction becomes visible, characterized by a craving for inclusive unity and a desire to overcome the small-state particularism for which Germany was notorious. The jurists played their part in this, especially those who admitted Montesquieu into their canon and applied to Germany his doctrine of varying national conditions for legislation.[41] Among them were Johann Heinrich Gottlob von Justi

---

[38]Friedrich Hertz, "Die Rechtsprechung der höchsten Reichsgerichte im römisch-deutschen Reich und ihre politische Bedeutung," *Mitteilungen des Instituts für österreichische Geschichtsforschung* 69 (1961): 331–58.

[39]"Das Deutsche Reich: Deutschland? Aber wo liegt es? Ich weiß das Land nicht zu finden. Wo das gelehrte beginnt, hört das politische auf." *Xenien von Goethe und Schiller*, in Johann Wolfgang von Goethe, *Gedichte in zeitlicher Folge*, ed. Heinz Nicolai, 5th ed. (Frankfurt a.M.: Insel, 1986), 372.

[40]Wolfgang Zorn, "Reichs- und Freiheitsgedanken in der Publizistik des ausgehenden 18. Jahrhunderts (1763–1792)," in *Darstellungen und Quellen zur Geschichte der deutschen Einheitsbewegung*, ed. Paul Wentzke (Heidelberg: C. Winter, 1959), 2:11–66.

[41]Rudolf Vierhaus, "Montesquieu in Deutschland: Zur Geschichte seiner Wirkung als politischer Schriftsteller im 18. Jahrhundert," in *Collegium philosophicum: Joachim Ritter zum 60. Geburtstag*, ed. Ernst Wolfgang Böckenförde (Basel: Schwabe, 1965), 403.

(1717–71), Heinrich Gottfried Scheidemantel (1739–88), and the Altdorf professor Johann Heumann von Teutschenbrunn (1711–69), author of the tract *Geist der Gesetze der Teutschen* (1760), which follows this line of reasoning.[42]

In addition to the practical, reformist "national spirit" harbored by the awakening middle class, there was also an enthusiastically anti-French, often anti-Enlightenment variety.[43] This direction is particularly exemplified by works such as the following: the 1756 *Edda* edition of the francophone Swiss Paul Henri Mallet; the bardic lyric; Johann Wilhelm Ludwig Gleim's *Preussische Kriegslieder* (1758); Thomas Abbt's *Vom Tode fürs Vaterland* (1761); the German translation of Macpherson's cleverly forged *Ossian* (1764); Friedrich Gottlieb Klopstock's trilogy on the national hero Hermann the Cherusker (Arminius), as well as his German songs and general enthusiasm for everything Scandinavian.[44] The irritation provoked by this movement in the adherents of the rationalistic Enlightenment can be felt as late as Georg Christoph Lichtenberg in his expression of scorn for

> eine gewisse Art Leute, meistens junge Dichter, die das Wort *Deutsch* fast immer mit offnen Naslöchern aussprechen. Ein sicheres Zeichen, daß der Patriotismus bei diesen Leuten sogar auch Nachahmung ist. Wer wird immer mit dem Deutschen so dicke tun?[45]

> [a certain type of person, mostly young poets, who almost always pronounce the word *German* with open nostrils. A sure sign that for these people patriotism too is a kind of imitation. Who else would be so puffed up with Germanness?]

---

[42]On Justi, see Stolleis, *Geschichte des öffentlichen Rechts*, 1:379–82 (see n. 11 above); on Scheidemantel, ibid., 295–96; and on Teutschenbrunn, see Hugo Eisenhart, "Johann Heumann Edler von Teutschenbrunn," in *Allgemeine Deutsche Biographie* (Leipzig: Duncker & Humblot, 1880), 12:331–32.

[43]Gerhard Masur, "Deutsches Reich und deutsche Nation im 18. Jahrhundert," *Preussische Jahrbücher* 229 (1932): 1–23, esp. 17–18; Ernst Rudolf Huber, "Volk und Staat in der Reichsrechtswissenschaft des 17. und 18. Jahrhunderts," *Zeitschrift für die gesamte Staatswissenschaft* 102 (1942): 593; cf. Huber, "Der preussische Staatspatriotismus" (see n. 36 above).

[44]The trilogy consists of *Die Hermanns Schlacht* (1769), *Hermann und die Fürsten* (1784), and *Hermanns Tod* (1787).

[45]Georg Christoph Lichtenberg, *Aphorismen*, ed. Friedrich Sengle (Stuttgart: Philipp Reclam, 1984), 79.

There were authors, however, even among the *Reichspublizisten,* who succeeded in combining the enlightened "antidespotic" line with the new sentiments. The best example is Friedrich Carl von Moser, a firebrand reformist from the ranks of the *Publizisten.* Moser was at the same time a devout Christian as well as an enthusiastic supporter of the imperial constitution and, as a member of the Imperial Aulic Court, performed certain duties for Vienna.[46] His work *Von dem Deutschen National-Geist* (1765) and his review *Patriotisches Archiv für Teutschland* (1784–90) have as their common goal the creation of a middle-class civil society based on constitutional reform of the empire. He envisioned progress along the lines of a "national assembly" and reforms in the territorial states.[47] Hence, imperial patriotism and bourgeois enlightened thinking were hardly contradictory terms. The so-called *Sturm und Drang* poets (such as Friedrich Klinger, Johann Michael Reinhold Lenz, the brothers Christian and Friedrich Stolberg, Johann Heinrich Voss, Leopold Göckingk, Georg August Bürger, Heinrich Boie, and the young Goethe and Schiller), as unpolitical as their break from the conventions and frustrations of society may seem, were oriented towards the fatherland and inclined toward imperial patriotism, especially after coming into contact with *Reichspublizistik* in the course of their study of law.[48] The much-touted "freedom" of these men, encapsulated in the famous motto to *Die Räuber* (1781): *in tirannos,* as antiabsolutistic as it was, was still very much the *altteutsche* freedom. With Schiller's motto, the Tacitean topos of *Libertas Germaniae* was restored to life, in part transformed into something human, in part reclaimed from the British and the Franks as a German national possession.[49]

[46]Stolleis, *Geschichte des öffentlichen Rechts,* 1:152, n. 318 (see n. 11 above).

[47]*Der aufgeklärte Absolutismus,* ed. Karl Otmar Freiherr von Aretin (Cologne: Kiepenheuer & Witsch, 1974).

[48]Rudolf Vierhaus, "'Patriotismus': Begriff und Realität einer moralisch-politischen Haltung," in *Deutsche patriotische und gemeinnützige Gesellschaften* (Munich: Kraus International Publications, 1980), 9–29. On the influence of *Reichspublizistik* on the Storm and Stress poets, see Gerrit Walther, "'… uns, denen der Name *politische Freiheit* so süsse schallt': Die politischen Erfahrungen und Erwartungen der Sturm- und Drang-Generation," in *Freies Deutsches Hochstift: Sturm und Drang* (Frankfurt: Freies Deutsches Hochstift, 1988), 307–27; Harro Zimmermann, *Freiheit und Geschichte: F. G. Klopstock als historischer Dichter und Denker* (Heidelberg: C. Winter, 1987).

[49]Friedrich Meinecke, *Weltbürgertum und Nationalstaat,* vol. 5 of *Werke,* ed. Hans Herzfeld (Munich: Oldenbourg, 1962).

Particularly after the French monarchy was destroyed and the revolutionary red dawn capsized into a radical democratic nationalism and the reign of terror, Germans turned to the protective function of inner peace, legal culture, and the imperial constitution.[50] Whereas up to this point the witticism had been permitted that the imperial constitution was a "confusion blessed by the gods" (confusio divinitus conservata), people now began to remember ever more clearly Voltaire's and Rousseau's praise of the imperial constitution.[51] As one famous *Reichspublizist* summarized it, "No happier establishment of a state can be imagined than this, because every member of the empire is certain in the possession of what is his and protected against the offences of others."[52] Now the advantages of the situation at home in comparison to those in France became increasingly clear. "We do not hang so in the air," wrote Wilhelm Heinse in 1792, "and are not pushed about by every breeze."[53] Even the widely traveled revolutionary Georg Forster thought in 1789 that "it is not a bad idea at all to consider how much quiet and warmth the old Gothic edifice,

---

[50]Albert Stern, *Der Einfluss der Französischen Revolution auf das deutsche Geistesleben* (Stuttgart: J. H. Cotta, 1928); Jacques Droz, *L'Allemagne et la Révolution française* (Paris: Presses universitaires de France, 1949); George Peabody Gooch, *Germany and the French Revolution* (1920; reprint, London: Frank Cass, 1965); T. C. W. Blanning, *The French Revolution in Germany: Occupations and Resistance in the Rhineland, 1792–1802* (New York: Oxford University Press, 1982), 255–85; Karl Härter, *Reichstag und Revolution: 1789–1806* (Göttingen: Vandenhoeck & Ruprecht, 1992); Stolleis, *Geschichte des öffentlichen Rechts*, 1:327–29, with further bibliography (see n. 11 above).

[51]Walther, "'uns, denen der Name *politische Freiheit* so süsse schallt,'" 318, with further bibliography (see n. 48 above). On Voltaire's influence on German literature of the eighteenth century, see Hermann August Korff, *Voltaire im literarischen Deutschland des 18. Jahrhunderts* (Heidelberg: C. Winter, 1917); on the relationship between Voltaire and *Reichspublizistik*, see Notker Hammerstein, "Voltaire und die Reichspublizistik," in *Voltaire und Deutschland*, ed. Peter Brokmeier, Roland Desne, and Jürgen Voss (Stuttgart: Metzler, 1979), 335.

[52]"Wie mag eine glückseeligere Einrichtung eines Staats erdacht werden, als diese, da ein jedes Mitglied des Reichs in Erhaltung des Seinigen sicher, gegen ander Beleidigungen geschützt." Johann Stephan Pütter, *Patriotische Abbildung des heutigen Zustandes beyder höchsten Reichsgerichte* (Göttingen: Schmidt, 1749), 7.

[53]"Wir schweben nicht so in der Luft, und lassen uns von jedem Wind hin und her bewegen." Wilhelm Heinse, "Aus Mainz und Aschaffenburg: 1793–1803," in *Sämtliche Werke*, ed. Albert Leitzmann (Leipzig: Insel, 1924), 8.3:21; see Manfred Dick, "Wilhelm Heinse in Mainz," in *Mainz—Centralort des Reiches: Politik, Literatur und Philosophie im Umbruch der Revolutions-Zeit*, ed. Christoph Jamme and Otto Pöggeler (Stuttgart: Klett-Cotta, 1986, 165–97).

the German imperial constitution, has offered its occupants."[54] And a year later he noted, "No volcano will erupt under the honorable Gothic landmark of our imperial constitution and throw its intricate little towers, its narrow bundles of columns, and its gruesome flying buttresses into the air, and baptize us with the fire and sulfur of political rebirth."[55]

Now the jurists from the Halle and Göttingen schools of *Reichspublizistik* had genuine reason to emphasize just how peaceful and blessed the imperial constitution had proved to be and how very much it was in the Germans' own interest not to discard it casually.[56] In 1792 the Helmstedt professor Carl Friedrich Häberlin wrote his famous article "On the virtues of the German State Constitution,"[57] and in 1794 he assured his readers that he was "still quite thoroughly convinced... that our constitution is one of the most excellent."[58] In the following year Günther Heinrich von Berg, also of the Göttingen school, wrote his article "On the German Constitution and the Preservation of Public Peace in Germany."[59]

Certainly the freer spirits among them were agreed on one thing: that the ceremonial rules and regulations with their staggering complexities, interminable delays, and inscrutable legal paths repre-

[54]"Darzuthun, in wiefern das alte gothische Gebäude der deutschen Reichsverfassung seine gute Seite habe, wie es seinen Insassen Ruhe und Wärme geben könne, ist gar nicht übel." Letter to Friedrich Heinrich Jacobi, 23 Nov. 1789, in *Georg Forsters Werke*, ed. Deutsche Akademie der Wissenschaften zu Berlin (Berlin: Akademie-Verlag, 1981), 15:374.

[55]"Kein Vulkan wird sich unter dem ehrwürdigen Gothischen Denkmal unserer Reichsverfassung entzünden, seine ziemlich geschnörkelten Thürmchen, seine schlanken Säulenbündel und schaurigen Spitzengewölbe in die Luft sprengen, und uns mit dem Feuer und Schwefel der politischen Wiedergeburt taufen." Review of "Reflections on the revolution in France," by Edmund Burke in "Geschichte der Englischen Literatur vom Jahre 1790," in *Georg Forsters Werke*, 7:280–81; see Winfried Dotzauer, "Johannes von Müller und Georg Forster im Mainz der Erthal-Zeit (1786/88–1792)," in *Mainz—Centralort des Reiches*, 198–235 (see n. 53 above).

[56]Karl Otmar Frh. von Aretin, "Reichstag, Rastatter Kongress und Revolution: Das Wirken Isaaks von Sinclair und seiner Freunde am Ende des Hl. Römischen Reiches," *Hölderlin-Jahrbuch* 22 (1980/81): 4–17; Härter, *Reichstag und Revolution*, esp. 11–31 (see n. 50 above).

[57]"Über die Güte der teutschen Staatsverfassung," *Braunschweigisches Magazin* (1792): 40–42; revised in *Deutsche Monatsschrift* (1793): 3–7.

[58]"... weil... ich noch immer lebhaft davon überzeugt bin, dass unsere Verfassung eine der vorzüglichsten ist." Carl Friedrich Häberlin, *Handbuch des Teutschen Staatsrechts*, 5th ed. (Berlin: Friedrich Viehweg, 1794), 1: introduction, n. *.

[59]Günther Heinrich von Berg, "Über Teutschlands Verfassung und die Erhaltung der öffentlichen Ruhe in Teutschland" (Göttingen, 1795).

sented leftovers from a "Gothic" Middle Ages inherited by a modern world positioned for revolution. Clearly, the imperial constitution was worn out, ossified. A whiff of melancholy filled the air whenever the subject turned to the imperial constitution, for everyone knew that its days were numbered. Just when the collapse would occur, however, nobody wished to predict. The stronger force came from nationalism, once enthusiasm for humanity had been discredited. Nationalism seemed to offer a bridge, at a time when the imperial institutions were collapsing, across which one could hope to reach the constitutional shore.[60] "The times," wrote Heinrich von Kleist in 1805 to his friend Otto August Rühle, "seem to be tending toward a new arrangement of things, and we will experience nothing other than the collapse of the old."[61] Eight months later the time had in fact come.

*   *   *

Late-eighteenth-century imperial patriotism was qualitatively different from the early-sixteenth-century enthusiasm of the humanists, and different also from the patriotic clinging to the empire during the crises of the Thirty Years' War and the wars of Louis XIV. Although the mood and the political situation were basically different, political longing for a half-imaginary "empire" continued; this empire did not succeed until 1806 in becoming a modern state, and for this very reason it managed to retain its sacred aura and remain a point of identification. Thus in 1817 in the positions and decisions of the university fraternities (*Burschenschaften*) we find in article 12: "The longing for an emperor remains unweakened in the chest of every German man and youth so long as there is a remembrance of an emperor and the

---

[60]Arnold Berney, "Reichstradition und Nationalstaatsgedanke (1789–1815)," *Historische Zeitschrift* 140 (1929): 57–86; cf. Masur, "Deutsches Reich und deutsche Nation" (see n. 43 above); von Aretin and Hammerstein, "Reich," 5:489, with further bibliography (see n. 33 above); Gerhard Schuck, *Rheinbundpatriotismus und politische Öffentlichkeit zwischen Aufklärung und Frühliberalismus* (Stuttgart: Steiner, 1994); Georg Schmidt, "Der napoleonische Rheinbund—ein erneuertes Altes Reich," in *Alternativen zur Reichsverfassung in der Frühen Neuzeit?* ed. Volker Press (Munich: Oldenbourg, 1995), 227–46.

[61]"Die Zeit scheint eine neue Ordnung der Dinge herbeiführen zu wollen, und wir werden davon nichts als bloss den Umsturz der alten erleben." Letter to Otto August Rühle von Lilienstern, Königsberg, Dezember 1805, in *Heinrich von Kleist: Sämtliche Werke und Briefe*, ed. Helmut Sembdner (Munich: Carl Hanser, 1964), 2:789.

Reich has not vanished."[62] The more secularized and rationalized the idea of the empire had become over the course of the seventeenth and eighteenth centuries, the more important appeared to be the legal structure of the empire and the public law that accompanied it. The mountain of scholarly books that arose on the subject may have a corollary in the disappearance of the sacred power and political capacity of the empire. Thus, in the course of time "imperial patriotism" became more and more "rational." Its argument was made increasingly in terms of the practical advantages of retaining the imperial constitution; in the end, when the political constitutional situation and the trusted lifestyle that attended it were visibly *in extremis,* imperial patriotism acquired, appropriately enough, an admixture of melancholy. As the empire collapsed around them and the national state remained aloof, the Germans fled—"gedankenvoll und tatenarm," rich in thought and poor in deed, as Hölderlin put it—into an empire of ideas, comforting themselves with the words of Schiller from 1797: "As the political empire began to crumble, the spiritual empire established itself ever more firmly and completely."[63]

---

[62]"Die Sehnsucht nach Kaiser und Reich ist ungeschwächt in der Brust jedes frommen und ehrlichen deutschen Mannes und Jünglings und wird bleiben, solange die Erinnerung an Kaiser und Reich nicht verschwunden ... ist." "Grundsätze und Beschlüsse des achtzehnten Oktobers," 2: art. 12, in Hans Ehrentreich, "Heinrich Luden und sein Einfluss auf die Burschenschaft," in *Quellen und Darstellungen zur Geschichte der Burschenschaft und der deutschen Einheitsbewegung,* ed. Herman Haupt (Heidelberg: C. Winter, 1913), 4:48–129, here 119; on the Wartburgfest, *175 Jahre Wartburgfest: Studien zur politischen Bedeutung und zum Zeithintergrund der Wartburgfeier,* ed. Klaus Malettke (Heidelberg: C. Winter, 1992).

[63]"Indem das politische Reich wankt, hat sich das geistige immer fester und vollkommener gebildet." "Deutsche Grösse," in *Werke,* ed. Gerhard Finke and Herbert Georg Göpfert (Munich: Carl Hanser, 1960), 1:474.

The Imperial Double Eagle, woodcut by Hans Burgkmair

The "Universal" and the "Local" in Episcopal Visitations

Edmund M. Kern

Scholars of the Reformation and its aftermath in Germany have sought to identify either the "success" or the "failure" of religious reform, social discipline, or confessionalization. The histories produced depend upon a number of implicit assumptions: they adopt the perspective of the reformers, accept society's division into elite and popular elements, and construct narratives outlining the origin, development, and results of reform. Accounts of a rich and complex religious life are thus reduced to evidence for either wins or losses in a zero-sum game. Instead, historians must assess religious practices in particular locations, where neither reform programs arrive at their idealistic ends nor the people's practices retain their presumably independent integrity. Even in the reports of episcopal visitations (ostensibly so one-sided, perspectively simple, and transparently biased), historians can recognize both "universal" projections and the "local" contingencies that interrupt and displace them. The false dichotomy between "success" and "failure" dissolves as historians recontextualize the "universal" and the "local" in terms of each other in site-specific settings.

WHAT DO YOU DO WITH A DRUNKEN CHAPLAIN? If you are that priest, you claim that you live a celibate life, wear the appropriate dress and tonsure of your order, and actively fulfill your clerical duties, reading the breviary, saying mass regularly during the week, and teaching the catechism on Sundays. You also admit that you have a fondness for drink, despite your best intentions. If you are the man's pastor, you pay him, provide for his upkeep, and keep a close watch on him. If you are his parishioners, you see him as a drunk, a distracting and disruptive influence in your parish, despite the pastor's close attention.

Edmund M. Kern

In 1617, episcopal visitors to the parish of Bruck in the duchy of Styria instructed the pastor to send the problem priest back to his monastery in Altenburg and to exercise better judgment in appointing assistants.[1] Now, I put the same question, again, to scholars: What do you do with a drunken chaplain?

Before providing an answer of my own to this question, I would like to comment at some length about how scholars of religious reform in the early modern period might answer it: A drunken chaplain is made an example of either the success or failure of religious reform. Note, for example, that in a recent article, Geoffrey Parker poses, again, a question raised by Gerald Strauss first in a 1975 article and then in his 1978 book, *Luther's House of Learning*: Should historians consider the Reformation a success or a failure?[2] As Parker makes clear, much subsequent research has focused on the programmatic aims of religious reform movements in not only Lutheran areas but Catholic and Calvinist ones as well. The questions of "success" and "failure" have framed much of this research. Perhaps the tendency to ask such questions should itself be questioned. Behind this approach stand a number of implicit assumptions about how stories of religious life in the early modern period should be told: from the reformers' perspective, set within a society divided into elite and popular elements, and as narratives emphasizing temporal change, with clear beginnings, middles, and ends. Further, these assumptions often prevent historians from seeing an undeniable and extremely intriguing aspect of that religious life—its presence only within specific locations, which allow (almost demand) practices that are sometimes coherent and sometimes contradictory.[3]

---

[1] Hill Monastic Manuscript Library, St. John's University, Collegeville, Minn., *Visitationsprotokoll 1617/19*, 952 F. saec. 17, Graz-Diözesanarchiv, codex no. XIX-D–18, project no. 27,429, fols. 466v–467r (hereafter cited HMML XIX-D–18); see also Andreas Posch, "Aus dem kirchlichen Visitationsbericht 1617—Ein Beitrag zur religiösen Lage in der Steiermark unter Ferdinand II.," in *Innerösterreich, 1564–1619*, ed. Alexander Novotny and Berthold Sutter (Graz: Das Steiermärkische Landesmuseum, 1967), 222.

[2] Geoffrey Parker, "Success and Failure during the First Century of the Reformation," *Past and Present* 136 (1992): 43–82; Gerald Strauss, "Success and Failure in the German Reformation," *Past and Present* 67 (1975): 30–63; idem, *Luther's House of Learning: Indoctrination of the Young in the German Reformation* (Baltimore: Johns Hopkins University Press, 1978).

[3] A number of works associated with the "linguistic turn" in scholarship inform my arguments about how historians allow the terms of their discourse to frame obser-

Reducing religious life to a series of wins and losses in a zero-sum game in which only the reformers fully participate replicates, at least in part, a view of the Reformation criticized by Bernd Moeller in 1965:

> To caricature the common description, Luther generally appears as a great sage, a kind of spiritual colossus, who attains his Reformation breakthrough, draws the broad consequences, and then drags people with him as he strides through history handing out truths right and left.[4]

Although Strauss is in full agreement with Moeller about the undesirability of such a depiction, his conclusions in *Luther's House of Learning* reinscribe the idea that only the perspective of reformers matters, by simply reversing the outcome of the process described by Moeller: The Lutheran reformers' pedagogical program for the creation of a "Christian society" ruled by "evangelical principles" failed ultimately, and hence so did the Reformation itself; accordingly, the common people were no more Christian in their beliefs, in the sense the reformers intended, than they had been before the start of the Reformation. Reversing the outcome of reform has done little to challenge assumptions about whose perspective historians should adopt. Recent work on confessionalization, which emphasizes similarities among Lutheran, Catholic, and Calvinist reform programs, has also done little to undermine overwhelmingly top-down approaches to the past. When we speak of "Lutheran confessionalization," "Catholic confes-

---

vations and to shape descriptions without recognizing that the choices they make (consciously or unconsciously) structure the texts they produce. Most historians present the form that their accounts of historical events take as somehow "natural," something found rather than something constructed. See in particular Hayden White, *Metahistory: The Historical Imagination in Nineteenth-Century Europe* (Baltimore: Johns Hopkins University Press, 1973); idem, *Tropics of Discourse: Essays in Cultural Criticism* (Baltimore: Johns Hopkins University Press, 1978); and idem, *The Content of the Form: Narrative Discourse and Historical Representation* (Baltimore: Johns Hopkins University Press, 1987). Dominick LaCapra, "History, Language, and Reading: Waiting for Crillon," *American Historical Review* 100, no. 3 (1995): 799–828, examines a "typology of important reading practices" (806) among historians and in doing so says a lot about the kinds of histories produced. See also the articles in *A New Philosophy of History*, ed. Frank Ankersmit and Hans Kellner (Chicago: University of Chicago Press, 1995).

[4]Bernd Moeller, "Problems of Reformation Research," in *Imperial Cities and the Reformation: Three Essays*, ed. and trans. H. C. Erik Midelfort and Mark U. Edwards (Durham, N.C.: Labyrinth, 1982), 13. See also the use of this quotation in R. W. Scribner, *The German Reformation* (Atlantic Highlands, N.J.: Humanities Press, 1986), 1–5.

sionalization," and "Calvinist confessionalization," have we really moved all that far from Moeller's caricature? In writing recently about "Luther, Loyola, Calvin und die europäische Neuzeit," is Heinz Schilling replacing a single spiritual colossus with a trinity of them?[5]

Further, in seeking to identify success or failure, scholars frame their accounts implicitly according to the terms of a binary opposition between either elite (external/learned/doctrinaire) programs or popular (internal/ignorant/traditional) practices, even though that opposition has been under attack for some time. Constrained within this frame, historians reduce rich and complex information from highly diverse territories to evidence for either a triumphant or a misfired confessionalization. As a result, they produce narratives with strikingly similar plots, regardless of detail. Whose success? Whose failure? To answer "the reformers'" simply begs a larger question. Frequently without pursuing other options, historians tell a particular kind of story from a particular point of view: the drunken seventeenth-century chaplain in Bruck, whose sorry story began this essay, must be interpreted as either a success or a failure.

Nevertheless, the glimpses of the past afforded us need not be interpreted through lenses ground to bring only success or failure—by the "elite" among the "popular"—into sharp focus.[6] Rather than

---

[5]Heinz Schilling, "Luther, Loyola, Calvin und die europäische Neuzeit," *Archiv für Reformationsgeschichte* 85 (1994): 5–31.

[6]Strauss himself cast the problem in these terms in the conclusion to *Luther's House of Learning*, 302–5 (see n. 2 above), and has picked it up again in responses to his critics in Gerald Strauss, "The Reformation and Its Public in an Age of Orthodoxy," in *The German People and the Reformation*, ed. R. Po-chia Hsia (Ithaca: Cornell University Press, 1988), 211–14. See also his critics' implicit acceptance of the dichotomy: James Kittelson, "Successes and Failures in the German Reformation: The Report from Strasbourg," *Archive for Reformation History* 73 (1982): 153–74, and idem, "Visitations and Popular Religious Culture: Further Reports from Strasbourg," in *Pietas et Societas: New Trends in Reformation Social History*, ed. Kyle C. Sessions and Phillip N. Bebb (Kirksville, Mo.: Sixteenth Century Journal Publishers, 1985), 89–101; and Steven Ozment, *When Fathers Ruled: Family Life in Reformation Europe* (Cambridge, Mass.: Harvard University Press, 1983). Ozment's recent *Protestants: The Birth of a Revolution* (New York: Image Books, 1991) can be read as a response to Strauss's thesis insofar as it emphasizes lay responses, activities, and beliefs within the "revolution." Important critiques of the popular–elite dichotomy include: Natalie Zemon Davis, "From 'Popular Religion' to Religious Cultures," in *Reformation Europe: A Guide to Research*, ed. Steven Ozment (St. Louis: Center for Reformation Research, 1982); Richard Trexler, "Reverence and Profanity in the Study of Early Modern Religion," in *Religion and Society in Early Modern Europe, 1500–1800*, ed. Kaspar von Greyerz (Boston: Allen & Unwin, 1984), 245–69; and R. W. Scribner, "Is a History of Popular Culture Possible?" *History of European Ideas* 10, no. 2 (1989): 175–91.

depict early modern religion as the story of a single practice (top-down reform and its ultimate implementation or rejection), I want to put reform programs in their place by paying attention to the spaces where they literally took place: in the parishes where reform was simply one religious practice among many.[7] I shall revisit diocesan visitations (so central to Strauss's claims as well as those of others) not simply as documents that record events identifiable as either successes or failures, but also as events themselves, which took place as "visits"—a going-to-see. Visitations were (among other things) a physical and mental projection of the putatively universal into the pragmatically local, requiring movement through space, a mapping of that space, and a mapping of movement within it. They were considered a means to an end (another place), but could that end ever be attained? Parishes, I shall maintain, were inherently, but not perfectly, unstable places—and not neutral sites—places where the mapping projects of reform, social discipline, or confessionalization were all doomed (if I may say so) to fall short.[8] In such a setting it seems counterproductive to locate and identify successes and/or failures by appealing to visitation reports. Local circumstances necessarily interrupted and disrupted attempted projections of universal ideals.[9]

[7]On the relative unwillingness of scholars in general to spatialize the social practices they study, see particularly Edward W. Soja, *Postmodern Geographies: The Reassertion of Space in Critical Social Theory* (New York: Verso, 1989), and David Harvey, "The Geopolitics of Capitalism," in *Social Relations and Spatial Structures*, ed. Derek Gregory and John Urry (New York: St. Martin's, 1985), 126–63. See also the articles in *Place/Culture/Representation*, ed. James Duncan and David Ley (New York: Routledge, 1993).

[8]I refer, in other words, to what Strauss labels "indoctrination" but what others label "rationalization," "the civilizing process," "social disciplining," "modernization," or most recently "confessionalization" (inter alia). See Thomas Winkelbauer's brief genealogy of "social disciplining" and "confessionalization," in "Sozialdisziplinierung und Konfessionalisierung durch Grundherren in den österreichischen und böhmischen Ländern im 16. und 17. Jahrhundert," *Zeitschrift für historische Forschung* 19 (1992): 317–24. Among the familiar authors he cites are Max Weber, Norbert Elias, Gerhard Oestreich, Ernst Walter Zeeden, Heinz Schilling, Wolfgang Reinhard. See also R. Po-chia Hsia, *Social Discipline in the Reformation: Central Europe, 1550–1750* (New York: Routledge, 1989), esp. 1–9, 188–90, for a discussion of pertinent literature.

[9]See Michel Foucault on space and geography in "Of Other Spaces," *Diacritics* 16, no. 1 (1986): 22–27; idem, "Questions on Geography," in *Power/Knowledge*, ed. Colin Gordon (New York: Pantheon, 1980), 63–77; and "Space, Knowledge, and Power," in *The Foucault Reader*, ed. Paul Robinow (New York: Pantheon, 1984), 239–56. Although I believe that Foucault allows for instabilities and interruptions within the discourses his work posits, his emphasis on epistemic (hegemonic) qualities has led several scholars to react in critical and productive ways. See especially Pierre Bourdieu, *Outline of a Theory*

Edmund M. Kern

It could be objected that I am overstating my case and that the analyses of Strauss and others are more nuanced than I allow. I am certainly willing to concede that Strauss himself allows for other questions in *Luther's House of Learning*, and he even makes, in a sense, the same point I hope to make: "The burden of proof ought now at last to be placed where it belongs: upon those who claim, *or implicitly or tacitly assume,* that the Reformation in Germany aroused widespread, meaningful, and lasting response to its message."[10] More recently, in a kind of final response to his critics, he seems to call for an understanding of ideological movements as projects necessarily limited by circumstances: "Although the book was not intended as a demonstration of how ideals succumb to reality, it became just that...."[11] It is also true that a number of recent works by anglophone historians undermine the categories of elite and popular, even as they employ them, and call into question the effectiveness of reform movements within city, town, or village settings.[12]

Nevertheless, these works still tend to emphasize a particular perspective and still tend to employ the language of success and failure, a tendency from which I as well have not been immune.[13] This tendency becomes even more pronounced when one turns to the German-language scholarship on the Reformation and its after-

---

of Practice, trans. Richard Nice (New York: Cambridge University Press, 1977), esp. 89–92, and Michel de Certeau, *The Practice of Everyday Life*, trans. Steven Rendall (Berkeley: University of California Press, 1984), esp. 91–130.

[10]Strauss, *Luther's House of Learning*, 307–8 (my emphasis; see n. 2 above).

[11]Strauss, "The Reformation and Its Public," 194–95 (see n. 6 above).

[12]Some excellent examples include: David Warren Sabean, *Power in the Blood: Popular Culture and Village Discourse in Early Modern Germany* (New York: Cambridge University Press, 1984); R. W. Scribner's essays in *Popular Culture and Popular Movements in Reformation Germany* (London: The Hambledon Press, 1987); Thomas Robisheaux, *Rural Society and the Search for Order in Early Modern Germany* (New York: Cambridge University Press, 1989); Lyndal Roper, *The Holy Household: Women and Morals in Reformation Augsburg* (New York: Oxford University Press, 1989); Marc Forster, *The Counter-Reformation in the Villages: Religion and Reform in the Bishopric of Speyer, 1560–1720* (Ithaca: Cornell University Press, 1992); and Philip Soergel, *Wondrous in His Saints: Counter-Reformation Propaganda in Bavaria* (Berkeley: University of California Press, 1993). An especially good use of "popular culture" in a way that undermines some of its less desirable implications is found in Scribner, "Is a History of Popular Culture Possible?" (see n. 6 above).

[13]Edmund Kern, "Confessional Identity and Magic in the Late Sixteenth Century: Jakob Bithner and Witchcraft in Styria," *Sixteenth Century Journal* 25 (1994): 323–40.

math.[14] In these works, neither perspective nor the language of success is questioned. They are tacitly assumed, as Strauss pointed out in 1978, and narratives following the same basic plot emerge: first the introduction of reform, then its development, followed by either reaction to it or its consolidation, and finally its successful completion. There is often little discussion of failure, since incomplete confessionalization is usually interpreted as the success of toleration.[15]

[14]American scholars whose own research interests are quite different have pointed to this fact when emphasizing the need to engage Strauss's claims: Mark U. Edwards, "The Luther Quincentennial," *Journal of Ecclesiastical History* 35, no. 4 (1984): 607; Susan C. Karant-Nunn, "Alas, a Lack: Trends in the Historiography of Pre-University Education in Early Modern Germany," *Renaissance Quarterly* 43, no. 4 (1990): 790, 792, 796–97; and James D. Tracy, "From Humanism to the Humanities: A Critique of Grafton and Jardine," *Modern Language Quarterly* 51, no. 1(1990): 133. Despite Heiko Oberman's central use of Strauss's ideas in "Martin Luther: Vorläufer der Reformation," in *Verifikationen: Festschrift für Gerhard Ebeling zum 70. Geburtstag*, ed. Eberhard Jüngel, Johannes Wallmann, and Wilfrid Werbeck (Tübingen: Mohr, 1982), two primary architects of "confessionalization" either casually dismiss or fail to mention *Luther's House of Learning* in foundational articles: Wolfgang Reinhard, "Zwang zur Konfessionalisierung? Prolegomena zu einer Theorie des konfessionellen Zeitalters," *Zeitschrift für historische Forschung* 10 (1983): 255–77, and idem, "Reformation, Counter-Reformation, and the Early Modern State: A Reassessment," *Catholic Historical Review* 75, no. 3 (1989): 383–404; and Heinz Schilling, "Die Konfessionalisierung im Reich: Religiöser und gesellschaftlicher Wandel in Deutschland zwischen 1555 und 1620," *Historische Zeitschrift* 246, no. 1 (1988): 1–45, and idem, "Confessional Europe," in *Handbook of European History, 1400–1600: Late Middle Ages, Renaissance and Reformation*, ed. Thomas A. Brady, Jr., Heiko Oberman, and James D. Tracy, vol. 2, *Visions, Programs, Outcomes* (Leiden: E.J. Brill, 1995), 641–81. The elite perspective and "success" are tacitly assumed.

[15]For Germany, see *Die reformierte Konfessionalisierung in Deutschland: Das Problem der "Zweiten Reformation,"* ed. Heinz Schilling (Gütersloh: Gerd Mohn, 1986); *Die lutherische Konfessionalisierung in Deutschland*, ed. Hans-Christoph Rublack (Gütersloh: Gerd Mohn, 1992); *Die katholische Konfessionalisierung in Europa*, ed. Wolfgang Reinhard and Heinz Schilling (Münster: Aschendorff, 1995); and *Die Territorien des Reichs im Zeitalter der Reformation und Konfessionalisierung: Land und Konfession 1500–1650*, ed. Anton Schindling and Walter Ziegler, vol. 1, *Der Südosten*; vol. 2, *Der Nordosten*; vol. 3, *Der Nordwesten*; vol. 4, *Mittleres Deutschland*; vol. 5, *Der Südwesten* (Münster: Aschendorff, 1989–93). Note the perspective assumed in the five points for discussion outlined in the opening remarks of Bernd Moeller in the recorded "Schlussdiskussion" to Schilling's *Die reformierte Konfessionalisierung*: "the concept of the 'Second Reformation,'" its "theological-historical origin," the "motives of the concerned parties," "those who carried it out," and "finally the social consequences" (440). Moeller provides a variation on the same theme in the discussion recorded in Rublack's *Die lutherische Konfessionalisierung*: "1. crisis, 2. confessionalization, 3. success and failure" (559). I can only assume that Reinhard and Schilling's volume on Catholicism approaches religious life in a similar fashion.

In the collections edited by Schindling and Ziegler, no overarching themes are

Edmund M. Kern

Once again, there are exceptions to this trend in the German-language scholarship, particularly insofar as *Alltagsgeschichte* is experiencing a renaissance of sorts.[16] Despite this fact, in his 1992 survey,

---

provided, since the articles are intended only to provide bases for comparison. Although specific events proceed very differently in each of the territories described, frequently recurring terms give most of the narratives a similar shape: (1) introduction of reform (*Einführung, Einfluß*), (2) its development (*Entwicklung, Fortschritt, Ausbreitung*), (3a) reaction to it (*Widerstand, Wiederbelebung, Ringen, Niedergang, Reste, Ausnahmen, Umschwung*), (3b) its consolidation (*Entscheidung, Durchführung, Kontinuität*), and (4) its successful completion (*Erfolg, Vollziehung, Sieg*). In his review of the first three volumes, Robert Bireley rightly points out that the authors are constrained by the format proposed by the editors and by the current state of research, but I believe that these facts in particular support the point that I want to make. Bireley also expresses his dismay over the fact that discussion of the most important issue—that of *results*—raised by *Luther's House of Learning* is almost wholly absent; *Sixteenth Century Journal* 23 (1992): 619–22.

The recent *Handbook of European History* (whose focus, as the title implies, is not limited to Germany), edited by Brady, Oberman, and Tracy, takes seriously the question of *results*, but again a clearly top-down perspective is explicit in the titles to volume 2's three sections: (1) "Visions of Reform," (2) "Programs for Change," and (3) "Outcomes." Contributors to the section titled "Outcomes" implicitly assume that same perspective by posing the familiar question of "success and failure." See, for example, Thomas A. Brady, "Settlements: The Holy Roman Empire," 360–62 and passim (see n. 14 above).

[16]See in particular Richard van Dülmen's excellent anthology presenting the work of many scholars, *Studien zur historischen Kulturforschung*, vol. 1, *Armut, Liebe, Ehre*; vol. 2, *Arbeit, Frömmigkeit und Eigensinn*; vol. 3, *Verbrechen, Strafen und soziale Kontrolle*; vol. 4, *Dynamik der Tradition* (Frankfurt am Main: Fischer, 1988–92). For earlier examples, see *Kultur der einfachen Leute*, ed. Van Dülmen (Munich: C. H. Beck, 1983); *Volkskultur: Zur Wiederentdeckung des vergessenen Alltags (16.–20. Jahrhundert)*, ed. van Dülmen and Norbert Schindler (Frankfurt am Main: Fischer, 1984); van Dülmen's own essays in *Religion und Gesellschaft: Beiträge zu einer Religionsgeschichte der Neuzeit* (Frankfurt am Main: Fischer, 1989); and Schindler's works, *Widerspenstige Leute: Studien zur Volkskultur in der frühen Neuzeit* (Frankfurt am Main: Fischer, 1992). A number of recent books on witchcraft also display some concern with the quotidian, notably, Eva Labouvie, *Verbotene Künste: Volksmagie und Ländlicher Aberglaube in den Dorfgemeinden des Saarraumes (16.–19. Jahrhundert)* (St. Ingbert: Röhrig Verlag, 1992), and idem, *Zauberei und Hexenwerk: Ländlicher Hexenglaube in der frühen Neuzeit* (Frankfurt a.M: Fischer, 1993). More generally, the social history of the Reformation is still vibrant, as evidenced by the articles in *Landgemeinde und Stadtgemeinde im Mitteleuropa: Ein struktureller Vergleich*, ed. Peter Blickle (Munich: Oldenbourg, 1991), *Historische Zeitschrift*, Beiheft (Neue Folge) 13. But note the cautionary tone struck by R. W. Scribner in "Communalism: Universal Category or Ideological Construct? A Debate in the Historiography of Early Modern Germany and Switzerland," *The Historical Journal* 37, no. 1 (1994): 199–207, as well as the question posed by John Theibault in "Towards a New Sociocultural History of the Rural World of Early Modern History?" *Central European History* 24, nos. 2–3 (1991): 304–24.

Konfessionalisierung im 16. Jahrhundert, Heinrich Richard Schmidt felt it necessary to remark upon a lack of scholarship on what he calls the "history of the believers."[17] Putting a positive spin on this state of affairs, Peter Burke has remarked that newcomers to the field of "popular piety" in previously ignored geographic areas ("undiscovered regions") could avoid the theoretical mistakes and assumptions of the mostly French and Italian pacesetters.[18] The task requires abandoning our implicitly elite perspective and our presumption of elite success.

To do so may be difficult, not least because historians like to tell stories with beginnings, middles, and ends, stories of people moving through time. Observing the construction of reform programs (which can be easily documented) provides useful beginnings, and assessing their successes and/or failures (or more frequently simply presuming success) can provide neat and simple ends. Although historians use a language of space and place in their narratives, the language of time provides an evolutionary coherence that dominates and represses other possible narratives that display more awareness of a specificity of place that might interrupt that temporal coherence. I feel more comfortable with the indeterminacies of middles, which can be understood as not just times, but places, where cultural practices become continuously repetitive contests over power, legitimacy, and identity. In those middles instability seems the norm, emerging from the absence of any truly complete control by any one person or faction.[19]

[17]Heinrich Richard Schmidt, *Konfessionalisierung im 16. Jahrhundert* (Munich: Oldenbourg, 1992), 119.

[18]"Popular Piety," in *Catholicism in Early Modern History: A Guide to Research,* ed. John O'Malley, S.J. (St. Louis: Center for Reformation Research, 1988), 127. Robert Bireley's contribution to the same volume, "Early Modern Germany" (11–30), confirms Burke's image of Germany as an "undiscovered region." For German contributions, see *Die Visitation im Dienst der kirchlichen Reform,* ed. Ernst Walter Zeeden and Hans Georg Molitor, 2d ed. (Münster: Aschendorff, 1977); and *Kirche und Visitation: Beiträge zur Erforschung des frühneuzeitlichen Visitationswesen in Europa,* ed. Zeeden and Peter T. Lang (Stuttgart: Klett-Cotta, 1984). But compare the relatively tentative examination of German visitations in these essays (some expressly treat other areas outside central Europe) with the vast literature for France and Italy cited by Burke, "Popular Piety," and Angelo Torre, "Politics Cloaked in Worship: State, Church and Local Power in Piedmont 1570–1770," *Past and Present* 134 (1992): 42–92.

[19]Cf. Wesley A. Kort, "'Religion and Literature' in Postmodernist Contexts," *Journal of the American Academy of Religion* 58, no. 4 (1990): 575–88; Alvin Vos, introduction to *Place and Displacement in the Renaissance,* ed. Vos (Binghamton, N.Y.: Medieval

Edmund M. Kern

I might account for my comfort with these indeterminacies by pointing to the work of David Harvey and Edward W. Soja. In separate works, each has argued that in general scholars grant priority to history and the temporal and simply ignore geography and the spatial. Space is presumed to be neutral, an inherently stable context for historical change. Soja claims that an "already-made geography sets the stage, while the wilful making of history dictates the action and defines the story line." The historical imagination is thus curiously blind and actively hostile to the geographical or spatial imagination—blind and hostile, that is, to a whole host of possibilities for the "triple dialectic of space, time, and social being."[20] Historians jettison direct attention to settings in their constructions of beginnings, middles, and ends, largely, I think, because they want to generalize—to elaborate upon the significant, to discover the principle that underlies all specific cases. But as David Sabean has reminded us, generalization is not without its dangers: does one generalize to illustrate typicality, to outline a particular narrative of development and progress, or to show how particulars conform to or diverge from abstract values? Drawing upon the work of Mikhail Bakhtin, Michel de Certeau, and James Clifford, among others, Sabean responds to the desire to generalize in the following manner:

> Once we center our attention on relationships, we are forced into research strategies which favor the local and the particular.... When interest is centered on how consciousness is formed in social intercourse, on dialogical processes of value, and on ideological construction, then "particular, concrete contexts" become the locus of serious work.... [A] reified notion of culture is giving way to socially specific, exacting accounts of power, resistance, and constraints *in loci*, where many voices contend each for its own view of reality. Rather than mapping and recoding the results onto new situations, the new perspectives offer a loose set of procedures and examples of

---

and Renaissance Texts and Studies, 1995), ix–xxii; and Annabel Patterson, "Local Knowledge: 'Popular' Representation in Elizabethan Historiography," in *Place and Displacement*, 87–106. Katherine L. French argues for a similar conception of place as integral to religious practice, in a microhistory of an English parish, "Competing for Space: Medieval Religious Conflict in the Monastic-Parochial Church at Dunster," *Journal of Medieval and Early Modern Studies* 27, no. 2 (1997), 215–44.

20Harvey, "Geopolitics of Capitalism," 141, and Soja, *Postmodern Geographies*, 10–16, 25, quoted at 12 and 14 (see n. 7 above).

possibilities for finding coherence or contradictions in any social context.

Sabean's attention to the local highlights the situatedness of events and the spatial qualities of what he labels the "contextual logics of performance."[21]

As Sabean's work makes clear, direct attention to space has not been entirely absent from historical scholarship. One of the first works to look at reform with an eye towards its spatial aspects was William Christian's *Local Religion in Sixteenth-Century Spain*, whose vocabulary of the "universal" and the "local" and whose questioning of the elite-popular dichotomy have so profoundly influenced my own thought on Lutheran, Calvinist, and Catholic reform in Germany. Christian distinguishes productively between religion as prescribed and religion as practiced, the first a manifestation of the ideally universal church, the second a manifestation of the particular, the local, the idiosyncratic, and the unique.[22] His understanding of each avoids the bind created in trying to define the popular, but it does not go far enough. For it is important to note that prescribing religion is a form of religious practice. Prescriptive religion as practice, too, must have a site, a location; it does not exist independently of movement through space. For this reason, what I have termed "the projection of the universal" differs somewhat from Christian's notion of universal religion, although I am in agreement when it comes to his discussion of local religion, which has the potential to absorb, resist, modify, accept, challenge, defeat, and, in a word, localize projections of the universal.

Certainly, historians can assess the impact of reformers' efforts on believers. Likewise, historians can reverse the opposition by assessing the impact of local practices and norms upon reform efforts.[23] But it seems to me that the appropriate third move entails not only (1) the recognition of both reformers' and believers' perspectives and/or (2) the reversal of a hierarchical arrangement that grants priority to elite

[21]David Sabean, *Property, Production, and Family in Neckarhausen, 1700–1870* (New York: Cambridge University Press, 1990), 7–12, quoted at 11 and 12.

[22]William A. Christian, Jr., *Local Religion in Sixteenth-Century Spain* (Princeton: Princeton University Press, 1981), 3–8, 178–79, 181, and passim.

[23]See Robert F. Berkhofer's interesting observations on the question of historical perspective, "A Point of View on Viewpoints in Historical Practice," in *A New Philosophy of History*, 174–91 (see n. 3 above).

views, but also (3) an exploration of how each perspective unravels when religious practices are placed within site-specific, local circumstances and the relationships that construct them.[24] In such a place, neither reform programs ("reform"/"social disciplining"/"confessionalization") arrive at their idealistic ends, nor do people's religious behaviors ("tradition"/"popular beliefs"/"custom") retain their ostensible integrity in the face of new introductions. There is no pure reform (or official religion) and there is no pure religion of the people (or popular religion). To follow James Clifford in borrowing a phrase from William Carlos Williams, I would argue that "the pure products ... go crazy."[25] Does such a move return us to a simple historicism or, worse still, devolve into nihilism? I think not. A continuous migration, but not vacillation, between the two perspectives opens greater interpretive possibilities as historians continuously recontextualize both the universal and the local in terms of the other. The distinctions between the two are not axiomatic categories—easily defined as either official religion or popular religion[26]—but rather the distinc-

[24]What I am proposing could be termed a "deconstructive" move indebted to the readings found, for example, in Jacques Derrida's *Of Grammatology*, trans. Gayatri Chakravorty Spivak (Baltimore: Johns Hopkins University Press, 1974), esp. 27–73 and 157–64; also "Structure, Sign, and Play in the Human Sciences," in *Writing and Difference*, trans. Alan Bass (Chicago: University of Chicago Press, 1978), 278–93; "Semiology and Grammatology" and "Positions," in *Positions*, trans. Alan Bass (Chicago: University of Chicago Press, 1981), esp. 19–24 and 41–47; and "Signature Event Context," in *Margins of Philosophy*, trans. Alan Bass (Chicago: University of Chicago Press, 1982), esp. 329–30. But I agree with Jeffrey T. Nealon, who proposes in "The Discipline of Deconstruction," *PMLA* 107, no. 5 (1992): 1266–79, that those who seek to reduce deconstruction to a "discipline" or "method" fundamentally misread Derrida's work as philosophy: "I still think it is important to distinguish among deconstructions—not, however, to save a deconstructive orthodoxy, but rather to recall the specificity at the heart of Derrida's itinerary and to pose a question to that still-dominant reduction of deconstruction which makes it into a method for producing readings. When deconstruction became a method, its singularity and its concern with alterity were smoothed out into an all-encompassing, easily iterable disciplinary project—one to which Derrida's texts pose an essential challenge" (1276).

[25]William Carlos Williams, *Spring and All* (1923), as quoted in James Clifford, "Introduction: The Pure Products Go Crazy," in *The Predicament of Culture: Twentieth-Century Ethnography, Literature, and Art* (Cambridge, Mass.: Harvard University Press, 1988), 1–17; clearly, Clifford's use of Williams has informed my own positions, but "pure products" were fantasies long before the twentieth century's ever more rapid changes brought about a crisis of modernity.

[26]See Craig Harline's use of these terms in "Official Religion-Popular Religion in Recent Historiography of the Catholic Reformation," *Archive for Reformation History* 81 (1990): 239–62. Although the author retains both "official" and "popular" as central to

tions between them are contingent, dependent upon particular times, settings, and relationships.[27]

There is no doubt that visitations were intended to be important parts of much larger reform movements. They were programmatic and executed in order to attain clearly stated goals and aims. For example, in 1617 the archbishop of Salzburg ordered the visitation of clerical institutions and parishes in the duchy of Styria that uncovered the hapless drunken chaplain we encountered. It was to be not only an assessment of the state of Catholicism, but an active step towards improving religious practice and uprooting error. Visitors made clear recommendations to the pastors, vicars, and superiors of the religious establishments, following the guidelines in their instructions. It was a clear effort to project a universal vision of the church into the individual localities of the archdiocese. We can ascertain this fact both in the literal movement of the archbishop's officers into these locales and in the mapping project they conducted during their visits, which included investigations of clergy and patrons (*circa personas*), liturgical items (*circa res*), places (*circa loca*), and services (*circa divina munera*) as well as reports on confraternities and guilds. Each report concludes with the commission's own decrees (*decretum/ decreta*).[28]

---

his calls for rewriting the history of the "official church," his own analysis explicitly calls attention to the concepts' shortcomings: "The more one chisels away at 'official' religion, the more elusive it becomes, just as many have been frustrated in trying to get at 'popular' religion" (241). Official and popular have little meaning unless they are understood in relation to site-specific settings—hence, my preference for "universal" and "local," which have a spatial resonance.

[27]Kerwin Lee Klein, "In Search of Narrative Mastery: Postmodernism and the People Without History," *History and Theory* 34, no. 4 (1995): 275–98, offers an informative discussion of "universal histories" and "local histories" in recent works on world history. Klein explores (among other issues) the "double plot" in many of these works, a double plot that simultaneously seeks to account for cultural homogenization (the universal) and cultural differentiation (the local). Although Klein is critical of the reification of both metanarratives and local narratives (especially since it tends to reinscribe formal distinctions between "historical" and "nonhistorical" modes of discourse), he is not disturbed by attempts to make sense simultaneously of general developments and non-assimilable particularities. Both gestures are necessary and proper—part of the contact and conflict among proliferating historical narratives. For Klein, a narrative's universal or local character derives from its power to subordinate other narratives— from, in other words, its discursive *position*, which is "always changing and historically specific" (297).

[28]See the report's preamble, HMML XIX-D-18, fol. 1v and passim, as well as Posch, "Aus dem kirchlichen Visitationsbericht 1617," 197–200, for a discussion of the instructions given visitors (n. 1 above).

One particularly good example of this effort can be seen in the commission's decree to the master of the municipal hospital for the aged, infirm, and destitute in Graz, but many others can be found. Both the building and its inhabitants had to conform to certain standards. Men and women were to be housed separately, linens provided for each bed, and every room equipped in a particular way with a font of holy water, a crucifix, and a rosary for each resident. An account had to be rendered to the parish's pastor every year. Priests were to be brought in to say mass and administer the sacraments, and the hospital's attendant was to ensure that patients confessed their sins at least once a year. Almost as an afterthought, the visitors noted, infirmities, both literal and figurative, were to be handled with patience.[29]

Just as the visitors mapped hospital rooms, so too did they map the collegiate houses, parish churches, vicarages, chapels, cemeteries, shrines, and pilgrimage sites of the archdiocese; but they went further in their efforts, mapping both movements within the parish as well as the bodies of clergy and believers. This literal mapping of the archdiocese went hand in hand with the intended mapping of people's beliefs. Visitors began by recording the names, locations, and patrons as well as any disputes over funds, authority, or jurisdiction. They described the conditions of churches and chapels, their contents, how they were arranged, and they duly informed pastors, vicars, and superiors what changes had to be made. Most notable were the frequent orders to erect a tabernacle above the main altar rather than to store the Eucharist beside it or within a nearby niche; to construct a baptismal font according to standards that outlined its form, decoration, and use; to maintain a sanctuary lamp; or to outfit the churches with specified altar cloths, chalices, ciboria, and other apparatus. Confessions were not to be heard in the sacristy but in the nave or, preferably, within a confessional; prelates or teachers had to teach the catechism in specified places and lead the children to mass; side altars were to be maintained, clearly identified, and distinguished from the main altar; heretics had to be denied burial within sacred ground; and confraternities and guilds had to attend mass and to participate in processions on certain holidays. Visitors instructed priests to wear clerical garb appropriate to their orders to distinguish them from the laity. The four-cornered biretta, signifying completion of a course of

---

[29]HMML XIX-D–18, fol. 16r.

training at a Jesuit school, was singled out as particularly important for this purpose since it indicated a higher level of expertise in Catholic doctrine.[30] Visitors also decreed that confraternities and guilds have standards made that bore the image or symbol of their patron saint, which they should carry on appropriate feast days. The mental landscape was similarly mapped through regularly held services, catechism classes for all children, preaching from the pulpit, setting moral examples, proper education and supervision for priests and teachers, and the careful recording of baptisms, communicants, and heretics.[31]

The visitors to Styria described mixed physical and mental landscapes in the duchy despite their overall impression that religion was improved, if imperfect. Although they frequently made recommendations for improvement, commented regularly on the poor quality of believers' piety and practices, and spent a good deal of time settling numerous disputes over jurisdictions and funding, they seemed satisfied with the quality of both clergy and church services. For every drunken chaplain, dissimulating priest, disturbed nun, or formerly Lutheran schoolteacher, there were numerous secular and regular clergy and teachers whose reports to the commission indicated that they were well educated and competent, and perhaps even learned, pious, and respected.[32] Frequently, it seems, the visitors' silences indicate more about their general satisfaction than specific corrections do about their unhappiness.

And yet I am struck by how few heretics one finds compared to the numerous priests, nuns, and parishioners who had to be corrected or whose disputes had to be settled by the visitors. May they not have been a permanent part of the landscape, along with the learned and the pious, just so many failures in what I can imagine the visitors saw as a mostly successful effort? This realization leads me away from the visitors' mapping project and towards the experiences of the locals, which can be gleaned from the report. When I do so, I begin to ascertain a very brief presence by outsiders, who seem serious and make

[30]Posch, "Aus dem kirchlichen Visitationsbericht 1617," 211 (see n. 1 above).
[31]HMML XIX-D-18, passim; Posch provides a useful summary, 197–200, 225–28.
[32]See HMML XIX-D-18, fols. 466v–467r (chaplain), fol. 628v (priest), fol. 47r (nun), and 25r–26v (schoolteacher). For only a few examples of those viewed in a more positive light, see fols. 31v–32r (pastor in Graz), 38v–48v (prioress of an Ursuline convent), 490v (pastor in Leoben), and 461v (teacher in the Latin school in Bruck).

demands but mostly leave well enough alone, sanction what is already taking place, and quickly depart. Dramatic glimpses of the local can be found if one chooses to look at already existing side altars, shrines and pilgrimage sites, guilds and confraternities, each with its own distinctly local identity, and the steady presence of problematic priests, nuns, and parishioners. Such persistent aspects of the local were not alien, unlike the visitors; rather, they were part of the normal, if constantly moving, landscape of religious life. Scholars have made much of the fact that visitation reports necessarily record negative impressions; after all, they constituted efforts to locate error and thus reflect the interests of the visitors and their superiors.[33] Yet if scholars turn from their own reductive efforts to locate and define the success or failure of reform efforts, this problem is lessened, since visitors' silences and the glimpses of the local that their reports provide can tell their own stories.

For example, questions addressed to the guild masters in Graz reveal no fewer than thirty-one guilds, most with their own patron saint, banners displaying their patron, and special feast days for communal celebration. Two confraternities are also listed for the parish of Graz and its vicarages and filial churches in the surrounding area. In their remarks, the visitors note the lack of piety and the existence of doctrinal error, inconsistent practices, and rivalries among the guilds in Graz; but they go on to authorize numerous guild activities under clerical supervision: every guild was expected to seek the approval of the duke, to have a patron and banner, to celebrate the appropriate feast days, and to participate in the funeral processions of fellow members and in the Corpus Christi procession. One wonders how much these reforms could have affected the guilds' perceived disruptive behavior. Put otherwise, the guilds were to continue what many, if not most, had been doing already, with perhaps the exception of participating in the Corpus Christi procession. Guilds fewer in number and less diverse can be found throughout Styria's larger cities and even in the countryside. Most pastors were admonished to improve and to regularize their activities, but nothing was done to disband them. The religious and social landscape, from the multiple perspectives available to local individuals and groups, looked pretty much

---

[33]See, for example, Marc Venard, "Die französischen Visitationsberichte des 16. bis 18. Jahrhunderts," in *Kirche und Visitation* (see n. 18 above), and James Kittelson, "Successes and Failures" and "Visitations and Popular Religious Culture" (see n. 6 above).

the same before, during, and after the visitation, save for a few literally ornamental changes.[34]

The notion of two distinct perspectives, the elite and the popular, unravels when reformers' attempts to project a universal ideal are placed within the elastic—simultaneously flexible and resilient—sites of the individual parishes. Reform affected the parishes, but the parishes also affected reform. Regularizing gestures on the part of the archbishop's officers appear frequently in the report, but little, if anything, was done to put a stop to local practices falling within certain parameters. What was true for guilds and confraternities also applied to the veneration of municipal patrons, the construction and maintenance of side altars, the visitation of pilgrimage sites and shrines, and numerous other examples.

The visitors expressly authorized local forms of religion while attempting to regulate, direct, and supervise them. Confronted with practices of local origin, the visitors simply reinscribed those already existing practices in particular, specific locales. The universal had, in effect, acknowledged and thereby absorbed the local. The messy realities of geographic distribution—diverse territories; a hodgepodge of parish churches, vicarages, and chapels; disparate shrines and pilgrimage sites; and dramatically different church buildings—had in fact been recognized and accepted by the very mapping project intended to make all practices and beliefs universal.[35] The inherent instability of multiple sites rendered reform programs not ineffective, but necessarily incomplete.

Local believers, too, absorbed aspects of the reformers' program; but within everyday life, did it really matter that a tabernacle was present, that the baptismal font was more elaborate, that feast days would be celebrated with greater fanfare? Local sources of instability likely had a more direct impact on affairs than the irregular and infrequent visitations. Inconsistent teachers and clergy, the irregular activities of guilds and confraternities as well as rivalries between them,

---

[34]See, for example, HMML XIX-D–18, fols. 8r–9v and 18v–24r (guilds and confraternities in and near Graz), fol. 24r (regulation of guilds), and fols. 458r, 459v–460r, 488r, 622v (instructions to pastors).

[35]HMML XIX-D–18, passim. Almost every page of the report, despite its formulaic composition (or perhaps because of it), bespeaks the kind of diversity I have in mind. Although Posch, "Aus dem kirchlichen Visitationsbericht 1617," is concerned exclusively with Styria's urban sites, this report too reveals a great variety of experiences (see n. 1 above).

and disputes over funds and jurisdictions shaped the realities of everyday life.[36] Other kinds of documents would reveal even more about such inherent instabilities, and yet I have examined only visitation reports precisely because they are so ostensibly one-sided, perspectively simple, and transparently biased in favor of concerns about reform. Local sites were inherently unstable places, which could and would disrupt all attempts to make them the same.

If we wish, we can review visitations in terms of either success or failure by comparing them to earlier and later visitations, but we risk eliminating a lot about religious life in the process. How do we measure transgressions? Do we define them, assign them different weights, and then add them up? According to this implicit calculus of success and failure, the visitation of Styria conducted between 1617 and 1619 seems a rousing success. Compared to what visitations of various kinds tell us about the periods of 1523–25, 1528, 1544–45, and 1581, Styria was more obviously Catholic and its believers adhered more clearly to prescribed Catholic doctrine, liturgy, and polity than they had done earlier.[37] But it seems to me that when local geographies and the multiple points of view within them are taken into account as well, evidence for either the success or the failure of religious reform becomes impossible to identify.

The question I posed at the beginning of this essay highlights the problem: What do you do with a drunken chaplain? Is he an example of successful religious reform insofar as his misdeeds were discovered and punished? Or is he an example of its failure insofar as his misdeeds occurred some two to four decades after the introduction of religious reform to the duchy? In Bruck in 1617, different parties had different views of the problem, views that cannot be made today to correspond entirely with one another, so that we might stamp this

[36]HMML XIX-D–18, passim; again, see Posch for brief examples.

[37]Cf. Karl Amon, *Die Salzburger Archidiakonenvisitation von 1523–1525 in der Steiermark* (Graz: Selbstverlag der Historischen Landeskommission für Steiermark, 1993), 36–42; HMML *Visitationsprotokoll*, 174 F. saec. 16. (1528), Graz-Diösesanarchiv, codex no. XIX-D–23, project no. 27,427, and Karl Eder, "Die Visitation und Inquisition von 1528 in der Steiermark: Gesamterscheinung und kritische Würdigung," *Mitteilungen des Instituts für österreichische Geschichtsforschung* 63 (1955): 312–22; Rudolf K. Höfer, *Die landesfürstlichen Visitation der Pfarren und Klöster in der Steiermark in den Jahren 1544/1545* (Graz: Selbstverlag der Historischen Landeskommission für Steiermark, 1992), 76–79; and Johann Rainer and Sabine Weiß, *Die Visitation steirischer Klöster und Pfarren im Jahre 1581* (Graz: Selbstverlag der Historischen Landeskommission für Steiermark, 1977), 9–27. Note also the conclusions in Posch, 225–28.

episode a success and a failure. Because it was both, it must also have been neither. Confronted by this aporia, this indeterminacy, we cannot decide between success and failure. Sometimes a drunken chaplain is just a drunken chaplain.

In concluding, I want to raise explicitly a final question, which has remained implicit in my critique of success and failure: Are historians' own mapping projects any less susceptible to the disruptive influence of the instabilities found in the Reformation landscape? Our endeavors, it seems to me, are not unlike the efforts of the episcopal visitors themselves, entrusted to implement a disciplinary program, but confronted with a flexibility and resiliency that render it necessarily partial and incomplete. How alike are we to the imperial cartographers described by Jorge Luis Borges in the parable "On Rigor in Science"? Their ultimate achievement, a map so detailed that it covered entirely the empire it was meant to represent, gradually deteriorated and was eventually abandoned.[38] In pursuing the similarly totalizing quest to understand the Reformation and its aftermath as either a success or a failure, we reenact the operations and recapitulate the aims of the empire's cartographers. We construct a narrative map, reducible to a single term or, perhaps, to a set of related terms intended to cover the entire Reformation landscape. This narrative map is no more permanent than the imperial map in Borges' parable.

We must accept that visitations reveal traces both of unifying gestures, within their very formulation, and emphasis on common concerns (the projection of the universal), and of diversifying gestures, through representations and reinscriptions of disparate and different practices (acknowledgment of the local). To reduce the productive and creative tension between these two tendencies is to fall into the

---

[38]"Del Rigor en la ciencia," in *El Hacedor* (Buenos Aires: Emecé Editores, 1967), 113. In this complete translation, I have slightly modified the English version of Mildred Boyer and Harold Morland from *Dreamtigers* (Austin: University of Texas Press, 1964), 90, with the help of my colleague at Lawrence University, Hugo Martinez-Serros: "In that Empire, the Art of Cartography reached such Perfection that the map of one Province alone took up the whole of a City, and the map of the empire, the whole of a Province. In time, those Excessive Maps did not satisfy, and the Colleges of Cartographers set up a Map of the Empire that had the size of the Empire itself and coincided with it point by point. Less addicted to the Study of Cartography, Succeeding Generations understood that this Widespread Map was Useless, and not without Impiety they abandoned it to the Inclemencies of the Sun and of the Winters. In the deserts of the West some mangled Ruins of the Map still exist, inhabited by Animals and Beggars; in the whole Country there are no other relics of the Disciplines of Geography."

conceptual trap of not only thinking dichotomously, but going a step further and granting priority to one term in the dichotomy as though it were the only thinkable alternative. Analyzing and depicting the visitation as an event that takes place within a space, a space that is inherently but not perfectly unstable, allows for the conscious recognition of simultaneously coherent and contradictory gestures in the same place. The landscape of the late Reformation is thus made a landscape within which one finds continuous movement—a complex system comprised of both reform movements and the activities that interrupt and displace them. Religious reform, social discipline, and confessionalization are not out of bounds in such a landscape, but as projections of the putatively universal, the pragmatically local necessarily disrupts them.

Clericalism and Communalism in German Catholicism

Marc R. Forster

Two central characteristics of Catholicism in Southwest Germany were clericalism and communalism. Clericalism meant, especially in the seventeenth and eighteenth centuries, that German Catholics demanded that priests, especially resident priests, perform and sanctify church rituals. Communalism meant that village communes played a central role in the supervision of the rural clergy and in the organization of village life. These two aspects of rural Catholicism reinforced each other, especially since the desire for more, and more active, priests led communes to press for the creation of new parishes and benefices. Once new benefices were created, communes consciously retained influence over the behavior and duties of the clergymen. The clericalism and communalism of rural religion both reflect the popular appeal of "baroque Catholicism" and provide a window on the popular role in the development of modern German Catholicism.

ON 16 APRIL 1764 THE NEIGHBORING COMMUNES of Langenschemmern and Aufhofen, located in Upper Swabia near the city of Biberach, wrote a long letter to the bishop of Constance.[1] The community leaders protested an episcopal ordinance that forbade church services in Langenschemmern on Easter Sunday and on a number of other high feast days of the Catholic calendar. The decree ordered that the villagers attend these services in the church in the neighboring village of Schemmerberg. But these peasants wanted to hear mass and receive communion in their village church on the most important day of the Christian calendar.

The residents of Langenschemmern and Aufhofen, like many other peasants in Southwest Germany, lived in a filial parish. By the mid-eighteenth century there was a priest living in Langenschemmern, but he was only a chaplain (*Kaplan*), and the legally recognized

[1]Generallandesarchiv Karlsruhe (henceforth GLAK) 98/3848.

parish priest resided in Schemmerberg, about fifteen kilometers away. This priest and the patrons of the parish, the Cistercian monastery of Salem, asserted the ancient rights of the "mother church." The monastery's incorporation of the parish of Schemmerberg justified its right to collect the tithe in the filial villages and permitted the parish priest to collect all fees and offerings made by the faithful. The fees and offering were, by tradition, given at Easter and three high feasts (Christmas, Pentecost, Corpus Christi).[2] The villagers from Langenschemmern and Aufhofen reluctantly paid these fees; they were not, however, willing to go to the services in Schemmerberg.

The villagers gave a number of reasons for wanting services in their own church. Some of these reflected the practical problems and dangers of rural life in the eighteenth century. The peasants did not want to leave their villages empty, for fear of robbers, vagabonds, and fire. They also claimed that there were many old and sick people who could not make the walk to Schemmerberg. Finally, they pointed out that at the mother parish the church was too small to hold all the parishioners, and that those coming from far away did not get seats. In fact, especially on Easter, the church in Schemmerberg was so full that many people had to stand outside and could neither hear the sermon nor see the priest and the altar.[3]

This latter objection points up the broad religious issues involved here. Certainly the practical problems concerned the villagers, as did the insult to their honor when they had to stand in the back of the church, or even outside, while the Schemmerbergers occupied the well-placed pews.[4] Because they did have a resident vicar, the people of Langenschemmern did not complain about the lack of a priest to do emergency baptisms or give communion and last rites to the

[2]On the liturgical year, see Robert W. Scribner, "Ritual and Popular Religion in Catholic Germany at the Time of the Reformation," in *Popular Culture and Popular Movements in the Reformation* (London: Hambledon Press, 1987); Charles Phythian-Adams, *Local History and Folklore: A New Framework* (London: Bedford Square Press, 1975), 21–25; Eamon Duffy, *The Stripping of the Altars: Traditional Religion in England, c.1400–c. 1580* (New Haven: Yale University Press, 1992), esp. chap. 1. Also Ludwig Veit and Ludwig Lenhart, *Kirche und Volksfrömmigkeit im Zeitalter des Barock* (Freiburg: Herder Verlag, 1956).

[3]See Marc R. Forster, *The Counter-Reformation in the Villages: Religion and Reform in the Bishopric of Speyer, 1560–1720* (Ithaca: Cornell University Press, 1992), esp. 36–38.

[4]The problem of seats was probably important to the leaders of the Langenschemmern *Gemeinde*, who were the elite of that village and surely had seats in their church. The poorer peasants probably did not have seats in either church.

dying, a major concern in many filial churches. However, their request highlights a number of other significant religious concerns. The inhabitants of Langenschemmern and Aufhofen wanted their own priest to give them the full range of services, with full ceremony, in their own church on Easter. The villagers considered both the "silent mass," held early on Easter morning, and the sermon by the chaplain insufficient. They rejected the argument of the priest in Schemmerberg who said that the villagers had a better opportunity to show their devotion in the filial than in the mother church:

> [The early mass and sermon] are more pleasing to God, and better for their souls, than going to one mass [in the afternoon] and spending the whole morning with nothing to do except hang around, especially the single men.[5]

The people of Langenschemmern wanted their village church elevated to a real parish, which would mean full services on all holidays in their community, complete with a sermon, communion, and the elevation of the host, and they wanted to witness all of this from inside the church. They also demanded that "their priest" perform this mass, not the priest from Schemmerberg. The villagers' Catholicism certainly required a priest, but their religion was also local and communal in spirit.

This incident illustrates two central and interlocking aspects of Catholicism in Southwest Germany. The first aspect was the laity's demand that priests, especially resident priests, perform and sanctify church rituals, an attitude I will call clericalism.[6] The second attribute was the continuing communal control of parishes. The coexistence of clericalism and communalism indicates that German Catholicism evolved differently than many church reformers envisaged. Most significantly, although the people honored the special role of the priest

---

[5]GLAK 98/3848: "Welches Got gefälliger, und ihren Seelen anspriesslicher seyn wird, als an einem so heyl. tag nur ein einzige mess anhören, und alsdan den ganzen vormittag unnuz und mit miessigang zu bringen, besonders von lediger Bursch." (All translations from documents are mine.)

[6]I have taken the concept of clericalism from Timothy Tackett, *Religion, Revolution, and Regional Culture in Eighteenth-Century France: the Ecclesiastical Oath of 1791* (Princeton: Princeton University Press, 1986). I realize that there are problems with using the term, especially since it evokes the nineteenth-century use of clericalism, which was often pejorative.

and even expected his leadership, just as Tridentine reformers hoped, communities did not give the priest control of the village parish.[7]

Clericalism and communalism were closely intertwined, and they even reinforced each other. The desire for more, and more active, priests led communes to press for the creation of new parishes and benefices. The ecclesiastical hierarchy was, mostly for financial reasons, generally reluctant to support such projects, and communities had to make monetary contributions as well as expend political capital to achieve their goals. Communes did not take this initiative without consciously retaining influence over the behavior and duties of the clergymen hired in the new positions. Furthermore, the central importance of the priest in the religious life of communities caused the people, and especially their leaders, to carefully monitor the professional performance of their pastors. Those priests who failed to carry out their duties were quickly criticized. If they continued to neglect their office, parishioners brought pressure to bear for their removal.

Neither clericalism nor communalism was new in the early modern period. The church had always sought to "clericalize" Christianity, although with mixed success. In the fifteenth century, for example, the church sought to control access to the sacred and to "professionalize" the clergy. The laity, however, often bypassed the parish priest, turning to mendicants for the sacraments and to lay confraternities for devotion.[8] Communes played a major role in the religious life of fifteenth-century Germany, and rural Catholicism in southern Germany and Switzerland was to a great extent communalized by 1500.[9] This was probably the logical outcome of the simultaneous creation of the parochial structure in the European countryside in the Middle Ages and the elaboration of communal institutions,

---

[7]John Bossy, "The Counter-Reformation and the People of Catholic Europe," *Past and Present* 47 (1970): 51–70.

[8]Robert Scribner, *The German Reformation* (Atlantic Highlands, N.J.: Humanities Press, 1986), 12–13.

[9]Peter Blickle, *Communal Reformation: The Quest for Salvation in Sixteenth-Century Germany* (Atlantic Highlands, N.J.: Humanities Press, 1992). Also Rosi Fuhrmann, "Die Kirche im Dorf," in Peter Blickle, ed., *Zugänge zur bäuerlichen Reformation: Bauer und Reformation* (Zurich: Chronos, 1987), and Franziska Conrad, *Reformation in der bäuerlichen Gesellschaft: Zur Rezeption reformatorischer Theologie im Elsass* (Stuttgart: Franz Steiner Verlag Wiesbaden, 1984).

especially in the German-speaking lands.[10] There is considerable debate among social and political historians over the extent to which peasant communes lost their autonomy to the rising state in the early modern period.[11] Whatever their fate as political players, the point here is that communes remained very influential in organizing local religious life through the eighteenth century.[12]

Clericalism

In seeking the origins of opposition to the Civil Constitution of the Clergy in revolutionary France, Timothy Tackett has argued that popular Catholicism in large regions of France was clericalized by the late eighteenth century. Clericalism (in this definition) "involved a relatively greater internalization of sacerdotal functions in one's view of the nature and workings of religion" and was strong in those parts of France, especially in the west, which resisted the revolutionary reorganization of the church in the 1790s.[13] Tackett argues that clericalization was in part a consequence of Tridentine reform:

> Perhaps, in practical terms, the ultimate measure of success of the push toward clericalization under the Old Regime was not the extent to which the clergy was able to crush popular religion—which was all but impossible in the short run—but rather the extent to which the clergy was able to impose its influence while still maintaining a viable and flexible *modus vivendi* with the popular expressions of religious sentiment. (235)

It appears that much of Catholic Germany experienced a similar process of clericalization. Here too there were "cultural and structural features" which made the people receptive to a clericalized religion. As in France, one can identify a "certain degree of tolerance and accommodation" on the part of the ecclesiastical hierarchy. Furthermore, the same "clustering of variables which converged to help fos-

[10]On communal institutions, see Heide Wunder, *Die bäuerliche Gemeinde in Deutschland* (Göttingen: Vandenhoeck & Ruprecht, 1986), and Peter Blickle, *Deutsche Untertanen: ein Widerspruch* (Munich: C. H. Beck, 1981).

[11]David M. Luebke, *His Majesty's Rebels* (Ithaca: Cornell University Press, 1997).

[12]On the communal church, see Forster, *Counter-Reformation in the Villages*, esp. chap. 1 (see n. 3 above). On communalism more generally, see Robert W. Scribner, "Communalism: Universal Category or Ideological Construct? A Debate in the Historiography of Early Modern Germany and Switzerland," *Historical Journal* 37, no.1 (1994): 199–207, esp. 204–5.

[13]Tackett, *Religion, Revolution, and Regional Culture*, 249 (see n. 6 above).

ter particularly strong clerical ... orientations..." in western France can be found in Southwest Germany. These variables included a large clerical establishment, local and rural recruitment of the parish clergy, and "a missionary tradition sympathetic to certain aspects of popular religion."[14]

One must also look beyond the structures of religious life and examine how the people interacted with the clergy, above all the parish priests. One aspect of this relationship was a clear decline in anticlericalism among German peasants between the Peasants' War (1525) and the end of the Thirty Years' War.[15] This trend was accompanied by growing pressure from the population for an expansion of the parochial structure, especially between 1590 and 1620, and again after about 1690. Although population growth explains some of the need for more priests, the content of the petitions from communities suggests something more: an increasing demand for the presence and services of qualified Catholic priests.

A certain kind of anticlericalism, in which peasants expressed hostility toward overly zealous priests, was dominant in whole regions of France. This attitude is difficult to find in Catholic Germany, even in the late eighteenth century.[16] Peasants resented priests too closely linked to repressive lords, but this problem was apparently not widespread. Conflicts between parishioners and priests over the tithe or other property conflicts were of course endemic, and sometimes the peasants drew on the older, and very rich, anticlerical tradition in criticizing the wealth and political power of the Catholic Church. Yet on the local level, peasants appear to have separated the religious function of the priest from his role as petty bureaucrat, property manager, and tithe collector.[17] In Southwest Germany, the peo-

---

[14]Tackett, *Religion, Revolution, and Regional Culture*, 248–49.

[15]On anticlericalism, see Peter Blickle, *The Revolution of 1525: The German Peasants' War from a New Perspective* (Baltimore: Johns Hopkins University Press, 1981), and Henry Cohn, "Anticlericalism in the German Peasants' War, 1525," *Past and Present* 83 (1979): esp. 16–31.

[16]For France, see Philip T. Hoffman, *Church and Community in the Diocese of Lyon, 1500–1789* (New Haven: Yale University Press, 1984); Tackett, *Religion, Revolution, and Regional Culture* (see n. 6 above).

[17]Conflicts between peasants and priests may have declined as the patrons, particularly the monasteries, collected the tithe themselves. In many places priests became less involved in day-to-day economic life after 1650. Peasants in the southern Black Forest fought the monastery of Saint Blasien tooth and nail, but rarely does one find anticlerical rhetoric in their conflicts with the monastery. See Luebke, *His Majesty's Rebels* (n. 11 above).

ple even viewed monks as useful for pastoral duties, thereby undermining the criticism of monasteries as "parasitic," a common anticlerical attack during the Reformation and throughout the sixteenth century.[18]

The search for new priests was another aspect of clericalization. Rural communities actively organized and supported the creation of permanent benefices for priests, or if this was not possible, they arranged for and funded temporary clergymen, mostly mendicants from nearby towns. The reasoning behind these measures was fairly standard. In 1651, for example, the residents of Waldmössingen asked the bishop for a priest of their own, or if this was not possible, for an Augustinian to come from the town of Oberndorf on a weekly basis. The one-and-a-half-hour journey to Oberndorf was too long for the villagers to undertake every week, and as a result many had not received communion in years. Many children were growing up having never been to mass or catechism class. The villagers were willing to contribute in several ways to the project: "With the donations and alms of generous and good-hearted people, and our own sweat and blood we have completed the building of a church."[19] Permission to bring a priest to this church would, the peasants informed the bishop, honor God, and "lead us weak mortal people to salvation."[20]

The request of the Waldmössinger, while couched in the grim language of the immediate aftermath of the Thirty Years' War, was echoed time and again in the seventeenth and eighteenth centuries by other peasants. In 1777 the community (*Gemeinde*) of Schlatt protested to the Austrian regime in Freiburg that they were poorly served by the Franciscan hired by their lords, the Knights of St. John.[21] The commune argued that the villagers paid enough tithe to support a resident priest, who would surely do a better job. The mendicants endangered the souls of the faithful because they could not always come to Schlatt in time for emergency baptisms or to give the sacra-

---

[18]See Marc R. Forster, "The Elite and Popular Foundations of German Catholicism in the Age of Confessionalism: The Reichskirche," *Central European History* 26, no.3 (1993): 313, 323.

[19]Hauptstaatsarchiv Stuttgart [henceforth: HStASt.] B466a/402. "So haben wir durch hilff Milte= undt Gottseelige Leiten hilff steür und allmossen, neben unseren armen Schweisend Bluott wider ein Kürch erbawt undt zu endt gebracht."

[20]HStASt. B466a/402: "auch uns schwache sterbliche Menschen zuer Seeligkheidt füern thutt."

[21]GLAK 79/825,no. 26; cf. 89/107.

ments to the dying. The villagers also considered the services that the Franciscans offered insufficient:

> The mendicant priests assigned to this parish read two masses a week, including Sunday and holidays. These services consist of a sermon, although not always, or sometimes a catechism lesson instead, and then the mass itself, all of which happens in quick succession, so that they [the Franciscans] can get home as soon as possible.[22]

Two central religious issues informed the demands for more priests. The first was the need for resident priests to baptize the newborn and confess the dying. In this area the Tridentine emphasis on the sacraments appears to have coincided with the traditions within popular Christianity that emphasized these rites of passage, especially baptism.[23] The second issue was the popular demand for complete services, particularly regular masses during the week, Sunday services with both a sermon and the mass, and extensive ceremonies on important feast days. The focus on the mass indicates its importance as the central moment in popular Catholicism.[24]

Village communes were willing to expend their own resources to get the religious services they wanted. In 1737 the commune of Molpertshausen agreed to contribute stones and other building material to repair its church, and in 1763 the same commune arranged for full services in this church on major feasts, in part by donating a field to the parish for the upkeep of a resident priest.[25] In other places villagers had fewer resources, but they offered to contribute work teams for

---

[22]GLAK 79/825, no. 26."[N]ebst den Kommt der jederzeit zu solcher Pfarrey versehend bestelte ordensgeistliche all wochen 2 mahlen zu Messen, dann an Sonntag= und gebottenen Feyr tagen, und bestehet dessen vorrichtung in abhaltung einer Predig, doch nicht allzeit, und statt desen der ChristenLehr, und H. Mess-opfer, welch alles nachinander beschiehet, und sich so dann wider nacher hauss begibet."

[23]Scribner, *The German Reformation*, chap.1, esp. p. 11 (see n. 8 above). Also Bernd Moeller, "Piety in Germany Around 1500," in Steven Ozment, ed., *The Reformation in Medieval Perspective* (Chicago: Quadrangle Books, 1971), 50–75, and Veit and Lenhart, *Kirche und Volksfrömmigkeit*, pt.1, chap. 2 (see n. 2 above).

[24]On the importance of the mass, see Eamon Duffy, *The Stripping of the Altars*, chap. 3 (see n. 2 above); John Bossy, *Christianity in the West, 1400–1700* (London: Oxford University Press, 1985); and Louis Châtellier, *La Religion des pauvres: Les Missions rurales en Europe et la formation du catholicisme moderne, XVIe–XIXe siècles* (Paris: Aubier, 1993).

[25]HStASt. B486/1273.

building or made regular contributions of wood from communal forests.[26]

Although clericalism was a permanent feature of both official and popular religion, there was an increased demand for priests in Catholic regions after 1650. This process kept the clerical council (*der geistliche Rat*) of the bishops of Constance busy in the first decades of the eighteenth century.[27] One way to expand the number of clergy was to hire assistant priests, primissaries (*Frühmesser*), and chaplains. In 1708, for example, the Teutonic Knights reported that the parishioners of the filial church in Dettingen wanted the priest in Dingelsdorf to hire a "permanent assistant."[28] Beginning in 1709, the inhabitants and a local nobleman in Laupheim attempted to force the monastery of Ochsenhausen to hire and pay a primissary in their parish.[29] Although the council supported this endeavor, Ochsenhausen tenaciously resisted, prompting episcopal officials to threaten legal measures in 1714. In both these cases the additional priest was eventually installed.[30]

The Clerical Council also discussed a number of projects for the creation of new parishes in this period, at Möhringen (1710), Ingerkingen (1711), and Dettingen (1712).[31] In general, episcopal officials responded positively to these schemes. The rigid parish structure of the period 1500–1650 was weakening; it is significant that in all cases monasteries resisted new parishes, while communes, with modest support from episcopal officials, applied pressure for change. The peasants could be most imaginative about the arrangements for new parishes, a sign that they wanted results. The residents of Immenriedt proposed that the property of the parish priest in Kißlegg, where the mother church was located, be freed from a number of taxes and dues. This would increase his income by 100 Gulden,

---

[26]See GLAK 61/13465, pp. 458–60 and 567–75, for one example of the complicated negotiations for the building of a new church in Mainwangen in 1707.

[27]Erzbischöfliches Archiv Freiburg (henceforth: EAF), Ha 216, 217, 218.

[28]EAF, Ha 217, pp. 301, 303.

[29]EAF, Ha 217, pp. 46–47, 70–71, 105–6, 184–85, 213. Ha 218, pp. 362–63, 382–83, 501–2, 522–24.

[30]Other examples of revival of secondary benefices: *Caplanei* in Hummertsried, HStASt. B486/438 and *Frühmesserei* in Nusplingen, HStASt. B467/684.

[31]EAF, Ha 218, pp. 52–55, 227–28, 235–36, 250, 291–93, 398–99.

allowing him to hire an assistant to conduct services in Immenriedt. The villagers were rewarded for their initiative.[32]

There are other indicators of the growing importance of the clergy. In the century after the Thirty Years' War, pastoral work absorbed many holders of *beneficia simplicia*, who theoretically were not required to provide such services.[33] Furthermore, mendicants and monks played a significant pastoral role by the mid-eighteenth century, something that in the 1770s and 1780s surprised Austrian officials intent on abolishing monasteries. Much of the monk/priests' work was unofficial, as villagers called on Capuchins, Augustinians, Franciscans, and Dominicans from nearby towns when they needed a priest.[34] The regular clergy performed especially important services in the many towns and small cities of the regions, where parish priests were few and overburdened.[35] When questioned in the 1780s about the usefulness of monasteries, magistrates almost uniformly applauded the regulars.[36] The Capuchins received the most praise, especially for their work in the mountainous regions near Waldshut, Stauffen, and Tettnang. One town council argued that "they are not just useful, but necessary."[37] The parish structure, which despite the efforts of the people changed only slowly, required that the Capuchins and other orders filled the needs of a clericalized religion. There is a certain irony that the success of clericalization, a fundamental goal of Catholic reformers, depended on the diversity and variety of the Catholic Church in Germany, which ran counter to the spirit of the organizational reforms of Trent.

The vehemence with which peasants attacked priests who did not fulfill their professional responsibilities is another indication of the importance of the clergy. In 1661 the Vogt (a kind of mayor) and council of the Black Forest village of Schönau criticized their priest, Father Giselbertus Strankhaar.[38] According to his parishioners, the

---

[32]Ibid., pp. 335–36, 418–19, 426–27.   [33]GLAK 79/837.   [34]GLAK 118/186.

[35]Richard Goldthwaite, *Wealth and the Demand for Art in Italy, 1300–1600* (Baltimore: Johns Hopkins University Press, 1993), 133, compares the density of parishes in Italy and Germany. There were far fewer parishes in German cities.

[36]HStASt. B17/426.

[37]HStASt. B17/426: "nicht nur nutzlich, sondern notwendig."

[38]GLAK 229/94055. Father Giselbertus was probably a Benedictine from St. Blasien. The parish was incorporated into the monastery, which also had extensive juridical rights, many serfs, and considerable estates in the area. See Luebke, *His Majesty's Rebels* (see n. 11 above).

Father did not teach the youth to pray the Our Father or the Hail Mary, had failed to preach on a Palm Sunday and a Good Friday, did not support the parish confraternity, and refused on several occasions to hear confessions. Father Giselbertus compounded his unpopularity with a personal lifestyle that did not fit the villagers' image of a priest. According to one report, the priest was raising several young dogs and a wolf in the parsonage. The peasants feared that the wolf would injure the village children, and even expressed deeper fears:

> Everyone knows the true nature of a wolf and the father should keep him under control so that it does not hurt anyone ... [and] it is not a good idea to raise a wolf in our valley ... and even less advisable that he enter the church. Serious trouble could easily result from this wolf.[39]

Father Giselbertus denied most of the charges, and called the Schönauer lazy, neglectful, superstitious, and "Idioten." In his view, the children's inability to say their prayers was the parents' fault. He maintained that his dogs and wolf had not harmed anyone, adding, "[I] must in passing comment, that it is nicer to live with dogs and wolves, and that one receives more loyalty from them than from my ungrateful parishioners."[40]

One should not be distracted by Father Giselbertus' eccentricities. The complaints about his professional performance were typical. Any priest who did not provide enough masses, or who failed to preach, risked the wrath of his parishioners. Equally important were the sacraments, especially baptism and marriage, as well as confession and communion at Easter. Finally, the Schönauer complained about the arrogance of the priest, particularly when he kept people waiting in the church while he finished preparing his sermon, when he did not show up for confessions, or when he unilaterally canceled sermons. The priest was vital for the practice of Catholicism in Schönau, and

---

[39]GLAK 229/94055. "Allein weiss man woll was ein wolff für ein Natur hat, so solle er herr deme im der gewarsame behalten damit niehmant kein schadt dar durch geschehe.... Allso ist diess nit rumlich ein wolff in einem thall auf zue ziehen...viell weniger dz er soll in die kirchen kommen, und leichtlich ein grosser unglück von dem Wolff entspringen kente."

[40]GLAK 229/94055. "Muss aber beynebens lehrnen, quod melius sit cohabitare inter canes et lupos und grösser trewheit bey ihnen zuefinden, als bey meinen undankbaren Pfahrkinderen...."

his parishioners had clear "expectations concerning the proper role and behavior of the priest." At the same time they surely did not obey him uncritically.[41]

It is easier to demonstrate the importance of priests in the villages than to explain the clericalization of Southwest German Catholicism. It is worth mentioning some tentative ideas. Certainly the clericalization of popular religious practice was a goal of Tridentine reform, yet the importance of the Catholic clergy in Southwest Germany is not just an indication of the victory of Catholic reform. In fact, an important element in the relationship between the church and the population was the weakness of Tridentine reform. The large number of monasteries and collegiate chapters, all with extensive rights (especially of patronage) in rural parishes, provided a buffer between aggressive Tridentine reformers and the population, preventing the alienation of the population from the church. Furthermore, the density of the Catholic clergy in this region, a source of anticlericalism in the early sixteenth century, was less threatening by 1600, and even a source of strength after 1650. The diversity of the clergy meant that the Catholic Church was less monolithic than the neighboring Protestant territories and precluded any coordinated attack on popular culture. Finally, most Catholic priests, monks, and nuns were local people, of small-town or even peasant background, which made it easier for the people to accept them.

The institutional and sociopolitical factors behind clericalism are only a part of the story.[42] The attachment of the population to the religious ceremonies in which the priest officiated was another characteristic of popular religion. An examination of these religious practices—whether they were sacraments like baptism, confession, and communion, or devotions of lesser theological significance, like processions, pilgrimages, and the rosary, and even sermons—are central for our understanding of popular Catholicism. An analysis of these practices is the subject for a separate study. At this point it is important to look at the communal context within which people practiced these devotions.

---

[41]Quoted from Tackett, *Religion, Revolution, and Regional Culture*, 229 (see n. 6 above). Also see Forster, *Counter-Reformation in the Villages*, esp. chap. 6 (see n. 3 above).
[42]Tackett, *Religion, Revolution, and Regional Culture*, esp. 229 (see n. 6 above).

COMMUNALISM

Clericalism did not mean that parish priests took control of parishes. In fact, the growing importance of the parish priest was in significant ways the result of the communalism of Catholicism in the Southwest. Communes promoted clericalism while continuing to administer church property, influence the appointment of priests, and organize village religious life. Even in the eighteenth century there were striking continuities with the communal church of the pre-Reformation era as described by Peter Blickle.[43] As they did around 1500, Catholic peasants demanded that the priest respond to their needs and desires, that he not require extra pay for basic services, and that he live as a member of the community. Furthermore, although lay people accepted the special power and position of the priest, they did not allow him the initiative in arranging and promoting religious devotions. Throughout the seventeenth and eighteenth centuries, peasants organized processions, pilgrimages, and confraternities; funded the building of chapels and the placement of stations of the cross, pictures, or new altars in parish churches; and demanded that priests lead prayer meetings and other devotions. An active laity was a central feature of rural German Catholicism.

There were, then, striking continuities in the ecclesiopolitical role of the rural communes between the sixteenth and the eighteenth centuries. One must, however, heed the warnings of Robert Scribner to avoid using communalism as an overarching or universal category in German history.[44] The communalism of religious life, for example, does not preclude a weakening of the communal role in local administration. When one examines the day-to-day management of parish life, one has to acknowledge the central role of the communes. Here too an oversimplification or romanticization of the commune is to be avoided. There is no doubt that a village elite dominated the parishes as they dominated the communes. With these caveats in mind, the

---

[43]Blickle, *The Communal Reformation* and *The Revolution of 1525* (see nn. 9, 15 above).
[44]Scribner, "Communalism" (see n. 12 above). See also Heinrich Richard Schmidt, "Die Christianisierung des Sozialverhaltens als permanente Reformation" in *Kommunalisierung und Christianisierung: Voraussetzungen und Folgen der Reformation, 1400–1600*, ed. Peter Blickle and Johannes Kunische, *Zeitschrift für historische Forschung*, Beiheft 9 (Berlin: Franz Steiner, 1980), 113–63.

concept of communalism contributes to our understanding of rural Catholicism.

The most obvious role played by the commune was in the administration of the parish. The commune always participated in the management of parish property. In Schönau in 1613, for example, the village council prepared the annual accounts (*Rechnungen*) without consulting with the priest. In 1624 the same village council asserted its right to draft these accounts, which clearly symbolized control of this property, without informing either the priest or the patrons of the parish, the monastery of St. Blasien.[45] Even when the Austrian government forced the Schönauer to make concessions, as happened in 1624, the priest was allowed only to witness the submission of the accounts, not to participate in their preparation.[46]

Overseeing the finances of the parish gave communal officials, especially the church overseers (*Kirchenpfleger*), some power over the priest. Most clergymen in parishes received a significant part of their income from parish property. In the village of Fischbach, admittedly an unusual case, the parish priest received his whole salary directly from the *Gemeinde* in the form of four cash payments, as well as grain and wine rents from the parish property and other fees.[47] Even more important for most priests was the small tithe, which in most places communal officials collected and then gave to the priest. This situation caused, of course, endemic conflict between priests and their parishioners.

Communal officials always possessed keys to the church sacristy, baptistery, and offering chest. Indeed, throughout the seventeenth century parish priests struggled to secure a key for themselves so that they would not have to seek out communal officials to enter the church.[48] Priests usually did get keys to the church, but often not to offering boxes. In Öwingen, the monastery of Salem supported the mayor of the village when he refused to give a copy of an offering box

---

[45]GLAK 229/94055.

[46]Rudolf Reinhardt, *Die Beziehungen von Hochstift und Diözese Konstanz zu Habsburg-Österreich in der Neuzeit: Zugleich ein Beitrag zur archivalischen Erforschung des Problems "Kirche und Staat": Beiträge zur Geschichte der Reichskirche in der Neuzeit*, vol. 2. (Wiesbaden: Franz Steiner Verlag, 1966).

[47]GLAK 98/3817; agreement from 1698.

[48]GLAK 229/94055, Schönau.

key to the priest.[49] The possession and control of keys, of course, also had great symbolic implications, which were not lost on the parties involved.

Priests complained that communal officials treated the parish church as if it belonged to the community. The priest in Schönau argued that the villagers should not hang pictures and install chairs without consulting him.[50] Chairs and pews became a big issue after 1650, as peasants built them into rural churches for the first time. Conflicts over seating took place at several levels: priests squabbled with communal officials over who should determine seating arrangements, and the villagers feuded with each other over the best seats in church, with the priest often taking sides. In Blumenfeld in 1726, Pfarrer Johan Thomas Metzger tried to bring, as he called it, "order" (*Ordnung*) to the new seating installed in his church.[51] He placed his mother, his housekeeper (*Haushälterin*), the chaplain's maid, and the wife of a local official (the *Obervogt*), in the front row. Although Metzger thought this arrangement came close to matching the way the women had previously stood during services, regularizing the seating caused an uproar. Several women did not like seating the priest's mother in the front row and protested by standing in the main aisle through a whole Sunday service. Communal officials then intervened, arguing that the new seating violated tradition, and complained to their superiors that the priest planned to take away "private chairs" and divide them among all parishioners. It seems in fact that Pfarrer Metzger may have wanted to go beyond arranging a good seat for his mother and supported the majority of his parishioners against a village elite. Village leaders asserted that Metzger was innovating, and that he was motivated by "ambition."[52] One thing is clear: The villagers played a major role in the administration of the parish, even when they were divided among themselves.

Communes also influenced the appointment, disciplining, and removal of parish priests.[53] In a small number of parishes villagers exerted this power through the direct patronage of the church, while

---

[49]GLAK 61/13463, p. 309r. This *Opferstock* also held money from an endowment given to keep up a roadside cross and picture.

[50]GLAK 229/94055.   [51]GLAK 93/252.

[52]Cf. HStASt. B467/47. In Altdorf/Weingarten the *Rat* tried to reorganize seating arrangements, a move that the *Pfarrer* and some of the poorer parishioners resisted.

[53]See Forster, *The Counter-Reformation in the Villages*, chaps. 1 and 6 (see n. 3 above).

in a much larger number of places they controlled secondary benefices. Furthermore, communities brought indirect pressure to bear on monasteries, chapters, and government officials who had the actual right to appoint priests. Finally, as we have seen, peasants kept a close eye on the performance of their priest and did not hesitate to seek the removal of unacceptable clergymen. The town council of the small Austrian town of Binsdorf held the right to nominate the community's parish priest, who was then proposed (officially "presented") by the emperor to the bishop of Constance.[54] All evidence indicates that Austrian officials respected the choices of the council. In 1587, at a time when the Hapsburg government aggressively sought to eradicate concubinage among parish priests, officials in Innsbruck approved the council's nomination of Jacob Armbruster, who was known to have a concubine. In 1589 the council and commune further consolidated their hold over the priest by permanently adding the income of a chapel, over which they had patronage, to the resources of the parish.[55] Binsdorf was an exceptional but not isolated case. There were other parishes where the commune had the right to appoint priests; in Fischbach, for example, the *Gemeinde* nominated twenty-two priests between 1580 and 1777 to the monastery of Salem.[56]

By the eighteenth century, the mayor, council, and commune of Binsdorf had legally lost some control over the appointment of the parish priest. In 1762 the Binsdorfers nominated three candidates for the vacant parish and sent their names to Austrian officials. A government commission then interviewed the three finalists, and one of them was presented to the bishop.[57] However, the final outcome seems to have been predetermined. The candidate recommended first and most strongly by the *Gemeinde* received the post. According to Austrian officials he did no better than the others in the examination but was appointed because he had good recommendations "from his whole flock where he will be the shepherd...."[58] The Binsdorfers had a juridical right to nominate a priest, which gave them a special role in appointments. Other communes were sometimes less successful in getting their candidates appointed. In 1588 the commune in Deilingen also recommended a priest who had a concubine, but Austrian

[54]HStASt. B37a/134. [55]HStASt. B37a/135. [56]GLAK 98/3819. [57]HStASt. B38/573.
[58]HStASt. B38/573: "besonders von dem ganzen Schaff=Stall. dene er als hirth vorgestanden."

officials appointed someone else.[59] More often, however, the intercession of the commune helped a candidate. In 1593 Jacob Dietpold became Pfarrer in Durbheim after a strong recommendation by the commune.[60] In this case, officials regretted having rejected Dietpold's application several years earlier, since the villagers liked Dietpold and treated the other priest whom the authorities had appointed very badly.

Village communes also exerted pressure on parish patrons after the finalists for a position became known. In 1755 the commune and many residents of Ingerkingen petitioned against the appointment of one Herr Belling to their parish.[61] Belling was, according to the villagers,

> nothing but a troublemaker, who interferes entirely too often in secular matters, so that when the peasants have business with one another, he reports the parties to the authorities and supports one side or the other.... [Furthermore], he goes around at night and listens at windows to hear what is going on. He even complained to the *Oberpfleger* [a Salem official] that the priest in [the neighboring village of] Schemmerberg kept poor order in his parish, although [this priest] receives the highest praise from everyone [else].[62]

This case was complicated by the fact that Belling was born in Ingerkingen and had friends as well as many enemies in the village. The abbot of Salem, patron of the parish, had the final say and appointed a different priest:

> [T]he said vicar [Belling] is little trusted by many, or even the majority of the parishioners in Ingerkingen, and, because of having enemies and other personal matters, he would probably cause them to stay away [from church].[63]

[59]HStASt. B37a/147.   [60]HStASt. B37a/156.   [61]GLAK 98/3841.
[62]GLAK 98/3841. "Der Mann seye nichts als ein Unruhe- Stiffter, mische sich allzuviel in die Weltl. geschäffts, so, daß wann die bauern einige händel oder sonst geschafft mit einander haben, er mit denen partheyen zu der herrschaftl. Obrigkeit lauffe und die sachen bald so, bald anders Vortrag helffe.... Er lauffe nächtlr. Weyle in dorff um und horche vor denen fensteren, was passire. Er habe sogar den h. Pfarrer von Schemmerberg bey titl. h. P. Oberpfleger daselbst verclagte, er halte einen so schlechte ordnung unter seinen Pfarrkindern, der doch von jedermann das beste lob habe."
[63]GLAK 98/384. "ersagter Vicarius bey sehr viel oder den meheren deren Inngerkingerische pfarrkinder kein vertrauen fünden, dise hingegen, vermutlich der gegenseytigen freundschafft halber, und wegen ein= so andere Personalien vielen austand bey den wurde."

Marc R. Forster

When necessary, communes often used well-placed and well-constructed letters to get rid of unwanted priests. In the 1580s and 1590s peasants knew to accuse unsatisfactory priests of concubinage in order to have them removed. In 1584 the commune of Weilen unter den Rennen petitioned the Austrian government for the removal of their priest, Jacob Krafftenfels.[64] The letter listed ten complaints emphasizing his difficult and combative behavior, especially conflicts over the tithe, and his unwillingness to obey communal regulations regarding the use of meadows. Almost in passing, in point number seven of the petition, does the letter mention Krafftenfels' concubine and nine children. The letter concludes with an appeal to get rid of this priest and "give us a competent and peaceful priest."[65] Leaving nothing to chance, the commune also denounced Krafftenfels to the episcopal court, angering Austrian officials. In the end, their concerted effort succeeded: Krafftenfels was removed.

By the late seventeenth century, concubinage was no longer widespread; consequently when communal leaders sought to remove a priest, they now emphasized his professional failings. The priest in Tafertsweiler, according to his parishioners in 1692, did not begin Sunday services at a regular time, neglected catechism lessons, and did not hold a series of votive masses against bad weather at five in the morning as required.[66] In the eighteenth century, parishioners often pointed to a "loss of trust" when criticizing priests.[67] Although communes knew how to pull the right strings with higher authorities, they were also genuinely concerned with the performance of the clergy. As we have seen, the ability and dedication of the priest was central to the success of clericalized Catholicism. Rural communes saw it as part of their job to monitor the performance of the local clergy.

Communes went beyond overseeing the behavior and effectiveness of priests and organized much of the religious life of the parish themselves. As we have seen, some of this function resulted directly from the communal role in the creation of new benefices. The

[64]HStASt. B37a/272.
[65]HStASt. B37a/272. "uns mit ainem tauglichen, fridtlichen Priester, ... begeben."
[66]GLAK 61/13463, pp. 320r–23r. There was a similar case in Hailtingen in 1750: HStASt. B467/500.
[67]GLAK 93/248 (Mindersdorf, 1747); HStASt. B38/574 (Binsdorf, 1783); HStASt. B468/661 (Kirchdorf, 1654).

Gemeinde of Nusplingen made sure that the holder of the new chaplaincy knew exactly what his duties were.[68] He was expected to assist the parish priest, especially with confession and Sunday services; to read mass on Tuesdays for the community and extra masses during Lent; and to read two additional masses a week for the souls of the benefactors of the chaplaincy.

Communes hired priests to perform religious functions, often without consulting ecclesiastical officials. Thus the commune of Böhringen brought in an Augustinian monk to conduct services in the village church. Both the commune and the monk were surprised and shocked when the Pfarrer in Gössingen, the official parish priest of this filial church, complained in 1719.[69] The villagers were even more stunned to hear the priest argue "that the honorable *Gemeinde* of Böhringen had no power to order a priest [to perform services]."[70] Indeed, the Böhringers asserted this right by withholding the tithe from the priest in Gössingen because he did not hold services in their church.

Processions and pilgrimages were central to popular piety, especially after the Thirty Years' War.[71] These were generally organized by the laity and led by the communes. Thus during the war, the commune of Birndorf instituted a regular procession, or pilgrimage, to the Marian shrine of Todtmoos. In the middle of the eighteenth century, the Birndorfers participated in at least eighteen major processions each year, most of which originated with vows made by the villagers.[72] Villagers often wanted their priests to lead, or at least accompany, processions, and in many cases priests were required to take part. Disputes sometimes broke out over this obligation. In 1750 the vicar general in Constance resolved such a conflict in Hailtingen in the following way:

> The parish priest must accompany the biannual communal procession to the chapel in Weiler, although this [procession] began and

---

[68]HStASt. B467/684. [69]HStASt. B467/473.

[70]HStASt. B467/473. "als hätte ein lobl. gemeind zu Böhringen keinen gewalt einer priester zu bestellen."

[71]Wolfgang Brückner, *Die Verehrung des heiligen Blutes in Walldürn: Volkskundlich-soziologische Untersuchungen zum Strukturwandel barocken Wallfahrtens* (Aschaffenburg: Paul Patloch Verlag, 1958). Brückner emphasizes that pilgrimages were often a kind of extended procession, and processions a sort of local pilgrimage.

[72]Jakob Ebner, *Aus der Geschichte der Ortschaften der Pfarrei Birndorf* (Karlsruhe: Verlag Leo Wetzel, 1938), 113–15.

Marc R. Forster

has taken place up to now as a freely held devotion of the community. Devotion and yearning [for salvation?] is as dependent on the [priest's] presence and eagerness as on that of his flock. [The priest] will receive the usual 40 kreuzer....[73]

Processions and pilgrimages were a perfect expression of a clericalized and communalized religion in that they required the participation of the priest yet were mostly organized and promoted by the communes.

Communes were enmeshed in almost all aspects of local religious life. Villagers as well as townspeople founded a large number of confraternities, sometimes in response to clerical initiatives, sometimes not.[74] Communes demanded that priests perform traditional blessings and benedictions, even when the church considered such practices suspect.[75] In the late eighteenth century, parishioners organized and funded the erection of Stations of the Cross in parish churches.[76] The laity clearly participated actively in religious life, not just as spectators at mass or recipients of the sacraments, but as organizers and innovators as well. This linked the church to popular religion and gave Catholicism a tremendous vitality through the eighteenth century.

*   *   *

Beginning in the 1760s and reaching a peak in the 1780s, the Austrian government instituted a thorough reform of Catholic institutions in its territories. Motivated by Enlightenment principles of rationalization and the promotion of economic productivity, "Josephine" reformers enacted a series of decrees, most of which encountered widespread opposition. Peasants and townspeople resisted not only the closing of shrines, convents, and monasteries but also the

[73]HStASt. B467/500. "h. Pfarrvicari die zweymahlig Jährliche zu der Capellen Weyller von der gemayndt haltendte Procession, obschon dise ausfreyen willens, und andacht der gemaynd aufgenohmmen, bis anhero löbl. gehalten worden, mit seiner gegenwarth und Eüfer, als von welchem der schaffen, als von ihrem fürten die andacht und begürde abhanget, für die gewöhnlich. 40 kr. ziehen, begleiten und halten soll...." See also B467/546.

[74]Ebner, *Aus der Geschichte der Ortschaften der Pfarrei Birndorf*, 111–12 (see n. 72 above); see also Jakob Ebner, *Geschichte der Ortschaften der Pfarrei Hochsal* (Wargen: Selbstverlag des Verfassers, 1958), 61–66, and EAF A1/340.

[75]HStASt. B467/500; EAF A1/329 and A1/483; cf. Veit and Lenhart, *Kirche und Volksfrömmigkeit* (see n. 2 above).

[76]HStASt. B61/1098, B481/77, B481/78.

dissolution of confraternities, and ignored the abolition of church holidays, processions, and pilgrimages.[77] One aspect of the reforms, however, received popular support: the effort to reorganize the parish structure and create a number of new parishes. Here reforms played right into the communal and clericalized structures of popular Catholicism. Austrian officials asked priests, local officials, and communes to indicate villages that deserved new parishes or chapels, thereby intimating that communities with more than seven hundred inhabitants and/or requiring more than an hour's walk to the nearest church would receive funding.[78] Communes, especially, responded energetically to this opportunity, providing the requested data, and often writing extensive petitions for new parishes. In this area at least, popular Catholicism and *Aufklärung*-Catholicism coincided.

The coexistence of clericalism and communalism suggests that there was no clear division between official and popular Catholicism in Southwest Germany. Catholicism became more dependent on the presence and performance of the parish priest, yet this clericalization occurred, at least in part, because of popular pressure. Communes maintained an important role, but the village elites who controlled them were both representatives of the village community and agents of higher authorities. Clericalism and communalism were fundamental aspects of the dynamic between popular and official religion that created the successful Catholicism of Southwest Germany.

---

[77]Thomas Paul Becker, *Konfessionalisierung in Kurköln: Untersuchungen zur Durchsetzung der katholischen Reform in den Dekanaten Ahrgau und Bonn anhand von Visitationsprotokollen 1583–1761* (Bonn: Edition Röhrscheid, 1989), esp. 311–15.
[78]HStASt. B61/213; GLAK 79/822.

ACKNOWLEDGMENTS

Research for this essay was funded by the Alexander von Humboldt Foundation, the National Endowment for the Humanities, and the R. F. Johnson Faculty Development Fund of Connecticut College.

A Priest Hearing the Confession
of a Kneeling Man

Terms of Loyalty
Factional Politics in a Single German Village (Nöggenschwihl, 1725–1745)

David Martin Luebke

In seeking to explain rural unrest in early modern Germany, historians typically argue that factional divisions corresponded to distributions of wealth and were overcome through institutional forms of communal coercion. But a dearth of evidence often prevents the proof of such assertions. This essay links data on status, kinship, and political ties in a single eighteenth-century village to show that kinship, not wealth or power, was the best predictor of factional allegiances, and that the patriarchal dominance of housefathers undermined the efficacy of communal institutions in enforcing political solidarities. The concentration of power and wealth in village elites so magnified their factional quarrels that no communal institution was able to contain them.

THROUGHOUT THE EARLY MODERN ERA, German peasants faced the difficult challenge of maintaining communal solidarity against forces of disunity emanating both from outside and within village boundaries. To the outside, peasants confronted princes, seigneurs, and their agents, who more often than not were intent on expanding the powers of state at the expense of autonomous decision making by village elders. But this essay is about social forces that undermined communal solidarity from *within* the village fence, as illustrated by the tormented experience of Nöggenschwihl, a tiny Black Forest community in the Hapsburg county of Hauenstein, during a highly divisive and long-winded peasant uprising called the "Salpeter Wars" (1725–45). During these turmoils Nöggenschwihl, like other villages in Hauenstein, failed to cohere politically, and split instead into two bitterly hostile factions. The roots of this disunity in patterns of interaction between local power, social stratification, kinship, and factional loyalties recommend a rethinking of historical interpretations that emphasize the ongoing vitality of communal institutions in the Holy Roman Empire during the final century of its existence. Specifically, institutions of communal government appear to have played only a small role in the formation of political thought and action among peasants. Rather, the influence of kinship over the configuration of political loyalties loomed far larger—so much so, indeed, that they undermined the ability of village elders to enforce political solidarity through the institutional means of coercion available to them. The village, in short, mattered hardly at all.

Nöggenschwihl was situated at both the geographical and political epicenter of an ancient and often violent struggle that pitted the Outer Austrian county of Hauenstein, led by eight annually elected cantonal magistrates (or *Einungsmeister*), against the prodigiously wealthy Benedictine abbey of St. Blasien. Starting in the mid-thirteenth century, St. Blasien had acquired seigneuries (and with them jurisdictions and serfs) inside the county, including an estate (*Fronhof*) and lower court (*Niedergericht*) in Nöggenschwihl, both purchased in 1279.[1] Hauenstein's eight cantons (*Einungen*) originated as a sworn defensive alliance among peasants against St. Blasien's efforts to expand its holdings within the county, and their continuing struggles to thwart it erupted in violence in 1370, 1412, 1525, and again in 1612. The outbreak of the Salpeter Wars in 1725 was a continuation of these struggles with St. Blasien over Nöggenschwihl and other abbatial jurisdictions like it. This time, a resistance movement grew around decades-old legal disputes over the monetized value of certain servile dues, the extent of St. Blasien's claims against the inheritances of its serfs, the weight of various fines imposed by its lower courts, and the abbey's claim to sovereignty over them.[2] Like many revolts elsewhere,

---

[1] On the abbey's gradual acquisition of seigneuries and jurisdictions in Hauenstein, see Hugo Ott, *Die Klostergrundherrschaft St. Blasiens im Mittelalter* (Stuttgart: Kohlhammer, 1969), and idem, *Studien zur Geschichte des Klosters St. Blasien im hohen und späten Mittelalter* (Stuttgart: Fischer, 1970); also Heinrich Schwarz, "Der Hotzenwald und seine Freibauern," in *Quellen und Forschungen zur Siedlungs- und Volkstumsgeschichte der Oberrheinlande*, ed. Friedrich Metz (Karlsruhe: Südwestdeutsche Druck- und Verlagsgesellschaft, 1941), 2:67–199, here 115–16.

[2] See David M. Luebke, *His Majesty's Rebels: Communities, Factions, and Rural Revolt in the Black Forest, 1725–1745* (Ithaca: Cornell University Press, 1997), 54–70; Karl F. Wernet, "St. Blasiens Versuche, sich der Grafschaft Hauenstein pfandweise zu bemächtigen," *Zeitschrift für die Geschichte des Oberrheins* [hereafter ZGO] 107 (1959): 161–82; and Günther Haselier, *Die Streitigkeiten der Hauensteiner mit ihren Obrigkeiten: Ein Beitrag zur Geschichte Vorderösterreichs und des südwestdeutschen Bauernstandes im 18. Jahrhundert* (Karlsruhe: Südwestdeutsche Druck- und Verlagsgesellschaft, 1940), 7–16.

an homage controversy provided the spark to open resistance.[3] Finally, a 1725 census of all abbatial serfs in Hauenstein transformed the resistance of the *Einungsmeister* into a full-blown political movement.

But the eighteenth-century confrontation differed fundamentally from earlier revolts in one key respect: The peasantry failed to form a united opposition to the abbey, splitting instead into two factions of roughly equal size. One of them was reformist in outlook and generally nonviolent; its members tended to seek redress of peasant grievances by litigating through officially sanctioned channels of judicial appeal. The other faction tended to reject the existing order as corrupt and offered more militant means to correct it: tax boycotts, personal petitions to Emperor Charles VI, and armed confrontations. After some twenty years of often bloody feuding, several lawsuits, three Austrian military interventions, and half a dozen rebel attempts to provoke the mediation of Emperor Charles, this internecine conflict resulted in the destruction of precisely those autonomies that Hauenstein's peasant elites had labored for generations to defend.

At the time, all parties to the conflict recognized the centrality of factional politics and developed a vocabulary to reflect it. Provincial Hapsburg officials availed themselves of a ready-made set of political labels that arrayed peasants according to the measure of ritual obedience they displayed toward the representatives of royal authority: the more rebellious majority of Hauensteiners were described as "unruhig" (restless or simply disobedient), while the others were called "ruhig" (peaceable or obedient). Organized as it was around deference, however, the official classification scheme grossly oversimplified the complexities of peasant politics, and in its place, peasants evolved their own factional nomenclature: "disobedient" peasants called themselves "salpeterisch," after the profession of their leader, an old and wealthy peasant in the village of Buch who supplemented his income by selling saltpeter, which he refined from manure smeared on livestock stalls (hence the term "Salpeter Wars").[4] Their

---

[3]André Holenstein, *Die Huldigung der Untertanen: Rechtskultur und Herrschaftsordnung (800–1800)* (Stuttgart: Fischer, 1991).

[4]The factional label *salpeterisch* may have been devised by "peaceable" peasants; see Generallandesarchiv Karlsruhe (hereafter GLA), 113:229, 9r–10v, Martin Thoma of Haselbach to Speaker Joseph Tröndle of Schmitzingen, 21? May 1728. Thoma accused the "peaceable" Georg Fluem of Dietlingen of saying that "all who are salpeterisch are

rebels' least incendiary term for the other faction was *müllerisch*, a reference to the profession of their leader, Joseph Tröndle, a miller in the village of Unteralpfen.

The event of factionalism in Hauenstein raises empirical questions with profound theoretical implications. First, why were village elders unable to enforce solidarity, given the institutional means of coercion available to them? Many, perhaps most, historians of peasant politics in early modern Germany tend to emphasize the decisive role of village institutions in the process of forging resistance movements from the raw ore of social or economic grievance. Intramural solidarity, it is argued, was crucial to the success of any resistance movement and could be achieved only if village elders were able to punish those who were unwilling to assume their share of common risk, for example, by excluding them from the use of common pastures. If elders themselves were hesitant to rebel, resistance movements formed only if they could be removed from authority. Either way, it is argued that villages were the primary "carriers" of peasant resistance.[5] But in Nöggenschwihl and the other villages of Hauenstein, peasant solidarity was the first casualty of the unrest: not only did the villages fail to produce a cohesive peasant syndicate, but collective interests also generated two increasingly incompatible articulations. These realities suggest the inadequacy of rigidly causal links between the socioeconomic bases of politics and their superstructural manifestations as a means to explain the variety of political thinking and action among subaltern groups.

Another empirical question pertains to the composition of peasant factions. The few historians who have inquired into the sources of dissension among peasants in time of rebellion have tended to attribute them either to inequities in the distribution of sociopolitical power or to intergenerational conflicts between housefathers and

---

scoundrels and self-perjured heretics." In any case, salpeterisch peasants adopted the label willingly. On the method of refining saltpeter from manure, see Rudolf Metz, *Geologische Landeskunde des Hotzenwalds* (Lahr: Schauenberg, 1980), 288.

[5]Peter Blickle, *Unruhen in der ständischen Gesellschaft, 1300-1800* (Munich: Oldenbourg, 1988); Andreas Suter, *"Troublen" im Fürstbistum Basel (1726–1740): Eine Fallstudie zum bäuerlichen Widerstand im 18. Jahrhundert* (Göttingen: Vandenhoeck & Ruprecht, 1985).

their offspring.[6] Yet neither of these perspectives explains the evidence from Nöggenschwihl. With respect both to wealth distributions and kinship, factional divisions were vertical rather than horizontal. Class distinctions do not appear to have coincided with factional divisions, which suggests that poorer peasants allied themselves politically with wealthier benefactors. By the same token, factional divisions more often ran between lineages than through them: vertical kinship ties proved more decisive than divisions between generations. Factions, then, amounted to coalitions of lineage groups.

A happy convergence of evidence in Nöggenschwihl makes it possible to establish linkages between data on kinship ties, factional sympathies, and in some cases, estimates of gross personal wealth for individual village residents. The primary basis for these linkages is the serf census that created a great stir in 1725 and after. Because the condition of abbatial serfdom was purely hereditary and unrelated to the terms of land tenure, it was necessary for St. Blasien to reconstruct the genealogical history of each village in which its serfs lived. The result amounts to a comprehensive genealogical cadaster of villages where almost all residents bore servile status. Nöggenschwihl was one such village, one of the few for which these cadasters survive. Indicators of factional loyalties survive in a variety of forms, among them lists of peasants who did or did not perform homage in 1727; rosters of Nöggenschwihl residents whom provincial authorities found guilty of rebellious activities after the Austrian military interventions of 1728 and 1739; and lists of *salpeterisch* and *müllerisch* peasants that village officials compiled in 1745. Because Nöggenschwihl was subject to St. Blasien's lower jurisdiction, finally, the contract for every sale, trade, or bequest was supposed to be registered and approved by functionaries of the so-called High Steward's Bureau (*Obervogteiamt*), located just to the east of Hauenstein in the village of Gurtweil, which managed St. Blasien's lower jurisdictions in Nöggenschwihl, Weilheim, and

---

[6]David W. Sabean, *Landbesitz und Gesellschaft am Vorabend des Bauernkrieges: Eine Studie der sozialen Verhältnisse im südlichen Oberschwaben in den Jahren vor 1525* (Stuttgart: Fischer, 1972); Hermann Rebel, *Peasant Classes: The Bureaucratization of Property and Family Relations under Early Habsburg Absolutism, 1511-1636* (Princeton: Princeton University Press, 1983); and Thomas Robisheaux, *Rural Society and the Search for Order in Early Modern Germany* (Cambridge: Cambridge University Press, 1989).

Birndorf.[7] Fortunately, contractual records from the High Steward's Bureau survive from 1739 through 1744, during the central period of the revolt.[8]

What do these linkages tell us? For one thing, they suggest that the shifting balance of factional loyalties in Nöggenschwihl reflected trends in the county as a whole. During the rebellion's initial phase (1725–29), *salpeterisch* arguments appear to have enjoyed an appeal that was wider than in later years, when factional allegiances hardened. An indication of this emerges from lists of Nöggenschwihlers who attended a *salpeterisch*-inspired rally of St. Blasien's juridical subjects in the neighboring parish of Waldkirch in November 1726. The rally was intended to whip up public support for a more confrontational policy than that of the sitting college of *Einungsmeister*.[9] Most of Nöggenschwihl's household heads were in attendance, including many who would later appear on lists of *müllerisch* peasants. Most notable among them were several abbatial officeholders from Nöggenschwihl: Johannes Bächle, for example, who farmed half of the entailed manse (*Fronhof*) in the village and who also served as abbatial bailiff (*Vogt*) for the lower court there. The following May, Bächle did homage to the newly elected abbot Franz II Schächtelin, a strong indication of his evolving *müllerisch* sympathies. Eventually, Bächle would emerge as the principal *müllerisch* peasant in Nöggenschwihl, though he paid a hefty fine for the indiscretion of having attended the "contentious gathering" at Waldkirch in 1726. Yet even in 1727, a year when *Einungsmeister* elections swept *salpeterisch* candidates into power in all eight cantons, the number of homage refusers in Nöggenschwihl still included many who subsequently disap-

---

[7]On the origins and duties of the High Steward's Bureau, see GLA 229:37331.I, "Deductio ex archivo S. Blasiano über das St. Gallische Lehen deß Thurn Guttenburg und Gerichts Weylheimb," 19 January 1723; GLA 229:37275, "Verzeichnis der zur Herrschaft Gutenburg gehörigen Vogteien, Gemeinden, Ortschafften und der hoch- und niedergerichtlichen, zu diesem Amt gehörigen Orte" [n.d.]; and Josef Bader, ed., "Das ehemals sanktblasische Amt Gutenburg," *ZGO* 3 (1852): 355–84, here 370–76.

[8]GLA 61:14160–14161, Kontraktenprotokolle des Obervogteiamts Gurtweil (hereafter cited as Kontraktenprotokolle). These records resumed in 1749, after the rebellion had ended.

[9]In a ceremony reminiscent of Einungsmeister elections, those who sided with the interests of the "Whole County" were asked to march around a pear tree and be counted. For details on the events at Waldkirch on 3 November, see the interrogation transcripts (Verhörsprotokolle) in GLA 113:224, especially 122v–127r (Bläsi Kayser of Neuenmühle) and 127v–136r, 137r–140r (Adam Schmiedle of Niedermühle).

peared from lists of the reliably "rebellious."[10] A great winnowing of allegiances took place in the aftermath of an Austrian military intervention in 1728 and 1729, when "culpable" peasants and their sympathizers in every village were identified and penalized. By 1739 the distribution of factional sympathies was roughly even; in 1745 the *salpeterisch* side enjoyed only a slight majority in Nöggenschwihl. Among all villages under abbatial jurisdiction, the *salpeterisch* majority comprised only 53 percent.[11]

The evidence from Nöggenschwihl also suggests that institutions of the village (*Gemeinde*) were unable to prevent the emergence of factions. To be sure, the only records of Gemeinde decisions that have survived pertained to individual villagers whose conflicts with the community had come to the attention of higher abbatial or Hapsburg authorities; as such, they cannot be regarded as a representative sample of Gemeinde decisions generally. On the other hand, these recorded conflicts typically involved peasants who allowed their cattle to overgraze common fields or who removed boundary markers from private forest plots, and in most cases, the transgressors later turned up among Nöggenschwihl's salpeterisch peasants. A notorious offender in this respect was Johannes Schaller, paterfamilias of one of the most reliably salpeterisch families in the village, whose actions had sown "great disunity [*große Uneinigkeit*] in the community."[12] Another overgrazer was Balthas Bächle, a strident *salpeterisch* dissenter within his predominantly *müllerisch* clan.[13] Of course, it is risky to make too much of such links; yet another villager accused of overgrazing was Johannes Bächle—in all probability the same Johannes Bächle who later functioned as Vogt and who proved to be a pillar of

[10]GLA 113:229, 71r, "Specification der jenigen Mindergerichtsunterthanen welche zu Wyhlen den 13ten May 1727 das Handgelübt abgelegt haben."

[11]See David M. Luebke "Factions and Communities in Early Modern Germany," *Central European History* 25 (1992): 281–301.

[12]See GLA 61:10759, Strafregister des Amts Gutenburg, 29, 3 August 1709 (fine of 10 Pfund against Johannes Schaller, Johannes Bächle, and Hans Georg Gamp for overgrazing contrary to "Gemeindsverbott"); ibid., 26 March 1718 (fine of 10 Pfund against Johannes Schaller for complaining about the "Gemeindts Waldt Markhung" and for having removed boundary markers); ibid., 14 May 1718 (fine of 10 Pfund against Johannes Schaller for having renewed his problems with the Gemeinde over forests).

[13]GLA 61:5795, Straf-, Zins und Gefällprotokolle des Amtes Gutenburg, 12 January 1737 (fine of 5 Pfund against Balthas Bächle for grazing his cattle on fields belonging to Vogt Johannes Bächle); ibid., 19 January 1737 (fine of 3 Pfund for doing the same again).

the *müllerisch* faction in Nöggenschwihl.[14] To be sure, no record survives that *müllerisch* peasants were excluded from the use of common pastures as punishment for refusal to join in sworn communities of opposition to St. Blasien. But if *müllerisch* peasants had experienced such discipline, we have every reason to suspect that they would have reported it to abbatial authorities—after all, there is no shortage of reports of less formal kinds of censure, such as slander and thefts of wood and horses.[15] The number of communal interventions against individual *salpeterisch* peasants suggests that if anything, the means of collective censure remained in *müllerisch* hands. If such was the case, however, communal institutions of coercion cannot have worked very well. In his 1751 letter of resignation, Vogt Johannes Bächle noted how difficult it had been to keep the community together. Throughout the rebellion, he remarked, the *salpeterisch* peasants had "held me in suspicion" so that "all became disobedient" [ist alles in Ungehorsam komen], "to the shame of communal and lordly authorities" [der gemaint und herrschafflichen Weesen].[16]

But was Nöggenschwihl merely a cranky exception to prove the rule that village communes "carried" peasant revolt? Evidence on the sociopolitical composition of factions in Nöggenschwihl suggests otherwise. An implicit (though certainly not inevitable) corollary of theories that stress the power of communal institutions is the proposition that factional divisions, if they existed at all, corresponded with unequal distributions of wealth and power. One Swiss historian has argued that nonrebels were typically well-to-do officeholders and others "in the entourage of the state" and *its* interests, people who were "integrated vertically" into state channels of command and who opposed their poorer "horizontally integrated" fellows, whose interests lay in preserving the values and institutions of the village against

---

[14]See n. 12 above.

[15]See GLA 61:5795, Straf-, Zins und Gefällprotokolle, 26 May 1736 (fine of 3 Pfund for slanders and disrespectful behavior against Vogt Johannes Bächle); ibid., 15 October 1736 (fine of 5 Gulden against the salpeterisch peasant Georg Bächle, who had called Joseph Mattner of Bierbronnen a "bläsmisch Schellm" [=abbatial scoundrel] and "bläsmisch Dieb" [abbatial thief]); GLA 61:5776, Verhörsprotokolle des Obervogteiamtes, 88, 12 February 1739 (fine of 2 Pfund against the *salpeterisch* [Hans] Peter Eisele of Nöggenschwihl for felling a fir tree in the private forests of the müllerisch Moritz Gantert); GLA 61:5777, Verhörsprotokolle OVA, 26, 22 May 1742 (notice given of the theft of a six-year-old horse with saddle and harness in value of 100 Gulden, owned by Vogt Johannes Bächle).

[16]GLA 229:75480, 4r–v, Johannes Bächle to OVA, 20 September 1751.

the intrusions of the state.[17] To be sure, this description fits the behavior of *Vogt* Johannes Bächle and of Georg Thoma, the village headman (*Dorfmeyer*), who between them farmed St. Blasien's manse in Nöggenschwihl. When in early 1739 a *salpeterisch* fund-raiser noted that "the most eminent ones give nothing" [die Fürnembsten geben nix], he probably had these two in mind. But other "eminent ones" did join the *salpeterisch* cause. A different Johannes Bächle, the Vogt's paternal cousin, served as St. Blasien's sexton in Nöggen-schwihl's parish church, yet in 1739 he was condemned to perform twelve days' forced labor on road repair for complicity in the second violent outbreak of revolt.[18] St. Blasien's forester (*Bannwart*) in Nöggenschwihl, Johannes Ebner, was also *salpeterisch*.[19] Finally, at least three of St. Blasien's eight quitrent collectors (*Träger*) in Nöggen-schwihl emerged as *salpeterisch* activists in the 1720s.[20] These rebellious officeholders were hardly less integrated "vertically" than their opponents.

Contrary to the assumption that nonrebels tended to be wealthier than their peers, moreover, a comparison of the estimated gross personal wealth of peasants in both factions shows a rough parity between them. The principal source of these data are records kept by the abbatial High Steward's Bureau of living bequests—mostly partial sales of patrimonies or matrimonies to heirs in exchange for a combination of payment and a retirement provision (*Leibdung*). These data are supplemented by less reliable information from a list of rebel activists and their estimated worth that was compiled by Austrian criminal investigators a few years earlier, in 1733. By this measure, the average wealth of *salpeterisch* peasants in Nöggenschwihl was 1,041 Gulden, that of *müllerisch* peasants 1,071 Gulden. This is, admittedly, a crude instrument: it does not reflect the wealth of all peasants on either side—only those whose gross worth was estimated at the time. It is further possible that the price tag attached to

[17]Suter, *"Troublen,"* 107–8 (see n. 5 above).

[18]GLA 113:250a, F4 (list of Nöggenschwihl residents sentenced to forced labor on road repair), 29 April 1739.

[19]A Bannwart was nominated by the Gemeinde and approved in office by St. Blasien; GLA 61:5777, 19, "Nöggenschwiel: Bestell. und Beeyd. Bannwart," 3 March 1742. The brief tenure of salpeterisch Johannes Stigler as Bannwart (1740–42) suggests that abbatial confirmation was not always a matter of course.

[20]GLA 66:7296, Zinsrodel des Waldamts, 1709. The collectors in question were Balthas Bächle, Georg Eckert, and Joseph Gerster.

bequests did not reflect the market value of the properties conveyed. Also, the Austrian investigators' estimates were quite rough. Finally, these data give no indication of how many paupers, with little or no property to transfer, allied themselves with one faction or the other. But there are other reasons for suspecting that the rough socioeconomic parity these data suggest is accurate. For one thing, it cannot be chalked up to a generally equal distribution of wealth within the community as a whole. Some indication of the degree of social stratification in Nöggenschwihl emerges from a thorough survey of individual peasant wealth compiled for the purposes of the *Rustical-Steuer* of 1761, a tax levied against the fruits of peasant land. The register shows that of 26,107 liters of wheat, rye, hops, and garden vegetables produced in Nöggenschwihl, the wealthiest decile produced just under one third (32.66 percent), while the poorest generated only 0.05 percent. One peasant alone held lands so extensive that they accounted for almost 10 percent of the village's total agricultural product. Of course, agriculture was not the sole source of wealth in Nöggenschwihl: millers such as Conrad Gerster, taverners such as the younger Balthas Bächle, and village artisans such as Benedict Dörflinger the wheelwright and Joseph Binkert the nail maker, all appear artificially poor. Nevertheless, in the absence of such protoindustrial innovations as rural weaving, land remained the sole source of income, directly or indirectly, for the vast majority of Nöggenschwihlers, and the 1761 cadaster may be taken as a broad indication of wealth distributions among them. In the canton of Dogern as a whole, such disparities were only slightly greater: the top decile of proprietors commanded 43 percent of agricultural production, the poorest 0.13 percent. In view of such crass inequalities, the rough factional parity of recorded wealth appears all the more remarkable. The clear implication is that factional divisions did not coincide with those of wealth. Rather, factional divisions cut across income strata.

What is more, evidence from real estate transactions leaves the impression that factional allegiance could work as powerful an influence on socioeconomic relationships as the reverse. Between 1738 and 1743 the High Steward's Bureau recorded a total of forty-two real estate transactions in Nöggenschwihl. If we exclude bequests from consideration, we are left with thirty real estate transactions *between* nuclear families. In only five of these cases—one-sixth of the total— did an exchange cross factional lines, where a *salpeterisch* peasant traded with or sold land to a *müllerisch* peasant, and vice versa. Eighty-three percent transpired *within* the bounds of factional community. To be sure, we cannot know how many land deals the peasants struck amongst themselves without the bureau's knowledge. That such deals occurred, however, is beyond doubt: the High Steward's Bureau often imposed fines for the misdemeanor (*Frewel*) of making real estate deals without official consent, but this is obviously no reliable indicator of the actual number of unapproved deals. In 1706, for example, *Vogt* Hans Thoma paid a fine of 3 Gulden 20 Kreuzer for selling land without permission. It had been a bad year for Thoma's relations with the High Steward: only a few months earlier, Thoma had been fined 6 Gulden 40 Kreuzer for stating publicly that the year's tithe assessment was too high, that it was a "dog's business," and that the peasants should refuse to pay.[21] Fines for the misdemeanor of concluding land deals without permission were also imposed on Johannes Schaller and Johannes Fluem in May 1709, Moritz Gantert in January 1737, and on Jacob Schäffer and Claus Albiez in January 1737.[22] But such documentary evidence records only those cases that came to the High Steward's attention and therefore cannot indicate the number of shady deals. An impression of the volume of unapproved real estate deals is reflected in a complaint registered in 1783 by Forest Steward von Spaun, who reported with some annoyance that, despite a series of decrees mandating that all abbatial subjects register all real estate exchanges with the abbey, the peasants recorded inheritance contracts infrequently and only then if it served their interests.[23]

The inescapable conclusion is that factional divisions did not coincide with those of wealth. But what might account for the willingness of some peasants to ignore factional fissures and trade across them? Sheer desperation seems to explain two of them, both involving the reliably *müllerisch* Moritz Gantert. By 1739 Gantert had accumulated so much debt that he was unable to pay it off, let alone provide a secure material basis for his heirs, without selling some of

---

[21]See GLA 61:10759, Strafregister des Amts Gutenburg 1701–1712, 17 (21 April 1706); ibid., 11 (11 January 1706).

[22]For Schaller and Fluem, see GLA 61:10759, Strafregister des Amts Gutenburg 1701–1712, 28; for Gantert, Schäffer, and Albiez, see GLA 61:5795, Straf-, Zins- und Gefällprotokolle des Amts Gutenburg.

[23]See GLA 113:16, "Jurisdiction in der Grafschafft Hauenstein," 26 May 1783.

the property away. In two sales, Gantert sold roughly one-quarter of his holdings to two *salpeterisch* peasants, Jacob Schäffer and Joseph Schaller. Gantert, in short, seems to have looked for help wherever he could get it—even if it meant selling to factional enemies.[24] In two other cases, kinship ties appear to have overcome factional differences. Both of these involved the *müllerisch* Joseph Ebner, who in early 1741 bought land worth 233 Gulden from his *salpeterisch* brother-in-law Joseph Schaller and from Michel Schaller, Joseph Schaller's brother.[25] Notwithstanding these exceptions, however, the larger point remains that, as far as we can tell, real estate deals tended to transpire between cofactionalists.

If neither officeholding nor wealth distinguished factions, what did? The balance of evidence suggests that kinship, not wealth or office, was the best predictor of factional allegiance. The most striking illustration of this emerges from linkages between St. Blasien's 1725 genealogical cadaster and the surviving documentary indicators of factional allegiance (see appendix). Factional unanimity prevailed in almost 70 percent of fifty-nine identifiable father-son pairs. Enmity separated fathers from sons in only ten cases, and in half of these, it resulted from a *salpeterisch* son's going *müllerisch* late in the revolt: these were the younger Balthas Bächle, Johannes Eckert, his second-cousin Simon Eckert, Georg Schaller, and Georg Gerster. The data

---

[24]See GLA 61:14160, Kontraktenprotokolle, 121, 7 May 1739 (sale by Moritz Gantert to Jacob Schäffer of 2 Viertel Acker "Langfuhren" for 42 Gulden); ibid., 430, 5 May 1741 (sale by Moritz Gantert to Johannes Dörflinger of about 1 Jauchert Acker for 81 Gulden, and sale by Johannes Dörflinger to Moritz Gantert of about 1 Vierling Feld for 27 Gulden); ibid., 513, 9 December 1741 (sale by Moritz Gantert to Joseph Schaller of 7 Vierling Feld for 100 Gulden, including debts [28 Gulden 48 Kreutzer to Meyer Bernheim, Jew of Tiengen, 20 fl to Johannes Eckert of Nöggenschwihl, 20 fl to Johannes Brutschi of Nöggenschwihl, and 30 fl to the buyer] for a balance of 1 Gulden 12 Kreuzer); ibid., 514, 9 December 1741 (sale by Moritz Gantert to his step-daughter, Catharina Gamp, of about 1 Tawen Matten, 1 Jauchert Wald for 200 Gulden); and GLA 61:14161, Kontraktenprotokolle, 5, 4 January 1742 (sale by Moritz Gantert to his step-daughter Catharina Gamp and her betrothed, Friedle Fluem, of one-half of his entire estate, including house, barn, fields, and household mobilia, for 600 Gulden [including Gantert's debts of 84 Gulden to Meyer Bernheim of Tiengen, 84 Gulden to the convent at Rindern, 100 Gulden to Joseph Brutschi of Nöggenschwihl, 39 Gulden 36 Kreuzer to Johannes Eckert of Nöggenschwihl, and 30 Gulden to Johannes Schaller]).

[25]See GLA 61:14160, Kontraktenprotokolle, 405, 30 March 1741 (sale by Joseph Schaller to Joseph Ebner of 1 Tawen Matten for 100 Gulden); ibid., 396, 20 February 1741 (sale by Michel Schaller to Joseph Ebner of 2 Vierling Matten for 133 Gulden 40 Kreuzer, including debts to the parish in Höchenschwand [50 Gulden] and to Adam Gerster's children in Fohrenbach [37 Gulden 12 Kreuzer]).

linkages that indicate unanimity between fathers and sons do not, by the way, result from some accountant's assumption that sons would follow in their fathers' political footsteps: in each case, the factional loyalties of sons were indicated by behaviors independent of filial obligation.

This factional cohesion within nuclear families, moreover, reproduced itself in extended families. On the *salpeterisch* side, for example, the Fink clan was comprised of three brothers (Johannes, Georg, and Lorenz) and their cousin Johannes "the Black" [*der Schwarz*]. All but Lorenz were registered in a list of *salpeterisch* supporters compiled in 1726; the same three refused to do homage to Abbot Franz II in 1727; all but Johannes "the Black" were fined for their rebellious activities in 1734; and one of the two Johanns (it is not clear which one) was sentenced to forced labor on road repairs after the Austrian military intervention of 1739. All four Finks, finally, were identified as *salpeterisch* in a list drawn up in 1745 by Georg Thoma, the village headman. In addition to the Finks, rebel organizers in the county could count on the sympathies of the Eckerts, Villingers, Schäffers, Jordans, Hüpfers, Brutschis, Vogelbachers, and Gersters. Among their enemies, the Thoma, Dietschi, Fluem, Keppeler, Ebner, Gantert, Gärtner, Kaiser, and Gamp families were more or less consistently *müllerisch* in behavior. Once again, the evidence of real estate transactions reinforces the impression of factional cohesion within clans. Among cofactional real estate transactions (excluding bequests), 40 percent occurred between siblings or brothers-in-law. In all the remaining instances, buyer and seller were either unrelated or the kinship tie was distant to the point of irrelevance—yet as noted above, the vast majority of these transpired between peasants of like factional mind. Among the latter were sales between the *müllerisch* Johannes Fluem and his father's mother's mother's husband's brother's great-grandson, Vogt Johannes Bächle; between Vogt Bächle and his third-cousin, the younger Balthas Bächle; and between the *salpeterisch* Joseph Schaller and his great-grandfather's wife's brother's grandson, Georg Eckert.[26] Taken together, these data paint a picture of peasants consolidating their holdings into more efficient units

---

[26]For the sale between Johannes Fluem and Vogt Bächle, see GLA 61:14160, Kontraktenprotokolle, 96, 26 February 1739; between Vogt Bächle and the younger Balthas Bächle, see GLA 61:14161, Kontraktenprotokolle, 407, 17 October 1744; and between Joseph Schaller and Georg Eckert, see ibid., 407, 20 October 1744.

David Martin Luebke

through sale or trade within a single degree of affinity and otherwise transacting only with cofactionalists. To reduce factionalism to struggles between rich and poor, or between representatives of "vertical" and "horizontal" integration, therefore, would appear to dilute the strongest variable of all: blood.

Where does this leave us? The vertical pattern of factionalism, both with respect to wealth distributions and familial cohesions, points to the patriarchal dominance of housefathers struggling to consolidate their tenancies into maximally efficient and productive estates and to bequeath them whole to a single heir. In this effort, the challenge for Nöggenschwihl's patriarchs (*müllerisch* and *salpeterisch* alike) was to maximize their freedom of action in land markets. To achieve it, however, they risked running afoul both of Hauenstein's partible inheritance customs and of St. Blasien, in its efforts to subordinate the land market to its own arbitration. From the housefathers' perspective, the difference between factions pivoted on the tactical question of whether litigation or more militant means would best achieve the desired result.

Small wonder, then, that disagreement between Hauenstein and St. Blasien in 1725 centered on a 1 percent real estate tax, subpoena fines in abbatial jurisdictions, limits on partible inheritance, and the requirement to register all land transactions with abbatial authorities.[27] Together, these legal devices threatened to equip St. Blasien with de facto veto authority over all land deals—an especially useful tool, given the abbey's heavy dependence on interest from loans to peasants: interest on capital loans was easily the abbey's biggest moneymaker and may have accounted for nearly a third (32.53 percent) of its annual revenues from Hauenstein.[28] This assault on the autonomy of peasant land markets triggered an allergic political reaction. Ten of the thirty-nine grievances Hauenstein presented in 1728, for example, raised objections to St. Blasien's innovations in the land mar-

[27]GLA 113:228, 145r–148v, "Copia St. Blasm. Taxordnung soviel selbe dessen Mindergerichtl. Unterthanen betrifft" (1728). In 1710 the abbey increased fines levied against juridical subjects who ignored summonses—the equivalent of 40 Kreuzer for the first failure to respond to a subpoena, 1 Gulden 20 Kreuzer for the second failure, and a hefty 6 Gulden 40 Kreuzer for the third—and increased the rigor with which these and other dues were collected; GLA 67:1725, Obervogt to Speaker of Hauenstein, 9 November 1714.
[28]See GLA 79:2875, "Jährlich-ohngefährlicher Ertrag des Gotteshauß St. Blasien ... in dem Österreichischen," ca. 1716.

ket;[29] the hottest controversy centered on the level of subpoena fines—and by implication, on St. Blasien's ability to impose its arbitration. Specifically, the *Einungsmeister* protested that custom set a cumulative maximum of 6 Gulden 40 Kreuzer on subpoena charges, instead of the cumulative 8 Gulden 40 Kreuzer levied by St. Blasien (abbatial officials countered that no single subpoena exceeded the customary amount and that the customary maximum was not cumulative).[30] Though all the *Einungsmeister* raised this objection repeatedly during the years prior to the outbreak of rebellion in 1725, each time their complaints met with the abbey's stubborn resistance.[31] In light of this and the interest of Nöggenschwihl's housefathers in maximizing their freedom of action in land deals, is it any wonder that the village's two *müllerisch* potentates, Johannes Bächle and Hans Georg Thoma, struggled for decades to have their entailed manses reclassified as quitrent estates, from which they could alienate properties at will?[32]

By the same token, however, the records of bequests expose the complicity of Nöggenschwihl's housefathers—again, regardless of factional ties—with St. Blasien in undermining customs geared to preserve the principle of egalitarian partible inheritance, specifically the "right of withdrawal" [*Zugrecht,* or *jus retractus*]. According to a territorial law of 1552, siblings could appropriate a portion of lands alienated by sale or trade from family patrimonies: if a peasant sold all his properties to a single heir, the "heir's brother" could legally appropriate half of the lands in question; similarly, the custom allowed any offspring to appropriate a share if their father sold part of his lands to

---

[29]GLA 65:11419, 5r–6r, "Gravamina des Schwarzwaldes," 8 June 1728.

[30]GLA 67:1725, 9 November 1714, case 2; and GLA 99:428, 229–331, "Huldigungs Prothocoll," 9–11 September 1721, §1.

[31]GLA 229:5658, "Puncta … der Graffschafft Hawenstein," 14 May 1719, §5; GLA 113:225, 128r–131v, "Protocoll und freundnachbarl. Verabschiedung vom 22. März 1720," §7; GLA 99:979, "Actum St. Blasien," 5 June 1720; GLA 99:428, 229–331, "Huldigungs Prothocoll," 9–11 September 1721, §1; GLA 99:979 and GLA 113:89, Juridical Subjects to Abbot Blasius III, 17 December 1723, §1.

[32]GLA 229:75482, "Extractus Hochamtsprotokol," 10 April 1709; GLA 67:1739, "Supplicationes auß denen drey Gerichten," 48r, 3 March 1751. For similar cases elsewhere in Hauenstein, see GLA 229:37289, "Fundamental-Ursachen des lobl. Gottshaus St. Blasien in dem Amt Gutenburg etwelchen Hoff zur Lehen ansreche, welch von denen Inhaberen allein für Zinßgüeter gehalten werden," 7–10 January 1671; and ibid., "Verzaichnus deren, in denen St. Blasmischen Reichsherrschafften ligenten Lehen welche Ehrschätzig seÿendt," 1701.

a "stranger"—anyone outside the immediate lineage group.[33] In all but a few instances, however, tenants bequeathed their lands to one heir; and although they were usually obliged to compensate siblings monetarily, the "right of withdrawal" was never allowed to interfere. The result was an arrangement similar to the unigeniture inheritance system of preferential legacy (*préciput*) that prevailed in parts of northern France.[34] According to the well-informed miller Joseph Tröndle of Unteralpfen, the habit was widespread throughout the county.[35] In this, however, Nöggenschwihl's *salpeterisch* housefathers were no more immune to undermining custom than their *müllerisch* compeers. Joseph Schaller, for example, remained *salpeterisch* throughout the 1730s and 1740s, but in 1750 he sold his lands to one son for 1,300 Gulden and a pension.[36] Even Martin Eisele, Nöggenschwihl's preeminent rebel activist, passed his lands undivided to his son Hans Peter, who bought out the inheritance claims of his two sisters.[37] In only one documented instance did a Nöggenschwihl peasant attempt to affect a sale of land by claiming the right of withdrawal—and St. Blasien nullified it, even though the claimant was *müllerisch* and the seller *salpeterisch*![38] Yet as the very existence of factionalism shows, there was no inevitable community of interest between housefathers and the abbey. Rather, the primary issue at stake was one of control: peasant elites sought to remove all constraints—whatever their origin—on the free disposition of property. In this connection, custom served as a defense against St. Blasien's innovations, even as Hauenstein's peasants violated it in the conduct of their private affairs. Given this consensus, the sociopolitical similarity of Hauenstein's two factions seems less surprising.

We will never know why individual peasants chose one path or the other—*müllerisch* or *salpeterisch,* reformist or radical. Why should a well-to-do Nöggenschwihler like Joseph Eckert have exposed him-

[33]"Landsordnung des Schwartzwalds," 19 December 1552 in "Nachträge zu den Mittheilungen über die Grafschaft Hauenstein," ed. Josef Bader, *ZGO* 12 (1861): 101–27, here 118–22 ("Von Verlassung der Güeter").

[34]For examples, see GLA 61:14160, 8, 14 June 1738; ibid., 25, 2 August 1738; ibid., 110, 30 April 1730; GLA 61:14161, 129, 12 May 1742; and ibid., 212, 8 January 1743.

[35]See GLA 99:1034, 24r–25v, Joseph Tröndle of Unteralpfen to Marquard Herrgott, 29 January 1732.

[36]GLA 61:14162, Kontraktenprotokolle, 278–79.

[37]GLA 61:14160, Kontraktenprotokolle, 364, 22 December 1740.

[38]GLA 61:14161, Kontraktenprotokolle, 64, 29 January 1742.

self to fines and forced labor when other *coqs du village* did not? The surviving evidence provides no unequivocal answers. Either way, though, the housefathers of Nöggenschwihl shared a common interest in improving the conditions of autonomous action, whatever means they chose to achieve it. The implications of this are several. First, one must be careful to distinguish between discourse and practice: custom, for example, meant one thing as an element of sociopolitical discourse between lords and subjects, quite another as a description of actual peasant practices, and in Hauenstein these two aspects contradicted each other squarely. Of course, the justice or injustice of "actual practices" was to some extent framed by popular discourses on kinship and property. But the sociopolitical context of discourse matters, and identical discourses may take on different meanings, depending on the identity of their participants.

Another implication only seems obvious. It is that, in the long run, patriarchal tendencies undermined communal solidarity. If the factional cohesion of families is any indication, the evidence from Nöggenschwihl presents us with tensions generated by the attempts of housefathers to monopolize and individualize access to means of production—by undermining the "right of withdrawal" and by instituting a system of de facto unigeniture inheritance. It matters not a bit that St. Blasien sought to rearrange the interactions of kin and property in similar ways: in relations between lord and subject, the crucial issue was control over the access to arable land, not the pattern of access as such. Perhaps, then, the socioeconomic integration of kin groups wider than the nuclear "monad" underlay the remarkable communal cohesion of villages in earlier rebellions, both in Hauenstein and elsewhere. The concentrations of power and wealth that resulted from an increasingly patriarchal and preferential system of inheritance both extended the distance between rich and poor and magnified the consequences of tactical quarrels among the peasant elite so much that, finally, no communal institution was able to contain these conflicts.

ACKNOWLEDGMENTS

Research for this paper was supported by the Deutscher Akademischer Austauschdienst (DAAD) and the Yale University Council on Western European Studies. I am also indebted to the staff of the Generallandesarchiv Karlsruhe for their generous help.

Appendix: Factional Affiliations in Nöggenschwihl, 1725–1745

Key

1721: Peasants who performed homage on abbot Blasius, 9 September 1721. GLA 99:428, 267–71.

1726: Peasants who attended a *salpeterisch* assembly at Waldkirch on 3 November 1726. GLA 99:975: Specification waß vor Mannschafft zuo Waltkirch erschinen ist.

1727: Peasants who did and did not perform homage to abbot Franz II on 24 May 1727. GLA 113:225, 147: Verzeichnuß was für personen zu Nöggenschweil die dem gnetigen herrn prelaten nit gehoidiget habm. 24 May 1727 (Bescheind Georg Thoma Dorffmeyer). GLA 113:229, 71r: Specification der jenigen Mindergerichts Underthanen welche zu Wyhlen den 13ten May 1727 das Handgelübt abgelegt haben. "No" indicates pro-*salpeterisch* sympathies.

1733: Peasants exempted from paying the expenses of Austrian military intervention. GLA 113:240, 4454-450v: Specifica[ti]o welche von der repartition ausgenohmen seindt: "Yes" indicates pro-*müllerisch* sympathies.

1734: Peasants required to pay punitive fines for rebellious activity. GLA 113:240, 272r: Specification der jenigen so ahn denen in der Grafschaft Hauensteinischen unrueh bis dahin aufgeschwollenen 50000 fl: unkösten nach dem steürfueß zu bezahlen haben (1734). Numbers indicate fines in Gulden and Kreuzer.

1739a: *Salpeterisch* donors. GLA 113:244, 100r-101v: Verzeichnuß waß für Manschafft in Neggenschwiell (February 1739). "Yes" is a strong indication of pro-*salpeterisch* sympathies.

1739b: Peasants granted an IOU for fines imposed. GLA 65:11426, 86r-87v: Versicherungs Schein für die unruehige der Gemeindt Nöggenschweyl und Düthlingen. (23 March 1739). "Yes" indicates *salpeterisch* activity.

1739c: Peasants sentenced to forced labor on road repair. GLA 113:250a, F4, 29 April 1739. "Yes" indicates *salpeterisch* activity.

1739d: Peasants fined to cover costs of Austrian military intervention. GLA 113:250a, F5, 29 April 1739. Numbers indicate fines in Pfund.

1745: *Salpeterisch* and *müllerisch* peasants. GLA 113:264: Specification der gemeint Neggenschwiel waß für rüehige Leüth wer heyrath, und lethig (1745); ibid.: Specification über die gemeint Neggenschwiel von denen waibliche Geschlecht der kleinen oder Salbeterschen (1745). *mül* = *müllerisch*, *sal* = *salpeterisch*.

Indicates who displayed adherence to the *salpeterisch* faction and when.

Factional Affiliations in Nöggenschwihl, 1725–1745

Cat. No.	Name	Birth Year	Occupation, Office	Serf-Lord	1721	1726	1727	1733	1734	1739a	1739b	1739c	1739d	1745
BÄCHLE, BECHLE														
i.3.2.5	Balthas Bächle der Alt	?	?	St. Blasien	yes	yes	no				yes	yes	40	
i.3.2.5.2	Balthas Bächle der Jung	1705	Wirt	St. Blasien	yes	no					yes			mül
i.3.2.5.6	Joseph Bächle	1720		St. Blasien										mül
i.3.2.5.7	Johannes Bächle der Schwarz	1717		St. Blasien										mül
i.3.2.6.1	Joseph Bächle	1710		St. Blasien										mül
i.5.4.2	Johannes Bächle "Hanselmännle"		Mesmer	St. Blasien	yes	yes					yes	yes		
i.5.4.2.1	Franz Bächle	c1692		St. Blasien	yes	yes								
i.5.4.2.3	Johannes Bächle	c1698		St. Blasien	yes	yes								
i.5.4.2.9	Benedict Bächle	1711		St. Blasien					3.4					
i.5.5.7.5	Johannes Bächle	c1694	1/2 Fronhofmeyer, Vogt	St. Blasien	yes	yes	yes	yes						mül
FINK														
iv.1.3.1	Johannes Fink	?	?	St. Blasien	yes	yes	no		14.0	yes	yes	yes		
iv.1.3.1.1	Joseph Fink	1717		St. Blasien					15.0	yes	yes	yes	10	sal
iv.1.3.2	Georg Fink	c1683		St. Blasien	yes	yes	no		14.4					sal
iv.1.3.2.3	Lorenz Fink	1722		St. Blasien										sal
iv.1.6.2	Johannes Fink	c1695		St. Blasien	yes	yes			9.1	yes	yes	yes		
iv.1.6.2.1	Joseph Fink	1720		St. Blasien										
ECKERT, EGGERT														
vii.1.1.3	Georg Eckert	?	Träger	St. Fridolin			no		55.0		yes?	yes?		
vii.1.1.3	Joseph Eckert	1707		(none)	yes	yes	no			yes?	yes?	yes?		
vii.1.1.3	Johannes Eckert	1710		(none)	yes	yes	no							
vii.1.3	Georg Eckert	?		St. Blasien	yes	yes								
vii.1.3.2	Georg Eckert der Jung	c1685		St. Blasien						yes	yes	yes		sal
vii.1.3.2.1	Joseph Eckert	1714		St. Blasien					11.0	yes?	yes?	yes?		sal
vii.1.3.3	Joseph Eckert	c1689	Schneider?	St. Blasien					11.0		yes?			sal

| | | | | | \multicolumn{10}{c}{Factional Affiliations in Nöggenschwihl, 1725–1745 (Continued)} |
Cat. No.	Name	Birth Year	Occupation, Office	Serf-Lord	1721	1726	1727	1733	1734	1739a	1739b	1739c	1739d	1745
vii.2.1	Balthas Eckert	?		St. Blasien	yes	no	no							
vii.2.1.1	Johannes Eckert	c1689		St. Blasien	yes	no	no							
vii.2.1.2	Melchior Eckert	c1691		St. Blasien	yes	no	no							
vii.2.1.3	Simon Eckert	c1692		St. Blasien	yes	no	no							*müi*
\multicolumn{15}{l}{SCHALLER}
viii.1.2	Johannes Schaller	?		St. Blasien	yes	no	no							
viii.1.2.1	Michel Schaller	c1690		St. Blasien	yes	yes	no					yes		*sal*
viii.1.2.3	Johannes Schaller	c1694		St. Blasien	yes	no	no							
viii.1.2.4	Joseph Schaller	c1695		St. Blasien										*sal*
viii.3.6	Melchior Schaller	?	Schneider	St. Blasien			no							
viii.3.6.2	Joseph Schaller	1707		St. Blasien										
viii.3.6.4	Georg Schaller	1711	Nagelschmied	St. Blasien						yes		yes		*müi*
viii.3.7	Jacob "Jogle" Schaller	?		St. Blasien	yes	no	no							
viii.3.7.1	Johannes Schaller	c1685		St. Blasien		yes	no							*sal*
\multicolumn{15}{l}{DIETSCHI}
ix.1.6	Johannes Dietschi	?		St. Blasien	yes	yes	yes	yes						
ix.1.6.2	Johannes Dietschi	1714		St. Blasien	yes	yes	yes	yes						*müi?*
\multicolumn{15}{l}{FLUEM}
x.1.3.3	Johannes Fluem der Alt	?	Mesmer	St. Blasien	yes	yes	yes	yes						
x.1.3.3.2	Johannes Fluem der Jung	?		St. Blasien	yes	yes	yes	yes						*müi*
x.1.3.3.6	Friedle Fluem	1710		St. Blasien										*müi*
x.1.3.3.8	Steffa Fluem	1714		St. Blasien						yes				*müi*
\multicolumn{15}{l}{THOMA}
xiv.1	Hans Thoma der alte Vogt	?	Vogt, Träger, 1/2 Fronhofmeyer	St. Blasien	yes									
xiv.1.2	Georg Thoma	?	1/2 Fronhofmeyer, Dorfmeyer	St. Blasien	yes	yes	yes	yes						
xiv.1.2.1	Johannes Thoma	1708	1/4 Fronhofmeyer	St. Blasien	yes?									*müi*

FACTIONAL AFFILIATIONS IN NÖGGENSCHWIHL, 1725–1745 (CONTINUED)

Cat. No.	Name	Birth Year	Occupation, Office	Serf-Lord	1721	1726	1727	1733	1734	1739a	1739b	1739c	1739d	1745
xiv.1.2.3	Hans Georg Thoma	1712	1/4 Fronhofmeyer	St. Blasien			no							mül
xiv.1.2.4	Joseph Thoma	1716		St. Blasien			no							
BÄCHLE, BECHLE														
xv.1.1	Georg Bächle	?	Wirt	St. Blasien	yes	yes				yes				
xv.1.1.1	Georg Bächle "Wirtsohn"	?	Sailer	St. Blasien	yes	yes	no			yes	yes			
xv.1.2	Johannes Bächle	?	Geschworener	St. Blasien	yes	yes	no							
xv.1.2.1	Conrad Bächle	1701		St. Blasien	yes		no		16.3	yes	yes	yes		sal
xv.1.2.3	Johannes Bächle	1711		St. Blasien			no							
xv.1.2.4	Joseph Bächle	1712		St. Blasien			no							
xv.2.1	Johannes Bächle	?	Schulmeister	St. Blasien	yes	yes	no							
xv.2.1.1	Johannes Bächle	1708		St. Blasien			no?							mül
THOMA														
xix.4.5	Georg Thoma[a]	?	Schindeldecker	St. Blasien	yes	yes	no		7.2	yes	yes			
xix.4.5.1	Georg Thoma[b]	1712	Schmied	St. Blasien	yes		no			yes				sal
xix.4.5.2	Johannes Thoma	1714	Weber	St. Blasien					22.0	yes	yes?	yes?		sal
EBNER														
xi.2.4	Johannes Ebner	?	Bannwart, Förster	St. Blasien			yes	yes						sal
xxi.2.9	Georg Ebner	1709		St. Blasien										
KEPPELER														
xxii.2	Franz Keppeler	?	Nagelschmied	St. Blasien	yes		no							
xxii.5	Hans Keppeler	c1665	Nagelschmied	St. Blasien		yes	no							
BINKER, BINKERT														
xxiii.1.2.	Johannes Binkert	?	Nagelschmied	St. Blasien	yes	yes	yes			yes	yes			sal
xxiii.2.2.1	Johannes binkert	1712		St. Blasien	yes	yes	yes			yes	yes	yes		
xxiii.1.2.2	Joseph Binkert	1716	Nagelschmied	St. Blasien	yes	yes								sal
xiii.3	Caspar Binkert	?	Schmied, Gastwirt	St. Blasien										

Factional Affiliations in Nöggenschwihl, 1725–1745 (Continued)

Cat. No.	Name	Birth Year	Occupation, Office	Serf-Lord	1721	1726	1727	1733	1734	1739a	1739b	1739c	1739d	1745
xiii.3.1	Joseph Binkert	?		St. Blasien	yes		no		36.4					
xiii.3.3	Johannes Binkert	c1699		St. Blasien			yes?							
DÖRFLINGER														
xxv.1.2	Johannes Dörflinger	c1690	Wagner	St. Blasien	yes	yes	no		16.3	yes	yes			*mül*
xxv.3	Claus Dörflinger	?		St. Blasien	yes	yes	no							
xxv.3.2	Johannes Dörflinger	c1685	Zimmermacher, Rath	St. Blasien	yes	yes	no			yes	yes			*sal*
xxv.4.1	Georg Dörflinger	?		St. Blasien	yes									
xxv.4.1.2	Johannes Dörflinger	1720		St. Blasien										*sal*
EISELE, ISELIN														
xxvii.2	Johannes Eisele der Alt	?		St. Blasien	yes	yes	no			yes	yes	yes		*mül*
xxvii.2.2	Johannes Eisele der Jung	1709	Soldat	St. Blasien	yes	yes	no			yes	yes			*mül*
xxvii.2.3	Joseph Eisele	1710		St. Blasien	yes	yes	no?							*mül*
xxvii.2.4	Hans Michel Eisele	1712		St. Blasien	yes						yes			*mül*
xxvii.3	Joseph Eisele	?		St. Blasien	yes	yes	no							
xxvii.5	Martin Eisele	c1682		St. Blasien	yes	yes	no			yes			30	*sal*
xxvii.5.3	Hans Peter Eisele	1715		St. Blasien					36.4					*sal*
STIGLER, STIGELER														
xviii	Friedle Stigler	?	Strohschmied	St. Blasien	yes	yes	yes	yes						
xviii.1	Johannes Stigler	?	Bannwart, Förster	St. Blasien	yes	yes	yes					yes		
EBNER														
xxx	Steffa Ebner	1734		St. Blasien	yes	yes	yes							
xxx.3	Joesph Ebner	c1696		St. Blasien	yes	yes	no							*mül*
LEBER														
xxxiii	Heinrich Leber der Alt	?		St. Blasien	yes	yes	yes	yes						
xxxiii.1	Heinrich Leber der Jung	c1682		St. Blasien	yes	yes	no		7.2	yes	yes	yes		
xxxiii.6	Georg Leber	1706	Sächler	St. Blasien	yes								8	*sal*

FACTIONAL AFFILIATIONS IN NÖGGENSCHWIHL, 1725–1745 (CONTINUED)

Cat. No.	Name	Birth Year	Occupation, Office	Serf-Lord	1721	1726	1727	1733	1734	1739a	1739b	1739c	1739d	1745
	VILLINGER													
xxxviii.2	Johannes Villinger	c1700		St. Blasien	yes				9.1	yes	yes	yes		sal
xxxviii.3	Adam Villinger	c1708		St. Blasien					7.2	yes	yes	yes		sal
	SCHÄFFER													
xxxviii	Jacob "Jogle" Schäffer	c1686		St.Blasien	yes	yes	yes	yes		yes	yes	yes		sal
	GAMP													
xxix	Hans Jacob Gamp			St. Blasien	yes		no			yes	yes	yes		sal
	JORDAN													
xl	Georg Jordan	?		(none)	yes	yes yes	no							
xl.1	Johnnes Jordan	1709		St. Blasien		yes	no							
xl.3	Steffa Jordan	1717		St. Blasien					47.4					sal
	HÜPFER, HUPFER													
xlii.1	Jacob "Jogle" Hüpfer	?		St. Blasien	yes	yes								
xlii.2	Michel Hupfer	c1695		St. Blasien	yes	yes	no		11.0	yes	yes			sal
	BRUTSCHI, BRUTSCHE, BERTSCHE													
xliii	Johannes Brutschi	?		St. Blasien			no							
xliii.3	Johannes Brutschi	1701		St. Blasien	yes									
xliii.1	Joseph Brutschi	?		St. Blasien	yes	yes	no			yes				
xliii.1.2	Steffa Brutschi	1721		St. Blasien	yes				23.5				24	
	GAMP													
xliv	Benedict Gamp	?		St. Blasien	yes									
xliv.1	Joseph Gamp	1704		St. Blasien	yes	yes								
	GANTERT, GANTHERT													
xlv	Moritz Gantert	c1681		St. Blasien			yes	yes						mül
	ALBIEZ, ALBÜEZ													
xlvi	Claus Albiez	?		St. Blasien			no							

FACTIONAL AFFILIATIONS IN NÖGGENSCHWIHL, 1725–1745 (CONTINUED)

CAT. NO.	NAME	BIRTH YEAR	OCCUPATION, OFFICE	SERF-LORD	1721	1726	1727	1733	1734	1739ᵃ	1739ᵇ	1739ᶜ	1739ᵈ	1745
MATTNER														
xlviii	Johannes Mattner c	?	Krämer, Wagner	(none)		yes	yes							
KAISER, KAYSER														
xlix	Johannes Kaiser	c1685		St. Blasien		yes	no							
VOGELBACHER														
1.3	Thoma Vogelbacher	c1690	Schmied	St. Blasien	yes	yes	no		18.2		yes	yes	8	*sal*
GERSTER														
li	Joseph Gerster		Träger	St. Blasien	yes	yes	no		25.4					
li.1	Valentin Gerster	1707		St. Blasien	yes	yes	no							
li.2	Georg Gerster	1709		St. Blasien			no				yes	yes	yes	*mül*
SCHALLER														
lii	Joseph Schaller "Birndorfer"	1702	Holzmacher	St. Blasien	yes	yes	no		73.2	yes?	yes?	yes?	yes	*mül*

a. Thoma was deprived of his voting rights for three years in 1730; GLA 113:237, 83r–84v: Specification deren Jenigen in der letzten vorgewesten ... ohnruhe interessierten Unterthanen welche ... von activä bey denen ämbter wahlen perpetuo vel ad tempus priviert (28 March 1730).

b. Identified as one who in 1739 distinguished himself with "slanders"; GLA 113:242, 215r–v: Specification etlich ledtigen Knaben welche sich In der Unrueh starckh des handtels mit schelten ohn genomen (1739).

c. Mattner was deprived of his voting rights for three years in 1730; GLA 113:237, 83r–84v: Specification deren Jenigen in der letzten vorgewesten ... ohnruhe interessierten Unterthanen welche von activä et passivä bey denen ämbter wahlen perpetuo vel ad tempus priviert (28 March 1730).

Blurring Genre Boundaries
Judas and His Role in Early Modern German Drama

Paul F. Casey

The figure of the apostle Judas Iscariot is a vital cog in the story of Christian salvation, but the biblical motivation for his betrayal of Christ has always been unclear. With Judas we are operating almost entirely in the realm of myth, for the Bible tells us virtually nothing about his background, and accounts of his role as an apostle are contradictory. Medieval dramatic conceptions focus on avarice as his sole motivation, but in sixteenth-century Germany, dramatists wedded a healthy portion of humor to the conventional motif of avarice. Focusing principally on Thomas Naogeorgus' *Judas Ischariothes* and drawing other sixteenth-century German dramas into the discussion, this paper examines the paradox of comical portrayals of the embodiment of the archtraitor in a period of strong religiosity. It concludes that Judas came to assume the role of the fool in drama, worthy of ridicule and pity rather than hatred.

THE POSITION OF THE DISCIPLE JUDAS ISCARIOT in the Christian theological framework is, at the very least, curious. He does not figure at all in any theological system, nor do any of the creeds mention him, yet his role in the greatest tragedy of all time is central and crucial. Without Judas and his betrayal of Christ, there is no redemptive incarnation. One might reasonably argue that without the integral role of Judas, there is no Christianity, for clearly someone had to hand Jesus over to the Jewish authorities to effect his self-sacrifice: Christ's death forms the essential part of his soteriological mission. There are even biblical passages (e.g., John 13:18–31[1]) which suggest that Jesus specifically chose Judas for this task of treachery: Christ singles him out for special attention by giving him the first Eucharist at

---

[1]Biblical citations are to *The Oxford Annotated Bible with the Apocrypha*, ed. Herbert G. May and Bruce M. Metzger (New York: Oxford University Press, 1965).

the Last Supper and sending him forth on his mission with the admonition, "What you are going to do, do quickly" (John 13:27). In his betrayal, then, has Judas not become an accomplice in Christ's own grand design? Is he not doing the Lord's bidding, merely an adjunct in a redemptive scheme initiated by Christ himself? Regardless of how one assesses his transgression, the comic function of this tragic figure in German dramas of the sixteenth century is, at first glance, not only jarring, but it disrupts established genre boundaries.

In the Christian narrative, Judas plays a pivotal role as an intermediary between good and evil: he belongs to the party of the good but acts as an agent of evil. His role functions as the inversion of Christ's role: Judas sells his master for money, whereas Christ "redeems" or buys back mankind with his self-sacrifice; taken together, both events imply a balanced commercial transaction. The story of Judas Iscariot as it descends to us is almost entirely fictional, yet that does little to affect its status as myth.[2] Myth adds texture to a narrative which, in the Gospels, is anything but detailed. What we know of Judas is paltry: we learn virtually nothing in the scriptures of his background or the meaning of his surname Iscariot. We must even exercise caution not to confuse him with another disciple of Jesus, Judas Thaddaeus, the son of James (Luke 6:16; Mark 3:18; John 14:22), who remained loyal.

Appointed treasurer of the group of disciples by Jesus, Judas Iscariot held the communal purse. By nature avaricious, he reputedly used his position to his own advantage, adopting a parsimonious attitude toward charitable donations and what he viewed as unnecessary expenditures. His reaction to the anointing of Jesus' feet by Mary of Bethany (John 12:1–8; Mark 14:4; Matt. 26:8) furnishes the one biblical reference to his niggardliness. His inquiry "Why was this ointment not sold for three hundred denarii and given to the poor?" draws John's editorial comment: "This he said, not that he cared for the poor but because he was a thief, and as he had the money box he used to take what was put into it."[3] John's report, however, postdates

---

[2]Hyam Maccoby, *Judas Iscariot and the Myth of Jewish Evil* (London: Peter Halban, 1992), 2. Maccoby's study is insightful and thorough, and I draw from it at various points in my introductory remarks.

[3]Luther refers to this incident in his *Sendbrief vom Dolmetschen* (Wittenberg,1530), where he questions the translation of "Ut quid perditio ista unguenti facta est?" as "Warum ist diese Verlierung der Salben geschehen?" Luther prefers the rendering: "Was soll doch solcher Schade? Nein, es ist schade um die Salbe."

the event by many years, and thus his comment sounds like a retroactive attempt to establish motivation for Judas' subsequent actions, when the real motivation is unclear. Ultimately, we arrive at the account of Judas' life by the process of amalgamating the versions found in the four Gospels, for none of the Evangelists spends time on filling in complete details. For them, his role was symbolic and uninteresting beyond his function in the text as a traitor: scripture furnishes no polemic against Judas, merely attaching repeatedly the tag "who betrayed him" to his name (e.g., John 6:70; Mark 3:19).

That the biblical accounts of Judas' life are at variance and sometimes contradictory is not surprising. We are used to filling in the lacunae of one Gospel with information from another, thus papering over the cracks. The biblical accounts of Judas' death, for instance, are incompatible with each other. Mark and John offer no account; Matthew describes the suicide of a penitent (Matt. 27:3–10); the Acts of the Apostles (Acts 1:18) has him bursting asunder in a field that he purchased with the thirty pieces of silver. One might profitably investigate the stages of evolution of the Judas story through the four Gospels, but such a task is clearly beyond the scope of this paper.[4]

The factual evidence in the New Testament is scanty, but that paucity has not noticeably altered certain widely diffused scholarly theories about Judas Iscariot, popularized in modern times by films and novels. For example, there is the widely held conviction that Judas was the only Judaean among the apostles, who were all Galileans. This hypothesis makes him by heritage an outsider, whose ancestry distances him from the rest of the disciples: it underscores the detachment of the other disciples from his deed. The Gospels say nothing explicitly about this theory, which is based on a questionable scholarly derivation of the name "Iscariot."[5] There is, as well, the popular theory that patriotism and zealotry motivated Judas' actions: he did not really wish to betray Jesus but was attempting to force him into action to overthrow the Romans. Again, the Gospels offer no support for this theory. All the apostles believed Jesus' kingdom was of this world, yet none of the others found this belief sufficiently motivating to betray him. Firmly held as well is the contention that

---

[4]Maccoby poses precisely this question in his work cited (see n. 2 above).

[5]Walter Bauer, *Das Leben Jesu im Zeitalter der neutestamentarischen Apokryphen* (Tübingen: J.C.B. Mohr, 1909), 173ff.

Judas and the Jews are somehow synonymous: whenever a scapegoat is needed to bear the burden of a disaster, the Jews are chosen and the name "Judas" applied to them. The Christian imagination repeatedly makes the identification of Jesus' own people, the Jews who betrayed him, with his disciple Judas Iscariot. Yet nowhere does the Bible indicate that Judas is a representative of the Jewish nation. He is not an allegory for the Jewish people but a symbol of betrayal, and it is in this context that he fits into German drama.

The portrayal of Judas in such enduring passion play traditions as that of Oberammergau reinforces the persistent misconception of his role. Regularly stamped as blatantly anti-Semitic, modern versions of the Oberammergau play (from 1970 onwards) attempt to dispel the charge by omitting such slanders of the Jews as appeared in the 1934 performance. That version casts the Jews as "a fiendish brood," "the murderous horde," "this evil band," a "murderous league," bloodhounds and fools who had come "up from the nethermost Hell."[6] But even with the deletion of such inflammatory descriptors, the play still casts Judas as representative of the Jewish people's willingness to betray Christ.[7] Although its roots are clearly medieval, the oldest extant manuscript of the Oberammergau play dates only from 1662. In 1880 August Hartmann established the authenticity of this 1662 playbook and demonstrated that it was a composite of four distinct versions of Christ's passion; for example, Sebastian Wild's 1566 version of the passion, *Die Passion und die Auferstehung Christi*, contributes several thousand lines to the Oberammergau play.[8] Just as the play itself represents a conflation of other works, so the figure of Judas in the Christian imagination results from a conflated and confused identification. Christian converts in the early days of the Church noted the many prominent figures named Judah in Jewish history and concluded that the name was synonymous with that of Jew. They further associated the name Judas with the ancient Jewish homeland

---

[6]Saul S. Friedman, *The Oberammergau Passion Play: A Lance against Civilization* (Carbondale: Southern Illinois University Press, 1984), 85.

[7]Ibid., 87.

[8]August Hartmann, *Das Oberammergauer Passionsspiel in seiner ältesten gestalt* (Leipzig: Breitkopf und Härtel, 1880).

(Judaea)—which in Latin (Iudaeus) even sounds the same—and came to connect the identity of the betrayer with the entire Jewish people.[9] In the passion plays of the German Middle Ages, the figure of Judas functions as the archetype of the traitor who sold his master for money. The telling image of the Jew as miser emerges in scenes in which Judas drives a hard bargain with the Jewish elders for his blood money, each party trying to outdo the other in avarice. Such encounters, meant to adumbrate the pettiness of Judas' actions, are the root of later comic characterizations of Judas. In the *Alsfelder Passionsspiel* (1501), for example, Judas argues with Caiphas, the high priest, about every coin that makes up his blood money:

Judas dicit:	Der pennigk ist roit!
Caiphas:	Der gildet der fleysch und broitt!
Judas:	Disser ist krangk!
Caiphas:	Judas, hore, bilch eyn gut klangk!
Judas:	Disser ist doch zurisßen!
Caiphas:	Judas, nym eyn andern und mach dich nit beschisßen!
Judas:	Disser hot eyn hole!
Caiphas:	Szo nym eyn andern! hie gildet dir woil.
Judas:	Disser hot eyn falsch zeychen!
Caiphas:	Willttu en nyt, ßo wel ich dir eyn andern reichen!
Judas:	Disser ist doch swarcz!
Caiphas:	Sehe eyn andern und ganck an eyn harcz!
Judas:	Disser rycz ist zumaile langk!
Caiphas:	Judas, wollestu dich hencken, hie gulde dir eyn strangk!

---

[9]Friedman, *The Oberammergau Passion Play*, 87 (see n. 6 above), makes this point in some detail. In the context of anti-Semitic renderings of Judas, it is noteworthy that one of the most infamous of modern anti-Semites does *not* emphasize the association of Judas with the Jews. In 1918, Joseph Goebbels penned "Judas Ischariot, eine biblische Tragödie": in iambic pentameter, the play tells the story of Judas, the outsider, intent on following the man he thinks will establish a new empire. Once installed as a disciple, Judas is disappointed that Christ's kingdom is not of this world: he considers the promise of salvation after death merely a sop to the masses. Judas betrays Christ so that he himself might establish the kingdom of God on earth. The play makes the point that Judas betrayed Christ out of idealism, not avarice. Goebbels had hopes of publishing the drama, which questions the premise that the Catholic Church will produce the just order. These hopes were dashed when his parish priest in Rheydt objected to the subject matter. See Rolf Georg Reuth, *Goebbels* (New York: Harcourt Brace & Co., 1993), 23. The Bundesarchiv in Koblenz houses the manuscript of the drama (NL 118/127).

Judas: Der ist blyen!
Caiphas: Wiltu uns dissen tagk gehygen?[10]

Such depictions of Judas lead to a predominance of Jewish misers in western literature—from Judas to Shylock—which is not in the least affected by the emphasis in authoritative Jewish rabbinic works on the exercise of charity and generosity to Jews and non-Jews alike, or the example of a long line of Jewish philanthropists.[11] The amplified Christian story of Judas furnishes a striking example of the power of myth over fact, for with the figure of Judas we are operating almost totally in the realm of invention.

The entire literature of the European Middle Ages knows Judas as a despicable traitor.[12] To the Germanic peoples, who after the sack of Rome had taken over a leadership role in Europe, the very idea of *Treubruch* (disloyalty) must have been horrifying. Little did they concern themselves with motivation for the deed; disloyalty was enough.[13] In the *Heliand* (ca. 830), for instance, Judas becomes sim-

---

[10]I quote from Richard Froning's reprint of the 1891/92 edition of the *Alsfelder Passionsspiel*, in his *Das Drama des Mittelalters* (Darmstadt: Wissenschaftliche Buchgesellschaft, 1964), 683–84. All translations into English in this essay are mine.
"*Judas:* The penny is red!
Caiphas: It buys meat and bread!
Judas: This one is worthless!
Caiphas: Judas, listen, what a good sound!
Judas: This one has a crack!
Caiphas: Judas, take another and don't make such a scene!
Judas: This one has a hole in it!
Caiphas: So take another! It will serve you well!
Judas: This one has the wrong image on it!
Caiphas: If you don't want it, I'll give you another.
Judas: But this one is black!
Caiphas: Look at another one and give it back!
Judas: This tear is very long!
Caiphas: Judas, if you wanted to hang yourself, you could buy a rope with it!
Judas: This one's made of lead!
Caiphas: Are you going to carry on like this all day?"
[11]Maccoby, *Judas Iscariot and the Myth of Jewish Evil*, 6 (see n. 2 above).
[12]Among works dealing with the legend of Judas, the following are useful: Wilhelm Creizenach, "Judas Ischarioth in Legende und Sage des Mittelalters," *Beiträge zur Geschichte der deutschen Sprache und Literatur* 2 (1876): 177–207; Paul Franklin Baum, "The Medieval Legend of Judas Iscariot," *PMLA* 31 (1916): 481–632; Paul Lehmann, "Judas Iskarioth," in *Erforschung des Mittelalters* (1941; reprint, Stuttgart: Hiersemann,1959) 2:229–85.
[13]Arthur Luther, *Jesus und Judas in der Dichtung: ein Beitrag zur vergleichenden Literaturgeschichte* (Hanau: Clauss & Feddersen, 1910), 31. "Das Grauen vor dem Treubruch an sich war so groß, daß die Veranlassung zum Verrat kaum beachtet wurde."

ply a Germanic *Dienstmann* (vassal) who has proven disloyal to his lord, the most grievous of sins:

> Da verheißen ihm die Herren dreißig Silbermünzen insgesamt zu seiner eigenen Verfügung, und er sprach zu dem Volke mit bösen Worten, daß er dafür seinen Herrn ausliefern werde. Dann wandte er sich von der Versammlung. Er war bösen Sinnes. Treulos überschlug er bei sich, wann ihm die Zeit kommen würde, daß er ihn dem Volke der Bösen, dem Volke der Feinde verraten könne.... Da machte sich Judas, der nach Bösem trachtete, auf, von dannen hinauszugehn. Der Degen war voll grimmen Sinnes wider seinen Herrn. Schon war es düstere Nacht, ganz bewölkt.[14]

A faithless ("treulos") vassal has betrayed his liege lord: the cause is unknown, but the atmosphere ("düstere Nacht, ganz bewölkt") forebodes an evil outcome for such reprehensible behavior.

Dante's *Inferno* confirms the severity with which the Middle Ages viewed disloyalty. There we find Judas in the very depths of hell (in the ninth circle reserved for those who were treacherous to their masters), where he is being chewed in the mouth of Lucifer along with Brutus and Cassius.

As the German Middle Ages progressed, literary representations of Judas increasingly stressed solely the motive of avarice for his actions. For hundreds of years, avarice seemed a suitable incentive: few paid attention to the fact that the payment stood in no relation to the deed. For his betrayal Judas received 30 pieces of silver (shekels), equal to 120 denarii. When we recall that the ointment used by Mary of Bethany (Matt. 26:8) had cost 300 denarii, the conclusion that Judas betrayed Christ for less than half the price of the ointment ought to spark some skepticism as to the sufficiency of the financial motive. In the passion plays—which underwent their own development in the course of centuries—Judas' depiction is consistent: we usually see him portrayed as bearing Semitic facial characteristics of

---

[14]I quote from the prose translation of the *Heliand* by Wilhelm Stapel, in *Der Heliand* (Munich: Carl Hanser Verlag, 1953), 127. "Then the masters gave him thirty silver coins and to the people he said, in evil words, that he would deliver the Lord for this amount. Then he turned away from the assembly. His heart was evil. Disloyally, he considered when he could betray him to the forces of evil, to the forces of the enemy....Then Judas, who was intent on evil, made preparations to leave. The warrior was consumed by wrathful evil intent against his master. Already it was gloomy night, completely cloud covered."

an ugly cast, dressed in yellow (the color of betrayal), wearing a red wig and beard, evidencing signs of covetousness, and aided and abetted by the devil.[15] Many of these plays stress the devil's active encouragement to betray Christ, for it was all but inconceivable in the minds of most contemporaries that any rational person would betray Christ without the collusion of demonic forces. Avarice, by itself, seemed an inadequate motivation.

Iconographic depictions of the deed of betrayal from the medieval and early modern periods also stress Judas' role as an *Einzelgänger* or his collusion with the devil. Facial stereotyping characterizes the painting of the Last Supper from the workshop of Lucas Cranach (1565) located in the Castle Church in Dessau. The work portrays all the Apostles, except Judas, as contemporary Reformation figures. Judas sits in isolation on the wrong side of the table, his Semitic features distinctly visible in profile. Clearly discernible as well are the money purse, which he holds behind him, and his traditional yellow garments. In Giotto's depiction of the receipt of the blood money (ca. 1305), the Judas figure is surprisingly young and handsome in contrast to the grave, long-bearded patriarchal priests. Here Giotto concentrates on the moment of Judas' transformation from apostle to traitor; hovering behind Judas is the shadowy figure of Satan, on the verge of corrupting the disciple.

In the German drama of the sixteenth century, the Judas theme does not figure as prominently as do other biblical themes; it in no way rivals in popularity the Prodigal Son, Susanna, Esther, Judith, Tobias, or Joseph as subject matter for dramatization. This dearth of dramas on the subject is partly a result of Luther's failure to recommend the material to aspiring dramatists, as he did with other themes. Luther views Judas as a thief, encouraged by the devil to betray his master, and his fate as an example of what happens to those who traffic with Satan: "Mit Juda helt es sich also, Er ist ein geytziger mensch, wie die Euangelisten etlich mal anzeygen, das, weyl der Herr ihn zum Schaffner verordnet, er vil abgetragen und gestolen hab."[16] It is doubtful whether Luther would have approved of subject

---

[15]For an overview of Judas' role in the passion plays, see Anton Büchner, *Judas Ischarioth in der deutschen Dichtung: Ein Versuch* (Freiburg i.B.: Guenther Verlag, 1920).

[16]Luther's pronouncements on Judas are contained in the *Hauspostille* of 1545. See *D. Martin Luthers Werke: Kritische Gesamtausgabe* (Weimar 1883ff.), 52:746. "With Judas the case was as follows: He was a greedy person, as the evangelists repeatedly note. Because the master made him treasurer, he secreted away money and stole it."

matter that smacked of the climate of the late medieval passion plays and would require the presence of the Savior on stage. The appearance of Christ as a stage figure may, of itself, not have imposed a risk, but dramatists were cautious to avoid verisimilitude that might awaken compassion in their audience.[17] Lutheran playwrights used biblical dramas to illustrate Reformation principles. One can well imagine the discomfort of dramatists trying to come to terms with the symbolism inherent in Judas' betrayal. Its application to Reformation ideas is not readily apparent, unless one merely wants to underscore the cautionary lesson of the passion plays, that merchants not become too greedy.

But sixteenth-century German drama does not totally neglect Judas. The first play devoted exclusively to the theme is Thomas Naogeorgus' *Judas Iscariotes tragoedia nova et Sacra lectu et actu festiva et iucunda* (Basel, 1552), quickly translated into German by Johann Mercur Morsheymer and published in Strasbourg in 1556.[18] With the theme, Naogeorgus has hit upon a subject matter uniquely suited to his satirical purposes. That he chose to write his drama in Latin indicates that he was not intent on an appeal to popular piety. Naogeorgus composed all his dramas in Latin, which was in keeping with the practice of German humanists of the period. Others quickly translated his plays into German, some as many as four times, and they received revivals well into the seventeenth century in both Latin and German.[19] Thus, regardless of the author's intention, the dramas had an impact on popular belief. Naogeorgus' five books of satires (*Satyrarum libri quinque*, Basel, 1555) belong to the best that the sixteenth century produced in this genre.[20] Judas also appears regularly,

[17]Cf. Hans-Gert Roloff, "Thomas Naogeorgs Judas—ein Drama der Reformationszeit," *Archiv für die neuen Sprachen* 208 (1971): 94–95.

[18]Karl Goedeke, *Grundriß zur Geschichte der deutschen Dichtung*, 2:335, misspells the name "Moesheymer." The German play appears in *Thomas Naogeorg: Sämtliche Werke*, ed. Hans-Gert Roloff, vol. 4, pt. 2 (Berlin: Walter de Gruyter, 1987), and bears the title page, *Judas Ischariotes / Ein neüw vnd sehr lustig Tragedia / von dem fürtreflichen gelerten Mann Thoma Nao-Georgio / Lateinisch beschryben aus der Heyligen Geschriffte vnd verdeüdschet durch Iohan: Mercvrivm Morsheymerum. Getruckt zu Straßburg / durch Paulum vnd Philippum Köpfflein Gebrüder. M.D.L.VI.* As far as I know, this is the only sixteenth-century drama in Germany devoted solely to the Judas theme. Roloff's article (see n. 17 above) is the first study to deal extensively with Naogeorgus' Judas drama.

[19]Cf. Goedeke, *Grundriß* 2:333–35.

[20]Roloff, *Archiv* (see n. 17 above), 85: "Die fünf Bücher Satiren gehören mit zu dem Besten, was diese Gattung im 16. Jahrhundert aufzuweisen hat."

Paul F. Casey

if marginally, as a wedding guest in the several sixteenth-century dramas on the Marriage-at-Cana theme, where his role as betrayer of Christ is all but overlooked.

Naogeorgus' drama is a work of hate and anger.[21] The author focuses on Judas as a metaphor for those early converts to the Reformation cause who, by midcentury, were returning to the Catholic fold and betraying the advances of Lutheranism. Further, by dedicating his drama to the city council of Strasbourg, he chastised civil authorities who were weakening in their allegiance to the cause before the *Augsburg Interim* (1548) imposed a certain degree of stability on religious matters. The tone of the work is tendentious and polemical, and literary historians understandably categorize it as *Kampfdrama*.[22] Appearing after Luther's death, and thus without his imprimatur, the drama occurs at a time after Reformation biblical drama had already reached its zenith. The work is thoroughly grounded in the medieval conception of the traitorous Judas, accompanied through the biblical events by the devil Sargannabus and the good counsel of Conscientia. These two allegorical figures battle throughout to gain ascendancy over Judas' soul and to influence his deed; their presence links the drama with the medieval mystery plays, where allegorical figures typically influenced the outcome. But although allegorical figures hold sway, Judas makes his choice through his own free will, giving in to the sin of *superbia*. Rampant avarice gains control of Judas' soul, strangling his more decent impulses, and spurs him on to his deed and ultimately to a suicide of desperation.

The subject matter, then, concerns a highly emotional event, central to the story of salvation, and any author dealing with it must exercise care to avoid a charge of blasphemy. Naogeorgus focuses on Judas as a tragic figure, adhering to the contemporary conception of tragedy as described by J. C. Scaliger and developing protasis, epitasis, catastasis, and catastrophe in the play.[23] The structure further emulates the classical conception of tragedy by including a prologue and

[21]Wilhelm Creizenach, *Geschichte des neueren Dramas* (Halle: Max Niemeyer Verlag, 1901), 2:135, characterizes Naogeorgus' drama as "ein Werk des Zornes und Hasses."

[22]Ibid., 136.

[23]Roloff, *Archiv* (see n. 17 above),102, describes the development of these tragic aspects of the play.

choruses to conclude each of the five acts. No extraneous stage business or subplots distract from the evolution of the main figure: "Nicht auf szenische Turbulenz, sondern auf die Luzidität des intellektuellen Beweisvorganges kam es Naogeorg an."[24] But despite the drama's serious nature—implicit in Naogeorgus' structuring it as a tragedy and the satirical point he intended it to make—the characterization of Judas is surprisingly and strikingly comical. Invariably the root of the humor is Judas' chrematistic (read: greedy) disposition, his avaricious nature. Naogeorgus quite pointedly constructs and refines this aspect of Judas' personality, and in doing so he deviates markedly from contemporary conceptions of the tragic genre: "Mit Stolz hat Naogeorg bekannt, daß die Einführung der Komik ... in die ernste Tragödie seine eigene Leisung sei."[25] In act 2, scene 2, Judas argues humorously with Malchus, doorkeeper to the high priest Caiphas, for admission to the authorities. As a fee for letting Judas enter, Malchus demands half of the money Judas will receive for his betrayal of Christ. Judas suggests a tenth of the amount, and they agree on a third, although Judas is intent on cheating Malchus out of even this reduced portion:

Iudas

Du thust warlich daran bößlich
Das solch gut werck würdt gwert durch dich
Ists nit ein plag / das der Lecker
So halßstärrig und zu wider
Mir ist / und mein nutz stets hindert
Ich wil (ob ich vleicht wirdt gewerdt)
Im etwas verheissen und doch
Dasselb im nit halten darnach
Dweil solchs auch ein Hoff bößlein ist
Wie ich vermerck auß seinem list.

Malchus
Was murmelst heymlich hinder mir?

[24]Ibid., 102. "Naogeorgus was not concerned with turbulent scenes, but rather with establishing the lucidity of a series of proofs."
[25]Ibid., 104. "Proudly Naogeorgus acknowledged that the introduction of the comic element into the serious tragedy was his own accomplishment."

Iudas
Ich denck was ich soll geben dir
Sehe hin / ich dir gewyß versprich
Den zehenden theyl hab ich für dich.

Malchus
Den zehenden theyl? da wirt nichs auß
Wos nit der dritt ist / so bleib drauß.

Iudas
Wolan dieweils nit sunst kan sein
So seys der dritt.

Malchus
So kom hinein.

(lines 1508–26)[26]

The repartee here is stichomythic, witty, and significant in length: these are not just intermittent comical remarks but claim some 160 lines of dialogue. The tone of the banter recalls the *Fastnachtsspiel* (shrovetide play) tradition of somewhat earlier decades in the sixteenth century and underscores Judas' prevailing obsession.

In act 3, scene 3, a similarly stichomythic encounter between Judas and Sebulius, the fictitious caterer of the Last Supper, produces another humorous episode. Peter has already paid the caterer to prepare the feast. Judas insists one should not pay for the meal before delivery, terms Peter an *Ertznarr* (arch fool; line 2321) for having done so, and makes a futile and ridiculous attempt to get the money back from the caterer:

---

[26]I quote from Hans-Gert Roloff's edition of the play (see n. 18 above).
   "*Judas:* Truly, you are ill-advised in this. You are preventing such good work by your action. This toady is so stubborn and despicable that he is hindering my purpose. I'll promise him something and then perhaps not keep my promise, because he himself is evil, as I can tell by his cunning.
   Malchus: What are you murmuring behind me?
   Judas: I'm considering what I should give you. Look, I'll promise you a tenth of what I get.
   Malchus: A tenth? That's nothing. If not a third, you stay outside.
   Judas: Well, if it can't be otherwise, then a third.
   Malchus: Okay, you can come in."

Iudas

....

Hörst Wirth gib wider her das gelt
Das dir ist worden dargezelt.

Sebulius
Habt nur fleyssig acht umb den herdt
Das das essen bald fertig werdt.

Iudas
Hörstu gib mir das gelt wider.

Sebulius
Jung bring mir den Morselsteyn her
Das ich die ding drin stoß bey zeyt
Und ich darnach nit zu lang beydt.

Iudas
Hörst auch was ich dir sag? gibs gelt
Das dir ist worden dargezelt.

Sebulius
Lieber gehe mir da auß dem weg....
(lines 2333–43)[27]

Sebulius ignores his entreaties and pleas, pretending not to hear the rantings of Judas, and continues with his preparations for the meal, ordering his help about and selecting the meal's components. Judas' repeated entreaties: "Es ist aber das gelt nit dein" (line 2359), "Geb du mirs gelt vil mehr jetz all // Darnach ich / was dir gebürt / bezall" (lines 2363–64)[28] fall on deaf ears, which drives him to comical paroxysms of impatience and hypocritical self-righteousness:

[27]*"Judas:* Hey, Caterer, give back the money you've been paid.
Sebulius: Be careful of the stove, the meal will be ready soon.
Judas: Do you hear me? Give me back the money.
Sebulius: Boy, bring me the Morselstein, so I can uncork and decant it, thereby saving time.
Judas: Do you hear what I say? Give me back the money that was paid to you.
Sebulius: You'd better get out of my way.... "
[28]"But the money isn't yours." "Give it all to me and afterwards I'll pay you what you deserve."

Iudas
Das hastu Petre als gemacht
Das du so närrisch unbedacht
Das gelt so hast geschlaudert hin
Ey was hastu doch für ein sinn?
Meynstu das gelt sey Haber stro
Oder gehe ich vergebens do
Mit lährem seckel für ein spott
Wie will ich den Armen thun raht
Waher will ich bezaln die leüt
Was solln wir hon zu essens zeyt
Wer will uns brod umb sunst geben
Oder solln wir des luffts leben
Das du doch so gar heyloß bist
Und machst das uns solchs alls gebrist.
(lines 2375–88)[29]

Judas' fixation on his role as keeper of the purse has totally corrupted his more decent impulses. The humorous undertones persist in act 4, scene 2, where Judas accompanies Nagidus, leader of the troupe that is to seize Christ, and insists on seeing his money before he betrays his master:

Nagidus
Du bist ein Narr.

Iudas
Neyn ich warlich
Dann wa mirs gilt / billich ich sprich
Das man mir geb was mir gebürt
Dann ich der untrew gnug gespürt
Drumb / das dus wüst / ich laß es sein
Und geh wider die strassen mein
Geht ir hin und sucht in eben

---

[29]*"Judas:* You've done all this, Peter, with your foolish thoughtlessness. You've wasted the money; what kind of sense do you have? Do you think the money is straw or am I supposed to walk around with an empty purse? How am I to help the poor? How am I to pay our people? What are we to eat? Who'll give us bread for nothing? Or are we to live on air? That you could be so heedless has put us all in this fix."

Solt ich mein mühe umb sunst geben.
(lines 2988–94)[30]

He perseveres relentlessly throughout the entire scene, until Nagidus finally shows him the money. In act 5, scene 1, Judas considers how he might obtain yet more money in his *seckel* (purse), thus intensifying, even after the betrayal, the motivation of avarice. On the plot level, this episode suggests Judas' awareness that he has struck a rather poor bargain in accepting the thirty pieces of silver, but on the authorial level it indicates Naogeorgus' suspicion that the price is inadequate as motivation for the deed. The final chorus concedes that Judas' behavior is risible, but urges spectators to profit from his example rather than merely laugh at him:

> So dürffen sie wol lachen dran
> Ey sagen sie / es gschicht in recht
> Dann sie allzeit darnach gefecht
> Darnach einr ringt / darnach im glingt
> Drumb jetzt ir straff auff sie eindringt
> Diß manen wir mit allem fleyß
> Das sie der sach nit so gar leyß
> Nachdencken wölln / und lern darbey
> Was Gotts gsetz / brauch / und recht art sey.
> (lines 4219–27)[31]

The Judas play, along with Naogeorgus' earlier *Kampfdramen* such as *Pammachius* (1538) and *Mercator* (1540), is among the sixteenth century's most successful satirical and propagandistic attacks on the Roman Church, even though it occurs at a time when the Lutheran Church had already gained a secure foothold, indeed an established position in various parts of the empire.[32]

---

[30]*"Nadigus:* You're a fool.
Judas: Truly not. What concerns me is that I be given what is due me, for I suspect deception. Therefore, so that you know, I'm leaving the matter alone and I'll go my own way. You go your way and look for him, so that I don't waste my efforts."

[31]"They may well laugh at him. They say it serves him right, for one sometimes achieves what one strives for and reaps the punishment. We warn assiduously that they not take the matter too lightly, but consider it and learn from it what God's law, custom and justice is."

[32]Barbara Könneker, *Die deutsche Literatur der Reformationszeit* (Munich: Winkler, 1975), 173.

Paul F. Casey

In the Marriage-at-Cana plays of Paul Rebhun (1538) and Wolfgang Schmeltzl (1543), Judas assumes a subsidiary role as a wedding
guest in an episode that constitutes Christ's first miracle. But aside
from Simon, the henpecked husband, Judas is the only humorous
character in these plays.[33] In act 4, scene 1, of the Rebhun version,
Judas reminds Jesus that the purse is empty, establishing and under-
scoring his preoccupation with money:

> Meister, das yr nicht vieleicht bey euch gedenckt
> Als obs gelts so viel da wer, davon man schenckt
> Drumb so wisset das der seckel schir ist lehr
> Wolt ihr dann viel schencken, dörfft zwar selbs wol mehr.[34]

He humorously prods Jesus on to action, giving Christ the opportunity to remark that when the time comes Judas, too, will be richly
rewarded:

> Lieber Juda darfst dich drumm nicht kumern fast
> Ob du viel odr wenig gelt im seckel hast,
> Diser sach ich selbs noch weis zu rhaten wol
> Wenn mein zeit wird sein, das ich nur schencken sol.[35]

Further, Judas wittily advocates the benefits of wine over water:

> Ich hab noch kaum genetzt ein zan
> Sol wir gereit kein wein mehr han?
> Ich wolt itzund erst trincken gern.
> ....
> Nach wasser sehn ich mich nicht sehr
> Es machet eim die schenckel schwer,
> Dazu bekümpts nicht iederman
> Drumb meid ich das so fast ich kan,

[33]Nicodemus Frischlin's play on the same theme, *Nuptiae Chananaeae* (1590),
omits Judas entirely.
[34]I cite from my forthcoming edition of Rebhun's *Hochzeitspil auff die Hochzeit zu
Cana Galileae* (1546) to appear in *Paul Rebhun: Das Gesamtwerk*, vol. 1 (Bern: Peter Lang
Verlag), act 4, scene 1: "Master, don't assume there is so much money that one can give
presents. You should know that the purse is empty. If you want to give a lot away, the
purse will need replenishing."
[35]Act 4, scene 1: "Dear Judas, you need not concern yourself about whether there
is a little or a lot in the purse. I'll take care of the matter when the time has come for
me to give presents."

Weil ich auch hab ein kalten magn
Der sich damit nicht kan vertragn,
Die genss das wasser bhalten solln
Die schnattern drinn so lang sie wolln.[36]

As Schmeltzl's version of the material derives from Rebhun's, his conception of Judas is similar. In both depictions, we encounter an extra-biblical Judas long before he has incriminated himself; his obsession with money and good wine, however, motivates the role he will subsequently assume. The comical aspects of Judas' role thus find confirmation in a number of sixteenth-century portrayals.

Striking in these Lutheran images of Christ's betrayer, produced during a period of intense religiosity, is a rudimentary grasp of psychological characterization. The medieval conception of Judas' avaricious and miserly behavior is inherent in sixteenth-century depictions of him, but Reformation dramatists wedded a healthy portion of humor to the standard characterization. Naogeorgus has used entire scenes, not just occasional witty remarks, to develop a comic depiction of the archetypical traitor. How was it possible for such serious men to conceive of the betrayer of Christ as in any way humorous? The explanation lies in the desire to develop motivating forces for Judas' deeds. In the Naogeorgus drama, Judas acts under the influence of Satan, the stock clown figure and jokester of the late medieval passion plays. By his sacrifice, Christ had conquered hell and the forces of evil: he had thoroughly discredited Satan and his cohorts who could no longer be taken seriously. By allying himself with the devil, the traitor Judas has made himself ridiculous and petty and has slipped into the role (and costume) reserved for the devil on the medieval stage, i.e., the fool. He is no longer solely responsible for his actions, and his role as archtraitor in the Christian legend recedes behind his characterization as a fool, who in the hands of Satan caves in to baser human instincts. It is no longer primarily a matter of *Treubruch*, but of Judas, in his human weakness, having given in to the disgraced forces of evil. By his greed, he has deceived himself. As a

---

[36]Act 5, scene 1: "I've hardly wet my whistle. Don't we have any wine left? I wanted to start drinking now.... I'm not longing for water, it makes the legs heavy. Also it doesn't appeal to everyone, thus I avoid it when I can because I have a cold stomach that doesn't tolerate it. The geese should keep the water and quack in it as long as they like."

fool, he becomes an object of pity and derision rather than a prince of treachery, and his behavior assumes humorous overtones. A veneer of the ridiculous in Judas' actions also aptly served Naogeorgus' political objectives—that is, the chastisement of recently fallen-away Lutherans—since, metaphorically, such behavior also characterizes them as shortsighted and ridiculous.

Sixteenth-century depictions of Judas as a comic figure, however, form something of an anomaly. The seventeenth century saw a return to a more conservative and less psychologically nuanced characterization. In Abraham à Santa Clara's voluminous work *Judas, der Ertz-Schelm* (four volumes), the title figure is externally and internally a monster, upon whom the author heaps abuse.[37] Among other unflattering phrases, Abraham terms him "der wilde und unflätige Misthammel," "großmäuliger Schmähler," "das verrüchte Lotterbürschel," "der schlimme Hund," "der elende Tropf," and "die Bestie."[38] Clearly, no redeeming personal qualities survive this depiction, and there is no room for situational humor. After somewhat enlightened consideration at the hands of Reformation dramatists, the figure of Judas had to wait nearly two centuries for as nuanced a treatment. In his *Messias*, whose first three cantos appeared in 1748, Friedrich Gottlieb Klopstock interpreted him as a handsome figure torn by dreams of earthly power and wealth:

> Ihm fällt ein schwarzes, lockichtes Haupthaar
> Über die breiten Schultern herab. Sein erstes Gesichte
> Ist voll männlicher Schöne. Dies Haupt, das über die Häupter
> Aller Jünger hervorragt, vollendet sein mänliches Ansehn.
> (Canto 3:375–78)[39]

---

[37]Abraham à Sancta Clara's work bears the title *Judas, der Ertz-Schelm, für ehrliche Leuth, oder Eigentlicher Entwurff, und Lebens-Beschreibung desz ischariotischen Böszwicht: Worinnen underschiedliche Discurs, sittliche Lehrs-Pincten, Gedicht und Geschicht ... / durch Pr. Abraham a S. Clara ... Saltzburg: bey Melchior Haan, 1686–1695.* The Beineke Library at Yale possesses a copy.

[38]"the wild and flatulent filthy beast," "big-mouthed slanderer," "the infamous dissolute," "the wicked dog," "the miserable drop," "the beast."

[39]I quote from Otto Hellinghaus, ed., *Klopstocks Werke: Der Göttinger Dichterbund* (Freiburg i.B.: Herder, 1748), 192. "Black, curly hair falls over his broad shoulders. His serious face is full of manly beauty. His head, which towers over the heads of all the other disciples, completes his manly appearance."

Klopstock's less obsessive and more differentiated portrayal harkens back to sixteenth-century conceptions of Judas as a foolish victim and rescues him once again from an unalleviatedly negative reputation.

The inclusion of comical portrayals of Judas within the framework of serious sixteenth-century German religious drama disrupts established genre boundaries, which, in this early period, would have precluded inserting comical figures into innately tragic situations, especially those that focus on the Savior himself. But precisely because the sixteenth century conceived of Judas' role within Christian salvation as at least as foolish as it is evil—a more perceptive and subtle view of his theological function than that of previous and subsequent generations—dramatists cause the figure of Judas to transgress the existing dramatic order, emphasizing his victimization and collusion with the devil rather than his perfidy. Perversion of traditional order and the crossing of genre boundaries result, in this case, in a more sympathetic and, indeed, more enlightened psychological conception of Christ's betrayer.

The Despair and Suicide of Judas
by Jean Duvet (Master of the Unicorn)

Architecture and Rhetoric in the Work of Johann Bernhard Fischer von Erlach

Friedrich Polleroß

Translated by Peter Ian Waugh

It is now commonplace that both the painting and sculpture of the early modern period are based on the principles of rhetoric. However, there is less information available on the connection between rhetoric and architecture, although the function of the most important buildings was also political or religious *persuasio*. The work of Johann Bernhard Fischer von Erlach (1656–1723) provides an exemplary case for studying that connection. Fischer was trained in Rome under Bernini and Bellori and went on to build notable churches and palaces in Vienna, Salzburg, and Prague. In his function as imperial architect he worked with *concettisti* such as Conrad Adolph von Albrecht and Carl Gustav Heraeus. Fischer was obviously aware of the rhetorical function of his buildings, and his understanding of the relationship between architecture and rhetoric can be analyzed according to three functions: the persuasive function of the architecture itself; the emblematic function of the buildings in the context of *inventio* and *dispositio*; and the question of *decorum* in connection with different styles in rhetoric.

THE CONNECTION BETWEEN RHETORIC AND THE VISUAL ARTS, above all in the painting of seventeenth-century Rome and France, has been a frequent subject of academic study over the past few years.[1] However, the relationship between Baroque rhetoric and architecture has so far received little attention.[2] In this study I shall examine this connec-

---

[1] Jacqueline Lichtenstein, *The Eloquence of Colour Rhetoric and Painting in the French Classical Age* (Berkeley: University of California Press, 1993).

[2] Bruno Contardi, *La retorica e l'architettura barocca*, Studi di storia dell'arte 8 (Rome: Bulzoni, 1978); Carsten-Peter Warncke, "Rhetorik der Architektur in der frühen Neuzeit," in *Johann Conrad Schlaun 1695–1773: Architektur des Spätbarock in Europa*, ed. Klaus Bußmann, Florian Matzner, Ulrich Schulze (Münster: Stuttgart Oktagon, 1995), 612–21.

tion in the work of Johann Bernhard Fischer von Erlach (1656–1723), the most important Austrian architect of his age, and in that of his son Joseph Emanuel.[3] This case study is motivated in part by the fact that Johann Bernhard Fischer von Erlach was not a traditional technician but learned and worked in Italy as sculptor and creator of ephemeral architecture. Religious painting and sculpture as well as absolutist decorations were the main fields of the visual arts in which rhetoric was used. Such a study joins the discussion of the emblematic function of Fischer's imperial architecture (Sedlmayr, Aurenhammer, Möseneder, Matsche, and Lavin); in addition, it promises to bring new insights into the relationship between architecture, sculpture, and literature when viewed in terms of rhetoric.

PERSUASIO

The main object of oratory was *persuasio*, i.e., the art of persuasion, directed primarily at the affections, but which had already been applied to the visual arts by Alberti.[4] Born the son of a sculptor in Graz, Fischer spent the years 1671 to 1687 studying and working as a sculptor in Rome and Naples. During this period he would certainly have encountered the theory of *docere*, *delectare*, and *movere*, as exemplified in the altars and celebratory apparatus for the forty-hour prayer constructed by the "theater architects" Cortona and Bernini.[5] Like Bernini's altars, Fischer's high altar for the church of pilgrimage in Mariazell, dating from 1693, was designed in the form of a stage. As in a *theatrum sacrum,* the spectator is exhorted to *compassio* by the angels flanking the crucifix held by God the Father and by the highly

---

[3]Hans Aurenhammer, *J. B. Fischer von Erlach* (London: Lane, 1973). Hans Sedlmayr, *Johann Bernhard Fischer von Erlach* (Vienna: Herold, 1976). For the latest state of research, see Friedrich Polleroß, *Fischer von Erlach und die Wiener Barocktradition*, Frühneuzeit-Studien 4 (Vienna: Böhlau, 1995).

[4]Joachim Knape, "Rhetorizität und Semiotik: Kategorientransfer zwischen Rhetorik und Kunsttheorie in der Frühen Neuzeit," in *Intertextualität in der Frühen Neuzeit: Studien zu ihren theoretischen und praktischen Perspektiven*, Frühneuzeit-Studien 2, ed. Wilhelm Kühlmann and Wolfgang Neuber (Frankfurt a.M.: Lang, 1994), 485–532.

[5]Karl Noehles, "Rhetorik, Architekturallegorie und Baukunst an der Wende vom Manierismus zum Barock in Rom," in *Die Sprache der Zeichen und Bilder: Rhetorik und nonverbale Kommunikation in der frühen Neuzeit*, ed. Volker Knapp, Ars Rhetorica 1(Marburg: Hitzeroth, 1990), 190–227, here 213–20; Mark Weil, "The Relationship of the Cornaro Chapel to Mystery Plays and Italian Court Theater," in *All the world's a stage...": Art and Pageantry in the Renaissance and Baroque*, Papers in Art History from the Pennsylvania State University 6/2 (University Park, Pa.: Pennsylvania State University, 1990), 458-86.

emotional gestures of the Virgin Mary and John below the cross (see fig. 1).

Like sacral sculptures and temporary architecture, the buildings of the Counter-Reformation and the Age of Absolutism had a persuasive function in general. An obvious example of this is provided by an engraving in the *Perspettiva de'pittori e architetti* by Andrea Pozzo (1693), which shows an equestrian monument of Emperor Leopold I (fig. 2). The architecture behind the statue has the same effect as a church apse, acquiring special dignity through the rows of double columns. The persuasive function of architecture is justified by Karl Eusebius of Liechtenstein on the grounds that the silent rhetoric of beautiful and impressive architecture enables it to draw attention automatically as well as arouse the admiration of both the educated and uneducated classes.[6]

Even one of Fischer's very first architectural manifestations, the utopian vision of the imperial residence in Schönbrunn (fig. 3) fulfills these conditions through its manipulations of perspective based on optical illusions, although it lacks any kind of realizable functionality. The design served either as an example of work submitted by the young artist in order to obtain a position at court or else as a teaching aid for his tutorship of the heir to the throne.[7]

ARCHITECTURA LOQUENS

It is probably no accident that the direct application of rhetorical terms recurs as an artistic credo in the life of Bernini. As Baldinucci mentions in 1682, the Roman artist recommended his students

> prima all'invenzione e poi riflettava all'ordinazione delle parti, finalmente a dar loro perfezione di grazia, e tenerezza. Portavia in ciò l'esempio dell'Oratore, il quale prima inventa, poi ordina, veste, e adorna, perchè diceva, che ciascheduna di quelle operzioni ricercava tutto l'uomo, e il darsi a più cose in un tempo stesso non era possibile.[8]

[6]Victor Fleischer, *Fürst Karl Eusebius von Liechtenstein als Bauherr und Kunstsammler (1611–1678)* (Vienna: C. W. Stern, 1910), 91–92.

[7]Sigurd Schmitt, "Johann Bernhard Fischer von Erlachs Schloß Schönbrunn in Wien: Studien über Schönbrunn I und das Schönbrunn-II-Realisierungsprojekt von 1696" (Ph.D. diss., University of Munich, 1990), 11–117.

[8]Filippo Baldinucci, *Vita del Cavalierre Gio: Lorenzo Bernino* (Florence: Vincenzio Vangelisti, 1682), 78. All translations are by Peter Ian Waugh unless otherwise noted.

Fig. 1. J. B. Fischer, *Hochaltar in Mariazell*, 1692, drawing, Landesmuseum Joanneum, Graz. Photograph: Kunsthistorisches Institut, University of Vienna. Used by permission.

Fig. 2. Andrea Pozzo, dedicatory page for Leopold I, 1693. Photograph: Kunsthistorisches Institut, University of Vienna. Used by permission.

[Firstly to consider the invention and then the arrangement of its parts and lastly to endow the work with its perfecting grace and elegance. In doing so he was following the example of an orator who first invents, then arranges, garnishes and embellishes, because he said that each of these steps demands the application of the whole man and that it is not possible to do everything at once.]

Significantly enough, the first examples of emblematic monuments that are no longer merely of a temporary nature are to be found in seventeenth-century Roman art, such as the design for a church with cupola, displaying the arms of the Chigi, attributed to Cortona, or Bernini's obelisk on an elephant.[9] The application of this practice to a Hapsburgian theme is demonstrated by a design for a stately carriage executed in 1673 by members of the immediate circle around Fischer's Roman teacher Philipp Schor. It shows a figure, personifying Spain and surrounded by allegories of war and peace, who not only displays the arms of Castile three-dimensionally in the form of a castle, but is also enthroned between the Pillars of Hercules, which display the royal motto *Plus Ultra* (fig. 4). It is therefore highly probable that Fischer, too, was familiar with the use of rhetoric and emblems in art, since the circles in which he moved included those of Bernini, Schor, the ecclesiastical art theorist Giovanni Pietro Bellori, and the scholarly Jesuit Athanasius Kircher.[10]

Characteristic of the following works is the fact that they are all examples of public architecture executed in collaboration with court scholars who shared a common humanistic or theological background. However, the personal—and thus methodical—relationship between ecclesiastical works and scholars on the one hand, and secular works and scholars on the other, has so far received little attention. Around 1690 the court architect had, in contrast to his work under Charles VI, primarily ecclesiastical concettists at his side. The first time Fischer worked with a secular scholar was on the triumphal arch built in 1699 in honor of the Roman king and his wife Amalie von Braunschweig-Wolfenbüttel. In 1712 Carl Gustav Heraeus (1671–1725), who was appointed director of the Imperial Collection of Coins and Antiquities by Joseph I in 1710, wrote the dedication for

[9]Karl Möseneder, "Aedificata Poesis: Devisen in der französischen und österreichischen Barockarchitektur," *Wiener Jahrbuch für Kunstgeschichte* 35 (1982): 139–75.

[10]Elisabeth Sladek, "Der Italienaufenthalt Johann Bernhard Fischers zwischen 1670/71 und 1686: Ausbildung, Auftraggeber, erste Tätigkeit," in Polleroß, *Fischer von Erlach* (see n. 3 above), 147–76.

Fischer's first handwritten version of *Historical Architecture,* which was subsequently presented to the new emperor.[11]

The conditions for the development of such syntheses of words and pictures in the "imperial style" were thus already in existence even before the accession of Charles VI. In 1712, on the advice of Heraeus, the second court architect Johann Lukas von Hildebrandt had designed a triumphal entrance to the Imperial Palace, constructed on the occasion of the coronation in Frankfurt. The connection between rhetoric and architecture in this case becomes clear from the following contemporary description:

> Die Zieraten dieses Thors (an welchem die Ordnung der *Architectur* dem Herrn Johann Lucas Hildebrand, Kayserlichen Hof-*Ingenieur,* allein obgelegen) hat man nach dem Exempel anderer Pforten nicht wollen ohne Bedeutung seyn lassen, um die Steine, wie bey der alten Römer Zeit, sowohl durch Figuren, als durch Schrifften redend zumachen.[12]

> [In accordance with the example of other arches, one did not want to omit endowing the decoration of this arch with significance, so as to make the stones speak through the figures as well as through the inscriptions, as in the time of the ancient Romans.]

INVENTIO

The first *officium oratoris* was traditionally *inventio,* the discovery of arguments to shock the affections, to produce pathos and ethos. As an aid to this, special handbooks were written. One of these works, the *Iconologie ou la science des emblèmes, devises etc., qui apprend à les expliquer, dessiner et inventer,* by Jean Baudoin (Amsterdam, 1698), presented itself as "most useful for orators … and in general for all those who are curious about the arts and the sciences."[13] As a result of his experiences in the circles of Bernini and the Roman and Neapolitan antiquaries, Fischer obviously saw himself from the very beginning

---

[11]On the work of the Fischers and their programs for Charles VI, see Franz Matsche, *Die Kunst im Dienst der Staatsidee Kaiser Karls VI.: Ikonographie, Ikonologie und Programmatik des 'Kaiserstils,'* Beiträge zur Kunstgeschichte 16 (Berlin: Walter de Gruyter, 1981), 1ff.

[12]Carl Gustav Heraeus, *Inscriptiones et symbola varii argumenti* (Nuremberg: P. C. Monath, 1721), 175–76.

[13]"très utile aux orateurs … et généralement à toutes sortes de curieux des beaux-arts et des sciences."

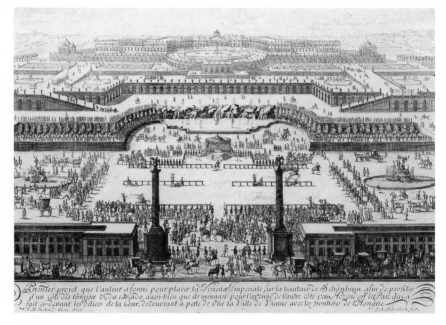

Fig. 3. J. B. Fischer, first design plan for Schönbrunn, ca. 1688; engraving by J. A. Delsenbach. Photo: Author's archive.

more as one of these "connoisseurs of the arts and sciences" than as a simple practitioner of architecture.

Fischer's own view of himself and his achievements as an ingenious designer and scholar is documented above all in connection with his first large-scale work in Vienna, the highly praised Trinity Column in 1679, which Leopold I dedicated to the memory of the plague epidemic. We learn from contemporary sources that it was *Ingenieur* Fischer who gave the impulse to invent something different and unusual. While the new invention of the cloud pyramids must be ascribed to the imperial *Ingenieur* Lodovico Burnacini, Fischer's contribution clearly displays the conscious and fitting artistic realization of a prescribed concetto. Namely, he demanded a change in the already existent basis so that the triangular figure on both pedestals could be more clearly seen, and he furthermore insisted upon a triangular balustraded platform instead of a circular one, so that it would match

Fig 4. Giovanni Paolo Schor, design for the Spanish ambassador's stately carriage, 1673, art market. Photograph: Author's archive.

the pedestals (fig. 5). The elaboration and development of the concepts for the reliefs that Fischer added to the architectural basis were made in close collaboration with the Jesuit Franz Menegatti. The result is a suitably convincing work of art, the concetto of which, both in its form and content, was the symbolism of the Trinity.

This use of a convincing visual symbolism also typifies Fischer's ideal design for Schönbrunn, with its numerous terraces (fig. 3). As later with the Court Library, the identification of the Hapsburgs here with Apollo and Hercules illustrates above all the ideal ruler's mastery of *arma et litterae*. Thus the medallion for the completion of the palace according to the second plan in 1700 expressly depicts the residence of Joseph I as the Palace of the Sun (fig. 6). Parallel to this, a Jesuit panegyric portrays the Roman king in front of his residence as Hercules (fig. 7).

However, in my opinion, more important than the traditional identifications of the ruler with the God of the Muses and the Virtuous Hero is the unique spatial extension and the hierarchical gradations of height found in Fischer's project. The optical impression corresponds to the iconographical hierarchy extending from the column portal, with its apotropaic representations of the demigod, to the quadriga of the Sun God above the central gable of the palace. Whereas the struggle of Good against Evil is illustrated by the victory of the virtuous heroes over Hydra and Cerberus, of Apollo over the python on the fountain, or indirectly, even of the battling knights, Phoebus-Apollo actually rises above the residence and thus into the realm of apotheosis inaccessible to terrestrial man.

Interestingly enough, the two pillars of Hercules and the steep ascent of the numerous terraces, as well as the depiction of the triumph of the Virtuous Hero over the Vices in the form of well-ordered architecture above artificial rocks, recur in Giovanni Francesco Guernerio's design for Wilhelmshöhe in Kassel, dating from 1701.[14] The two architects, both of whom were trained in Rome, obviously delivered variations of concepts that Bernini considered for the projects for Louis XIV. In 1665 the Roman architect had the idea of erecting two columns like those of Trajan and Antonine, flanking a pedestal which would support a statue of the Sun King on horseback and the motto

[14]Giovanni Francesco Guernerio, *Delineatio Montis a Metropoli Hasso-Cassellana Uno Circiter Milliari Distantis* (Rome: H. Harmes, 1726).

Non Plus Ultra, in allusion to Hercules. In the planning for the Louvre, Bernini combined the allegory of Hercules not only with the sun symbolism, but also with the visualization "of a moral and architectural progression."[15] Whereas, in Paris, Bernini's idea of Hercules, which he described as "contained in the mountain of labor, which is the rock," could only be illustrated metaphorically in the form of a rustic socle, Fischer and Guernerio employed the landscape in such a way that the difficult path of virtue to the Temple of Glory was represented in tangible form.

Furthermore, the main axis contains geographical allegory, since the sun quadriga symbolizes the East, whereas the Pillars of Hercules mark the western end of the world. Indeed, Fischer's illustration of the status of the Ruling Monarch of the Earth in both a historical and a geographical dimension is based on a tradition of pictorial and literary panegyric that goes back to the 1660s. It refers, on the one hand, to the *translatio imperii* of the ancient kingdoms of the Babylonians, Persians, Greeks, and Romans, up to the Hapsburgs, and on the other, to the claim, involving the question of Spanish succession, to a dominion *Plus Ultra* in all four continents.[16]

Under Charles VI, the two monumental pillars of Hercules acquired additional and more concrete meanings in relation to the sovereign. Since the motto *Plus Ultra* was the symbol of the Spanish monarchy and its dominions overseas, this motif was interpreted by the pretender to the Spanish throne as a symbol of the double sovereignty that had existed under his Hapsburg predecessor Charles V (fig. 8). A new layer of meaning was added with the imperial motto *Constantia et Fortitudine*, chosen by Charles VI, since these two virtues were also symbolized emblematically in the pillars.

This aspect also characterizes the program for the monumental columns of the Karlskirche in Vienna (fig. 9), constructed after 1715: according to Heraeus, they serve as "silent speakers" and allegorically refer to the founder's motto: *columnae muta et secundaria tantum significatione symbolum fundatoris loquantur* (in the hidden secondary

[15]Irving Lavin, "Bernini's Image of the Sun King," in *Past and Present: Essays on Historicism in Art from Donatello to Picasso* (Berkeley: University of California Press, 1993), 138–200, 288–302.

[16]Friedrich Polleroß, "Sol Austriacus und Roi soleil: Amerika in den Auseinandersetzungen der europäischen Mächte," in *Federschmuck und Kaiserkrone: Das barocke Amerikabild in den habsburgischen Ländern*, Ausstellungskatalog Schloßhof (Vienna: Bundesministerium für Wissenschaft und Forschung, 1992), 54–84, here 63–80.

Friedrich Polleroß

Fig. 5. Schönbrunn as residence of Plague Column, Vienna, ca. 1690 (copper
engraving, eighteenth century). Photograph: Author's archive.

Fig. 6. Schönbrunn as the seat of the Sun God, 1700; engraving of the medal celebrating the laying of the foundation stone. Photograph: Author's archive.

Fig. 7. Joseph I as Hercules Austriacus; copper engraving by A. Trost, 1701.
Photograph: Author's archive.

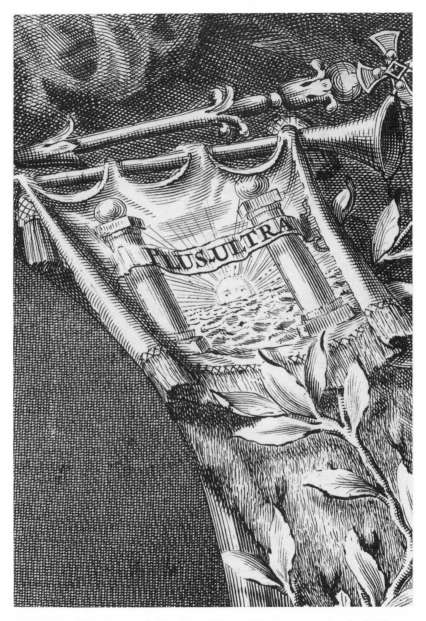

Fig. 8. Heraldic device of Charles as King of Spain; engraving by J. Blommendaal and Ph. Bouttats, ca. 1703/05. Photograph: Author's archive.

Fig. 9. Karlskirche, Vienna, engraving by Salomon Kleiner, ca. 1725. Photograph: Kunsthistorisches Institut, University of Vienna.

meaning the columns bespeak the founder's symbol). The two triumphal pillars are thus rightly associated with the columns of Jachin and Boaz, which were erected in front of the Temple of Jerusalem and, like the emperor's device, also symbolize the motto *Ne ruat* (that he might not fall). Especially interesting for us is an emblem of the Jesuits in Graz, dating from around 1600. It shows the Temple of Jerusalem as a central building with cupola, as well as two pillars and two obelisks (fig. 10).

The iconography of the Karlskirche should thus also be regarded from a typological point of view. The statues of *ecclesia* and the synagogue in front of the church explicitly indicate this. However, the typology of the imperial church, which was consciously constructed from the unwilling contributions of the estates and is thus a symbol of the Hapsburg Empire as a whole, presents Vienna above all as a New Jerusalem, Rome, and Constantinople in one, and Charles VI as

Fig. 10. The Temple of Jerusalem with its two columns; emblem of the Jesuits in Graz, ca. 1603. Photograph: Author's archive.

the new Solomon, Augustus, and Constantine.[17] The typology of sovereigns, which is set out in numerous texts by Heraeus, also informed the preface to Fischer's *Historical Architecture*, although, in my opinion, the real statement of this is to be found first and foremost in Fischer's artistic implementation. It is well known that the principal architectural characteristic of the Karlskirche is its conscious combination of classicistic elements and Baroque solutions, for most of which the original inspiration was provided by Bernini's designs for the facades of St. Peter's and Borromini's S. Agnese in Piazza Navona.

Confronted with this duality of the Karlskirche, I would interpret the portico, with its two driveways and columns, as forming the ancient Roman basis, upon which were placed the Roman Catholic cupola and the two bell towers. Such an interpretation corresponds with the fact that these consciously classicistic elements are dedicated to a modern and Christian hero, namely, Carl Borromaeus, who was the patron saint both of plague victims and of the emperor. In fact, this idea of the *aemulatio*, i.e., the supersession of Judaism and heathen antiquity by Christianity, had already been very clearly expressed by Heraeus in a poem dating from 1712. The emperor, who is there referred to as His Apostolic and Catholic Majesty and as King of Jerusalem, is apostrophized as the direct and legitimate successor of the biblical kings. However, owing to the sinfulness of the kings of Israel, God has entrusted the sovereignty to Charles VI, who will surpass even David and Solomon.[18] There can therefore hardly be any doubt that the Karlskirche was intended as the ideal theological and artistic realization of a house of the Almighty, which was only vaguely prefigured in the Temple of Solomon.

Proceeding from the allegorical interpretation of the Karlskirche, Fischer's Court Library has also been analyzed from this aspect, once again taking the columns as a starting point (fig. 11). However, the pillars as an "architectural motto" makes reference not only to its founder, Charles VI, but also to the traditional emblem *Ex Utroque*

---

[17]On the iconography of the columns of the Karlskirche, see Paul Naredi-Rainer, "Johann Bernhard Fischer von Erlach und Johann Joseph Fux: Beziehungen zwischen Architektur und Musik im österreichischen Barock," in *Barock: Regional–International: Kunsthistorisches Jahrbuch* 25 (1993), ed. Götz Pochat and Brigitte Wagner, 275–90, here 276–79; Matsche, *Die Kunst* (see n. 11 above), 201–5; Irving Lavin, "Fischer von Erlach, Tiepolo und die Einheit der bildenden Künste," in Naredi-Rainer, 251–74.

[18]Quoted in Matsche, *Die Kunst* (see n. 11 above), 283–89.

Fig. 11. Interior of the former Court Library, ca. 1730. Photograph: Verlag Pietsch, Vienna.

Caesar.[19] An illustration of this theme is to be found on the title page of a work by Athanasius Kircher. Here Minerva is seen presenting the pillars of Wisdom and Martial Combat as the foundations of a Christian prince's rule (fig.12).

ELOCUTIO

At least as important as good ideas to a speech was the linguistic expression of those thoughts, once they had been discovered by *inventio* and ordered by *dispositio*, through skilled mastery of the forms of embellishment and effect, known as *elocutio*. Of the *virtutes elocutionis*, that of decorum became a central category in the art theory of the Renaissance and the Baroque.[20] Ever since Vitruvius, the correspondence of form and content had been exemplified in the different styles of scenery employed in the theater for tragedy and comedy. The Renaissance architect Sebastiano Serlio reproduces a modernized version of Vitruvius in his book.[21] Fischer's scenic reliefs on the Plague Column evidently constitute a direct implementaton of this doctrine.[22] For here, too, the events are presented in a theatrical manner, the architectural backdrops being clearly accentuated both spatially and stylistically. It can hardly be accidental that the Last Supper is associated with classical column architecture, and the Old Testament prefiguration of the Eucharist with contemporary interior design and the use of conventional stuccowork.

As in the case of Baroque stage scenery, Baroque architecture had to correspond to the customary *decorum*. A particularly impressive example of this is provided by the *Wienerische Tugendspiegel* (Viennese

---

[19]Möseneder, *Aedificata Poesis* (see n. 9 above), 166ff.; Franz Matsche, "Die Hofbibliothek in Wien als Denkmal kaiserlicher Kulturpolitik," in *Ikonographie der Bibliotheken*, Wolfenbüttler Schriften zur Geschichte des Buchwesens 17, ed. Carsten-Peter Warncke (Wiesbaden: Harrassowitz, 1992), 199–233, here 224–25.

[20]Ulrike Mildner, "Decorum, Malerei, Architektur," in *Historisches Wörterbuch der Rhetorik*, vol. 2, ed. Gert Ueding (Tübingen: Niemeyer, 1994), 434–51.

[21]Serlio distinguishes between the old-fashioned comic scene, where "the houses must be right for citizens," and the elegant "Houses for Tragedies," which "must bee made for great personages, for that actions of love, strange adventures, and cruel murthers (as you reade in ancient and modern Tragedies) happen alweys in the houses of great Lords, Dukes, Princes, and Kings." Sebastiano Serlio, *The Five Books of Architecture: An Unabridged Reprint of the English Edition of 1611* (New York: Dover, 1982), 3: fol. 25.

[22]On the "classical and academic tendencies" of this relief, as well as its Roman influences (Raphael, Poussin, and Sacchi), see Christian Theuerkauff, "Johann Ignaz Bendl: Sculptor and Medallist," *Metropolitan Museum Journal* 26 (1991): 227–75, here 245–47.

Fig. 12. Allegory of the princely art of war and peace; frontispiece engraving for *Princeps Christiani Archetypon* by Athanasius Kircher, Amsterdam, 1672.

Fig. 13. Allegory of Decentia, engraving in the *Wienerische Tugendspiegel* by J. Chr. Weigl, 1687. Photograph: Author's archive.

Mirror of Virtue) by Erhard Weigel, published in 1687 (fig. 13). It describes the virtue of *decentia* (appropriateness) as a representation that corresponds to a certain social status and presents it in personified form with a scales, standing in front of the various pillars. As a result of their order, these vary in height and display the insignia of the different social classes, ranging from the lowest to the highest pillar, according to rank.

The importance of this question can be demonstrated by referring to one of Fischer's buildings that has not yet been considered from this point of view, namely, the Palais Trautson. In the first plan, the palace facade was designed with a simple Ionic order. However, during the construction work, Trautson, as Lord High Steward, was made a prince of the Holy Roman Empire in 1711; this fact then had to be incorporated in the *decorum* of his residence as well, so that the Ionic arrangement of the central projection was replaced by a composite order of columns. Yet their narrower proportions required the height of the gable to be raised, so that an inelegant overlapping of the beams resulted (fig. 14). This has been wrongly understood by architectural historians as "intended severity" and as the dynamic penetration of two building blocks.[23]

Against the background of the question of rhetorical style should also be seen the express decision of the emperor or his artistic advisors in favor of the two Fischers and against the second court architect, Johann Lukas von Hildebrandt. In fact, Hildebrandt's decorative, more two-dimensional style had an influence on bourgeois architecture and is opposed to the "high" Roman and Palladian style of the Fischers, as may be seen from the plans for the facade of the Imperial Palace in Michaelerplatz.[24] For the main facade of the imperial residence Hildebrandt planned an almost barracklike office building consisting of three-and-a-half storeys, decorated only in the middle by an entrance cylinder covered by a cupola, a pilaster arrangement, and a balustrade with statues. In his first alternative designs, Joseph Emanuel adopted the basic structure but replaced the rather modest portal with a monumental triumphal arch and embellished the plain barracklike facade with a projection that included a colossal arrangement of pillars. In actual fact, it was precisely these forms of architecture that expressed that *magnificentia*, which in its turn represented, in the *genus grande* of rhetoric, the goal to be achieved through a wealth of verbal embellishment (*ornatus*), conscious enlargement (*amplificatio*), fullness (*copia*), and variety (*varietas*).

CONCLUSIO

Obviously the court scholars who designed the iconography of these buildings, Carl Gustav Heraeus and Conrad Adolph von Albrecht,

---

[23]Peter Prange, "Das Palais Trautson: 'eine ungemeine Architecture,'" *Pantheon* 52 (1994): 101–19, here 103, fig. 4; Michael Krapf, *Palais Trautson* (Vienna: Bundesministerium für Justiz, 1990), 25–26.

[24]Richard Bösel and Christian Benedik, *Der Michaelerplatz in Wien: Seine Städtebauliche und architektonische Entwicklung,* exhibition catalogue (Vienna: Kulturkreis Losshaus, 1992), 66ff., cat. nos. 30–33.

Fig. 14. Palais Trautson, Vienna, ca. 1711, detail of the facade.
Photograph: Author's archive.

Fig. 15. The Colossus of Memnon, emblem of the triumphant arch of the city of Vienna; engraving by J. B. Fischer, 1690. Photograph: Author's archive.

were quite as skilled at rhetoric as the Jesuits at the court.[25] However, the question of whether Fischer himself was actually familiar with the basic principles of oratory still remains to be answered. It is true that the architect was confronted with Jesuit emblems as early as 1688 in Graz and 1689 on the Viennese Plague Column. It is recorded that Fischer designed emblems for the triumphal arch of 1690 (fig.15). He was evidently familiar both with the theory of emblems and with poetics; and the fact that he combined the use of word and picture, of the senses and reason, in a way similar to that of rhetoric is not only due to his training in Rome. For in his *Historical Architecture* Fischer

[25]Edwin P. Garretson, "Conrad Adolph von Albrecht: Programmer at the Court of Charles VI," *Mitteilungen der österreichischen Galerie* 24/25 (1980/81): 19–92.

Fig. 16. Benedikt Richter, reverse of the portrait medallion of J. B. Fischer, 1719. Photograph: Kunsthistorisches Institut, University of Vienna. Used by permission.

mentions that the engravings are provided with explanatory texts, since "illustrations, as silent speakers, demand a speaking picture. Because one of these without the other does not make its presence clearly enough felt."[26] With these words, the architect follows the traditional definition of emblems, which states that universal pictures should be determined by their inscriptions.

The final proof of the theory that the architecture of the imperial style is rhetorical, and that Fischer consciously combined the arts of oratory and architecture, is provided by the architect's portrait medallion, executed by the court medallist Benedikt Richter and dating from 1719. This personal emblem displays architecture of a deliberately eclectic and historicized nature, as well as the motto *Docent et Delectant* (fig. 16). The function of *docere* and *delectare*, which may be shown to have formed the theoretical basis of the architecture of Johann Bernhard Fischer von Erlach, was therefore exactly the same as that of the *officia oratoris*, first formulated by Cicero and Horace and a familiar part of modern art theory ever since Leon Battista Alberti.[27]

[26]"Abbildungen / als stumme Redner / eine redende Mahlerey erforden. Weil eine von diesen ohne die andere sich nicht deutliche genug zu erkennen giebet." *Entwurf einer historischen Architektur*, 5th ed., ed. with afterword by Harald Keller (Dortmund: Harenberg, 1988), fol. 12.

[27]An extended version of the present essay, together with further information on this subject, is found in German as "Docent et delectanti: Architektur und Rhetorik am Beispiel von Johann Bernhard Fischer von Erlach," *Wiener Jahrbuch für Kunstgeschichte* (1996): 155–206, illus. nos. 335–50.

The Jesuit Church of St. Michael's in Munich

The Story of an Angel with a Mission

Jeffrey Chipps Smith

Wilhelm V, Duke of Bavaria (r. 1579–97), was born on the feast day of the Archangel Michael. Whether a coincidence or a preordained congruence, this linking of prince and saint would result in the construction of St. Michael's in Munich, the first great church of the Catholic Reformation in Germany. In concert with the Jesuits, Wilhelm orchestrated a careful campaign to establish St. Michael as the new patron saint of this church, of Munich, and of the duchy of Bavaria. This essay explores Wilhelm's fascination with the saint as well as the artistic and theatrical efforts to promote St. Michael as the spiritual protector of Bavaria.

ON 1 JANUARY 1582, THE FEAST DAY OF THE NAME OF JESUS, Wilhelm V, Duke of Bavaria, proclaimed his intention to construct an imposing new church dedicated to the archangel Michael for the Jesuit order in Munich, his capital city.[1] With this announcement, one of the most significant episodes in German art commenced. It signaled the resurgence of the German Catholic Church and, critically, of religious art following almost sixty years of retrenchment during the Reformation.[2] From the outset, one must keep in mind St. Michael's uniqueness. It was the first significant church for any denomination built in the German-speaking lands since the 1520s. Wilhelm V and the Jesuits planned St. Michael's as a glorious symbol of post-Tridentine Catholic militancy. Elsewhere I have stressed the Jesuits' activism,

---

[1]This essay forms part of a much broader project, a book entitled *Sensuous Worship: Jesuits and the Art of the Early Catholic Reformation in Germany*, in which a thorough analysis of this church and a detailed citation of the literature are provided.

[2]For an overview of the previous period, with additional literature, see Jeffrey Chipps Smith, *German Sculpture of the Later Renaissance, c. 1520–1580: Art in an Age of Uncertainty* (Princeton: Princeton University Press, 1994).

educational ideals, and the critical impact of Ignatian spirituality upon their art. In this essay I shall focus upon Wilhelm's choice of St. Michael as patron and upon the archangel's visual manifestations. As we shall see, Michael was indeed an angel with a mission.

The story of this church begins indirectly with Wilhelm's birth on 29 September 1548.[3] Since this also happens to be the feast day of the archangel Michael, the young prince believed that God had intentionally intertwined their destinies. This sentiment is hardly surprising since Wilhelm grew up in a staunchly Catholic environment. His father, Albrecht V, was an aggressive supporter of the Catholic Church, particularly in the aftermath of the Peace of Augsburg of 1555. Albrecht used the Jesuits to strengthen the University of Ingolstadt, where young Wilhelm was educated, and he sponsored their rapid expansion within Bavaria. For instance, in 1559 he introduced the society into Munich and gave them the former Augustinian cloister.[4] Then in 1572 Albrecht established the Jesuit college, or school, here. For Wilhelm, his association with the Jesuits and with the church of St. Michael would be one of the defining characteristics of his reign. Indeed, the extensive revenues that he devoted to the church and college contributed to his administration's financial crisis. His youthful vow to build a church to St. Michael was realized shortly after he succeeded his father in 1579. Although Wilhelm would live until 1626, he abdicated in favor of his more politically adept son, Maximilian I, in 1597, just three months after the consecration of the Jesuit church. That is, he ruled until his pet project was completed (fig. 1).[5] Thereafter he often resided in his new palace, later known as

[3]"Wilhelm V. der Fromme, Herzog von Baiern," *Allgemeine Deutsche Biographie*, vol. 42 (Leipzig: Dunker & Humblot, 1897): 717–23; "Albrecht V., Herzog von Bayern," *Neue Deutsche Biographie*, vol. 1 (Berlin: Dunker & Humblot, 1953): 158–60; Herbert Schade, "Die Berufung der Jesuiten nach München und der Bau von St. Michael," in *Der Mönch im Wappen: Aus Geschichte und Gegenwart des katholischen München* (Munich: Verlag Schnell & Steiner, 1960), esp. 228–31; Paul Mai, *Sankt Michael in Bayern* (Munich: Verlag Schnell & Steiner, 1978), 33–36; and Helga Maria Andres, *Rekonstruktion der Herzog-Maxburg in München* (Munich: Tuduv-Verlag, 1987), 12–14.

[4]For a brief history of the Jesuits' early years in Munich, see Bernhard Duhr, *Geschichte der Jesuiten in den Ländern deutscher Zunge*, vol. 1 (Freiburg i. B. : Herdersche Verlagshandlung, 1907), 183–88; and Schade, "Die Berufung der Jesuiten nach München," esp. 214–17.

[5]Gabriele Dischinger, "Entstehung und Geschichte des Kirchenbaues (1583–1883)," in *St. Michael in München*, ed. Karl Wagner and Albert Keller (Munich: Verlag Schnell & Steiner, 1983), 220–43; idem, "Ein Plan des Münchner Jesuitenkollegiums," *Jahrbuch des Vereins für christliche Kunst* 15 (1985): 79–86.

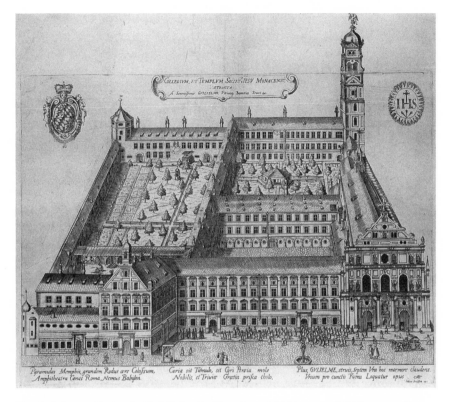

Fig. 1. Johann Smissek, *St. Michael's Church and College*, ca. 1650, engraving. (Munich, Stadtmuseum). Used by permission.

the Maxburg, located directly north of St. Michael's on a site now bound by the current Pacellistrasse, Maxburgstrasse, and Lenbachplatz. Linked by an arched passageway, the "Wilhelmsbogen," the palace permitted him immediate and constant access to the Jesuit church and specifically to the Holy Cross Chapel, his private oratory.[6] From its inception, St. Michael's also was intended as the new Wittelsbach family mausoleum with the tomb of the duke and his wife to be located in the choir.[7] Interestingly, the burial crypt, where Wilhelm

[6]What remained of the Maxburg and the second story of his oratory was destroyed in WWII. See Andres, *Rekonstruktion der Herzog-Maxburg*, esp. 20–21, 30, and figs. 8 and 24 (see n. 3 above).

[7]Dorothea Diemer, "Quellen und Untersuchungen zum Stiftergrab Herzog Wilhelms V. von Bayern und der Renata von Lothringen in der Münchner Michaelskirche," in *Quellen und Studien zur Kunstpolitik der Wittelsbacher vom 16. bis zum 18. Jahrhundert*, ed. Hubert Glaser (Munich: Hirmer Verlag, 1980), 7–82.

and his wife are interred, is linked perpetually with the choir by two special grilles that allow a glimpse of the high altar and permit the services to be heard from below. In death as in life, Wilhelm and his patron saint are allied.

What was the allure of St. Michael for Wilhelm other than their common date? The simplest response is that Michael offered the duke a perfect model for his princely aspirations. The *Trophaea Bavarica Sancto Michaeli Archangelo,* a short book published in Munich in 1597 to commemorate the consecration of the new Jesuit church, opens with St. Michael's appearance to Emperor Constantine. The archangel proclaims, "I am Michael, the archduke of the Lord of Lords, the protector of the Christian faith, who fights for you against impious tyrants, [as a] true and faithful servant, who bestows helpful arms."[8] This passage is highlighted in bold letters to assure the reader's attention. Upon awakening, Constantine, the first Christian emperor, realizes the importance of the dream and orders the construction of the first church honoring St. Michael, a clear precedent for Wilhelm's own actions. Here and in other texts, such as the *Golden Legend,* Michael is God's agent who can accomplish wondrous acts that no one else can perform.[9] Indeed Michael means he "who is like unto God."[10] It is Michael who transported the Virgin Mary's body to heaven and will be present holding the passion instruments at the Last Judgment. He is often portrayed with the scales of judgment or standing at the gate of heaven. Throughout the *Trophaea Bavarica* and the church's art, Michael's role as the defender of faith is stressed. It was Michael who drove Satan and the rebel angels out of heaven. And it was Michael who vanquished Satan when he threatened the Apoca-

---

[8]*Trophaea Bavarica Sancto Michaeli Archangelo* (Munich, 1597), A1v: "Ego (inquit) sic, sum Michael Archidux Domini Sabaoth virtutum Christianorum fidei tutor: qui tibi conra impios Tyrannos belligeruti, fideli & germano illius ministro, auxiliaria arma contuli." Although this book is often briefly cited in the literature on the church, there exists no critical study of its content.

[9]*The Golden Legend of Jacobus de Voragine,* trans. Granger Ryan and Helmut Ripperger (1941; reprint, New York: Arno Press, 1969), 578–86; Mai, *Sankt Michael in Bayern* (see n. 3 above); and Paul Imhof, "Der Kirchenpatron St. Michael," in Wagner and Keller, *St. Michael in München,* 9–21 (see n. 5 above).

[10]The words "Quis ut Deus" accompany some of the angel heads on the choir stalls that Martin Ernst and Georg Bendl completed in 1589. Lothar Altmann, "Die ursprüngliche Ausstattung von St. Michael und ihr Programm," in Wagner and Keller, *St. Michael in München,* 96 and figs. 49–50.

lyptic Woman—that is, the Virgin Mary in the book of Revelation (chap. 12). Wilhelm fashioned himself as God's agent, a devout Christian ruler, and staunch protector of the true faith. In 1582, just months after announcing that he would build the Jesuit church, Wilhelm sent a Bavarian army, led by his brother Ferdinand, into the lower Rhine to depose Gebhard Truchsess von Waldburg, the renegade archbishop of Cologne.[11] Wilhelm feared, perhaps with good reason, that the archbishop's recent conversion would give Protestants a majority among the imperial electors. The unsettling specter of a Protestant emperor and, ultimately, empire prompted Wilhelm's actions that ended successfully and inaugurated two centuries of Wittelsbach authority in Cologne. When viewed against the backdrop of the growing Counter-Reformation in Germany, his was the most dramatic victory over the foes of Catholicism since 1547. Like St. Michael, Wilhelm offered armed support to *Ecclesia*.

Normally a church, city, diocese, or region will have a long-established association with a particular saint. Think of the links between Heinrich and Kunigunde with Bamberg, or St. Willibald with Eichstätt, or St. Kilian with Würzburg.[12] Each is allied with the ancient history of the city or diocese. Similarly, their veneration was intimately bound with local identity and worship practices, including the display of relics, special celebrations on feast days, and often the establishment of confraternities. Occasionally, saints, such as Wenzel for Bohemia and Stephen for Hungary, were invested with the power to protect an entire region or nation from catastrophic harm.

In 1582 Bavaria had no preeminent regional patron or patroness. The belief that a guardian saint was needed typifies the reaffirmation of the power of saints voiced by the post-Tridentine Catholic Church.[13] Was it anything more than a token gesture? Faced with

---

[11]Günther von Lojewski, *Bayerns Weg nach Köln: Geschichte der bayerischen Bistumspolitik in der zweiten Hälfte des 16. Jahrhunderts* (Bonn: Ludwig Röhrscheid Verlag, 1962), 346–404; idem, "Bayerns Kampf um Köln," in *Wittelsbach und Bayern*, ed. Hubert Glaser, vol. 2, pt. 1 (Munich: Hirmer Verlag, 1980), 40–47.

[12]For instance, see *Hl. Willibald 787–1987: Künder des Glaubens—Pilger, Mönch, Bischof*, ed. Brun Appel and Emanuel Braun (Eichstätt: Bischöfliches Ordinariat Eichstätt, 1987); and *Kilian: Mönch aus Irland—aller Franken Patron 689–1989*, ed. Haus der Bayerischen Geschichte, Munich (Würzburg: Mainfränkisches Museum, 1989).

[13]In January 1583 Petrus Canisius, Germany's "second apostle" and Wilhelm's occasional advisor, touched upon the need for an intimate dialogue between individu-

Protestantism's potential to overrun all of Central Europe, Wilhelm found strength in St. Michael. Next, the duke had to translate his personal affinity for the archangel into a spiritual tie binding Michael with Bavaria. How does one initiate the selection of a patron saint and, more critically, how does one then construct a lasting bond between the saint and the community or region? I know of no official procedures for adopting a saintly protector. Such affiliations usually evolved slowly over time. Yet lacking such a historical precedent in Bavaria, Duke Wilhelm and the Jesuits worked energetically together using art and theater to promote Michael.

The first critical step in this process was the erection of the St. Michael's church, whose foundation stone was laid on 18 April 1583. As already noted, this was the most ambitious church building campaign in over half a century. Within Munich, only the Frauenkirche was larger, yet the contrast between the two buildings could not have been greater. The Frauenkirche, founded in 1468 by one of Wilhelm's predecessors, Albrecht IV, is a hall church characterized by its dark interior with tall columns, Gothic decorative features, and brick construction.[14] St. Michael's is, however, luminous. The spacious, columnless interior is airy and covered with white stucco. The width of its nave, at 20.29 meters, is second only to St. Peter's in Rome. Georg Dehio aptly characterized its visual impact as one of "majestic unity and quiet power."[15] Its singular design offered a modern aesthetic to match the Jesuits' militant spiritual and educational missions.

What was the archangel's role in all of this? In answer we must turn to his artistic presentations. In 1597 court artist Friedrich Sustris designed and Johann Sadeler engraved the elaborate fold-out frontis-

---

als and their saintly protectors when he wrote to Claudius Aquaviva, his Jesuit superior general: "When for the first time one enters a land or a city, one should ... invoke and venerate the angels and archangels and, moreover, the better known saints in every region, and recommend their assistance in the care of souls under your protection; because of your prayers God certainly will grant great help despite your own unworthiness"; cited in Schade, "Die Berufung der Jesuiten nach München," 209 (see n. 3 above).

[14]Peter Pfister and Hans Ramisch, *Die Frauenkirche in München* (Munich: Erich Wewel Verlag, 1983). The extensive renovations and repainting of the interior, completed in 1994, have brightened the church, but it still lacks the brilliance of St. Michael's.

[15]"[M]ajestätische Einheitlichkeit und ruhige Macht." Cited by Erich Hubala, "Vom europäischen Rang der Münchner Architektur um 1600," in Glaser, *Wittelsbach und Bayern*, vol. 2, pt. 1, 145 (see n. 11 above).

Fig. 2. Johann Sadeler, *The Holy Family before St. Michael's Church*, frontispiece to *Trophaea Bavarica Sancto Michaeli Archangelo* (Munich, 1597), engraving. (Munich, Bayerische Staatsbibliothek). Used by permission.

piece in the *Trophaea Bavarica* (fig. 2).[16] As Mary and the Christ Child sit in the foreground, the archangel as master builder prepares their spiritual house. Joseph assists by diligently measuring and cutting wood for the Schöner Turm, or Beautiful Tower, under construction behind. Under Michael's direction, a team of angels transports the wood, stone, and mortar. The texts allude to the significance of the enterprise. "[T]his is none other but the house of God, and this is the gate of heaven" reads the passage from Gen. 28:17 on the cradle.[17] "Thy testimonies are very sure: holiness becometh thine house, O Lord, for ever" (Ps. 92[93]:5) proclaims the passage held by an angel above.

St. Michael's position before the Jesuit church and college, specifically between the two doors of the south or main facade, coincides

---

[16]Isabelle de Ramaix, *Les Sadeler: Graveurs et éditeurs* (Brussels: Bibliothèque royale Albert Ier, 1992), 11 and no. 36.

[17]All biblical quotations come from the King James Version.

with the literal placement of Hubert Gerhard's monumental bronze statues of the archangel vanquishing Lucifer that dominate the lower zone of the facade (fig. 3).[18] Public access to the church was then possible only through the two doorways flanking the sculptural group as seen in another of the four engravings for the *Trophaea Bavarica* (fig. 4).[19] Onlookers stop to admire the bronzes. Others kneel in prayer. Although the statues' visual impact has been exaggerated in the print, their true scale, at over four meters in height, must have startled contemporaries. As modern observers we are accustomed to large civic, princely, and religious monuments. We forget, however, that in 1588 when Martin Frey cast Gerhard's two figures, there existed nothing in bronze even remotely comparable in Germany, Northern Europe, or, excluding a handful of equestrian statues, in Italy. Michael's prominence was intended to attract the viewer and to remind him or her that the archangel was indeed the powerful guardian of Bavaria. The prominent inclusion of Wilhelm's coat of arms and Golden Fleece collar, which he was awarded in 1585, on the wall just beneath the statue links patron and protector.

Yet size was actually secondary to the vivid portrayal of the struggle between Michael and Satan. The archangel stands calmly and confidently upon the writhing body of Satan. The scene is one of order versus chaos, good versus evil. Once perfect, like Michael, the fallen angel's body is now a hybrid of human, animal, and serpent parts. His physical power is held temporarily in check by Michael's staff. Significantly, the figures project out beyond the confines of their brilliant gilt niche, which recalls Satan's expulsion from heaven. Their combat literally extends into the space of the viewer. Satan's face, twisted in agony, still stares down at us. We quake nervously as we recall that for the moment Satan is subdued yet his power in our world is always potent. His glowering countenance and muscular body are unsettling. Gerhard's composition is frighteningly memorable. The pair reminds the viewers, such as those in Sadeler's print, of the constant mortal battle between good and evil waged within the world and, critically,

---

[18]Dorothea Diemer, "Bronzeplastik um 1600 in München: Neue Quellen und Forschungen, I. Teil," *Jahrbuch des Zentralinstituts für Kunstgeschichte* 2 (1986): 110.

[19]Plate IV is placed between leaves F2 and F3. De Ramaix, *Les Sadeler*, 11, questions the attribution of this engraving to Johann Sadeler (see n. 16 above). Originally there was a door on the west to the Jesuit college. The small doorway off the east transept was added only after WWII.

Fig. 3. Hubert Gerhard, *St. Michael Vanquishing Lucifer*, St. Michael's Church, approx. 1588, bronze statues. (Munich, Bayerisches Landesamt für Denkmalpflege). Used by permission.

Fig. 4. Johann Sadeler, *The Facade of St. Michael's Church*, in *Trophaea Bavarica Sancto Michaeli Archangelo* (Munich, 1597), between leaves F2 and F3, engraving (Munich, Bayerische Staatsbibliothek). Used by permission.

within one's own soul. The iconography of this group and indeed the whole church was influenced greatly by Ignatius of Loyola's *Spiritual Exercises*, the Jesuits' fundamental manual for promoting a reconsideration of one's faith.[20] In the section entitled the "Two Standards," he explains that there are two great opposing forces in this world: God's and Satan's. Ignatius calls Satan the "mortal enemy of our human nature" (136), who enlists all means, including riches, honors, and pride, to trap humanity. At stake are one's soul and one's eternal fate—salvation or damnation.

Gerhard's statue reminds us that, with the help of God's agents, Satan can be defeated. His physical bearing evokes St. Paul's advice to the Ephesians (6:10–13):

> Finally, my brethren, be strong in the Lord, and in the power of his might. Put on the whole armour of God, that ye may be able to stand against the wiles of the devil. For we wrestle not against flesh and blood, but against principalities, against powers, against the rulers of the darkness of this world, against spiritual wickedness in high places. Wherefore take unto you the whole armour of God, that ye may be able to withstand in the evil day, and having done all, to stand.[21]

In *Spiritual Exercises* Ignatius provided a clear, carefully structured method of meditation in order to assist the individual towards a heightened knowledge of self and of God. Put succinctly, first one constructs a sensuous memory of a topic, such as the fall of Satan, then one brings the power of the intellect to analyze it, and finally the will is engaged in order to personalize the meditation. Each stage permits a deeper level of comprehension. To stimulate the memory one should use the five senses to create a vivid mental picture. Ignatius recognized, as had many before him, that mental recall is far greater when tied to an image. Although ideally one constructs an imageless imagining, Ignatius encouraged those who needed help to begin with actual pictorial prompts, whether a print, painting, or sculpture. I think that this approach, which was so ingrained in Jesuit

---

[20]The relationship between the *Spiritual Exercises* and the church will be examined in Jeffrey Chipps Smith, *Sensuous Worship* (see n. 1 above). On what follows, see *The Spiritual Exercises of Saint Ignatius*, trans. David L. Fleming and Elder Mullan (St. Louis: Institute of Jesuit Sources, 1978), 136–48, here 84–91.

[21]Also cited in part in Imhof, "Der Kirchenpatron St. Michael," 11 (see n. 9 above).

spiritual and educational practices, influenced Gerhard's design. The sculptor devised a group, which through its scale, its material, its expressiveness, and its prominent placement, was intended literally to be memorable. It operates both as a stark image of the perpetual struggle between the two banners and as mnemonic prompt to promote a deeper understanding. The archangel's calm strength and clear stance contrast with the malevolent grimace and contorted pose of Satan. In an age in which German Catholicism struggled to reassert its authority in the face of the Protestant heresy, which many, including the Jesuits, dubbed the handiwork of Satan, Gerhard's St. Michael offered dramatic reassurance of God's power. Standing boldly before all who entered this church, the archangel held much promise as a patron saint. He ensured that heresy and the enemies of *Ecclesia* would never enter these portals.

The worshiper, albeit indirectly, could also take Gerhard's statues home. At least two quite elaborate engravings of the ensemble appeared around 1597, probably to coincide with the church's consecration.[22] Johann Sadeler's print after Peter Candid's design identifies the saint, the artists, the patron, and the height (fourteen "feet") of the ensemble. Here and in Lukas Kilian's larger engraving, Gerhard's *St. Michael Vanquishing Satan* proved reproducible, portable, and still mnemonically powerful. The multiplication of the image assures that the intercessory as well as protective potentials of St. Michael transcend their fixed locus or point of origin in Munich. Prints, like other religious tokens, can have inherent iconic efficacy.

The facade of St. Michael's church sets the archangel within a distinctly Bavarian context, one that localizes his protective responsibilities while simultaneously glorifying Wilhelm and his illustrious lineage. "To the supreme God, Almighty and Holy, and in honor of Michael, the puissant Archangel, this building is dedicated by its founder Wilhelm V, Count Palatine of the Rhineland and Duke of the two Bavarian domains," reads the prominent facade inscription.[23] Located between Christ as Salvator Mundi at the apex of the facade

---

[22]Dorothea Diemer in Glaser, *Wittelsbach und Bayern*, vol. 2, pt. 2, no. 76 (see n. 11 above); and Friedrich W. H. Hollstein, ed., *German Engravings, Etchings, and Woodcuts, ca. 1400–1700*, vol. 17 (Amsterdam: M. Hertzberger, 1949–), nos. 105A,105B.

[23]"DEO OPT. MAX. SAC. IN MEMORIAM D. MICHAELIS ARCHANGELI DEDICARI CURAVIT GUILIELMUS V. COMES PALATINUS RHENI UTRIUSQUE BAVARIAE DUX PATRONUS ET FUNDATOR." The text and translation are given in Herbert Schade, *St. Michael München*, 4th English edition (Munich: Verlag Schnell & Steiner, 1992), 3.

and St. Michael nearest the street stand statues of Wilhelm (who as patron supports a model of the church), Albrecht V, and thirteen other nobles who were either former rulers or allies of Bavaria. All were staunch supporters of the Catholic Church. Without delving into the iconographic complexities of this singular program, I merely wish to point out that the duke and the Jesuits were so intent upon having a prominent show facade opening onto this major street that they altered the original building plans in order to provide the church with a northern rather than an eastern orientation.[24]

Linking facade and interior, duke and St. Michael, are the three stained glass windows by Hans and Georg Hebenstreit of about 1590.[25] Set in the second story of the south wall, the two armorial windows flank the facade statues of Wilhelm and his father, Albrecht V. The much larger image of St. Michael vanquishing Satan occupies the central window on the primary vertical axis of the facade. Prior to the construction of the new organ in 1697 and the devastations of 1944, these stained glass windows, the only ones in the building, were readily visible from anywhere within the sacred space of the interior as well as from the secular realm of the street. Without romanticizing the experiential effect, to see the reassuring figure of St. Michael, who appears to float amid the ample field of surrounding blank glass, must have been impressive at night when the church was illuminated only from the interior.

St. Michael's pictorial presence is also the focal point of the interior, though he has a considerable supporting cast (fig. 5). Upon entering the Jesuit church, one is immediately struck by the profusion of angels. Gerhard and Carlo Pallago's over-lifesize terra-cotta angels holding the passion instruments line the nave and transept.[26] Their

---

[24]On the religious and political messages of the facade, see Herbert Schade, "Die Monumentalisierung des Gewissens und der Kampf zwischen Licht und Finsternis— Zur Fassade der St. Michaelskirche in München und zur 'Genealogie' ihrer Herrscherbilder," in Wagner and Keller, *St. Michael in München*, 23–80 (see n. 5 above). On the orientation, see Gabriele Dischinger, "Die Jesuitenkirche St. Michael in München: Zur frühen Planungs- und Baugeschichte," in Glaser, *Wittelsbach und Bayern*, vol. 2, pt. 1, 152–66 (see n. 11 above).

[25]Altmann, "Die ursprüngliche Ausstattung von St. Michael," 102 and figs. 3 and 129 (see n. 10 above). Father Karl Wagner informs me that the St. Michael window and the tops of the armorial lights are original but the lower sections of the latter, lost in WWII, are replicas.

[26]Dorothea Diemer, "Hubert Gerhard und Carlo Pallago als Terrakottaplastiker," *Jahrbuch des Zentralinstituts für Kunstgeschichte* 4 (1988): esp. 61–96.

Fig. 5. Interior of St. Michael's Church. (Munich, Bayerisches Landesamt für Denkmalpflege). Used by permission.

somber tone yields to the more celebratory character of the host of stucco angels that adorn the vaults and especially the majestic heavenly wreath of the crossing.[27] The layout of the church permits an unimpeded view of the high altar that fills the north wall of the apse (fig. 6).[28] This is the earliest of the monumental, wingless altarpieces that would become a staple of post-Tridentine Catholic churches in Germany. Set within a frame that consciously evokes a triumphal arch, Christoph Schwarz's painting vividly portrays St. Michael and the other angels driving the rebels from heaven. Michael calmly dispatches the prince of darkness into the fiery pit below. Clearly legible against the golden backdrop of heaven, even amid the chaos of the moment, the resplendent St. Michael offers hope and protection to the church's worshipers. St. Michael's struggle is given a Christian and specifically Catholic context as the painting is placed between Andreas Weinhart's Salvator Mundi statue above and the high altar, which once supported a prominent eucharist tabernacle. Additionally, Wilhelm V commissioned Augsburg goldsmith Christoph Lencker to make a tremendously expensive (2,534 Gulden) reliquary with statues of St. Michael vanquishing Lucifer.[29] Completed in 1596, this lavish ensemble likely stood on the high altar during certain feast days.

The choir with its altarpiece, the accompanying inscriptions on the frame, and the twenty-four surrounding niche statues consciously evoke the book of Revelation's image of heavenly Jerusalem.[30] This apparition of the eternal paradise awaiting the faithful signals the ultimate defeat of Satan and his legions. It is also the reward to the faithful who complete the process of spiritual reflection articulated in the artistic program of this church. Revelations offers the most detailed account of St. Michael's exploits, notably his role in defend-

[27]Eva Christina Vollmer, "Der Stuckdekor in St. Michael," in Wagner and Keller, *St. Michael in München,* 112–26 (see n. 5 above).

[28]Altmann, "Die ursprüngliche Ausstattung von St. Michael," 90–92 (see n. 10 above).

[29]This now lost reliquary, which contained relics of St. Christopher, is recorded in a drawing made between 1605 and 1607 by Michael Müller for the church's two-volume treasury book, which is still in St. Michael's. See Monika Bachtler, "Der verlorene Kirchenschatz von St. Michael," in Wagner and Keller, *St. Michael in München,* 132 and fig. 87 (see n. 5 above). I wish to thank Father Karl Wagner for letting me examine these beautiful volumes.

[30]Ibid., 92–96; see also Alfred Kaiser, "St. Michael in München: Ein Abbild des himmlischen Jerusalem," *Ars Bavarica* 65/66 (1991): 71–106.

Fig. 6. Christoph Schwarz, Wendel Dietrich, and Andreas Weinhart, *The High Altar of St. Michael's Church*, 1586, detail (Munich, Bayerisches Landesamt für Denkmalpflege). Used by permission.

ing the Virgin Mary from Satan. Originally, Gerhard's *Apocalyptic Woman* may have hung from the choir vault as part of Duke Wilhelm's tomb.[31] When the tomb project was abandoned, Gerhard's Virgin was moved to the high altar of the Frauenkirche in 1608 and to the column in the Marienplatz in 1638 (see page 169). We must therefore use our imagination to visualize the Virgin Mary floating in the air while, behind, Michael dispatches her foes.

These images of St. Michael on the facade, in the central window, in the monumental high altar, and occasionally in Lencker's reliquary, offer permanent reminders of the archangel's power and his ties with the Jesuits, Wilhelm V, and Bavaria. These representations, however potent, needed to be introduced to the public. Otherwise, what truly distinguishes this saint's identification with a church and a place from that of any other holy figure? Wilhelm and the Jesuits recognized that something else was needed to encourage popular acceptance of St. Michael as a patron saint. On 7 July 1597, the day after the official consecration of the church, the Jesuits staged an elaborate public play entitled the *Triumph of St. Michael,* likely composed by fathers Jakob Gretser and Matthäus Rader.[32] The event was performed in the streets before the main facade of the church and the adjacent Jesuit school. Theater, long an integral part of Jesuit education in Germany, now became public spectacle. Elaborate costumes, sharp dialogue in both German and Latin, stirring music, and the latest innovations in staging props, often moved with complex machines, addressed the audience's minds and senses. The five-act play, which lasted eight hours, involved more than nine hundred actors, with burghers and courtiers supplementing the core of Jesuit students. The thousands of spectators were provided with a rousing, at times harrowing, account of St. Michael's exploits.

---

[31]Diemer, "Quellen und Untersuchungen," 13–14, 22, and figs. 22–26 (see n. 7 above).

[32]*Triumph unnd Frewdenfest Zu Ehren dem heiligen Erzengel Michael als Schutzfürsten und Patron der Newgeweychten Herrlichen Kirchen vor und von dem Gymnasio der Societet Iesv angerichtet und gehalten auff den sibenden Tag Julij* (Munich, 1597). I have used both the German and Latin texts available in the Bayerische Staatsbibliothek in Munich: 4° Bavar. 2193/I, 1–57 (= Film R –710/6) and Clm 19575/21, pp. 561–714 respectively. See also Schade, "Die Berufung der Jesuiten nach München," 252–57 (see n. 3 above); and Jean-Marie Valentin, *Le Théâtre dans les pays de langue allemande (1554–1680)* (Bern: Peter Lang, 1978), 455–58.

The gist of the story is the ongoing battle between St. Michael and Satan, who is intent upon destroying the "Catholic Christian Church." In the first act, the Apocalyptic Woman hovers in midair between the ground and the church tower, thanks to the miracle of a hidden rigging. Lucifer is made as memorably hideous as possible. St. Michael, resplendent in his polished armor—which incidentally was lent by the duke—is Lucifer's moral and physical antithesis. Lightning and thunder accompany their skirmishes. In the fifth and concluding act, St. Michael, standing alone on the stage, declares that he has had enough of Lucifer's perfidity, especially as it causes dissension among Christians; this is a reference to the Reformation and, in the New World, an allusion to the Jesuits' missionary activity. In a sequence that must have enthralled the audience and anticipated the excesses of modern cinema, the archangel, as the divinely sent avenger, throws down the apocalyptic dragon from its high throne and vigorously dispatches three hundred vile devils. Victory assured, Michael pierces the clouds with his lance to reveal a jubilant choir of saints brilliantly bathed in celestial light. In act 5, scene 8, St. Michael, turning to the spectators, announces once again that because of the construction of the beautiful new church in Munich, he will forever protect Bavaria and its ducal house. He accepts his charge as the guardian of Bavaria, its Catholic Church, and its people.

Following the play a procession of actors led the crowd into the new church for high mass. The people must have delighted at staring at St. Michael and the other actors in their exotic costumes. The Jesuits intentionally fashioned details, such as these costumes, to stimulate the viewers' senses and, through these, their minds. For those who witnessed the play, their image of St. Michael was forever shaped or, at least shaded, by this event. A spiritual association between the audience and their new patron saint was initiated.

Duke Wilhelm gave Munich a glorious new church. The Jesuit community there simultaneously emerged both as the city's foremost educational institution and as the vanguard of the Catholic Reformation movement in southern Germany. The populace gained a new guardian saint whom they came to know through the consecration play and his careful imaging. In another of the engravings from the *Trophaea Bavarica* of 1597 an enthroned Bavaria rules secure in the knowledge that St. Michael will keep Satan and his legions, who include a Protestant preacher, in check (fig. 7). The accompanying

Fig. 7. Anon., *St. Michael Protecting Bavaria,* in *Trophaea Bavarica Sancto Michaeli Archangelo* (Munich, 1597), between leaves C4 and D1, engraving (Munich, Bayerische Staatsbibliothek). Used by permission.

inscription reads "Behold Michael, one of the foremost leaders, come in my aid. Daniel 12."[33] Wilhelm's affection for his birth saint is understandable. To his credit, he translated this coincidence, or put differently, pre-ordained congruence, into a plan of action to bolster the Bavarian Catholic Church. He provided St. Michael with a local identity and a specific spiritual mission.

Ultimately, however, how successful were Wilhelm's efforts? The church and its art did set both aesthetic and spiritual standards for the period. St. Michael remained venerated locally. Nevertheless, Wilhelm's desire to establish St. Michael as Bavaria's patron saint never took hold. One factor was his abdication in 1597. Once out of power, Wilhelm lacked the public stage for championing St. Michael. He was content to attend to his personal spiritual life rather than that of the duchy. Although his son and successor, Maximilian I, honored the archangel and reportedly helped make the silver statue of him now in the Residenz in Munich, he adopted the Virgin Mary as his primary patron.[34] Raphael Sadeler's engraving from the Jesuit Matthäus Rader's *Bavaria Sancta* of 1615 shows St. Michael, now wearing the Golden Fleece collar like both Wilhelm and Maximilian, displaying a map of Bavaria to Mary and the Christ Child (fig. 8).[35] A glimpse of Munich is visible below. His geographic ties are still emphasized even though he is clearly subordinate to the holy pair. He is their agent. Mary's primacy is signaled first in a medal of 1610 in which she floats above the city and then again, more significantly, in 1616 when Hans Krumper's bronze statue of her for the new facade of the Residenz was set into a marble niche boldly inscribed: "Patrona Boiariae."[36] Then

---

[33]"Ecce Michael Vnus De Principibvs Primis Venit in adivtorivm mevm. Dan. XII." This is a very loose paraphrase of Dan. 12:1, which reads in part: "And at that time shall Michael stand up, the great prince which standeth for the children of thy people: and there shall be a time of trouble, such as never was since there was a nation even to that same time: and at that time thy people shall be delivered...."

[34]This was also a time of considerable growth of the Jesuit-sponsored Marian congregations in Munich and several other Bavarian towns. See Peter Bernhard Steiner, "Der gottselige Fürst und die Konfessionalisierung Altbayerns," in Glaser, *Wittelsbach und Bayern*, vol. 2, pt. 1, 252–63; and Glaser, vol. 2, pt. 2, no. 276, for the ivory and ebony statue reportedly made by Maximilian (see n. 11 above).

[35]Albrecht Liess, ed., *Die Jesuiten in Bayern 1549–1773* (Weissenhorn: Anton H. Konrad Verlag, 1991), nr. 192.

[36]Michael Schattenhofer, *Die Mariensäule in München* (Munich: Verlag Schnell & Steiner, 1971), 9, with illustrations of the 1610 and 1640 medals; Diemer, "Bronzeplastik um 1600 in München," 122–23 (see n. 18 above); and David Crook,

Fig. 8. Raphael Sadeler, *St. Michael as Protector of Bavaria*, in Matthäus Rader, *Bavaria Sancta* (Munich, 1615), engraving (Munich, Bayerisches Hauptstaatsarchiv). Used by permission.

Jeffrey Chipps Smith

in the aftermath of the expulsion of the Swedish troops from Munich in 1634, a deliverance that Maximilian credited to the Virgin Mary, her statue by Gerhard, once in St. Michael's, was placed on a tall column in the middle of the modern Marienplatz on 8 November 1638, the anniversary of Maximilian's victory over the Protestants at White Mountain near Prague, which he credited to Mary's personal intervention (fig. 9).[37] Even today the Virgin is regarded as Bavaria's protectress.

Does this mean that St. Michael ultimately failed in his spiritual mission to Bavaria? I would argue that Wilhelm and the Jesuits found in St. Michael a very potent and enduring symbol. An equally lavish play honoring the archangel was performed in Munich in 1697, the centennial anniversary of the church's consecration.[38] Michael was an ideal advocate for the beleaguered Bavarian Catholic Church that struggled to reassert itself in the aftermath of the Council of Trent. With a different patron, Maximilian I, and a more desperate time, as Central Europe stumbled into the Thirty Years' War, St. Michael yielded to the Virgin Mary, whose multiple and deeply rooted spiritual roles made her both a more immediate, better loved, and even more potent protectress.

Orlando di Lasso's Imitation Magnificats for Counter-Reformation Munich (Princeton: Princeton University Press, 1994), esp. 65–82. An inscription plaque above further details her role as protectress of Bavaria.

[37]Schattenhofer, *Die Mariensäule in München*, esp. 3–20; and Louis Châtellier, *The Europe of the Devout* (Cambridge: Cambridge University Press, 1989), 115. Mary as Bavarian patron appears on the title page of *Annales virtutis et fortunae Boiorum*, vol. 2 (Munich, 1629), which was reissued as an independent print in 1635 in the aftermath of the expulsion of the Swedish invaders; see Wagner and Keller, *St. Michael in München*, fig. 148 (see n. 5 above). Maximilian and his successors also looked to St. Benno, whose relics are in the Frauenkirche in Munich, for support. See Karin Berg, *Der "Bennobogen" der Münchner Frauenkirche* (Munich: Tuduv-Verlag, 1979); and Georg Schwaiger and Hans Ramisch, eds., *Monachium Sacrum*, vol. 1(Munich: Deutscher Kunstverlag, 1994), fig. 27 (print of Benno as the protector of Munich and Bavaria, ca. 1705) and 2:505–20.

[38]Munich, Bayerische Staatsbibliothek, 4° Bavar. 2193/V; and Elida Maria Szarota, *Die Jesuitendramen im deutschen Sprachgebiet—eine Periochen-Edition: Texte und Kommentare*, vol. 3, pt. 1 (Munich: W. Fink, 1983), 439–50.

ACKNOWLEDGMENTS

I wish to thank the Alexander von Humboldt Stiftung of Bonn and the University Research Institute of the University of Texas at Austin for their continued financial support over the years. I have benefited from my discussions with Father Karl Wagner, S.J., the former rector of St. Michael's.

Fig. 9. Marc Anton Hannas (after Jacob Custos), Hubert Gerhard's *The Virgin Mary as the Apocalyptic Woman*, Munich, Marienplatz, after 1641, woodcut (Munich, Stadtmuseum). Used by permission.

Woodcuts by Jost Amman, from *Cleri totius*.
Top, left, A Cathedral Canon, *top, right,* A Jesuit.
Bottom, left, A Spanish Flagellant, and *right,* A Hieronymite.

Constructing the Boundaries of Community

Nationalism, Protestantism, and Economics in a Sixteenth-Century Broadsheet

Pia F. Cuneo

In this essay, a broadsheet from circa 1530 illustrated by the Augsburg art-ist Jörg Breu the Elder is examined. As an example of Reformation propa-ganda, the broadsheet raises critical issues about the function and use of cultural products as historical documentation, and about the nature of the relationship between text and image. In considering the specific ideologi-cal work that the broadsheet performs, this essay demonstrates how Prot-estant identity and community are constructed in both text and image along national, moral, social, and economic lines. The inclusion of national and economic components provides a broader understanding of how Protestant identity was fashioned than scholarship tending to focus exclusively on doctrinal debates.

As a genre of cultural production, single-leaf broadsheets are used widely by scholars for their documentary potential. Indeed, broadsheets provide primary and fundamental evidence of Reforma-tion ideas, ideals, and strategies, combining as they do the persuasive powers of both image and text. Because the evidence that broadsheets provide is so tantalizingly tangible, however, many historians are seduced into regarding them as transparent windows affording a direct and unmediated view of Reformation reality, instead of treating them as tendentious cultural constructs. The other academic group often availing itself of broadsheets, namely, art historians, frequently succumbs to another hampering temptation: to look only at the image and neglect its relationship with the text. The assumption in this case is that either the text is entirely extraneous to understanding the image, or that the relationship between text and image is entirely uncomplicated, whereby the image simply illustrates what is stated in the text.

To consider broadsheets critically, then, is to confront directly such key issues as the function and use of cultural products as historical documentation, and the nature of the relationship between text and image. In this paper, I will argue for the complexity of both of these issues by examining one German broadsheet that is representative of an entire genre of pro-Protestant cultural production. I will demonstrate how I believe the broadsheet functions: rather than passively reflecting "wie es eigentlich gewesen ist" in the Rankian sense, it instead performs ideological work by actively constructing subject positions for its audience to embrace and reject accordingly. I will also demonstrate that the relationship between the broadsheet's text and image is complicated: while there is important overlap between information conveyed in both text and image, each one also provides additional commentary upon the other.

In addition to questioning assumptions about how broadsheets work, I argue for a more nuanced understanding of the construction of Protestant identities and thus of Protestant community.[1] Examining the broadsheet reveals that a Protestant identity was constructed as positive and attractive not only with reference to religious issues. Furthermore, I will show how economics, nationalism, and Protestantism are all mutually inflected and are woven together in the broadsheet's textual and visual narratives in a mutually supportive manner. This identification of and emphasis on economic and national strands within Reformation critique provides an important corrective to the largely religious focus of historical scholarship.

---

[1]A word needs to be said here about my use of the word "Protestant." By using this term, I in no way wish to imply a single, undifferentiated Reformation identity. I am fully aware that, in terms of the broadsheet's context in 1530 Augsburg, both Zwinglians and Lutherans were vying with the Catholics for power and official sanction (the Anabaptists had been dealt with by and large by 1528 in Augsburg). However, my analysis of the broadsheet does not reveal any specifically Lutheran or Zwinglian position. I have thus used "Protestant" for lack of a better word; it implies in this context a combination of anticlerical, nationalist, and economically and socially conservative attitudes.

Anon. broadsheet, *The Minter's Reply*, illustrated by Jörg Breu the Elder, published ca. 1530 by Wolfgang Roesch. (Photo Constantin Beyer, Weimar; used by permission of Schloßmuseum, Schloß Friedenstein)

Pia F. Cuneo

The broadsheet to which I will refer as *The Minter's Reply,* was published around 1530 by the type-cutter Wolfgang Roesch.[2] The text, written by an unknown author, is illustrated by the Zwinglian artist Jörg Breu the Elder from Augsburg.[3] The text poses the question to a minter of coins: How can he explain the fact that he is busy day and night minting money when everyone else in the German lands is complaining of its scarcity?[4] The five columns of text and Breu's illustration elucidate the minter's reply to the question. From the reply, it is clear that the economic issue raised in the initial query is inseparable from religious and moral issues. In fact, the broadsheet knits economic, religious, and moral practices together to provide an answer to the currency question. In providing this answer, the broadsheet also constructs a resounding critique of Roman Catholicism and early modern capitalism, while simultaneously fashioning a desirable Protestant identity. This identity, as we shall see, is also constructed along nationalist lines, with the audience designated as German and its adversaries as either foreign or dealing with foreign goods.

Aside from brief mention, no work has been done on this broadsheet, and the interesting issue it raises of the economic and national-

[2]The broadsheet has received scant scholarly attention: Heinrich Röttinger, "Zur Holzschnittwerk Jörg Breu des Aelteren," *Repertorium für Kunstgeschichte* 31 (1908): 49; J. Guey, "Le Monnayeur de Jörg Breu L'ancien," *Revue numismatique* 11 (1969): 220; exhibition catalogue *Welt im Umbruch: Augsburg zwischen Renaissance und Barock* (Augsburg: Augsburger Druck- und Verlagshaus GmbH, 1980), 1:169–70; exhibition catalogue *Martin Luther und die Reformation in Deutschland* (Frankfurt a.M.: Insel Verlag, 1983), 253–54. A copy after Breu's original woodcut exists in Nuremberg (Germanisches Nationalmuseum) published by Niclas Meldemann; the original woodcut with text exists in one exemplar, in Gotha (Schloßmuseum, Schloß Friedenstein). Permission to reproduce the broadsheet has been kindly granted by the Schloßmuseum. The broadsheet is reproduced in Max Geisberg, *The German Single-leaf Woodcut 1500–1550,* 4 vols., ed. Walter Strauss (New York: Hacker Art Books, 1974), 1:323.

[3]For information on Breu, see Pia Cuneo, "Art and Power in Augsburg: The Art Production of Jörg Breu the Elder" (Ph.D. diss., Northwestern University, 1991).

[4]"Frag an den Müntzer. // Sag lieber Müntzer bistu frumm // Wa mainst das sovil gelts hinkumm // Daran Teütsch land groß mangel hat // Und ir doch müntzet frü und spat." This combination of moral and economic critique is also signaled by the couplets appearing directly below the image: "Wann wir hetten rechten glauben // Gott und gemainen nutz vor augen // Recht Elen/ darz°u maß und gwicht // G°ut frid und auch gleich Recht und Ghricht // Einerlay Müntz und kain falsch Gelt // So stünd es wol in aller welt" (If we had the right faith, God and the common good before our eyes, just measures of length, volume and weight, good peace and also equal rights and judgments, a common currency and no counterfeit coinage, then all would be well in the world).

istic dimension of Reformation critique has not been pursued. In addition to considering this issue, I will demonstrate how this broadsheet performs ideological work in creating alternative subject positions for its readers/viewers/listeners.[5] Each of these subject positions skillfully blends economic, moral, religious, and national issues, and each is ideologically weighted, thus prompting the audience to align itself accordingly. But because one of these positions is clearly constructed as positive, and the other, in dialectical opposition, as negative, the didactic thrust of the broadsheet is to prompt the audience to identify with the subject position clearly signaled as the correct one.[6] This is the position that constructs an identity that is German, anticlerical, socially and fiscally conservative,[7] and morally upright. It is, in fact, an effective fashioning of Protestant identity. By encouraging the audience to take up this position, the broadsheet actively defines a community based on national identity, similar ethics and morals, and opposition to several key concepts of otherness.

The broadsheet's text is very explicit in its construction of otherness and community. As narrator, the minter identifies three enemies of the German economy who will bring about financial ruin unless the audience recognizes who these enemies are and agrees to offer resistance. In response to the question posed, the minter answers:

> Täglich hör ich diß frag und klag // Ligt doch die antwort hell am tag // Wann wir nit weren sunst als plind // Und sehen unsers gelts drey find // Den Babst/ New sitten/ Frembde wahr // Die unser land erschöpfen gar.[8]

In his narrative, the minter defines both the communal position and its opposition. The audience is meant to identify with the minter, who addresses his public, consistently throughout the narrative,

---

[5]It is important to remember that many of these broadsheets were meant to be recited or sung aloud for the benefit of those who could not read, and so we must add the illiterate to the list of the broadsheet's potential audience.

[6]The critical positioning of the viewer in the broadsheet makes it similar in function to Lucas Cranach's *Christ and Anti-Christ*, 1521, although Cranach's pamphlet does so without any textual aid.

[7]My use of the term "conservative" implies values that uphold the status quo, are opposed to social mobility, are suspicious of both the accumulation and expenditure of large sums of money, and promote a specifically German identity.

[8]"I hear this question and complaint daily, although the answer is right there in front of us [to see] if we weren't so blind and would recognize the three enemies of our money: the pope, new customs, and foreign wares, which exhaust our land."

Pia F. Cuneo

inclusively with the first and second person plural. Furthermore, the audience is also clearly constructed as German; throughout the text, the minter refers to his public as "wir Teütschen selber" and as "uns teütsch narren." The Germans are in trouble; they are being duped out of their money because they are spending it on foreign wares, amounting to what would be termed in modern economic parlance as a trade deficit. However, if the audience adopts the critical stance of the minter, as it is linguistically and rhetorically encouraged to do, and resists these foreign temptations, the Germans will solve the currency drain, save the country, become better people, and escape God's wrath.

According to the minter, the German community is endangered by others who desire their money. By exploring how these others are constructed, we learn more about the German community through this negative foil. The others presented in the text represent the negative subject positions offered the audience, which is discouraged from adopting these positions because the others are made linguistically (described in the third person singular instead of the inclusive first person plural used to designate the minter and his German audience) and physically foreign, besides being labeled as the enemy. We will see that by rejecting these others, the audience aligns itself with a Protestant, nationalist, and conservative position. By adding Protestant to national and conservative values, Reformation ideals are made infinitely respectable, and decidedly not revolutionary. This is an important strategy for making the Reformation *salonfähig*, that is, socially acceptable.

First on the minter's list of enemies is the pope. The pontiff is likened to a sly merchant who exchanges tainted wares for good money; he has commodified spirituality by selling indulgences, dispensations, offices, and ultimately, salvation itself:

Der Bapst kan uns gantz höflich fatzen // Mit Bullen/ Abblaß/ Dispensatzen // Umb böse war gůt gelt er nimpt // Wie aim geschwinden kauffman zimpt.... Und es im alls umbs gelt ist fail // Gnad / Pfründen und das ewig hail.[9]

[9]"The Pope can, very generously, load us down with his bulls, indulgences, and dispensations. He takes good money for bad goods, as befits a sly merchant.... For him, everything is for sale: mercy, prebends, and eternal salvation."

In contradistinction to the pope as the merchant of spiritual wares, the minter describes Christ as the true and only source of salvation. To further highlight the distinction between Christ and the pope, the minter includes the use of economic terms in his description of Christ,

> der milch und wein // *On gold und silber gibt zukauffen* // Haist uns zum gnaden prunnen lauffen // Begert nichts darumm dann danckbars hertz // Er hat selbs tragen unsern schmerz // Sein plůt und todt *zalt unser schuld* // Durch in allain kumpts Vatters huld.[10]

This rejection of all means to salvation other than the gift of God's faith and Christ's sacrifice is the very essence of Luther's teachings, thus identifying the minter's position (the desirable one) as Protestant. This position is also clearly constructed as the morally correct one.

In the minter's narrative, the pope is not only spiritually corrupt, he is also foreign. His business deals are labeled as "der Römisch gwerb" (Roman craft) and the true path to salvation is described as leading not "durch die Römisch gulden port // Sunder Christum den gnaden hort."[11] By selling spiritual commodities, the pope in Rome is emptying German coffers, according to the minter: "Glaub mir/ Rom het uns gar auß gsogen // Den seckel mit dem gelt entzogen."[12] The minter mentions twice, however, that the pope's days of wheeling and dealing are numbered, thanks to the Germans: "Doch hat der Römisch gwerb ein end // Wa icht wir Teütschen selber wend"; and because the Germans have recognized the true source of salvation, "Drumb hats Bapsts grempel yetz ein ent // Wa icht wir Teütschen selber went."[13] These quotations surely refer to the institution of the Reformation in Germany. They further define the Protestant position as spiritually correct, while constructing the pope as oppositional and

[10]"who gives us milk and wine, which *we don't need to buy with gold and silver,* beseeches us to come to the fountain of mercy; He desires nothing more [from us] than a thankful heart. He Himself has felt our pain, His blood and death *pays our debt.* Through Him alone comes the Father's grace." (Emphasis added.)

[11]"through the golden Roman portal but [through] Christ, the treasure trove of grace."

[12]"Believe me, Rome has sucked us dry and made off with the purse and the money."

[13]"Yet the Roman craft comes to an end wherever we Germans turn our attention" and "Therefore, the pope's cup of bitters is now finished wherever we Germans ourselves turn our attention." I thank Max Reinhart for his help with this translation.

foreign other. The minter's explication of the first enemy thus provides a fundamental critique of Roman Catholicism based on economic and moral practices.

The minter's second enemy is the merchant. Although he is mentioned nowhere as foreign, the merchant's crime is that he drains currency from the German lands by selling imported luxury goods: "Den andern Feint nun auch verstand // Der unser gelt furt auß dem land // Ich main den Kauffman der on rů // Frembd unnütz war uns furet zů."[14] The consequences of this can be found both within moral/social and economic categories. In addition to the implicit moral critique of living a life of luxury, a distinctly social problem arises: with everyone wearing fine clothing and eating delicacies, one cannot tell anymore who belongs to what social class. It is particularly this blurring of social boundaries that earns the minter's righteous indignation ("Pfuch pfuch es ist ein grosse schand // Das es sich yetz hat alls verkert").[15] The economic consequences follow. With the solid middle class and even the lower classes spending money on exotic clothes and food, they eventually fall into financial ruin and become dependent on charity, and thus a burden on the community.

The minter's third enemy is closely related to the second. The plethora of new social customs, especially those of fashion, is denounced by the minter in tones similar to his castigation of the imported luxury goods sold by the merchant. If one spends all her money on clothes, how can one "save any cash" (Parschafft bhalten)? In addition, one is indulging oneself in the sin of pride and thus risking God's extreme displeasure. Here economic and moral consequences are linked. However, it is particularly the adoption of foreign customs that leads to these dangerous consequences:

> Wir tragen yetz die welschen schlappn // Seltzam Paret und Spannisch kappen // Wo kompt doch einr her über mer // Der uns nit gleich sein sitten lehr // So vol sind wir des wanckeln můts // Warlich ich sorg es bringt nit gůts.[16]

---

[14]"Now also understand the second enemy who diverts our money from the land; I mean the merchant who without surcease supplies us with foreign and useless wares."

[15]"Fie, fie, it's a great shame that everything is now topsy-turvy."

[16]"Now we wear Italian trains, strange berets, and Spanish caps. Who comes here from across the sea who doesn't straight away teach us all about his customs? We're so easily swayed. Really, I'm worried, nothing good will come of it."

The minter's narrative on the second and third enemies of German currency provides a critique of early modern capitalism and its attendant consumer culture. Money is spent, but not on necessary, life-sustaining items; instead, it is wasted on wares purchased for their power to signify status. Monetary excess is equated with moral excess. The minter describes the consequences of this consumer culture as particularly dire: Germans will be turned into fools, they will become arrogant, wars will break out, and God will turn against them. Implicitly, the minter would like the audience to save money by purchasing those locally produced goods that are suitable both socially and economically for the individual consumer. Thus the broadsheet's presentation of a positive subject position, which we have seen to be decidedly Protestant, is also constructed along highly conservative economic, moral, and national lines.

The Minter's Reply is hardly a novel text. It comes from a long line of moralizing literature, perhaps the best known example of which is Sebastian Brant's *Narrenschiff* (1494). Like *The Minter's Reply* some thirty-six years later, Brant's text excoriates consumer culture with its excessive fashion-consciousness and moral laxity.[17] Brant also critiques certain attitudes towards money and particular economic practices, such as greed, love of wealth, and usury.[18] But Brant's main concern is to exercise a general moral critique of "modern" society. He nowhere specifically mentions merchants, nor does he make foreign influences responsible for German society's ills.[19]

However, during the decade of the 1520s, a large number of texts were published that specifically combined social and moral critique with the economic. All of these texts were surely responding to the current debates on monopolies and currency held during the imperial diets of roughly that decade, necessitated by the need to regulate merchant and banking activities.[20] The formation of monopolies was

[17]See, for example, "Von neuen Moden" and "Von schlechten Sitten" in *Das Narrenschiff* (Leipzig: Verlag Philipp Reclam, jun. 1979), 34–35 and 46–47.

[18]Ibid., "Von Habsucht," "Von unnutzem Reichtum," and "Wucher und Aufkauf," 32–33, 66–67, 274–75.

[19]Brant, "Von ausländischen Narren," 286–87, does devote a whole chapter to "foreign fools," but they are described as fools within their own national boundaries and exert no deleterious effects on German society, as they do in the broadsheet under discussion.

[20]For information on economic practices and situations in Augsburg, see Hermann Kellenbenz, "Wirtschaftsleben der Blütezeit," in *Geschichte der Stadt Augsburg von*

discussed at the imperial diets of 1522/23 and 1530, while the state of currency was at issue at the diets of 1518, 1524, and 1530.[21] A cursory list of such texts providing economic commentary, in chronological order, includes Wilhelm Rem's chronicle entry from 1519. Rem was an Augsburg merchant with Protestant sympathies. His entry describes how wealthy merchants engage in unethical business practices and cheat each other out of enormous sums of money.[22] In *Ain Sermon von dem Wucher* (1520) Luther condemns usury as immoral, using quotes from the Old and New Testament. Usury is also, according to Luther, a danger to both the soul and a territory's economic system. Luther again addresses economic issues in their relation to morality and territory in his text *An den christlichen Adel* (1520). Here Luther specifically blames the availability of luxurious and foreign wares for corrupting good German morality and for draining the land of currency. He particularly mentions the Fuggers in this context, as well as in his critique of the papal business of selling indulgences. The connection between usury and clergy is the subject of the pamphlet *Hie kompt ein Beüerlein zu einem reichen burger von der güldt den wucher betreffen...*(1522).[23] Narrated from the clearly Protestant perspective of a humble but savvy peasant, the dialogue reveals that the rich, the clergy, and the religious all practice usury for their own personal enrichment but call it interest and refuse to see that it is immoral. In his *Sermon von Kaufhandlung und Wucher* (1524), Luther states that monopolies as well as trading for profit (especially on the international market) are immoral and are bleeding the Germans dry. Luther further describes the tricks merchants play to cheat their clients. The Protestant preacher Eberlin von Günzburg also attacks the social and moral consequences of merchant practices in

---

der Römerzeit bis zur Gegenwart, ed. Gunther Gottlieb et al. (Stuttgart: Konrad Theiss Verlag, 1985), 258–301.

[21]Clemens Bauer, "Conrad Peutinger's Gutachten zur Monopolfrage," *Archiv für Reformationsgeschichte* 45 (1945): 151–57; see also *Neue und vollständigere Sammlung der Teutschen Reichsabschiede* (Frankfurt a.M., 1747), 169–344.

[22]*Cronica newer geschichten von Wilhelm Räm,* ed. Friedrich Roth, Die Chroniken der deutschen Städte vom 14. bis ins 16. Jahrhundert, vol. 25 (1896; reprint, Göttingen: Vandenhoeck & Ruprecht, 1966), 116–17.

[23]"Here comes a little peasant to talk about usury with a rich citizen"; reproduced in *Die Wahrheit muß ans Licht: Dialoge aus der Zeit der Reformation,* ed. R. Benzinger (Leipzig: Verlag Philipp Reclam, jun. 1983), 261–68.

his pamphlet *Mich wundert das kein gelt ihm land ist* (1524).[24] Günzburg describes how merchants tempt Germans to spend their money
on foreign food and clothing. The Germans become accustomed in
this manner to luxury, continue to spend their money, and then,
when the money runs out, turn to usury, theft, and prostitution.
Finally, a 1529 entry in a city chronicle written by the broadsheet's
artist Jörg Breu castigates the Augsburg city council for caving in to
the city's powerful merchant interests, thus hindering the process of
institutionalizing the Reformation in Augsburg.[25]

Several factors, however, unite all of these texts: All except the
chronicles were immediately available in printed form in and around
Augsburg; all singled out the figure of the merchant for criticism; and
all authors were pro-Protestant.

The parameters of this paper do not permit me to carry out an
analysis of each text here. Nor do I want to suggest that the broadsheet in question merely reflects concerns voiced primarily in these
other texts. Instead, I mention them in order to point to a particular
constellation combining pro-Protestant arguments, social and moral
critique, and a negative presentation of the merchant. I want to indicate how economic discourse, of which the figure of the merchant is
the signifier, was appropriated by Protestants and used to construct a
positive Protestant identity. The point here is not whether the merchants were actually ruining German society, but how the figure of
the merchant acts as a discursive construct into which Protestant
writers and artists inserted their critique of the status quo and produced their own identity in opposition.[26]

In constructing the merchant, the Protestants were able to
expand their opposition to current religious practices of the Catholic
Church (particularly the sale of indulgences) in order to include criticism of current economic practices (particularly usury, the artificial

[24]*Eberlin von Günzburg: Ausgewählte Schriften,* vol. 3, ed. Ludwig Enders, Flugschrif-
ten aus der Reformationszeit: Neudrücke deutscher Literaturwerke des XVI. und XVII.
Jahrhunderts, vol. 18 (Halle: Max Niemeyer, 1902), 147–81. Hoffmann, *Martin Luther
und die Reformation in Deutschland,* 253–54, makes reference to Günzburg in his catalogue entry on Breu's broadsheet (see n. 2 above).

[25]*Die Chronik des Malers Georg Preu des Aelteren,* ed. Friedrich Roth, 2d ed., Die
Chroniken der deutschen Städte vom 14. bis ins 16. Jahrhundert, vol. 29 (1906; reprint,
Göttingen: Vandenhoeck & Ruprecht, 1966), 45.

[26]Certainly, concern existed as to how to regulate and control merchant activity
and practices, as the debates at the imperial diets attest (see n. 21 above).

markup of prices, and the establishment of monopolies). In relation to both religious and economic practices, the Protestants argued for a return to the values of the early Church, when, they posited, a person's relation to God was spiritually pure and people's relations to one another were not motivated by profit. By this appeal to an earlier presumed state of religious and economic purity, the Protestant position was made both fundamentally revolutionary and reassuringly conservative.

As I have shown, *The Minter's Reply* participates in the discursive formation of Protestant identity by using, among other tactics, the construction of the merchant. So far, however, we have considered this only in terms of the broadsheet's text. I would now like to demonstrate how the broadsheet's image both underlines and expands upon that identity.

Iconographically, Breu's woodcut illustration responds to and combines two types of images: the older, traditional triumphal procession, and the recently (i.e., since the end of the fifteenth century) established image of the hoarding rich man.[27] In Breu's woodcut, the clerical triumphal procession occurs in the right half, where two canons on foot precede a mounted cardinal and monk. The image of the hoarding man occurs in the left half, where a man is seated at a table, counting coins from sacks and purses full of money, while two clients stand before him. These two parts of the image responding to two different iconographical traditions, and separated into a religious sphere on the right and a secular sphere on the left, are literally hinged together by the figure of the minter, seated at a barrel and minting coins. For both the text and the image, the figure of the minter is thus rhetorically and compositionally at the center.

Breu's image supports the text in a number of other ways. In the figure of the hoarding man, Breu has illustrated the merchant. The man is dressed in a *Schaube*, a type of German sixteenth-century mantel, here with a broad fur collar.[28] This seems to have been the preferred garment of men of power and station, as seen, for example, in

---

[27]Examples of these iconographical traditions are Jörg Breu the Elder, *Adventus of Charles V,* ca. 1530; all ten sheets in Herzog Anton Ulrich Museum in Braunschweig, reproduced in Geisberg, *German Single-Leaf Woodcut,* 1:327–37 (see n. 2 above); clerical adventus illustrated in Ulrich von Reichenthal, *Chronik des Konstanzer Konzils* (Augsburg: Anton Sorg, 1483); illustration to Brant, "Von Habsucht" (see n. 18 above); title page of *Hie kompt ein Beüerlein* (1522; see n. 23 above).

[28]Carl Köhler, *A History of Costume* (1928; reprint, New York: Dover, 1963), 247–49.

Lucas Cranach's 1510 engraved double portrait of Kurfürst Friedrich der Weise of Saxony and his brother and co-regent Johann der Beständige (from the Wittenberger *Heiltumsbuch*). That successful merchants appropriated this garment as their own, with all its signification of authority and prestige, is indicated in such works as Dürer's portrait of Jakob Fugger and Amberger's portrait of Wilhlem Merz.[29]

The "Roman craft" involving dispensations, papal bulls, and indulgences is also indicated in the woodcut by the presence of papal documents in the right half of the image. The Catholic Church itself, as institution, is represented by the religious procession.

But the woodcut does not simply illustrate the text word for word. There is, for example, no indictment of new fashions or of foreign influence in the image, factors that feature prominently in the text. Furthermore, the merchant's activities in the text are described primarily in terms of international trading. But in the woodcut, the merchant is depicted as engaged in another kind of activity, namely, banking.[30] From the woodcut, it is unclear exactly what sort of monetary transaction is taking place, whether currency exchange, money lending, or investment. But no matter what the exact transaction is, the woodcut clearly emphasizes the merchant as financier, not trader, as a man involved more with financial commerce than with the buying and selling of goods. The critique of the merchant in the woodcut thus focuses not on the crafty merchant continually creating demand with his foreign wares, but on the merchant/banker making profits in the highly abstracted world of the money market. This activity is interpreted as negative since the image draws upon the iconography, recently established in moralizing literature and Protestant broadsheets, of the hoarding rich man.

The woodcut also expands the text's critique of the Catholic Church. Although the pope is not depicted, his emissaries are, and they come from all levels of the Church hierarchy. The Church is represented as spiritually bankrupt; instead of the figure of Christ, a

---

[29]Both portraits are in the Staatsgalerie in Augsburg (Schaetzlerpalais). Dürer's portrait of Fugger (inv. no. 717) is dated, probably falsely, 1500; Amberger's portrait of Merz (inv. no. L.1699) is likely from 1533. See Gisela Goldberg, *Altdeutsche Gemälde Katalog*, 3d ed., Städtische Kunstsammlungen, Staatsgalerie Augsburg (Munich: Verlag F. Bruckmann, 1988), 58–62 and 12–13 respectively.

[30]Cf. Jacques Le Goff, *Merchands et Banquiers du Moyen Age*, Que Sais-Je, vol. 699 (Paris: PUF, 1956), and Hermann Kellenbenz, "Wirtschaftsleben der Blütezeit" (see n. 20 above).

papal indulgence hangs from the cross. This shocking replacement indicates that the Church no longer worships God but Mammon; not Christ's sacrifice but the pope's authority and greed are now the Church's touchstone.

Furthermore, the tradition of a clerical triumphal procession is undermined in the woodcut by showing the religious processing towards the merchant in order to join the line of the merchant's clients. As in the image of the merchant/banker which is based on the hoarding rich man, recourse to iconographic tradition furthers the commentary here through the process of inversion. By showing the religious lining up to do business with the merchant, the woodcut suggests a direct connection between the financial enterprises of the merchant and those of the Church. In fact, the merchant's activities, as well as the actual making of money by the minter, explicitly receives the Church's blessing as revealed by the cardinal's gesture of blessing the activities in front of him. In the text, these secular and sacred deals remain in completely separate spheres. The audience is led to understand that this alliance between the Church and the merchant is an unholy one: the fool at the extreme right margin imitates, but also inverts, the cardinal's gesture of blessing to one of being cuckolded. This gesture clearly makes a negative commentary on the activities represented as involving deceit and dishonesty.

There was, of course, a close connection indeed between the Church's sale of indulgences and the merchants, particularly in Augsburg. Archbishop Albrecht of Brandenburg had been given authority from the pope to supervise the sale of indulgences in Germany. But part of the money he collected he used to repay loans from the Fuggers of Augsburg, who were helping him meet the debts he owed to Rome for holding several ecclesiastical offices simultaneously.[31] In fact, the canon in Breu's woodcut bears a certain resemblance to Albrecht of Brandenburg, as comparison with a 1537 medallion depicting the cardinal indicates.[32] It was the blatantly personal use of these monies that contributed to the protest against the sale of indulgences, thus sparking off the long process of the Reformation.

---

[31]See Werner Hofmann, ed., *Köpfe der Lutherzeit* (Munich: Prestel Verlag, 1983), 154.

[32]Located in Berlin, Staatliche Museen, Münzkabinett; illustrated in exhibition catalogue *Kunst der Reformationszeit* (Berlin: Elefanten Press Verlag, 1983), 133, catalogue no. B71.6.

Furthermore, the Augsburg Fuggers remained staunchly Catholic, despite the rapid institutionalization of the Reformation in the city. This was dramatically illustrated by the visit of the papal legate, Cardinal Lorenzo Campeggio, to Augsburg in 1524.[33] Because of strong anti-Catholic sentiment in the city, his entry was not celebrated with the usual pomp and ceremony. He spent four days visiting with the Fuggers, no doubt combining business with pleasure. Perhaps the figure of the cardinal riding a mule in Breu's woodcut refers to Campeggio and his connection with Augsburg merchants, since it was Breu himself who mentions the visit in the artist's city chronicle.[34]

One further connection between Breu's woodcut and Augsburg finance is the fact that the city had been granted the privilege to mint its own silver and gold coins by Charles V in 1521. A year later a mint was built in Augsburg under the supervision of the new mint-master, Balthasar Hundertpfund(!), near the city's Franciscan monastery.[35] Because of these local references, the images of the minter, as well as that of the merchant and the clergy as business partners, would all have been familiar ones to an Augsburg audience.

Although text and image sometimes lay different accents upon the critique of the German economy, moral standards, and Roman Catholicism, they both work together to construct a desirable Protestant subject position for the broadsheet's audience. By blending economic, moral, and religious practices with nationalism in a reassuringly conservative manner, the broadsheet successfully performs its ideological work; it defines the Protestant position as a desirable one. *The Minter's Reply* is thus an instructive case study of the kinds of work performed by cultural production in constructing boundaries that define community. It also admonishes us to pay careful attention, both to the different narrative accents laid by text and image as well as to the national and economic facets of Reformation critique.

---

[33]Breu, *Die Chronik*, 24 (see n. 25 above).
[34]Röttinger, "Zur Holzschnittwerk," 49 (see n. 2 above), in fact identifies Breu's cardinal as Campeggio, but does so on the basis of the cardinal's presence at the 1530 Reichstag in Augsburg. Röttinger does not mention the 1524 visit.
[35]Friedrich Blendinger and Wolfgang Zorn, eds., *Augsburgs Geschichte in Bilddokumenten* (Munich: C. H. Beck Verlag, 1976), 162.

Investiture of Charles V with his son Ferdinand I,
on September 5, 1530, in Augsburg (anon. engraving)

Der Kaiser als Künstler

Ferdinand III and the Politicization of Sacred Music at the Hapsburg Court

Steven Saunders

Boundary formation and the maintenance of political order and stability were persistent concerns for the Hapsburg emperors throughout the seventeenth century. The dynasty faced these challenges by adopting the precept that religious unity would ultimately prove more fundamental to the security of the realm than political union. Consequently, the Hapsburgs came to believe that Catholic cultural hegemony was crucial to maintaining political cohesion. This interaction between religious, political, and cultural ideals can be seen with particular clarity in sacred music from the reign of Ferdinand III. Music's presentation within particular liturgical, ceremonial, and institutional contexts helped to make musical statements of political ideas, yet even individual compositional gestures in works by court composers, including compositions by Emperor Ferdinand III himself, carried political meanings.

THERE WERE FEW CENTERS in early modern Germany where the tensions between separation and unity were so keenly felt as at the imperial court in Vienna. The Austrian Hapsburgs, nominal rulers over that most precarious of unions, the Holy Roman Empire of the German Nation, remained preoccupied with challenges to German unity throughout the early modern era.[1] The challenges that the dynasty faced from within the Reich were compounded by even more vexing religious, economic, and constitutional dilemmas in the lands under more direct Hapsburg rule (Bohemia, Hungary, and the hereditary lands). Faced with threats on so many fronts, the Hapsburgs came to adopt the precept that religious unity would ultimately prove more

---

[1]See, e.g., R. J. W. Evans, "Introduction: State and Society in Early Modern Austria," in *State and Society in Early Modern Austria*, ed. Charles W. Ingrao (West Lafayette, Ind.: Purdue University Press, 1994), 14.

fundamental to the security of the realm than political union.[2] From this guiding political principle flowed its cultural corollary: Catholic cultural hegemony was crucial to maintaining political cohesion. Sacred music played a pivotal role in articulating this political program; music was a crucial instrument for the propagation of the Catholic faith, as well as an important means of articulating the power and prestige of the House of Austria. The present study will explore the intersections between music and politics, concentrating on the reign of a single Hapsburg emperor, Ferdinand III.

Ferdinand III (r. 1637–57) remains an amorphous, even shadowy figure. In contrast to the vast literatures that have grown up around his father, Ferdinand II, and his son, Leopold I, Ferdinand III has been relatively neglected by historians. He has yet to find a modern biographer; indeed, one writer summed up the state of research on Ferdinand by claiming that history had denied him an identity of his own.[3] Nevertheless, Ferdinand's reign proves intriguing from a musical perspective. Ferdinand maintained a large and thoroughly Italianate music chapel, which cultivated virtually every style and genre of the mid-seventeenth century.[4] An entry in an eighteenth-century music dictionary summarized the emperor's contemporary reputation by noting simply that Ferdinand was "praised by all the writers of his time as a great connoisseur and patron of music."[5] Even more fascinating, Ferdinand III was himself a poet and composer.[6] The title of

[2]See, e.g., R. J. W. Evans, *The Making of the Habsburg Monarchy: An Interpretation* (Oxford: Clarendon Press, 1979), and Paula Sutter Fichtner, "Religion in the Counter-Reformation: Introduction," in Ingrao, *State and Society*, 33 (see n. 1 above).

[3]Charles W. Ingrao, *The Habsburg Monarchy, 1618–1815* (Cambridge: Cambridge University Press, 1994), 47.

[4]See esp. Herbert Seifert, "Die Entfaltung des Barock," in *Musikgeschichte Österreichs*, vol. 1, *Von den Anfängen zum Barock*, ed. Rudolf Flotzinger and Gernot Gruber (Graz: Verlag Styria, 1977), 351–68.

[5]Ernst Ludwig Gerber, *Historisch-biographisches Lexikon der Tonkünstler* (Leipzig, 1790–92; reprint, Graz: Akademische Druck- und Verlagsanstalt, 1977), col. 404. (Unless otherwise noted, translations are by the author.)

[6]On Ferdinand's compositional activity, see Guido Adler, *Musikalische Werke der Kaiser Ferdinand III., Leopold I. und Joseph I.* (1892; reprint, Farnborough Hants: Gregg International Publishers, 1972); Theophil Antonicek, "Die italienische Textvertonungen Kaiser Ferdinands III.," in *Beiträge zur Aufnahme der italienischen und spanischen Literatur in Deutschland im 16. und 17. Jahrhundert*, ed. Alberto Martino (Amsterdam: Rodopi, 1990); Antonicek, "Musik und italienische Poesie am Hofe Kaiser Ferdinands III.," *Mitteilungen der Kommission für Musikforschung*, no. 42 (Vienna: Verlag der Österreichischen Akademie der Wissenschaften, 1990); and Steven Saunders, "New Discoveries Concerning Ferdinand III's Musical Compositions," *Studien zur Musikwissenschaft* 45 (1996): 7–31.

this essay, "Der Kaiser als Künstler," then, is meant to be taken literally; yet it also seeks to evoke an even broader arena in which the emperor exercised considerable creative control, namely, in fashioning the *Gesamtkunstwerk* that was the imperial court itself.

Before Ferdinand's music chapel sounded a single note, it served as a vehicle for the articulation of political ideas. One of the first impressions of the imperial music chapel that a visitor to court would have received was visual: on major feasts, an observer would have been confronted with one of the largest, most impressive musical organizations in early modern Europe. At the beginning of his reign, for example, Ferdinand's chapel included twenty-seven singers, twelve choirboys, twenty-two instrumentalists (not including some ten trumpeters), and various ancillary personnel.[7] The Hapsburg public relations machinery ensured that the aura surrounding performance was widely known, even among those who had never heard the imperial musicians. Contemporary chroniclers generally describe only the musical pinnacle of most court festivities, the singing of the Te Deum. Their descriptions, however, are remarkably consistent. Again and again they stress those aspects of performance that were most intimately tied up with courtly representation: the size, diversity, and virtuosity of the imperial music chapel; the sheer volume of sound; the obligatory nonmusical accompaniment of church bells, cannons, and musket salvos; and the presence of trumpets and drums:

> His Majesty the emperor with the most eminent legate [the papal nuncio, Cardinal Dietrichstein] received the most serene couple in St. Augustin, where in singing the Te Deum, forty trumpets and drums filled all of the church with sound.[8]

[7]Ludwig Ritter von Köchel, *Die kaiserliche Hof-Musikkapelle in Wien von 1543 bis 1867* (1869; reprint, Hildesheim: Georg Olms Verlag, 1976), 58–65. See also Gabriel Bucelinus, *Germania topo-chrono-stemmato-graphica sacra et profana* (Ulm: Johann Görlin, 1655), 279–81; Adolf Koczirz, "Exzerpte aus den Hofmusikakten der Wiener Hofkammerarchivs," *Studien zur Musikwissenschaft* 1 (1913): 285; Peter Webhofer, *Giovanni Felice Sances (ca. 1600–1679): Biographisch-bibliographische Untersuchung und Studie über sein Motettenwerk* (Rome: Pontificio Instituto di Musica Sacra, 1964), 3–6; and the Haus-Hof- und Staatsarchiv (Vienna), Hofarchiv, Obersthofmeisteramt, Sonderreihe, vols. 186–87.

[8]*Relatione della solenne pompa celebrata nelle nozze delle Maestà delli Serenissimi Regi Ferdinando III. ... e C. Maria Infante Cattolica di Spagna* (Rome: Lodovico Grignanni, 1631), fol. [A3]: "La Maestà dell'Imperatore con l'Eminentissimo Legato riceverano li

Thereupon, in the choir, the Te Deum was sung with all sorts of musical instruments, military drums, trumpets, and beautiful voices; twenty-four cannons were fired, three salvos were discharged by the infantry in the square in front of the church, and all the bells, great and small, tolled.[9]

Meanwhile they began to play every sort of musical instrument and to sing the Te Deum laudamus, which along with the mass and motets, were new works by Signor Giovanni Valentini, chapel master of his majesty the emperor, [and] at the same time, on the square, the soldiers shot three musket salvos, and from the walls and bastions a great number of artillery were fired off, and in all the churches the bells tolled.[10]

Court artists, too, communicated messages similar to those broadcast by the chroniclers of court spectacle. An engraving celebrating Ferdinand's coronation as King of the Romans in 1636, for example, displays a large instrumental and vocal ensemble seemingly overflowing a loft above the choir in the Regensburg cathedral.[11] Similarly, a well-known engraving from 1648 invokes musical imagery to make a grand gesture of courtly representation. The artist, Michael Frommer, depicts Ferdinand riding triumphantly above an angel consort consisting of representatives from all the constituent groups of an extraordinarily well equipped princely music chapel.[12] The musicians include a string consort with members of both the modern violin family and viol families; wind instruments of various types; singers; a

---

serenissimi sposi nella Chiesa di Frati Agostiniani, dove cantandosi il Te Deum, quaranta trombetti, e gnaccheri con bellissimo concerto empirno tutta la Chiesa di rumore."

[9]*Relationis historicae semestrailis continuatio* (Frankfurt a.M., 1627), 73–74: "Darauff ist am Chor das Te Deum laudamus mit allerley Musicalischen Instrumenten, Heer-Paucken, Trommetten und lieblichen Stimmen gesungen 24 grosse Stück loss gebrent, von der Infanteria am Platz voer der Kirche 3. Salve geschossen, und alle grosse und kleine Glocke geleut."

[10]*Le quattro relationi sequite in Ratisbona ... Relatione dell' incoronatione del re de Romani* (Vienna, 1637), fols. CIv-CIIr: "Si diede nel mentre principio a suono d'ogni sorte de stromenti da Musici à cantare il Ve [*sic*] Deum laudamus, come anco la Messa, e Mottetti, opere nove del Signor Giovanni Valentini Maestro di capella di Sua Maestà Cesarea; su la piazza all'istesso tempo la soldatesca fece tre salve con moschetti, su le mura, e bastioni si spararono molti pezzi, in tutte le chiese si toccorono le campane."

[11]Reproduced in Steven Saunders, *Cross, Sword, and Lyre: Sacred Music at the Imperial Court of Ferdinand II of Habsburg (1619–1637)* (Oxford: Clarendon Press, 1995), 202.

[12]Walter Salmen, ed., *Bilder zur Geschichte der Musik in Österreich* (Innsbruck: Musikverlag Hebling, 1979), 55.

large and variegated continuo group; and a corps of trumpeters with the obligatory *Heerpaucker* (military timpanist). We need to be wary about reading the engraving too literally, of course; nevertheless, the value of a large music chapel (and of verbal and iconographic representations of that chapel) as instruments of courtly representation is fairly self-evident. Indeed, the projection of the authority and majesty of the ruler through the outward grandeur of his court was a commonplace of courtly life in the early modern era, as we know from numerous *Fürstenspiegel* and handbooks on court ceremonial.[13] Significantly, however, it was the music chapel, with its intimate connection to the church and its liturgy, rather than palace architecture or sumptuous banquets, that became the primary vehicle for courtly representation in seventeenth-century Vienna.[14]

In addition to the chapel's size, the institution had another significant attribute that would not have been lost on contemporaries: it was completely dominated by Italian musicians. Nearly all of the singers, string players, and composers at court were Italian, and the court actively broadcast its Italian orientation: published lists of the imperial household sometimes included not only the names of the musicians, but also their native cities.[15] In addition to the strongly Italian character of the chapel itself, Italianate musical genres were cultivated intensively at the imperial court. In the sphere of sacred music these included the Lenten oratorio or *sepolcro*, sacred opera, and spiritual madrigal. Ferdinand himself wrote an Italian madrigal, a short operalike "dramma musicum," as well as numerous Italian texts intended for musical setting. He also participated in Italian literary academies,[16] and frequently discussed Italian poetry in his correspon-

[13]Julius Bernhard Rohr, *Einleitung zur Ceremoniel-Wissenschaften der grossen Herren* (Berlin, 1733), cited in Hubert Christian Ehalt, *Ausdrucksformen absolutistischer Herrschaft: Der Wiener Hof im 17. und 18. Jahrhundert* (Vienna: Verlag für Geschichte und Politik, 1980), 65.

[14]See, e.g., Hellmut Lorenz, "The Imperial Hofburg: The Theory and Practice of Architectural Representation in Baroque Vienna," in Ingrao, *State and Society*, 93–109 (see n. 1 above); Saunders, *Cross, Sword, and Lyre*, 10–14 (see n. 11 above); and Josef Fiedler, ed., *Die Relationen der Botschafter Venedigs über Deutschland und Österreich im siebzehnten Jahrhundert*, vol. 1, Fontes rerum Austriacarum, no. 26 (Vienna: Kaiserlich-königliche Hof- und Staatsdruckerei, 1866), 387–88.

[15]Bucelinus, *Germania topo-chrono-stemmato-graphica*, 279–81 (see n. 7 above).

[16]Marcus Landau, *Die italienische Literatur am österreichischen Hofe* (Vienna: Carl Gerold's Sohn, 1879), 10–12; Herbert Seifert, *Die Oper am Wiener Kaiserhof im 17. Jahrhundert* (Tutzing: Hans Schneider, 1985), 195–96; Antonicek, "Musik und Italienische Poesie," 1–3; and Saunders, "New Discoveries," passim (see n. 6 above).

dence with his brother, Archduke Leopold Wilhelm. Indeed, the obsession with Italian poetry and music on the part of the Hapsburg dynasty spawned a huge repertoire of poetic, devotional, and musical works in Italian. Ironically, just as the German language gained respectability among Protestant intellectuals as a vehicle for serious literary expression, the Hapsburgs, titular rulers of the Holy Roman Empire of the German Nation, embraced Italian as the preferred language for cultivated discourse, turning it into a second vernacular.

The Hapsburg dynasty's intense identification with and cultivation of the work of Italian artists was no idle pastime.[17] The reliance on Italian musicians, the writing of Italian verse, the cultivation of Italian genres, the participation in academies founded on Italian models all served to confirm the Hapsburgs' confessional and dynastic bonds with the Italian peninsula. Yet such activities were also part of the studied cultivation of Ferdinand III's reputation—visible signs of the emperor's erudition.[18] A thoroughly Italianized musical establishment amounted to empirical confirmation of the emperor's artistic astuteness since, for any prince with artistic pretensions, garnering the best musical talent meant turning to Italy, the birthplace of nearly all the noteworthy innovations in seventeenth-century music, including monody, opera, the *concertato* style, and a variety of other new genres and techniques.

Cultivating the most up-to-date strains of seicento music came at a price, however. Ferdinand frequently dispatched musicians to Italy to recruit performers and to procure new music. Similarly, promising German musicians in the imperial service were frequently sent to study with Italian masters. The best known examples from Ferdinand's chapel were two keyboard virtuosi, Johann Jakob Froberger and Johann Kaspar Kerll, whose study with the most illustrious Italian teachers of the day, Girolamo Frescobaldi and Giacomo Carissimi, was supported financially by the emperor.

---

[17]Visiting ambassadors consistently remarked on Ferdinand's musical abilities. See, e.g., the report of the Venetian representative Girolamo Giustiani from 1654, quoted in Fiedler, *Die Relationen der Botschafter Venedigs*, 387: "La musica è l'unica sua deletatione, compone bene, e giudica delle uoci e dell'arte esquisitamente" (see n. 14 above).

[18]On reputation as one of the monarch's main tools of state, see Robert Bireley, *The Counterreformation Prince: Antimachiavellianism or Catholic Statecraft in Early Modern Europe* (Chapel Hill: University of North Carolina Press, 1990), 9–11, 55, 222.

Still other aspects of sacred music's presentation invested it with political significances. Ferdinand III did not retreat to the privacy of his court chapel for liturgical observances. Instead, he traveled frequently from the imperial palace (or *Hofburg*) to hear the two primary public religious celebrations, mass and vespers. The emperor, his family, and significantly, his court chaplains and musicians went along, turning individual parish churches, in effect, into branch offices of the imperial chapel.[19] In the context of mid-seventeenth-century Vienna, the Catholic emperor's presence in the parish churches was momentous. In 1624 Vienna's Protestant population had been ordered to begin instruction in Catholicism, or to risk confiscation of property. During the same period, the religious topography of Vienna was transformed as the Hapsburgs transferred Viennese churches to religious orders sympathetic to their program for the Counter-Reformation. The House of Austria underwrote the construction and renovation of many edifices and filled the new pulpits with Catholic preachers. This program of expansion served not only to accommodate the increased number of worshipers but also provided a visible proclamation of Hapsburg triumph over Protestant heresy.[20]

In this climate of forced conversion, the Catholic liturgy—which was made audible in musical settings performed by members of the emperor's own chapel—served didactic, even propagandistic functions. Indeed, the Hapsburgs recognized clearly music's potential for influencing their subjects: one of the four main thrusts in imperial decrees between 1628 and 1658 was to eliminate the singing of "non-catholic songs."[21] Thus, in the Hapsburg lands, even the most commonplace Catholic texts had political ramifications, for, during the Thirty Years' War, accepting Catholicism was not merely a religious statement; it was a political one, amounting to the legitimization of the sole sovereignty of the Hapsburg dynasty.[22]

---

[19]Archival records record payments for "carrying the organ, regal, and other instruments to various religious observances held in the city." See Paul Nettl, "Zur Geschichte der kaiserlichen Hofmusikkapelle von 1636–1680," *Zeitschrift für Musikwissenschaft* 16 (1929): 79–80.

[20]See, e.g., Ingrao, *The Habsburg Monarchy*, 97 (see n. 3 above).

[21]Robert Douglas Chesler, "Crown, Lords, and God: The Establishment of Secular Authority and the Pacification in Lower Austria, 1618–1648" (Ph.D. diss., Princeton University, 1979), 316–17.

[22]Ibid., 351.

If broad aspects of music's presentation and institutional context suggested political ideas in quite general ways, individual musical works proved capable of articulating specific tenets of the Hapsburg worldview. Forceful examples of such political statements in music occur in two Masses that seem to have been written for imperial coronations under Ferdinand III, the *Missa coronationis* and *Missa non erit finis*, by the imperial chapel master Giovanni Valentini.[23] One of the most arresting features of these works is that they contain written-out parts for trumpets. The trumpet could be particularly useful in making musical statements of political ideas, since the instrument's royal connotations were ancient. In fact, during the Middle Ages, only the *Reichsfürsten*, the greatest princes of the empire, were allowed to employ trumpeters. This tradition was very much alive in the seventeenth century, though in this, as in all else, inflation had taken its toll. When the Hapsburgs renewed the imperial patent for trumpeters in 1630, they recognized their right to play for "the emperor, kings, electors, princes, counts, barons, noble knights, and other highly qualified persons."[24]

In addition to these royal connotations, the use of trumpets also had strong military associations, owing to the instrument's traditional role in sounding military fanfares and signals. We can see how strong such military connotations remained, even in the seventeenth century, from a decree issued by the procurators of St. Mark's in Venice, which banned trumpets in 1639 for being too "warlike ... [and] more suitable for armies than for the house of God."[25] These associations were equally clear to a Florentine ambassador, who reported from Innsbruck in 1628 that the use of trumpets and drums in sacred music rendered a performance of Vespers "military, yet lively and devout."[26] Such resonances made the trumpet ensemble an apt

[23]The *Missa coronationis* is preserved in a copy from ca. 1665–70 in Kroměříž, Státni Zámek a Zahrady, Historicko-Umelecké Fondy, Hudební Archív (Czech Republic), shelfmark A1/Breit. I.1. The *Missa non erit finis* is contained in the Benediktinerstift Kremsmünster (Austria), ser. C, fas. 15, no. 715.
[24]Detlef Altenburg, "Zum Repertoire der Hoftrompeter im 17. und 18. Jahrhundert," in *Bericht über die erste Internationale Fachtagung zur Erforschung der Blasmusik: Graz 1974*, ed. Wolfgang Suppan and Eugen Brixel (Tutzing: Hans Schneider, 1976), 31–32.
[25]Quoted in Lorenzo Bianconi, *Music in the Seventeenth Century*, trans. David Bryant (Cambridge: Cambridge University Press, 1987), 113.
[26]Steven Saunders, "Sacred Music at the Hapsburg Court of Ferdinand II (1615–1637): The Latin Vocal Works of Giovanni Priuli and Giovanni Valentini" (Ph.D. diss., University of Pittsburgh), 249.

expression of Hapsburg policies, which inseparably linked religion and militant confessional politics.

Today, of course, the participation of trumpets in instrumental music is taken for granted. At the beginning of the seventeenth century, however, trumpets were typically not a formal part of a princely music chapel; instead the so-called *Hof- und Feldtrompeter* remained administratively part of the court stables and were added to the regular musicians of the chapel as a kind of special effect for particularly festive occasions. Moreover, the court-and-field trumpeters cultivated a distinct repertoire of military signals, fanfares, and sonatas, which were generally improvised and handed down in oral tradition rather than preserved through musical notation.[27] The fact that the *Missa coronationis* and *Missa non erit finis* have notated trumpet parts, then, is significant, for it allowed the trumpets to be incorporated musically into compositions performed by the regular instrumental ensemble.[28] In fact, when more that a decade earlier Valentini published works that were among the first to include notated trumpet parts, he stressed this new integration. In the dedication to his seven-choir *Messa, Magnificat et Iubilate Deo*, the composer claimed that he had struggled in these works "to invent [a] new way of combining trumpets with voices and instruments."[29] As the result of this new integration of the trumpet corps, composers could evoke in church music the military connotations of the court-and-field trumpet style.[30]

Imitations of the military trumpet style—particularly the use of sustained triads, rapid repeated notes, arpeggiated figures, and dactylic rhythms—acquired a kind of iconic significance during the

[27]Altenburg, "Zum Repertoire der Hoftrompeter," 47–60 (see n. 24 above); Manfred Hermann Schmid, "Trompeterchor und Sprachvertonung bei Heinrich Schütz," *Schütz Jahrbuch* 13 (1991): 38–45.

[28]It is probably no coincidence that the first published parts for trumpets come from Germany in the years just before the outbreak of the Thirty Years' War; see Steven Saunders, "The Hapsburg Court of Ferdinand II and the *Messa, Magnificat et Iubilate Deo a sette chori concertati con le trombe* (1621) of Giovanni Valentini," *Journal of the American Musicological Society* 44 (1991): 386.

[29]Giovanni Valentini, *Messa, Magnificat et Iubilate Deo a sette chori concertati con le trombe* (Vienna: M. Formica, 1621), fol. [A1v]: "Nell'Anno 1618. con l'occasione, che il Sacratissimo Imperatore mio Signore Clementissimo, fù coronato Rè di Ungheria, composi il presente Magnificat, & nel medesimo Anno poi, la Messa à Sette Chori, nelle quali mi affaticai d'inventare questo nuovo modo di concertare le Trombe, con Voci, & Istromenti; & ultimamente, hò fatto nell'istesso stile il Motetto Iubilate Deo."

[30]Saunders, "The Hapsburg Court," 387–93 (see n. 28 above).

seventeenth century in the so-called *battaglia* style, and in the famous *genere concitato* developed by Claudio Monteverdi. (It probably was no coincidence that Monteverdi introduced and defended this "agitated genere" in his *Madrigali guerrieri et amorosi*, a collection dedicated to Ferdinand III.) Trumpetlike musical gestures were invoked even in works that did not actually employ trumpets. Ferdinand III's own music hints occasionally at this military style (example 1).

Example 1. Ferdinand III, "Deus tuorum militum," Ratsbücherei (Lüneburg), K.N. 28, measures 78–88.

The passage at the *piu presto* marking in example 1, from Ferdinand's setting of the hymn "Deus tuorum militum," uses trumpetlike gestures to set words that have both military and political overtones: "in hoc triumpho Martyris" (in this triumph of the martyrs).[31]

Music was capable of still more specific statements of political ideas. Valentini's *Missa non erit finis* employs another common conceit found in sacred music from Ferdinand III's court: the linking of the ideas of temporal and divine kingship. The *Missa non erit finis* takes its name from a portion of the text of the Credo of the Ordinary, "cuius regni non erit finis" (whose reign shall have no end). Ferdinand's chapel master singled out those words for special treatment, first by introducing them with a long instrumental sonata, which, not coincidentally, includes music for trumpets, and second—and even more strikingly—by extending the setting of the five words "cuius regni non erit finis" over no fewer than eighty-four measures.[32]

An even more clearly articulated musical assertion of the Hapsburg notions of power and the divine right of kings occurs in another work by Valentini, *Cantate gentes*. This motet was written for the *Landtag* in Pressburg in 1647, a convocation at which Ferdinand III's son, Ferdinand IV, was crowned King of Hungary.[33] The text divides into four sections:

[Sonata]	[Sonata]
Cantate gentes in conspectu Regis Domini.	Sing, all peoples, in the sight of God the King.
[Sonata]	[Sonata]
Exultate principes in conspectu Regis Domini.	Exalt, ye princes, in the sight of God the King.
[Sonata]	[Sonata]
Jubilate reges in conspectu Regis Domini.	Make a joyful noise, kings, in the sight of God the King.
[Sonata]	[Sonata]
Quoniam est Rex Regum et Dominus dominantium.	For He is King of Kings and Lord of Lords.

[31]Ferdinand's hymn setting is preserved in the Ratsbücherei (Lüneburg), K.N. 28.

[32]Elisabeth Urbanek, "Giovanni Valentini als Messenkomponist" (Ph.D. diss., University of Vienna, 1974), 34.

[33]Joseph Sittard, "Samuel Capricornus contra Philipp Friedrich Böddecker," *Sammelbände der Internationalen Musik-Gesellschaft* 3 (1901/2): 99.

The first three sections of the motet are exhortations addressed, in turn, to the people, to princes, and to kings, while the final section presents a triumphant acclamation of kingship: "for he is King of Kings and Lord of Lords." Valentini emphasizes and confirms the Hapsburg view of confessional absolutism inherent in the text through his compositional choices, specifically by using increasingly elaborate musical gestures for each succeeding section. The wind instruments are excluded from the first two vocal sections, joining the singers only for the third, "royal" section, at the words "Jubilate reges in conspectu Regis Domini." Musical class distinctions extend further still: the instrumental sonata that introduces the final or "divine" section includes the most virtuosic music yet heard, with *cornetti* (the instrument is a sort of cross between a trumpet and a recorder) echoing one another in rapid sixteenth-note figures. What is more, at the final words "Dominus dominantium," the vocalists abandon the syllabic declamation to which they have been restricted throughout the piece in favor of long melismas (passages in which many notes are sung to a single syllable). Such melismas were conventional for depicting divine omnipotence in south-German music of the seventeenth century.[34] Musically, the work provides a mirror of confessional absolutism: the ruler is set above the *Volk* and lower nobility, a concept built into virtually every facet of the court ceremonial.[35] Yet the motet also contains a reminder that the monarch's authority derives, ultimately, from God. These were hardly old ideas in the Hapsburg territories of the mid-seventeenth century; in fact, Robert Bierley has shown that true absolutism was only established at the Hapsburg court during the reign of Ferdinand III's father, Ferdinand II.[36]

Cantate gentes and the *Missa non erit finis* go beyond the usual bounds of courtly representation, verging into an area known in the seventeenth century as *musica politica*.[37] The notion underlying

[34]Craig Allan Otto, "Symbol Structures in Central European Church Music: Aspects of the Word-Tone Relationship in the Mid- to Late-Seventeenth Century" (Ph.D. diss., University of Syracuse, 1978), 176–87 and 218.

[35]See esp. Ehalt, *Ausdrucksformen absolutistischer Herrschaft*, 117–27 (see n. 13 above).

[36]Robert Bireley, S.J., "Confessional Absolutism in the Hapsburg Lands in the Seventeenth Century," in Ingrao, *State and Society*, 36–39 (see n. 1 above).

[37]Volker Scherliess, "Musica politica," in *Festschrift Georg von Dadelsen zum 60. Geburtstag*, ed. Thomas Kohlhase and Scherliess (Neuhausen, Stuttgart: Hänssler-Verlag, 1978), 270–83.

musica politica was that music, both in the harmonious balance of its constituent parts and in its numerical order and proportion, might reflect the structure of the ideal state. One seventeenth-century music theorist, Giovanni Andrea Bontempi, described *musica politica* as "that well-proportioned harmony that joins together persons of high, middle, and low estate in the composition of a perfect republic."[38] Bontempi's words read almost like a description of the motet *Cantate gentes*: as the various estates symbolically heed the exhortation to music-making, using increasingly elaborate musical gestures, they also emblematize and extol the social order, balance, and consonance of the absolutist state.

The term *musica politica* was coined by Athanasius Kircher, a Jesuit polymath whose musical connections to the Viennese court were intimate.[39] In fact, some of Ferdinand III's musical works were created using a mathematically ordered system of mechanical composition propounded in Kircher's mammoth treatise, the *Musica universalis*.[40] These works—composed by the emperor himself and modeled on Kircher's mathematical tables—provide particularly noteworthy examples of the numerical order and harmony that were the basis of seventeenth-century *musica politica*.

Another means through which music could transmit political messages, though a fairly crude one, should be mentioned in passing, namely, the technique of pictorialism or madrigalism. Johann Jakob Froberger's celebrated *Lamento sopra la dolorosa perdita della Real Msta. di Ferdinando IV* ends with an upward sweeping scale that depicts the emperor's son ascending into heaven. It has been suggested that a series of twenty-one repeated chords in an instrumental lament written on the death of Ferdinand III by Johann Heinrich Schmelzer symbolizes not only the tolling of church bells but the twenty-one-year reign of the emperor.

Sacred music also had more subtle means through which to express political ideas, particularly through the interaction of music with a verbal text. Liturgical texts and sacred poetry served, among other things, to encourage devotion and, perhaps more importantly,

---

[38]Ibid., 273.
[39]Ulf Scharlau, *Athanasius Kircher (1601–1680) als Musikschriftsteller: Ein Beitrag zur Musikanschauung des Barock,* Studien zur hessischen Musikgeschichte, vol. 2 (Kassel: Bärenreiter, 1969), 41.
[40]Saunders, "New Discoveries" (see n. 6 above).

to direct those devotions into particular channels. A musical setting of a religious text could add yet another layer to this polyvalent process of religious persuasion. As a final example of the ways in which such music functioned as quasi-political statement, let us consider another piece written by Ferdinand III himself, a setting of the hymn "Ave maris stella." As background to this hymn setting, we need to begin by exploring Ferdinand III's special devotion to the cult of the Immaculate Conception.

It has long been recognized that the Hapsburgs developed a characteristic brand of catholic piety in the seventeenth century, the so-called *Pietas Austriaca*.[41] Two pillars of the *Pietas Austriaca* acquired special prominence under Ferdinand III: veneration of the Eucharist, and ardent devotion to the Cult of the Virgin, in particular, the promotion of the doctrine of the Immaculate Conception. Significantly, these ideas served to underline two of the main doctrinal differences between the Catholic Hapsburgs and their "heretic" Protestant subjects, and they acquired the character of anti-Protestant affirmations in the seventeenth century.[42] It should come as no surprise, then, that we have an inordinate number of sacred vocal works from the imperial court dealing with Eucharistic and Marian themes (including many works dealing with the Immaculate Conception).[43]

In the seventeenth century, the question of whether or not Mary had been conceived without original sin remained highly controversial. In fact, the Immaculate Conception was not finally defined as church dogma until 1854. Yet the Feast of the Immaculate Conception had been celebrated in Vienna since 1629, at the specific behest of Ferdinand III's father.[44] Significantly, Ferdinand III himself had

---

[41]Anna Coreth, *Pietas Austriaca: Ursprung und Entwicklung barocker Frömmigkeit in Österreich* (Munich: Oldenbourg, 1959).

[42]Neils Krogh Rasmussen, O.P., "Liturgy and Liturgical Arts," in *Catholicism in Early Modern History: A Guide to Research*, ed. John W. O'Malley, S.J. (St. Louis: Center for Reformation Research, 1988), 282.

[43]See, e.g., Giovanni Felice Sances, *Antifone e litanie della Beatissima Vergine a più voce* (Venice: Bartolomeo Magni, 1640); also idem, *Antiphonare sacrae B. M. V. per totum annum una voce decantandae* (Venice: stampa del Gardano, 1648); and Giovanni Valentini, *Ragionamento sovra il Santissimo da recitarsi in musica* (Vienna: M. Cosmerovius, 1642). A striking example is provided by a list of motets by Sances in a seventeenth-century inventory, the so-called Distinta specificatione dell'archivio musicale in the Österreichische Nationalbibliothek (Vienna), suppl. mus. 2451. Nine of the first ten motets in the list deal with Marian or Eucharistic themes.

[44]Coreth, *Pietas Austriaca*, 50 (see n. 41above).

been crowned King of Hungary on the Feast of the Immaculate Conception, and he subsequently penned Italian poetry in honor of the "Immaculata."[45] When, in 1642, Urban VIII issued a papal bull that declared the feast invalid, the emperor refused its publication in his lands.[46] In 1645 he placed his lands placed under the "protection, shelter, and patronage" of the "Immaculata," and ordered that a Marian column be erected where litanies and other devotions were to be celebrated.[47] Two litanies for this event, both employing trumpets, were composed by Giovanni Felice Sances; one of these, in fact, is described in a court inventory as "Litanie Cesare per l'Assunta alla Collonna." The column was dedicated in 1647, and in 1649 Ferdinand III ordered the university faculty to take part in a yearly procession to this Mariensäule on the Immaculate Conception.[48]

In the same year (1649) that he prescribed these processions, Ferdinand III composed a work that manifests musically his advocacy of the Immaculate Conception: the hymn "Ave maris stella." The composition is transmitted in the most comprehensive source for Ferdinand III's musical works—one that, amazingly, has been overlooked in previous discussions of the emperor's compositional activities. This manuscript is of Viennese provenance and is housed today in the *Ratsbücherei* in Lüneburg under the shelfmark K.N. 28.[49] The scribe who copied Ferdinand's hymns into K.N. 28 also recorded the dates of composition (see example 2), and these dates document two distinct patterns to Ferdinand's compositional activity. First, Ferdinand chose to set either hymns whose texts were used with some frequency, or texts that were employed on important feasts in the Viennese liturgi-

---

[45]His poem "In una pellegrinatione ad una Madonna miracolosa" begins: "Vergine Pia, e Santa, e Immaculata, // Che Cinthia tiene sotto i piedi tuo"; see *Poesie diverse composte in hore rubate d'Academico Occupato* (n.pl., n.d.) [B7r].

[46]Theodor Wiedemann, *Geschichte der Reformation und Gegenreformation im Lande unter der Enns*, vol. 5 (Leipzig: G. Freytag, 1886), 4–5. In 1641 Ferdinand III had introduced a requirement that papal bulls receive the imperial *placet* before their publication in the Hapsburg lands; see Bireley, "Confessional Absolutism," 45 (see n. 36 above).

[47]See Coreth, *Pietas Austriaca*, 52 (see n. 41 above), and Österreichische National-bibliothek (Vienna), Suppl. mus. 2451, fol. 65v.

[48]Ernst Tomek, *Kirchengeschichte Österreichs*, vol. 2: *Humanismus, Reformation und Gegenreformation* (Innsbruck and Vienna: Tyrolia Verlag, 1949), 524, and Ingrao, *The Habsburg Monarchy*, 38 (see n. 3 above).

[49]Description in Friedrich Welter, *Katalog der Musikalien der Ratsbücherei Lüneburg* (Lippstadt: Verlag Kistner & Siegel, 1950), 23. On the provenance and dating of the manuscript, see Saunders, "New Discoveries" (see n. 6 above).

Hymn	Feast	Composition Date	Feast Date
1. Ave maris stella	Feasts of BVM Immaculate Conception?)	18.XI.49	8.XII
2. Jesu corona virginum	Feasts of Virgins & Martyrs (St. Lucy?)	20.XI.49	13.XII
3. Iste confessor	Feasts of Confessors (St. Nicholas?) (St. Ambrose?) (St. Damasus?)	20.XI.49	6.XII 7.XII 11.XII
4. Jesu Redemptor omnium	Christmas	3.XII.49	25.XII
5. Deus tuorum militum	Common of One Martyr	17.XII.49	25–31.XII[a]
6. Crudelis Herodes	Epiphany	20.XII.49	6.I
7. Egregiae Doctor Paule	Conversion of St. Paul	18.I.50	25.I
8. Humanae salutis sator	Ascension	21.V.50	25.V.1650
9. Veni creator Spiritus	Pentecost	1650	5.VI.1650
10. Pange lingua	Corpus Christi	1650	16.VI.1650

Example 2. Dates of Composition and Feast Days for Hymns
by Ferdinand III in D–Lr, K.N. 28

a. Includes a verse marked "a Nativitate Domini e[t] totam octavam inclusive."

cal calendar.[50] Second, and more important for our purposes, Ferdinand set out to compose hymns that would be immediately useful; the date of composition recorded in the manuscript generally precedes by one to three weeks the date of the feast on which the hymn was to be sung.

The date of composition for "Ave maris stella" recorded in the Lüneburg manuscript is 18 November 1649. Given the emperor's compositional routine (works were generally completed within a few

---

[50]The feast days and dates are based on the calendar published in *Officia propria sanctorum cathedralis, ecclesia et totius diocesis Viennensis* (Vienna: M. Rickhes, 1632) and on a Gradual prepared for Ferdinand III by Georg Moser in 1651, Österreichische Nationalbibliothek (Vienna), cod. 15952.

weeks of the feast for which they were needed), only one Marian feast comes into question for the performance of "Ave maris stella": the Feast of the Immaculate Conception, which falls on 8 December, just under three weeks after the date of composition.[51]

It is one thing to know that Ferdinand created this hymn with the intention that it be performed for the first time on the Feast of the Immaculate Conception in 1649, a year in which that celebration was to assume special significance; it is quite another to show how his own devotion to the "Immaculata," a cornerstone of the *Pietas Austriaca*, is somehow encoded within the work itself. In order to explore this last level of musico-political signification, we need to begin with the hymn's text (example 3). Ferdinand chose to highlight one portion of the text to "Ave maris stella" by setting it in a musical style dramatically different from the remainder of the work. Most of "Ave maris stella" is set to a type of dancelike, triple-time music that had become quite conventional for portraying positive affects in sacred texts by the 1640s. These framing sections are indicated in example 3 by the sign C 3/1 (the seventeenth-century triple-time signature used in these portions of the piece.)

However, seven lines of text (shown in boldface), are set off starkly from the rest by being cast in a markedly different musical style. The lines abandon the characteristic dancelike, triple-meter music in favor of declamatory duple meter. Even more strikingly, they embody an abrupt shift in what the seventeenth century would have called cantus, roughly analogous to our key signature. (The change of cantus, marked by the appearance of a flat sign in the original, is likewise indicated by a flat in example 3.) The measures containing this abrupt change of musical style are shown in example 4. To modern ears, the change in cantus for the passage shown in example 4 resembles a shift from the key of G-major to G-minor. Such a change seems rather odd to twentieth-century sensibilities because of the connotations of sadness or lugubriousness that minor keys have acquired. In the seventeenth century, however, the introduction of a flat key signature (or in contemporary terms, a change to the flatsystem, or *cantus mollis*) often connoted softness, mildness, or piety.[52] Moreover,

---

[51]The text of "Ave maris stella" is a sort of multipurpose one. It is used regularly, not only on the Feast of the Immaculate Conception, but at a wide variety of Marian celebrations.

[52]See esp. Eric Chafe, *Monteverdi's Tonal Language* (New York: Schirmer Books, 1992).

$C_1^3\natural$

Ritornello
Ave maris stella,
Dei mater alma,
Atque semper Virgo,
Felix caeli porta.

Ritornello
Hail star of the sea,
God's loving mother,
And, though always a virgin,
The fertile gate of heaven.

Sumens illud Ave
Gabrielis ore,
Funda nos in pace,
Mutans Hevae nomen.

You who received that "Ave"
From Gabriel's lips,
Establish us in peace,
Reversing the name of "Eva."

Ritornello
Solve vincla reis,
Profer lumen caecis
Mala nostra pelle,
bona cuncta posce.

Ritornello
Loosen the chains of sin,
Bring light to the blind,
Drive away ills from us,
And ask for us all blessings.

Monstra te esse matrem:
Sumet per te preces,
Qui pro nobis natus,
Tulit esse tuus.

Show yourself to be a mother,
Let him receive our prayers through you,
Who was born for us,
Who deigned to be your Son.

$C\flat$

Ritornello
**Virgo singularis,
Inter omnes mitis,
Nos culpis solutos,
Mites fac et castos.**

Ritornello
**Peerless Virgin,
Gentle beyond all others,
Make us free from sins,
Spotless and mild.**

**Vitam praesta puram,
Iter para tutum:
Ut videntes Jesum,**

**Guarantee us a pure life,
Prepare a safe way,
That seeing Jesus**

$C_1^3\natural$

Semper collaetemur.

We may rejoice together forever.

Ritornello
Sit laus Deo Patri,
Summo Christo decus,
Spiritui Sancto,
Tribus honor unus.

Ritornello
Give praise to God the Father,
Give glory to Christ most high,
And to the Holy Spirit,
To the Three in One be equal honor.

Amen.

Amen.

Example 3. Ferdinand III, "Ave maris stella," Ratsbücherei (Lüneburg), K.N. 28.

Example 4. Ferdinand III, "Ave maris stella," measures 76–92.

one type of imagery associated with sudden shifts to "flat" music—pastoral imagery emphasizing what might be called mildness, sweetness, softness, or spotlessness—was also one of the main types of imagery used in connection with the Immaculate Conception in seventeenth-century painting, scriptural exegesis, and the Catholic liturgy itself.

Perhaps the most common source for such pastoral imagery was the Song of Songs, particularly those passages that were understood as allusions to Mary in her quality as the "Virgo tota pulcra."[53] To cite one of the most obvious examples, Song of Songs 4:7 was associated in scriptural exegesis with the "Immaculata" for quite obvious reasons. Its text runs "Tota pulchra es, et macula non est in te ("Thou art fair, my love; there is no spot in thee" [KJV]). These words turn up in the liturgies for the Feast of the Immaculate Conception no fewer than four times.[54]

We see the same confluence of symbols in a work by Giovanni Felice Sances. When Sances set the line "O quam pulchra es, et macula non est in te," he employed almost exactly those musical gestures used by Ferdinand III: a metrical shift, coupled with a sudden turn to the soft (*mollis*) sonorities of the flat system (example 5).

Since Ferdinand seems to have written "Ave maris stella" for the Feast of the Immaculate Conception in 1649, we can make a reasonable interpretation of the reading of the hymn's text that he had in mind. Clearly, Ferdinand seized upon the key images "castus" (pure or spotless), "mitis" (soft or mild), and "purus" (pure), setting them to flat (*mollis*) sonorities that suggested softness, gentleness, and piety. In original performance context, the strong emphasis on this portion of the text would have evoked more than just Mary's general purity and virginity. It would have emphasized musically—and thereby singled out for special attention, consideration, and devotion—an

---

[53]Suzanne Stratten, *The Immaculate Conception in Spanish Art* (Cambridge: Cambridge University Press, 1994), see esp. pp. 39–46, 60–66. On seventeenth-century exegesis of Canticle texts and its relationship to musical settings, see Robert Kendrick, "'Sonet vox tua in auribus meis': Song of Songs Exegesis and the Seventeenth-Century Motet," *Schütz Jahrbuch* 16 (1994): 87–98.

[54] This text is used as an antiphon at first and second Vespers, and at Matins; it is used also as the Alleluia verse at Mass. In addition, the Offertory for Mass on the vigil of the feast is drawn from Song of Songs 2:16, and the Communion comes from Song of Songs 6:9. Song of Songs texts also form the basis of portions of lessons four, five, seven, and eight at Matins, and the fifth antiphon at Lauds.

Example 5. Giovanni Felice Sances, "Ardet cor meum," measures 19–48.

attribute that the seventeenth century associated strongly with the Blessed Virgin in her quality as "Immaculata," namely, Mary the "Virgo, tota pulcra."

The palette of musico-political expression at the imperial court under Ferdinand III was rich indeed, ranging from broad features of music's presentation (e.g., the use of trumpets), to individual musical gestures (e.g., the *cantus mollis* section of Ferdinand's "Ave maris stella"). In order to understand how all of these elements coalesced, we might try to envision that first performance of "Ave maris stella" in 1649—perhaps given within sight of the newly erected Marien-säule. Such a performance would have been richly communicative. The hymn would doubtless have been performed by some of Ferdinand's finest Italian virtuosi, who encourage devotion to the Blessed Virgin while simultaneously proclaiming the grandeur, opulence, and noble taste of the House of Austria. The fact that Ferdinand himself had composed a work in honor of the Virgin confirms his own erudition and religiosity. What is more, the emperor's activity as a composer of sacred music provides a fundamentally anti-Machiavellian statement: religiosity and Christian virtue are not incompatible with political rule.[55] In addition, in accordance with the precepts of *musica politica*, the work's order and proportion mirror the structure of the absolutist state over which Ferdinand III rules. And the text of the hymn, and even its individual musical gestures, promote a catholic doctrine to which the entire dynasty is ardently devoted. In the context of seventeenth-century Vienna, therefore, this music also carries a distinctly anti-Protestant message.

Ferdinand III's setting of "Ave maris stella"—indeed, sacred music in general—was far more than a passing entertainment, or even a necessary adornment to the liturgy. Sacred music was capable of providing the eloquent embodiment of the entire ethos of court life under confessional absolutism.

---

[55]See Bireley, *The Counterreformation Prince*, passim (see n. 18 above), and Coreth, *Pietas Austriaca*, 9 (see n. 41 above).

𝔚hat 𝔇id 𝔅urckhardt's 𝔎enaissance 𝔖ound 𝔏ike?

Paul Walker

The first important cultural study of early modern Europe, Jacob Burck-hardt's *Die Kultur der Renaissance in Italien*, treats music in a brief, self-contained section near the end of the book and makes virtually no attempt to integrate it into the larger arguments that form the book's central thesis. In the intervening century and a quarter, music still finds itself something of an "outsider" in general cultural studies of the period. The following essay considers the reasons for music's marginalized status: the extent to which Burckhardt, even though he himself was musically very capable, could have encountered Renaissance music; the role played by performing institutions (especially the symphony orchestra and the opera) in determining which styles of classical music are most often heard; the relationship of music to general intellectual thinking; the performance emphasis of music education; and even recent theories about music as a separate "intelligence." In conclusion, suggestions are made for ways in which non–music specialists might approach the music of early modern Europe as well as speculation about the use of modern technology to integrate sound into our scholarly work.

WHEN JACOB BURCKHARDT, professor of history at the University of Basel, published his *Die Kultur der Renaissance in Italien* in 1860, his neighbor in nearby Zurich, Richard Wagner, had just completed the score for *Tristan und Isolde*. *Tristan* is perhaps the most "symphonic" opera that Wagner ever wrote, and its completion could be said to announce the beginning of the last and arguably the greatest golden age for the symphony orchestra, an age that added to the symphonies of Beethoven the great music dramas of Wagner, the tone poems of Richard Strauss, and the symphonies of Bruckner, Mahler, and Sibelius. In this light, it is not surprising that Burckhardt would have this to say about the music of the Italian Renaissance:

Höchst bezeichnend für die Renaissance und für Italien ist vor Allem die reiche Specialisierung des Orchesters, das Suchen nach neuen Instrumenten d.h. Klangarten, und—in engem Zusammenhang damit—das Virtuosenthum, d.h. das Eindringen des Individuellen im Verhältniß zu bestimmten Zweigen der Musik und zu bestimmten Instrumenten.[1]

[Extremely characteristic of the Renaissance and of Italy is the abundant specialization of the orchestra, the search for new instruments, i.e., types of sound, and—intimately connected with it—virtuosity, i.e, the incursion of the individual in relation to certain branches of music and to certain instruments.]

Burckhardt's book paints for the reader a rich, colorful picture of life in Renaissance Italy, but it is to a considerable extent a mute picture. Whereas significant buildings, classic paintings, and famous sculptures are skillfully woven into Burckhardt's text and serve to reinforce many of his principal arguments, his description of Renaissance music appears, compartmentalized, near the end of the book. There, after a passing reference to Palestrina and the predominance of Franco-Flemish musicians (no names given), the author devotes most of his seven brief paragraphs to sixteenth-century instruments and their players. Not a single piece of music is mentioned. He closes his remarks with this comment:

In einer Zeit da noch keine Oper den musicalischen Genius zu concentriren und zu monopolisieren angefangen hatte, darf man sich wohl dieses Treiben geistreich, vielartig und wunderbar eigenthümlich vorstellen. Eine andere Frage ist, wie weit wir noch an jener Tonwelt Theil hätten, wenn unser Ohr sie wieder vernähme.[2]

[At a time before opera had begun to concentrate and monopolize musical talent, one may imagine this [musical] activity as something ingenious, varied, and wonderfully original. It is another question how far we today could relate to that sound-world, if our ear were to hear it again.]

There certainly have been general histories of early modern Europe since Burckhardt's time, such as Thomas Munck's *Seventeenth-Century Europe*, that integrate music into their narrative and argu-

---

[1]Jacob Burckhardt, *Die Kultur der Renaissance in Italien*, 2d ed. (Leipzig: E. A. Seemann, 1869), 309–10. All translations are my own unless otherwise noted.
[2]Ibid., 312.

ments.[3] There have also been essays focused on music from a nonspecialist's perspective; for instance, Paul Oskar Kristeller's "Music and Learning in the Early Italian Renaissance," originally published in 1956.[4] Nevertheless, music still seems to lie outside the mainstream of early modern cultural studies. Not only do most authors of such general cultural studies, following Burckhardt's lead, continue to appear rather more comfortable with literature, art, and architecture than with music, but musicology itself has a reputation as a discipline somewhat "apart" from its intellectual neighbors. I wish first to consider possible reasons behind the current relationship between music, musicology, and early modern German studies; then I should like to offer a few modest suggestions toward the goal of helping each other attain a better, more complete understanding of our subject, early modern German culture.

Jacob Burckhardt clearly loved art history. In an admiring biography published a few years after Burckhardt's death, a former student, Hans Trog, described several ways in which his teacher's enthusiasm for older art manifested itself. For instance,

> Burckhardt sprach von diesen kunsthistorischen Vorträgen, die mit einer immer größer werdenden Fülle von Abbildungen den Hörer überschütteten, in höchst bescheidener Weise: sein Zweck sei nicht gewesen, Kunsthistoriker heranzubilden—welcher Gedanke ihm ein wahrer Abscheu war—, sondern seinen Hörern eine Anleitung und Orientierung zu geben für Reisen oder Galeriebesuche; nur zum Kunstgenuß anzuregen, war sein Ziel, nicht ein spezielles Kunstwissen mitzuteilen.[5]

> [Burckhardt spoke of these art history lectures, which overwhelmed the listener with an ever greater abundance of pictures, in most modest fashion: It was not his goal, he said, to train art historians—a thought that was truly loathsome to him—but to give his listeners an introduction and orientation for travels or gallery visits. His stated purpose was simply to instill an enjoyment of art, not to impart a specialized knowledge of art.]

---

[3]Thomas Munck, *Seventeenth-Century Europe: State, Conflict, and the Social Order in Europe 1598–1700* (New York: St. Martin's Press, 1990).

[4]Paul Oskar Kristeller, "Music and Learning in the Early Italian Renaissance," in *Renaissance Thought and the Arts: Collected Essays* (Princeton: Princeton University Press, 1990), 142–62.

[5]Hans Trog, *Jakob Burckhardt: Eine biographische Skizze* (Basel: R. Reich, 1898), 139.

In another passage, Trog paints a moving portrait of Burckhardt's love for the works of Raphael:

> Wer Burckhardt über Raphael hat sprechen hören, weiß, was wir meinen: man muß ihn gesehen haben, wenn er das Portrait eines Julius II. oder die Sixtinische Madonna vorwies; da übernahm ihn im eigentlichen Sinne des Wortes die Bewegung, und der seltene Fall trat ein, daß der Ausdruck für die tiefe Empfindung versagte.[6]

> [Whoever has heard Burckhardt speak about Raphael knows what we mean: one has to have seen him when he showed the portrait of Julius II or the Sistine Madonna; he was at that moment overtaken by emotion in the true sense of the word, and the rare instance occurred that words to express his deep feelings failed him.]

One reads page after page of Trog's biography, however, without finding a single significant reference to music: Burckhardt's many trips to Rome come and go without a word of any attempt to hear the Sistine Chapel choir, famous since the sixteenth century for its performances of Palestrina; Burckhardt's lectures are described in loving detail but with no indication that music played the slightest role; even mention of Heinrich Glarean, the sixteenth-century music theorist who lived in Basel, passes without any indication that Burckhardt ever entertained an interest in the most important musical figure of his hometown. Finally, a few pages from the end, Trog surprises us with a paragraph describing his teacher's passionate love of music. Here is how Trog puts it:

> Eine lichtere, sonnigere Welt fand Burckhardt auf dem ihm ganz besonders lieben Gebiet der Musik. Er war durch und durch musikalisch, spielte selbst Klavier und sang schön. Viele Abendstunden hat er am Klavier zugebracht, denn gearbeitet hat Burckhardt niemals in die Nacht hinein.... Seine musikalischen Lieblinge waren die eigentlichen Klassiker, namentlich Mozart, und die Italiener, die er aufs genaueste kannte.... Bei italienischen Opern oder Mozartstücken konnte man fast sicher sein, ihn zu treffen.... Selbst der musikalischen Theorie war Burckhardt in hohem Grade mächtig, und er konnte etwa seine kunsthistorischen Vorträge mit prachtvollen Vergleichen aus der Welt des musikalischen Schaffens schmücken. Wagner fand bei ihm wenig Gnade; ... Beethoven war ihm schon fast zu herb, Mozart war sein musikalischer Raphael.[7]

[6]Ibid., 138.
[7]Ibid., 150–51.

What did Burckhardt's Renaissance Sound Like?

[A brighter, sunnier world was for Burckhardt the realm of music, which he particularly loved. He was musical through and through, played the piano and sang beautifully. He spent many evening hours at the piano, for he never worked into the night.... His musical favorites were the true classics, namely, Mozart and the Italians, which he knew down to the last detail.... One could be almost certain to encounter him at performances of Italian opera or Mozart pieces.... Burckhardt was even to a high degree knowledgable about music theory, and he was able to embellish his art history lectures with marvelous comparisons from the world of musical creativity. He did not have high regard for Wagner; ... Beethoven was already almost too harsh for him; Mozart was his musical Raphael.]

When I quoted this last sentence recently to an art history graduate student at the University of Virginia who is specializing in Italian Renaissance art and who also happens to be a very fine singer of Monteverdi, she was incredulous. How could anyone lump Mozart and Raphael together in this kind of metaphor? Why would anyone so enamored of the Italian Renaissance not also be enamored of its music?

But let us ask ourselves the question in a somewhat different way. What was it possible for Jacob Burckhardt in 1860 to know about music before Mozart and Haydn? The answer is not too difficult to imagine if we perform a little thought experiment. Suppose you live in New York City in the late twentieth century and have season tickets to the Metropolitan Opera, the New York Philharmonic, and Carnegie Hall. Suppose further that sound recordings do not exist. If we then ask how much music written before, say, 1700 you will hear, the answer must be, "Almost none." Yet you could go across town to the Metropolitan Museum of Art and see many first-rate examples of medieval and Renaissance painting and sculpture. Why is this so?

The reasons are many. One of the most important, it seems to me, must be the symphony orchestra itself: that large, many-faceted ensemble of 40 to 120 musicians all playing as one. The orchestra in its modern sense did not exist before the middle of the eighteenth century, and its precursors can be traced back barely another century and a half before that. Likewise the piano, that ubiquitous parlor instrument of the pre-sound-recording age, was invented only in the first half of the eighteenth century. Now, it is the nature of performing ensembles that they first arise in order to perform a particular repertoire (say, the Beethoven symphonic works) and then continue to seek out music that fits their makeup. Naturally, then, any musical culture in which the symphony orchestra and the piano occupy such central positions will be a culture that focuses on music since 1700.

By contrast, the basis of Renaissance and early Baroque music was vocal, and its venue was the church and the private chamber, not the concert hall. It may surprise a modern classical music lover, for instance, to learn that a great many of the best composers of that time, including Josquin des Prez, Palestrina, Victoria, Tallis, Monteverdi, and Schütz, wrote no or almost no music at all for instruments without voices. The ensemble best suited to the works of these composers is therefore the small chamber choir or the small group of soloists more interested in ensemble singing than in solo singing. This is not to say that a group like the Charlottesville-Albemarle Oratorio Society, with its hundred-member chorus, could not perform these pieces. But whereas the earlier style cries out for clean lines and excellent tuning, in order to supply the proper give and take between bright, ringing consonances and sharp, biting dissonances, the later style wants power and the contrasts of volume and tone color that a large chorus and orchestra provide so well. A singer who has joined the ensemble in order to experience the latter will frequently find the former to be by contrast rather dull and colorless.

For those of musical inclination who lived during that second great age of western self-confidence, the nineteenth century, the symphony orchestra and the piano—and the musical styles that came with them—had brought music to a zenith against which all previous musics could not possibly measure up. As James Harr has written in "Music of the Renaissance as Viewed by the Romantics," this age saw the first modern attempts at the scholarly study of historical music, but of the music itself only the sacred works of Palestrina were at all well known.[8] To those of a neo-Gothic bent, the Renaissance was, first and last, the great age of unadulterated, pure church music; E. T. A. Hoffmann described the music of Palestrina as "simple, true, childlike, pious, strong and powerful"; strong and powerful, in other words, because of its childlike simplicity.[9] Not only is this a very one-

---

[8]James Haar, "Music of the Renaissance as Viewed by the Romantics," in *Music and Context: Essays for John M. Ward*, ed. Anne Dhu Shapiro (Cambridge, Mass.: Harvard University Department of Music, 1985), 126–44.

[9]"Palestrina ist einfach, wahrhaft, kindlich, fromm, stark und mächtig—echt-christlich in seinen Werken, wie in der Malerei *Pietro von Cortona* und unser alter *Dürer*

dimensional view of sixteenth-century music, but it is also quite at odds with Burckhardt's characterization of Renaissance Italy as a time of strong personalities and rampant individualism.

The view of music before the eighteenth century as something inferior and even primitive still survives in many of our music conservatories and can even be encountered in general cultural histories. Here, for instance, is a professor of history at Oxford writing in 1970 in a book on seventeenth-century Europe:

> The painter, the sculptor, and even for most purposes the architect had in 1600 materials that were as good as any available today. This was not true of the musician. There could not have been a musical equivalent of St. Peter's because the instruments that existed were incapable of the range and richness of sound it would demand. The lute and viol, the virginals and clavichord, imposed severe limitations on the composer. It was in the course of the seventeenth century that the essentials of the modern orchestra appeared. The violin evolved slowly into the form produced by Nicolo Amati and his apprentice Antonio Stradivari. The oboe now gave more quantity than quality of sound; but the introduction from about 1690 of the clarinet made possible the successful combination of strings and woodwind.[10]

But music's place in our modern scholarly dialogue is determined by much more than simply the centrality of the symphony orchestra. One such factor must certainly be that musical sounds were not capturable or preservable over time until the invention of tape recording in the twentieth century. Although its colors may be yellowed or faded with age, Van Eyck's Ghent altarpiece still stands in St. Bavo's Church, and a twentieth-century person can still walk up to it and see the very angel musicians that Van Eyck painted. That person cannot, however, hear Bach play his Goldberg Variations. One can look at a Bach autograph score, of course, but, as the German words *Noten* and *Musik* illustrate so nicely, musical notation is not music. And because performers have over time adapted their manners of performance as

---

...," E. T. A. Hoffmann, *Schriften zur Musik: Nachlese* (Munich: Winkler Verlag, 1963), 216 (italics original). The original article from which this quote is taken is "Alte und neue Kirchenmusik," *Allgemeine Musikalische Zeitung* 16 (September 1814). The translation is by Lewis Lockwood in his edition of Palestrina's *Pope Marcellus Mass* (New York: W. W. Norton, 1975), 135.

[10]D. H. Pennington, *Seventeenth-Century Europe* (Essex: Longman, 1970), 171.

well as their instruments and styles of vocal production in order to keep up with the changing times, older pieces and styles have either been performed in "updated" manner or dropped from the repertory altogether. Considerably more stands between Josquin des Prez and a twentieth-century listener, in other words, than between Van Eyck and a modern viewer.

Nor has music instruction been particularly friendly to the aims of its integration into the scholarly dialogue. The emphasis in this country, from the local public school to the prestigious conservatory, has always been on performing. In fact, participation in band, orchestra, or choir is often the only musical encounter most individuals ever have, and it reflects what most laymen think the study of music is. Anyone announcing the intention to major in music at, say, Indiana University (to name one of our most famous music departments) can expect to be asked, "And what will you be studying? Voice? Piano? Organ?"

Musicologists are also acutely aware that their discipline is much younger, and even today faces much more spadework, than most of its sister disciplines. When I chat with my colleagues in English literature, for instance, I marvel at the existence of bibliographies of bibliographies for virtually any significant figure, and I have watched graduate students in English agonize over the struggle to carve out a small corner of unexplored turf for their own. By contrast, my wife and I recently published a checklist of German sacred music between 1650 and 1700, which we compiled for the simple reason that I wanted to study this repertoire and found it to be under virtually no bibliographic control at all.[11] The seventeenth century, that rich, experimental time between the perfection of Palestrina and Lassus and the mastery of Bach and Handel, remains filled with unedited, untranslated music treatises and collections of music by significant composers that have never even been scored out for our examination. Research in music can be, as a result of these various factors, discouragingly intimidating to the uninitiated.

Taken together, the emphasis on performance and the relatively young tradition of musical scholarship have produced a field of musicologists most of whom started out as performers, and whose training

---

[11]Diane Parr Walker and Paul Walker, *German Sacred Polyphonic Vocal Music between Schütz and Bach: Sources and Critical Editions* (Warren, Mich.: Harmonie Park Press, 1992).

is probably much stronger in music than in the other liberal arts. In fact, many may be drawn to music *because* it is "its own thing." In his widely cited book *Frames of Mind*, the Harvard sociologist Howard Gardner concludes that intelligence is not a single, monolithic thing, but that each human being possesses many different "intelligences."[12] Gardner identifies seven, including verbal, logical-mathematical, spatial, and musical. Musicians, it turns out, *do* pursue something that works according to its own laws, and human beings *do* have varying innate, inborn levels of musical ability and sensitivity. It is no wonder, then, that music has tended to develop its own vocabulary and that its concepts, such as counterpoint and tonal harmony, do not easily relate to other manifestations of the human experience.

All of this talk of music's autonomy leads us to a related question: Did music in fact contribute to the thinking of early modern Europeans about their world? Has it, in other words, failed to insinuate itself into our modern cultural studies because it was also thought of as "its own thing" by persons of the time? In a recent book on the rise of the musical canon in eighteenth-century England, William Weber suggests that such may have been the case:

> Music had [in earlier times] a status within intellectual life that was quite inferior to that of poetry, sculpture, or even the drama.... Musicians had their own learned tradition, a process of writing in strict polyphonic styles, but it had few links with the wider intellectual life.[13]

In this context it is interesting to read the following description of Haydn and Mozart given by a contemporary woman of letters named Karoline Pichler:

> Mozart und Haydn, die ich wohl kannte, waren Menschen, in deren persönlichem Umgange sich durchaus keine andere hervorragende Geisteskraft und beinahe keinerlei Art von Geistesbildung, von wissenschaftlicher oder höherer Richtung zeigte. Alltägliche Sinnesart, platte Scherze, und bei dem ersten ein leichtsinniges Leben, war alles, wodurch sie sich im Umgange kundgaben, und welche Tiefen, welche Welten von Fantasie, Harmonie, Melodie und Gefühl lagen doch in dieser unscheinbaren Hülle verborgen!

[12]Howard Gardner, *Frames of Mind: The Theory of Multiple Intelligences*, reprinted with new introduction (New York: BasicBooks, 1993).

[13]William Weber, *The Rise of Musical Classics in Eighteenth-Century England* (Oxford: Clarendon Press, 1992), 2.

[Mozart and Haydn, whom I knew well, were men in whose personal intercourse there was absolutely no other sign of unusual power of intellect and almost no trace of intellectual culture, nor of any scholarly or other higher interests. A rather ordinary turn of mind, silly jokes and, in the case of the former [Mozart], an irresponsible way of life, were all that distinguished them in society; and yet what depths, what worlds of fantasy, harmony, melody, and feeling lay concealed behind this unpromising exterior.][14]

A similar disjunction between music and intellectual pursuits may be perceived in the thinking of my good neighbor in Charlottesville, Thomas Jefferson. Jefferson called music "the passion of my soul," played the violin, made sure that his daughters learned keyboard, and systematically collected music manuscripts and prints. When it came time for him to donate his library to Washington, D.C., to form the basis for the present Library of Congress, however, his collection of notated music was not included and is now mostly lost. And whereas today Jefferson's University of Virginia boasts one of the finest professional schools of architecture in the country, it still lacks a doctoral degree in any aspect of musical study or training.

Whether by the second half of the eighteenth century music had "few links with the wider intellectual life," as Mr. Weber puts it, is an issue I do not intend to debate, but evidence strongly suggests, as I read it, that such a divorce was rather less characteristic of the sixteenth and seventeenth centuries. Of course, one must admit from the outset that musicians of the Renaissance found themselves in the uncomfortable position of having not a scrap of music from ancient Greece and Rome on which to build any sort of rebirth. And the training that is needed to become a musical creator (i.e., a composer or improvisor) has always been highly technical and specialized. Nevertheless, humanism and its emphasis on rhetoric and persuasion played perhaps the decisive role in the creation of the High Renaissance style of Josquin des Prez and his contemporaries, as they began to take great care to provide music that both *declaimed* the text correctly and clearly and *expressed* the text as effectively and beautifully as possible. Certainly, the musical developments that took place

[14]Quoted from Karoline Pichler's "Errinnerungen" (Vienna 1843–44) in *Mozart: Die Dokumente seines Lebens*, ed. Otto Erich Deutsch, *Neue Ausgabe sämtlicher Werke*, series X, vol. 34 (Kassel: Bärenreiter, 1961), 473. The translation is taken from Otto Erich Deutsch, *Mozart: A Documentary Biography*, trans. Eric Blom, Peter Branscombe, and Jeremy Noble (Stanford: Stanford University Press, 1965), 557.

in Italy during the decades before and after 1600, especially in the genres of madrigal and opera, are inconceivable without the revival of Greek *ideals* (if not the particulars) concerning music's expressive and dramatic potential. It also occurs to me to wonder whether our post-Enlightenment focus on secular intellectual culture blinds us to music's significant role in theology and the religious culture of the early modern era. Music had been from the beginning a key element in Christian liturgy, and its importance, if anything, increased during the age of Reformation and denominational factionalism: Luther admired the works of Josquin des Prez and gave music a defining role in Lutheran liturgy and education; Calvin was suspicious of its entertainment value and banned nearly all of it from his religious experience; the Council of Trent weighed its role at length; the Venetians blurred the divisions between sacred and secular and performed ostensibly liturgical pieces for principally nonliturgical occasions; the Anglicans admired it so much that they allowed the first great composer of liturgical music in the English language, William Byrd, to remain Catholic.

In the spirit of interdisciplinary cooperation sought by this organization and this conference, I would like to close with a few remarks that I hope will remove at least a bit of the mystique and vaguely exotic air surrounding pre-Bach music and that will embolden the timid to engage it.

First of all, music of this era was, as I have already noted, predominantly vocal, and both Renaissance and Baroque musicians were very much of the humanist times in their insistence that the purpose of music should be to express its text. This contrasts markedly with the later "common-practice" style of Mozart and Beethoven, which, because it is to a large extent independent of words, relies much more on purely musical phenomena, in particular on tonal harmony. Nonspecialists should also know that our music teaching, like our concert programming, is heavily weighted toward this later style. They may be surprised to learn that the musicological community is still unsure how to evaluate the older style systematically and that practitioners of the sister discipline of Music Theory seldom consider it at all. In short, anyone with at least some understanding of consonance and dissonance has the preparation needed to engage the text of a piece of music and to grapple with the composer's attempt to convey that text to the listener.

Paul Walker

Second, the only way for Burckhardt to experience Renaissance music was by looking at it on the page; in other words, he could examine the *Noten*, but his opportunities to hear the *Musik* were few. In fact, in 1860 most of it lay only in partbooks and had not even been scored out to assist the scholar in gaining a sense of the whole piece and how the parts went together. Today, by contrast, one can buy recordings or attend concerts of this music performed by musicians who specialize in it. For about the last hundred years, and with increasingly greater activity since World War II, a number of musicians have undertaken to learn what can be known about the performance of earlier music. As it turns out, a fair amount can be learned. Furthermore, western musical notation has grown more detailed and prescriptive over the centuries, which is to say that there is often more to earlier music than one sees on the page. Listening will probably never completely replace examination of the score for a thoroughgoing scholarly investigation, and yet it certainly allows the nonspecialist access to music that would otherwise be a closed book. Included with this article is a discography of music from the fifteenth through the seventeenth century; it is highly selective and reflects very much my own taste in performances.

(Two asides: Liner notes to recordings, once the butt of music teachers' jokes, can today often provide better and more up-to-date sources of musicological information than articles and books. And nonspecialists may be surprised, and pleased, to learn that it is today, for various reasons, sometimes easier to find recordings than scores of earlier compositions.)

Finally, present developments in computer technology now enable us to include sound in an article or book. The Society for 17th-Century Music has recently "published" the first issue of an electronic journal that can include both visual and aural illustrative material.[15] It has always seemed to me a disadvantage to the scholar of music that pictures could easily be incorporated into a book but that only through notated examples (undecipherable by much of the general public) could music be so incorporated. The day is already upon us when technology can facilitate the true integration of music into our exploration of early modern culture. Let's all rediscover together what the Germany of Luther, Dürer, and Maximilian I sounded like.

[15]The journal can be accessed at http://www.smscm.harvard.edu/jscm/.

APPENDIX
SELECTIVE LIST OF RECORDINGS OF THE MUSIC OF EARLY MODERN EUROPE, WITH EMPHASIS ON GERMANY

THE INTERNATIONAL STYLE OF FRANCO-FLEMISH POLYPHONY IN THE 15TH AND 16TH CENTURIES

1. Many, many recordings.

2. Composers:
   Guillaume Dufay, Johannes Ockeghem, Josquin des Prez, Adrian Willaert, Jacobus Clemens non Papa, Heinrich Isaac, Roland de Lassus, G. P. da Palestrina, T. L. da Victoria; also the English John Taverner, Thomas Tallis, William Byrd, Orlando Gibbons

3. Performing ensembles:
   sacred repertoire: The Tallis Scholars, The Sixteen, The Hilliard Ensemble, various English and American cathedral choirs
   secular repertoire: The Medieval Consort of London, The Hilliard Ensemble, The King's Singers

ITALIAN MUSIC 1550–1650

1. Venice of the Gabrielis
   A Venetian Coronation 1595, performed by Gabrieli Consort, Paul McCreesh (Virgin Classics, 1990)
   Giovanni Gabrieli, Canzonas, Sonatas, Motets, performed by Taverner Consort, Andrew Parrott (EMI, 1991)
   Giovanni Gabrieli, Symphoniae Sacrae II, 1615, Selections, performed by A. Parrott (L'Oiseau-Lyre, 1978)

2. Monteverdi
   Madrigals (all performed by The Consort of Musicke)
   Book II (Virgin Classics, 1993)
   Book III (Virgin Classics, 1993)
   Book IV (L'Oiseau-Lyre, 1986)
   Book V (L'Oiseau-Lyre, 1984)
   Book VI (Virgin Classics, 1990)
   Book VIII: Madrigali Amorosi (Virgin Classics, 1991)
   Book VIII: Madrigali Guerrieri (Virgin Classics, 1991)

221

Book VIII: Balli (Virgin Classics, 1990)
Madrigali erotici (many from Book VII) (L'Oiseau-Lyre, 1982)

3. Operas

Orfeo, performed by Chiaroscuro & London Baroque, Nigel Rogers (EMI, 1984)
L'Incoronazione di Poppea, performed by concerto Vocale, René Jacobs (Harmonia Mundi France, 1990)

4. Sacred Works

Vespro della Beata Virgine [1610], performed by Kammerchor Stuttgart, Frieder Bernius (Deutsche Harmonia Mundi, 1989)
Festive Music in San Marco, performed by Frieder Bernius (FSM Adagio, 1991)
Mass of Thanksgiving 1631, performed by Taverner Consort, Andrew Parrott (EMI, 1989)
Venetian Vespers, performed by Paul McCreesh (Deutsche Gramaphon Archiv, 1993)

5. Carissimi

Jephte, Jonas, Judicium Extremum, performed by Monteverdi Choir, John Eliot Gardiner (Erato, 1990)

6. Instrumental

Early Italian Violin Music, performed by Musica Antiqua Köln (Deutsche Gramaphon Archiv, 1979)
Venetian Music at the Habsburg Court, performed by Musica Fiata (Deutsche Harmonia Mundi, 1991)

GERMAN, 1600–1650

1. Praetorius

Lutheran Mass for Christmas Morning, Paul McCreesh (Deutsche Gramaphon Archiv, 1994)

2. Schütz

Psalmen Davids, performed by Frieder Bernius (Sony, 1992)
Symphoniae Sacrae I, performed by Concerto Palatino (Accent, 1991)
Symphoniae Sacrae II, performed by E. Kirkby and Purcell Quartet (Chandos Chaconne, 1994)
Symphoniae Sacrae III, performed by Frieder Bernius (Deutsche Harmonia Mundi, 1989)
Musicalische Exequien, performed by John Eliot Gardiner (Deutsche Gramaphon Archiv, 1988)
Christmas and Easter Stories, performed by Frieder Bernius (Sony, 1990)
Matthäuspassion, performed by Hilliard Ensemble (EMI, 1984)

3. J. H. Schein

Diletti pastorali (secular vocal), performed by Cantus Cölln (Deutsche Harmonia Mundi, 1989)

Opella Nova II, performed by Musica Fiata (Deutsche Harmonia Mundi, 1990)

4. Organ Music

Die Norddeutsche Orgelkunst I, performed by Harald Vogel (Organa, 1982)

Das goldene Zeitalter der Norddeutschen Orgelkunst, Harald Vogel (Organa, 1985)

GERMAN, 1650–1700

1. Buxtehude

Cantatas

Membra Jesu Nostri, performed by Ton Koopman (Erato, 1988)

Cantatas, performed by Ton Koopman (Erato, 1988)

Organ works: Organ Works (7 vols.), Harald Vogel (Dabringhaus und Grimm, 1987–1993)

Chamber Music: Trio Sonatas, performed by Trio Sonnerie (Academy Sound and Vision, 1989)

2. Bach Family

The Bach Family Before Johann Sebastian: The Cantatas, performed by Musica Antiqua Köln (Deutsche Gramaphon Archiv, 1986)

Motets of the Bach Family, performed by Collegium Vocale Gent, Philippe Herreweghe (Ricercar, 1982)

17TH-CENTURY GERMANY IN GENERAL

1. Vocal

Deutsche Barock Kantaten (9 vols. to date), Ricercar Consort (Ricercar, ca. 1987–)

De Profundis (sacred vocal), performed by Musica Antiqua Köln (Deutsche Gramaphon Archiv, 1986)

2. Instrumental

Deutsche Barock Kammermusik (5 vols. to date), Ricercar Consort (Ricercar, ca. 1989–)

Deutsche Kammermusik vor Bach, performed by Musica Antiqua Köln (Deutsche Gramaphon Archiv, 1981)

Orpheus Lulling the wild Beasts
by Hans Ulrich Pilgrim (Hans Wechtlin)

Germany's Blind Renaissance

Christopher S. Wood

The German Renaissance was notoriously inattentive to the "look" of antiquity. But this blindness has actually been celebrated as the distinctive feature of German art, and not only by art historians with nationalist or irrationalist leanings. A wide variety of philosophers, critical theorists, and art historians have stressed the incommensurability of an anti-optical or "tactile" visuality with the representational models installed by the Italian Renaissance. But the historiographical preoccupation with the opacity of the German image has led to a disciplinary preference for those artifacts that seem to point forward to the modern work of art. "Memorial" artifacts, short on meaning and long on reference to real people and places—for example portraits or tombs—have been comparatively neglected. It may turn out, however, that the fine discriminations made by those antiquarians who deciphered antique inscriptions and designed modern memorials were not so different from the discriminations made by the proto-aesthete. In other words, the antiquarian's striving toward ideal transparency was a symptom of the same uneasiness with vision that produced the strange-looking German paintings.

THE GERMAN RENAISSANCE WAS PERVERSELY INDIFFERENT to the way ancient works of art looked. The encounter between the German sixteenth century and antiquity was played out on the field of the word, in textual criticism, epigraphy, or compilations of historical material. Symptomatic is the case of Conrad Peutinger of Augsburg, the imperial advisor with a large collection of antiquities. Peutinger's curiosity yielded a true novelty: his *Romanae vetustatis fragmenta* of 1505, which is the first published sylloge, or anthology of ancient inscriptions based on original research. Yet Peutinger never seemed to have much to say about how his coins or objets d'art looked. And the artists close to him, like Hans Burgkmair and even Albrecht Dürer, made

Christopher S. Wood

scant use of the collection.[1] Antiquity had no characteristic face, no "look," even for the learned. The German Renaissance was, apparently, a blind Renaissance.

All this is distressing to some art historians, since the reintegration of antique content with antique form is believed to be an indispensable attribute of an authentic Renaissance.[2] The early modern German artist often seems mistrustful of vision, as if vision were a mere prosthesis for the sense of touch. The German artist generally did not share the ambitions of artists elsewhere in Europe to reproduce optical experience—either through projective geometry as in Florence, or through impressions of color and atmosphere as in Venice, or through scrupulous descriptions of the surfaces of things as in the Netherlands. The German artist seemed to want to close the gap between eye and object and to produce an image that represented not the results of vision, but the results of a kind of optical palpating of the world. This paradoxical effort to see with the hands, or with the body, has in fact been prized by many art historians as the distinctive attribute of German art.

For example, the Viennese art historian Otto Pächt, in an essay on the characteristic German *Bildauffassung* or "concept of the image" of the late Gothic and Renaissance periods, describes a pictorial space generated by an active, creative gaze, a gaze that swerves and pokes about, shifting position from side to side and back to front.[3] Space in the German painting is seen from more than one point of view at the same time. Space is not projected plausibly onto the picture plane but rather shaped to produce eloquent rhymes with the picture's content and strange psychosomatic effects. Konrad Witz's allegorical image of *Synagogue,* from his Speculum altar in Basel of about 1435, is pressed down, defeated, by the angle of the doorway, bending in unison with the broken banner (fig. 1). The German painting tries to recreate the experience of space, the entry of the body into space, the constant

[1]Max Hauttmann, "Dürer und der Augsburger Antikenbesitz," *Jahrbuch der preussischen Kunstsammlungen* 42 (1921): 34–50; Erwin Panofsky, "Albrecht Dürer and Classical Antiquity," in *Meaning in the Visual Arts* (Garden City, N.Y.: Doubleday, 1955), 236–94. But see Tilman Falk, *Hans Burgkmair: Studien zu Leben und Werk des Augsburger Malers* (Munich: Bruckmann, 1968), on Burgkmair's close association with Peutinger.

[2]For example, Erwin Panofsky, *Renaissance and Renascences in Western Art* (New York: Harper, 1969).

[3]Otto Pächt, "Zur deutschen Bildauffassung der Spätgotik und Renaissance," in *Methodisches zur kunsthistorischen Praxis* (Munich: Prestel, 1977), 107–20.

Fig. 1. Konrad Witz, *Synagogue,* ca. 1435, Basel, Kunstmuseum.
Used by permission.

shifting of the relationship between the body of the subject and the surrounding bodies.

Pächt derived his notion of a "tactile" vision that would somehow verify the shimmering, shifting phantasms served up by the eye from the work of Alois Riegl, the great art historian of turn-of-the-century Vienna. But any number of German and Austrian art historians, aestheticians, and perceptual psychologists of the later nine-

Christopher S. Wood

teenth century were deeply interested in the relationship between touch and vision.[4] Very often this sort of thinking got correlated with nationalist and racist views in unscholarly and repugnant ways. The German artist's lack of detachment from the world, his tendency to in effect pounce bodily upon things, seemed to imply his sincerity and spirituality. For what things meant to the recipient subject, what effects they worked on the soul, was surely more important than merely how they looked. Thus the blindness of the German artist was seen as a prized relic of a premodern consciousness, a mind that observed no debilitating split between itself and the cosmos, a mind that refused the false consolation of a detached and artificially fixed point of view. The taste for tactility permeated the writings of many early-twentieth-century art historians. For example, Wilhelm Worringer, a kind of vulgarizer of Riegl who made a sensation in 1908 with his dissertation, an ingenious meditation on art and nature called *Abstraction and Empathy*; or Fritz Burger, a painter, a brilliant critic, and a prolific art historian, a pioneering exegete of modern painting, a kind of German Roger Fry; or Wilhelm Pinder, a reactionary and rather diabolical figure, an insightful reader of form, a synthesizer in a Spenglerian spirit, and a very effective popular writer. The books of Worringer, Burger, and Pinder had a real influence on artists, critics, younger German scholars, and the general educated readership.[5]

This was a powerful interpretive model, and even the young Erwin Panofsky was vulnerable to it. In his book on German medieval sculpture, or his early essay on Albrecht Dürer and antiquity, Panofsky was not shy about characterizing the "Germanness" of German art. He later recovered German art for the side of enlightenment through his monograph on Dürer, the synthesizing figure who tamed his native obscurantist impulses through his study of perspective, proportion, and classical iconography.[6] For Aby Warburg, meanwhile, this failure of the early modern German mind to take its distance from the world, to open up a measured gap between subject and

[4]Michael Podro, *The Critical Historians of Art* (New Haven: Yale University Press, 1982); Harry Francis Mallgrave and Eleftherios Ikonomou, eds., *Empathy, Form, and Space: Problems in German Aesthetics, 1873–1893* (Malibu: The Getty Center, 1994).

[5]Udo Kultermann, *The History of Art History* (New York: Abaris, 1993), esp. chap. 18.

[6]Erwin Panofsky, *Die Deutsche Plastik des 11. bis 13. Jahrhunderts* (Munich: Wolff, 1924); idem, "Dürer and Classical Antiquity" (see n. 1 above); idem, *The Life and Work of Albrecht Dürer* (Princeton: Princeton University Press, 1943).

object, this lack of perspective or *Denkraum,* was from the start an alarming symptom of irrationalism and fatalism, associated with the Orient and illiberalism. Warburg saw his own scholarly project as an extension of the original philological and archeological project initiated by the humanist scholars of the Renaissance.[7]

It could be argued that a certain anti-optical and nationalist current survived in writing on German art until as late as the 1970s in the works of art historians born early in the twentieth century, such as Alfred Stange or Franz Winzinger. But by and large, the Second World War dispelled this sort of rhetoric. After the war the dominant art historical models were associated with Heinrich Wölfflin and Panofsky, who were neo-Kantians and had nothing to fear from opticality, and with Warburg. The result was that for quite a long time academic art history, suspicious of tactility and experiential encounters with images, did not so much reconsider early German art as leave it alone.

But recently there has been a resurgence in creative scholarship on German art. And somehow, even in this country, the old anti-optical model has not really been abandoned. What scholarship does now is historicize the anti-optical mode by connecting it to real social circumstances and by explicating the choices cultures have made in adopting one mode over another. Indeed, paradoxically, the anti-optical mode turns out to be the key to everything that is "Renaissance" about German Renaissance art. What emerges is a kind of Renaissance in spite of itself. I am thinking here of Michael Baxandall's already classic book on German Renaissance wood carving, Bernhard Decker's imaginative monograph on Hans Leinberger, and Joseph Koerner's wide-ranging study of the German artist's self-representation.[8] Such scholarship has suggested how the German nonparticipation in the international project of optical painting was related to the idea of the stylish flourish as a direct trace of the author, an idea itself rooted in craft traditions; or to the German extreme inven-

[7]Ernst Gombrich, *Aby Warburg: An Intellectual Biography* (London: Warburg Institute, 1970); the study by Silvia Ferretti, *Cassirer, Panofsky, and Warburg* (New Haven: Yale University Press, 1989), is outstanding.

[8]Michael Baxandall, *The Limewood Sculptors of Renaissance Germany* (New Haven: Yale University Press, 1980); Bernhard Decker, *Das Ende des mittelalterlichen Kultbildes und die Plastik Hans Leinbergers* (Bamberg: Universität Bamberg, 1985); Joseph Leo Koerner, *The Moment of Self-Portraiture in German Renaissance Art* (Chicago: University of Chicago Press, 1993).

Christopher S. Wood

tiveness in narrative strategies; or to the persistence and prestige of the altarpiece, with its theatrical stagings of cultic presence, and symbolically remembered function as repository of relics; or, conspicuously, to the Protestant reformers' mistrust of the religious image, rooted in part in the fear that the visual data would provoke responses that exceeded the didactic brief that theology had given it. The blindness of German art, in other words, is still its source of interest and appeal.

This approach to the problem of the blindness of the German Renaissance is good historicism; but it is not only good historicism. If the German Renaissance artist was unwilling to offer up a lucid view of the world, or to organize the data of sense into clear contrasts between figure and ground, or to distinguish decisively within the framed picture between center and margin, then in a sense the German Renaissance foreshadows the pictorial preoccupations and achievements of Modernism. Certainly it is the overwrought tension between the center and the periphery of the image, the disruptive urge to break the continuous contour, the attraction to and fear of the excessive and the violent in the image, that make the German Renaissance so absorbing to us moderns. This was the epoch that initiated the realignment of the boundaries between the work of art and the world, between religious devotion and aesthetic reception, between artist and craftsman, that were only later institutionalized by modernity and modern art.

It is no surprise to learn that early-twentieth-century Modernists were in fact drawn to German art. Wassily Kandinsky and Franz Marc's *Blaue Reiter* almanac of 1912 reproduced on the very first page a woodcut from the *Ritter vom Turn*, a profane text published in Basel in 1495. They had seen the woodcut reproduced in Worringer's book on early German book illustration.[9] The German Renaissance antioptical space was constantly being resurrected in Expressionist painting; or in film, as in the famous sets for Robert Wiene's *Cabinet of Dr. Caligari* of 1920.[10] Expressionist painters recreated the very inside-outside quality that Pächt was writing about in his analyses of Ger-

---

[9]Wassily Kandinsky and Franz Marc, eds., *The Blaue Reiter Almanac*, new documentary edition, ed. Klaus Lankheit, trans. Henning Falkenstein (New York: Viking, 1974); see also Lankheit's introductory essay, 11–48.

[10]Siegfried Kracauer, *From Caligari to Hitler: A Psychological History of the German Film* (Princeton: Princeton University Press, 1947), chap. 5, esp. 67 ff.

man altar paintings. At the Bauhaus, meanwhile, the guru Johannes Itten was using early German painting—for example, the *Nativity* by Meister Francke, from the Thomas altar in Hamburg, of the 1420s—to illustrate his principles of pictorial rhythm or "form as movement" (fig. 2).[11] This culture that sought out and cultivated tension and disorienting participation is still our culture. In other words, there is a hidden continuity between our art history and the so-called Expressionist art history of the 1910s and 1920s.

Something of this preference for the anti-optical mode also survives in more recent philosophical writing on art, often in unexpected places. It is not surprising that some of the earlier German art history that resisted Wölfflin's or Panofsky's neo-Kantianism, with its trust in vision as a metaphor for the cognitive negotiation between subject and object, would ally itself crudely with versions of phenomenological thought. Phenomenology was dissatisfied with any spectatorial gap between consciousness and object. The full philosophical flowering of this mistrust of vision had to wait a generation, until Merleau-Ponty, who singled out Cézanne as the practitioner par excellence of a tactile painting.[12] Less well known than Merleau-Ponty, but in many ways just as interesting as a writer on art, is the French philosopher Henri Maldiney, a phenomenologist and opponent of structuralist linguistics. Maldiney wrote wistfully about objects that would be at once the signs and the incorporations of thoughts, where expression would be one with formation. He invoked the concept of the *Mal,* the German root of *Denkmal,* which is derived from Latin *macula,* the stain, the irreversible intervention into the world. The concept of the *Mal,* we are not surprised to learn, lay at the root of Cézanne's painting.[13] Maldiney, meanwhile, found a reader in Gilles Deleuze, and evidently introduced Deleuze to the ideas of Riegl and Worringer. Deleuze, in his own writings, has described several versions of a nonoptical vision: his smooth or nomadic mode, for example, which involves moving through a land-

[11]Johannes Itten, "Analysen alter Meister," in Bruno Adler, ed., *Utopia: Dokumente der Wirklichkeit* (Weimar, 1921); reproduced in Itten, *Bildanalysen,* ed. Rainer Wick (Ravensburg: Maier, 1988), 112.

[12]Maurice Merleau-Ponty, "Cézanne's Doubt," trans. Hubert L. Dreyfus and Patricia Allen Dreyfus, in *Sense and Non-Sense* (Evanston, Ill.: Northwestern University Press, 1964), 9–25.

[13]Henri Maldiney, "L'art et le pouvoir du fond," *Regard, parole, espace* (Paris: L'Age d'Homme, 1973), 173–207. See also idem, *Art et existence* (Paris: Klincksieck, 1985).

Fig. 2. From Johannes Itten, "Analysen alter Meister," in Bruno Adler, ed., *Utopia: Dokumente der Wirklichkeit*, Weimar, 1921. Used by permission.

scape, experiencing it without clear orientation and without really seeing it; or his concept of the diagram, which involves a kind of catastrophic, centrifugal presence of the painter within the canvas, and of which Bacon is the great exemplar.[14]

But even poststructuralist theory firmly rooted in semiotic doctrine, and therefore in principle hostile to phenomenology, will often celebrate a tactile, somatic, and performative visuality. This visual mode is characterized by deliberate obscurity, opacity, and incoherence. It is offered as an alternative both to classical or Cartesian visuality—supremely optical—and to the empirical, descriptive mode associated with Netherlandish painting. This anti-optical, nondetached mode is associated with Modernism and the sublime, but also with the Baroque or even the Gothic—never the German. And yet the schema of classical-descriptive-sublime *Sehformen,* or forms of seeing, seems to repeat the traditional Italian-Netherlandish-German triad of the older art historians.[15] The poststructuralist art historian Norman Bryson, meanwhile, advocates a mode of visuality unembarrassed by the physicality and temporality of the art-making process and unruffled by the disruption of the myth of pure, innocent vision by social and material reality.[16] Such interests in the tactile, the material, and the irreducible trace of the body's labor, seem to betray regret and impatience with the imperfection of re-presentation, and a perhaps justifiable fear that signifiers are too easily manipulated by the wrong forces. In a word, the interest in the tactile may betray a latent mistrust of semiosis.

The persistence of this mode of thinking within the historiography of German Renaissance art has encouraged a certain preselection of art history's objects. Most of the interesting recent scholarship on German Renaissance art, for instance, addresses in one way or another the process of the secularization of the image in the fifteenth and sixteenth centuries. According to the dominant model of this process, the devotional image increasingly relied on nonsemantic, or non-message-bearing, elements to hold the attention of beholders.

[14]*The Deleuze Reader,* ed. Constantin V. Boundas (New York: Columbia University Press, 1993).

[15]See for example the essays in *Vision and Visuality,* ed. Hal Foster (New York: Dia Art Foundation, 1988).

[16]Norman Bryson, *Vision and Painting* (New Haven: Yale University Press, 1983); see also Bryson's essay in Foster, *Vision and Visuality.*

Christopher S. Wood

Artists began producing artifacts that frankly delighted their owners: appealing scenes of ordinary life, landscapes, ingenious allegories.

But there were many artifacts produced in this period that do not fall along the secularization axis. I am thinking of what can be called memorial artifacts: portraits, statues, tombs, epitaphs, inscribed tablets. These are works that neither make awkward claims to signify remote and intangible objects nor resign themselves to pleasing their beholders in the present tense. I want to stress that such artifacts refer to their objects and do not merely signify.[17] That is, they offer verifiable information about real objects. And as such they fulfill their purpose through the mere fact of their existence and through the preservation and display of information.

This is by no means a secondary class of objects. Certainly they were close to the center of things in the minds of contemporaries. Renaissance humanists were obsessed with portraits, emblems, and epitaphs. Major artists like Dürer or Holbein who got their start in more or less traditional painting workshops, and who channeled their early talents into large altarpiece projects, eventually devoted considerable time to memorial artifacts. A major talent like Hans Burgkmair devoted much of his energies to monumental work for Emperor Maximilian. Such projects were prestigious and few artists would resist the opportunity to get involved. In fact, many of the outstanding younger talents were moving away from religious painting and sculpture and towards monumental art already in the 1510s and early 1520s, before the success of the Reformation gave those artists clear reasons to do so. The generation born around 1485 to 1495—artists like Peter Flötner, Peter Vischer the Younger, Loy Hering, Hans Daucher, Sebastian Loscher, Hans Schwarz, and Peter Dell—were declining the traditional career path of apprenticeship in a painting workshop in favor of bronze sculpture, medals, plaquettes, but also antiquarian prints and book illustrations. I believe this trend was in large part driven by the young artists themselves, and not only by the wishes of patrons. This hypothesis helps explain why there was so little good German painting after the deaths of Dürer (1528), Matthias Grünewald (1528 or 1532), and Albrecht Altdorfer (1538)—there was still talent around, but it was otherwise occupied.

---

[17]On the distinction between signification and reference, see Umberto Eco, *A Theory of Semiotics* (Bloomington: Indiana University Press, 1976), 58ff., 163ff.

How should scholarship address these "memorial" artifacts? Ideally, there would be no need for scholarship at all; we would just read the information we wanted straight off the monuments. But in practice the monuments are not so easy to read. The original procedures of archeological inquiry were developed by Renaissance antiquarians precisely for the purpose of deciphering the monuments of antiquity. Inscribed monuments—coins or epitaphs—are scholarship's primordial objects. What antiquarian method does is identify through forensic procedures the aberrations and tics that make it possible to locate the text in space and time and ultimately to "purify" the text. Antiquarianism is supposed to stabilize and fix the reference of the monuments so that they will testify more credibly to historical reality. It is a method that is designed to further the ambitions of the monuments themselves.

But our intellectual culture tends not to take seriously the monument's own voice. Why should we be content with what the inscription wants to tell us? The scholarly mode that the monument asks of us—straightforward reading of offered information—seems too naive, too flat. To read these lucid artifacts on our own terms, we prefer to betray them, and in effect revert to the old familiar blindnesses, the ones that we learned from German painting. We prefer to read between the lines, against the intentions of the makers; to ignore the referential character of the tombs or portraits and instead treat them as representations, whose relationship to any event, fact, individual, or historical discourse is itself a backwards construction by an interpreter. We subject the artifacts to semiotic analysis, which transforms them and puts them to use, our use. The semiotic method thus mimics not the Renaissance antiquarian's recovery of texts but the secularization process, the *Kultwerk*-to-*Kunstwerk* transformation. The semiotic method, not surprisingly, tends to privilege the most beautiful and complex objects. Art history in particular is a discipline caught in an oscillating pattern: seduced and then repelled by the phenomenal presence of its object; fascinated by that presence, but then driven to read it as a sign pointing away from itself. This is exactly why social or economic historians often find art historical writing so irritating.

By the same token, the semiotic method is unfair to the memorial objects. Certainly the monument can be read as a complex sign. The monument is a physical presence that is meant to initiate a train of thought, such as remembrance of an absent other, or perhaps reflec-

tion on one's own mortality. Often it engages in tropes like prosopo-
peia, where the monument pretends to speak in the voice of the dead
person. Still, in comparison with self-styled works of art, or fictions,
the monument is inevitably deficient; the very concept of "work of
art" seems inappropriate, and in most cases so does the concept of the
"author." The result is that modern scholarship has had little to say of
interest—beyond the basic cataloguing, or forensic work—about
monuments and medals. One subfield that has seen some very good
work is the print, particularly the informational, propagandistic, or
polemical print.[18] But in the field of German Renaissance sculpture
there is still much to do. Nearly all treatments of the subject privilege
the "painterly" or "florid" sculpture of the eve of the Reformation,
from the mid-1480s to the mid-1520s.[19]

I would like to offer a few reflections on some of these objects and
on the ways in which historical research might directly address the
asymmetry between the semiotic premises of modern interpretive historical scholarship and the referential claims of the objects.

One category of object that remains somewhat lost in the art history of the German Renaissance is the statue. The statue is strictly a
freestanding sculpture of a human body. The statue doubles the body,
in real space that is continuous with its beholder's space, and therefore bears a more than semiotic relationship to the body. The psychosomatic basis for the affective power of the statue reveals itself in
marginal formats and institutions like the effigy, objects that we cannot always classify as works of art.[20] In the Christian West, taboos
and conventions severely restricted the production and display of
statues. The freestanding statue had strong associations with the
pagan idol, and indeed the false gods were easily identified in Chris-

[18]See Peter Parshall, "Imago contrafacta: Images and Facts in the Northern Renais-
sance," *Art History* 16 (1993): 554–79; and the essays in *New Perspectives on the Art of
Renaissance Nuremberg*, ed. Jeffrey Chipps Smith (Austin: Archer M. Huntington Art
Gallery, 1985).

[19]Including Baxandall, *Limewood Sculptors* (see n. 8 above) and Michael Liebmann,
Die Deutsche Plastik (Leipzig: Seemann, 1982). The recent and outstanding survey by
Jeffrey Chipps Smith, *German Sculpture of the Later Renaissance, c. 1520–1580* (Prince-
ton: Princeton University Press, 1994), is by contrast free of this prejudice.

[20]See the remarkable studies by Wolfgang Brückner, *Bildnis und Brauch: Studien zur
Bildfunktion der Effigies* (Berlin: Schmidt, 1966) and Adolf Reinle, *Das stellvertretende
Bildnis* (Zurich: Artemis, 1984), as well as the many important examples and discussions in David Freedberg, *The Power of Images* (Chicago: University of Chicago Press,
1989).

tian painting by their pedestals (usually round columns), their material (usually bronze), and their nudity. The Christian holy personages were virtually never sculpted and displayed on freestanding columns. Some potentially dangerous, quasi-idolatrous Madonnas were legitimated by reduction in scale: the Schöne Madonnas, for example, which were occasionally exhibited on columns inside churches, were much smaller than life-size. To distinguish it from the dangerous effigy, the powerful double of the human form, the sculpted body in late-medieval and Renaissance Germany was normally trimmed and embellished, shrunk and enlivened, in such a way as to pull it unequivocally into the camp of art. The surfaces of figures carved in the "florid" manner were painted and gilded; drapery was animated and billowed in imitation of the linear extravagances of engraving; the body was typically pulled and prodded in the direction of narrative or given an anecdotal or homely flavor. Some were freestanding, but on a small scale; most were embedded in the theatrical machine of the altarpiece, even if in today's museums they are misleadingly displayed on freestanding pedestals. In effect, this was painterly sculpture, continuous in function and form with painting, capable of nearly the same range of iconographic performances and dramatic or narrative effects. This was sculpture that was clearly legible as fiction. The stone Madonna by Erhard Heydenreich erected outside the pilgrimage chapel at Regensburg in 1520, on the other hand, was a revolutionary and controversial breach of convention.[21] Living persons, incidentally, were never portrayed in full-length statuary.

Although young German artists learned from travel, from local collections, and from prints and drawings about antique statuary, they found few opportunities to experiment in public. One venue was the municipal fountain, where the function (real or vestigial) of the water spout had for centuries provided safe cover for iconographic experimentation. In one interesting episode in Augsburg, Protestant objections to a statue of a local saint apparently opened the way to a radical iconographical move. In 1537 the city replaced the figure of St. Ulrich on a fountain with a life-size, bronze, nude Neptune—apparently the very first life-size bronze figure standing free in a

---

[21]See Christopher S. Wood, "Ritual and the Virgin on the Column: The Cult of the Schöne Maria in Regensburg," *Journal of Ritual Studies* 6 (1992): 87–101, with references to the earlier literature.

Christopher S. Wood

public space north of the Alps (fig. 3).[22] There was nothing like it even in Italy, although certainly there was more elegant sculpture to be found there. What is interesting is that Augsburg Protestants later objected to humanist interest in the ancient local cult of Cybele. One local worthy complained that "heathen poets and historians had filled the city with idolatrous images."[23] This response suggests that they suspected there was more to the archeological interest in antique gods than met the eye.

Another category of object that hovers on the periphery of art historical inquiry is the epigraphic monument. Epigraphy was a major interest of the German humanists. The humanists were eager to crown their own existences with inscribed tablets in good Latin and in finely formed antiqua capitals. They could reintegrate what they learned about antique inscriptions with the native tradition of epitaphs. A similarly hybrid object is the medal. The Germans started later than the Italians but eventually produced a huge corpus of medals. The medal is a modern phenomenon with an antique flavor. Although it resembles an antique coin, it actually had its origins in the fifteenth century.

The epitaph's or the medal's connection to the individual—the collection of facts—is offered as an absolute connection. The lettering of an inscription is a transparent vehicle; it represents its object—namely, language—perfectly. But the medal also records and publishes other facts about an individual, not only linguistic data but also an image. Ordinarily, a picture refers less reliably to its object than an inscription does. In this case, the instability of the image is minimized by the format of the profile, which reduces the complexity of the skull to a more easily remembered linear form and which mythically remembers the origins of art in an indexical, completely reliable tracing of a silhouette on a wall. The profile partially overcomes the blindness of drawing, the inevitable dependence of drawing on schemas or memory. The profile grounds form in touch. The epitaph and the medal are objects that could almost be read with the fingers.

---

[22]*Welt im Umbruch: Augsburg zwischen Renaissance und Barock,* exhibition catalogue (Augsburg: Augsburger Druck- und Verlagshaus, 1980), 2: no. 502.
[23]Friedrich Roth, "Das Aufkommen des neuen Augsburger Stadtpir mit dem Capitäl und dem Cisa- oder Cybelekopf um 1540," *Zeitschrift des Historischen Vereins für Schwaben und Neuburg* 35 (1909): 115–27.

Fig. 3. Neptune fountain, 1537, Augsburg, Jakobsplatz.
Used by permission.

It is no wonder that such monuments appealed to antiquarians. The antiquarian hoped to exclude subjectivity, or rise above it. And the basic purpose of the monument was to grant its beholder as little room for interpretive freedom as possible. Antiquarianism embraced writing as its medium in order to overcome oblivion, which is after all the sorry result of a biological deficiency. The same goes for the acceptance of contour, or indexical form, the perfect antidote for impatience with the contingency and perspectivalism of experienced vision.

In many ways it is more helpful to think of epitaph inscriptions and medals together with prints. Modern inscriptions were published in the sylloges along with the ancient. And crucial to the phenomenon of the medal was the concept of replication. Contour was apprehensible, publishable; it was form as a kind of writing. This understanding of form stands behind the late medieval fascination with the *Urform* of Christ's face or body. An indulgence woodcut of the late fifteenth century, for example, claimed to illustrate the almond-shaped wound of Christ in actual size: "This is the length and breadth of the wound," the text insists; "the little cross measured out forty times equals the length of his body" (fig. 4).[24] Pope Innocent promised insurance against death for one day to anyone who kissed this printed cross. The impulse was to repeat, publicize, and eventually publish such powerful forms. Published form—either the linear contour or the nonmaterial, dispensable form of letters—would survive the corrosion of time. The inked sheets of paper were meant to outlive even stone buildings, and indeed in many cases they have. I would argue that the intense interest in authentic, authoritative, palpable forms is consistent with the antiquarian mentality.

The inscribed monument represents its object less problematically than a picture. An individual is, among other things, a compilation of socially shared information, above all a name, but also facts such as titles, public positions, ancestors, dates of birth and death. Such facts exist only as linguistic units; they are extensions of the name attached to the body. Lettering imitates language perfectly, in its own medium, so to speak. There is no need to worry about the link between the monument and its object.

---

[24]Richard S. Field, comp., *Fifteenth Century Woodcuts and Metalcuts* (Washington: National Gallery of Art, 1965), no. 260.

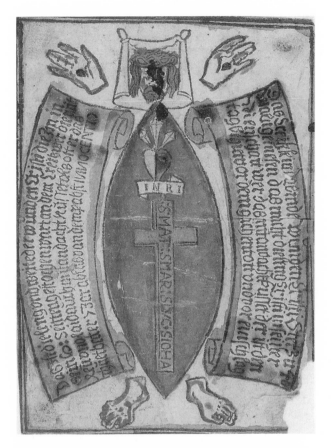

Fig. 4. Wounds of Christ, indulgence woodcut, southern Germany, ca. 1490, Yale University Art Gallery, inv. no. 1971.53.3. Used by permission.

But there are hints of rebellion within this purism. Such monuments also deliberately leave little room for the artist, for the public unfolding of an authorial persona, of the sort that German painting so dramatically permitted in the first decades of the sixteenth century. The German medals and epitaphs are notoriously difficult to attribute. There is little margin for the individual handwriting of the artist to show itself. Thus the paradoxical spectacle of a community of

Christopher S. Wood

young, talented, and ambitious artists in the 1520s and 1530s, all striving forward in the field of bronze plaquettes or medals. One curious outlet that the German medalists found for their own ambition was making portrait medals of each other, no matter how obscure and unaccomplished they were. For example, the Strasbourg sculptor Friedrich Hagenauer made a medal of his friend Laux Furtnagel in 1527 when Furtnagel was only twenty-two years old—a mere journeyman, not admitted to the painters' guild until 1546![25] (See fig. 5.) Meanwhile, these artists seized every opportunity to mark or sign the medal by distorting, or as we would say, "stylizing" the profile—for example, by sloping the shoulders or dipping the hat in the Furtnagel medal.

Moreover, there are actually important distinctions to be made among antiqua capital forms, distinctions that contemporaries seem to have had an eye for, as much as they were sensitive to latinity itself, to grammar and abbreviations. A remarkable example is the monument for Vitus Meler in the Augsburg cathedral cloister, carved probably by Gregor Erhart in 1518 and adorned with beautiful, confidently incised Roman majuscules (fig. 6).[26] Strikingly, no precise chronology of the development of the "antiqua" epigraphic majuscule in Germany has been established. Yet Peutinger himself, both in a letter to Conrad Celtis and in the preface to his 1505 sylloge, boasted of the "delightful" capital letters that the printer Erhard Ratdolt had specially designed for him.[27]

Pressure builds up beneath the grid of writing and writerly form, and the optical returns, as if to rescue the monuments from semiotic death. Although such aberrations are harder to detect on medals and tombs, because the arena is so much narrower, we are dealing with essentially the same phenomenon that fueled the dissent over religious statues and paintings. And in fact, the blindness of the antiquarian is the same blindness that produced all the weird-looking paintings. The forensic eye is indeed blind: it ignores the obvious in favor of the insignificant, the aberrations that make the artifact reveal

[25]Stephen K. Scher, ed., *The Currency of Fame: Portrait Medals of the Renaissance*, exhibition catalogue (New York and Washington: Frick Collection and National Gallery of Art, 1994), p. 233, no. 94.
[26]Karl Kosel, *Der Augsburger Domkreuzgang und seine Denkmäler* (Sigmaringen: Thorbecke, 1991), p. 157, no. 87.
[27]Conrad Peutinger, *Briefwechsel,* ed. Erich König (Munich: Beck, 1923), no. 35.

Fig. 5. Friedrich Hagenauer, portrait medal of Laux Furtnagel, 1527, Munich, Bayerisches Nationalmuseum, inv. no. R3461. Used by permission.

more information about itself than it wanted to. But this eye, this capacity for detecting the aberration, is what makes it possible to smooth out the aberration in the chastised text, the critical edition. And this blindness is identical in structure to the blindness of taste, or appreciation: the sensitivity to the free play of signification that is at the heart of aesthetic judgment. This structural overlap between the sensitivity to minute aberrations that expand the referential range of the monument—that is, beyond its intentionality—and the sensitivity to semiotic difference that makes an image into a work of art, manifests itself conspicuously in the institution of connoisseurship.

Fig. 6. Attributed to Gregor Erhart, epitaph of Vitus Meler, 1518, Augsburg, Cathedral. Used by permission.

Our own interpretive scholarship, which dismisses the reading of referential monuments as a mere *Hilfswissenschaft,* prior and inferior to hermeneutic or semiotic reading, inevitably patronizes these monuments. Instead, we might see their straining towards perfect lucidity and universality as symptoms of the same uneasiness with vision that produced both the strange German paintings and the iconoclastic reaction to them.

The "Other" in the Age of the Reformation

Reflections on Social Control and Deviance in the Sixteenth Century

Hans J. Hillerbrand

This essay attempts, in the context of a broad survey of the sixteenth century, to analyze what society found offensive in the various manifestations of the Other in the century: Jews, Anabaptists, witches, beggars, prostitutes. The essay finds that the societal verdict always included both an intellectual and a moral censure, that social control increased in the course of the sixteenth century, and that a universal effort was made during the time to make the Other visible. The essay concludes with observations about the role of religion in the tightening of social control.

"I ONCE SAW AMONG US some men brought by sea from a far country," wrote Michel de Montaigne in his *Apology for Raymond Sebond*, "and because we did not understand their language at all, and because their ways, moreover, and their bearing and their clothes were totally remote from us, which of us did not consider them savages and brutes?"[1] Thomas Cranmer's 1549 Prayer Book, in turn, implored the faithful in every Good Friday service to call on God "to have mercy upon all Jews, Turks, infidels, and heretics and to take from them all ignorance, hardness of heart, and contempt of Thy word." The meaning of Montaigne's and Cranmer's felicitous phrases takes us straight to our topic. For both Montaigne and Cranmer, there existed men (and women) whom they did not consider their equals, whom they deemed inferior, and for whom in fact special prayerful intervention was necessary and appropriate.[2] Fundamentally, both

---

[1]Michel de Montaigne, *Essays*, 2.12.343.
[2]There is a voluminous literature; I note a few publications of special importance: Michael Theunissen, *The "Other": Studies in the Social Ontology of Husserl, Heidegger,*

Montaigne and Cranmer meant to distance themselves from the Other.

While clearly not pivotal for the Reformation of the sixteenth century, our topic of the "Other" seems to pertain to a well-worn aspect of the sixteenth century, one nowadays very much in scholarly vogue. Such also was the case a century ago, when a similar vogue prevailed: theological questions were not highly esteemed and scholars were more interested in Calvin's role in Servetus' execution than in Calvin's Christology. Indeed, had my title preferred the nomenclature of "Persecution and Toleration" and the Reformation, it would have had a familiar ring with a fairly substantial literature. A generation ago the French historian Joseph Lecler wrote no less than two volumes on that topic, not so much on tolerance, of course, as on intolerance.[3] And the general interest has continued. In short, there is hardly uncommon courage in my selection of the topic; if anything, questions might well be asked about the author's lack of imagination.

All the same, things are a bit more complicated. I judiciously (so I think) observed that my topic "seems to pertain to a well-worn aspect" of the Reformation. In actual fact it does not. For to talk about the Other is not to talk about toleration; rather, it is an intriguingly different way of looking at the mentality of the Reformation and the entire sixteenth century.

Needless to say, the sixteenth century did not know of the Other. It did know, as Montaigne's and Cranmer's words neatly indicate, savages and brutes, heretics, schismatics, and infidels. It also knew of those who stood at the margin of society: lepers, witches, beggars, vagabonds, gypsies, prostitutes, tavern keepers, gamblers, not to mention American Indians, moneylenders, soldier-mercenaries, laundry-

---

Sartre and Buber (Cambridge: MIT, 1955); Richard Wentz, *The Contemplation of Otherness: The Critical Vision of Religion* (Macon: Mercer University Press, 1984); Emmanuel Levinas, *Totality and Infinity* (Pittsburgh: Duquesne University Press, 1969), esp. 251: "The 'Other' is situated in a dimension of height and abasement ... he has the face of the poor, the stranger, the widow, and the orphan and, at the same time, of the master called in to justify my freedom." See also Jonathan Z. Smith, "Differential Equations: On Constructing the 'Other,'" *Arizona State University Lectures in Religion* (Tempe: Arizona State University, 1992).

[3]Of course, the literature on tolerance and intolerance in the Reformation is extensive, but Lecler's two volumes are a good place to start: Joseph Lecler, *Toleration and the Reformation*, trans. T. L. Westow (New York: Association Press; Longmans, 1960).

men, and henchmen. All these were the Other, and even this lengthy list makes no claim to completeness. Each conjures up a specific connotation; collectively, the terms refer to men and women on the outside, on the margins, whom society did not accept as its own. Societal ethos always includes those who are in and those who are out, who is and who is not included in the great feast of life, and who are, precisely because they are out, seen as inferior, despicable, ignoble, despised, belittled. The Age of the Reformation is no exception.

Obviously, the general label Other subsumes a broad spectrum of specific manifestations. Edward Said's provocative study on the notion of "orientalism" suggested that there is external Other, that is, an Other who is not part of the community.[4] Of course that external Other existed very much in the sixteenth century—the Turks, the American Indians, also generically the "foreigners," the Italians for the Germans, for example, and conversely the Germans for the Italians. And in that religiously turbulent age there was the religious Other as well: Protestants for the Catholics, Catholics for the Protestants. The religious Other may well have been the most blatant characteristic of the age; most of the time (though by no means always) manifesting itself as the external Other. In Elizabethan England, for example, the Catholic Other was both external and internal, embodied by Philip II no less than by the Jesuit priests who had come from Douai to restore England to the Catholic fold.

Whether external or internal, the crux of the matter is clearly control. Society draws boundaries regarding acceptable and unacceptable values and behavior. The Other is the evaluative societal designation for individuals or groups who do not accept—or are not seen to accept—the norms that society embraces and imposes on its members.[5] The designation of the Other is a societal verdict. Society declares who is, and who is not, the Other. Society constructs and reduces social control, norms, and thus negatively deviance.[6] And by society we mean those exercising political power that allows to control or intellectual power that allows to create consciousness. The rank and file of the people are a different matter. Bereft of power, they

---

[4]Edward Said, *Orientalism* (New York: Vintage, 1978).

[5]This is a variation of the definition found in Hans Mayer, *Outsiders: A Study in Life and Letters* (Cambridge, Mass.: MIT, 1982), xiii.

[6]See the interesting discussion in Nanette J. Davis and Bo Anderson, *Social Control: The Production of Deviance in the Modern State* (New York: Irvington, 1983).

cannot control. They display prejudice, that is, intellectual or emotional stances that are powerful in their own way, but at the same time bereft of the power to control. In fact, prejudice will remain ineffective unless it is accompanied by the societal exercise of power to declare some to be the Other.

In his essay "Differential Equations: On Constructing the Other," Jonathan Z. Smith distinguishes—in his customarily provocative way—three models of the Other in terms of "cultural traits," "center and periphery," and "intelligibility."[7] Otherness for Smith means difference and distinction, and not what I might call "judgmental censure," as the key element. While Smith calls attention to the importance of "difference," he fails, in my opinion, to realize that the crucial element in the construction of social control (and, thereby, deviance) is a value judgment. The point is not so much "otherness" as difference as it is "otherness" as different values. To say (as, for example, Europeans might be wont to do) that the Chinese are the Other because they use chopsticks as eating utensils instead of forks and knives, is one thing. To add the judgment of concomitant inferiority (because of their eating customs) is something else. In the sixteenth century the observation, neutral in itself, that the native Americans did not wear (European-style) clothes became relevant the moment the judgment was added that they were, therefore, morally inferior. The question remains, of course, if difference inescapably leads to value judgments.

Which takes us back to Montaigne and Cranmer. Montaigne distinguishes between the "stranger" and the "Other," and he is quite clear as to what makes the difference. It is more than geographic distance and difference. Of course the men Montaigne talks about come from a different place; their language, ways, clothes, and bearing are different. But what begins as a descriptive statement is promptly turned into judgment. Empirically discernible differences become the ground on which the strangers are turned into the Other, namely into savages and brutes.[8] In other words, "different"-ness in itself is not

[7]Smith, "Differential Equations," 2 (see n. 2 above). This perspective is echoed by William Green, "Otherness Within: Towards a Theory of Difference in Rabbinic Judaism," in Jacob Neusner and Ernest Frerichs, eds., *"To see ourselves as others see us": Christians, Jews, Others in Late Antiquity* (Chico, Calif.: Scholars Press, 1985).

[8]See here the comments on the Good, the True, and the Beautiful by Donald Black, "Social Control as a Dependent Variable," in *Toward a General Theory of Social Control*, vol. 1, ed. Black (New York: Academic Press, 1984), 26ff. Black has a lengthier treatment as well: *The Behavior of Law* (New York: Academic Press, 1976).

Other-ness. Only when evaluative labels are applied does the stranger become the Other.

In his own way, Cranmer very much addresses the same issue. He is more specific than Montaigne in his appellation—he names Jews, Turks, infidels, and heretics, but these are only specific (and expanded) categories of Montaigne's men. Importantly, however, Cranmer picks up where Montaigne ended. Cranmer focuses on ideological differences with the Other. He is unwilling to accept the Other, and he psychologizes the difference by explaining that "ignorance" and "hardness of heart," together with "contempt for God's word," turns humans into the Other. Obviously, the last characteristic—contempt for God's word—is the crucial one for Cranmer, but equally important is the imputation of certain moral shortcomings in the Other, which makes the Other inferior. The themes of obstinacy, ignorance, and contempt for God's word (here simply understood as the source for all moral norms) as a characteristic of the Other recurs repeatedly throughout the sixteenth century, as for example, in Sebastian Castellio, who also noted the conflux of theological deviance and moral shortcoming.[9]

This essay seeks to do two things—to explore several specific illustrations of the sixteenth-century Other and to offer some general observations about the phenomenon. It will distinguish four exemplars, each one of them representing a distinctive type of the Other. Importantly, this essay will employ the category of "visibility" as the identifying characteristic of the Other. In other words, for any societal pronouncement on the Other to become meaningful, the Other must be visible or made visible. This essay will confine itself to manifestations of the internal Other. This means the omission of two rather important and intriguing sixteenth-century manifestations: the Turks and the American Indians. In would be intriguing to comment on the sixteenth-century European perceptions of both. In particular, the American Indians as Other pose the important question as to what prompted their ultimate degradation: the questioning of the Indians' humanity.[10]

[9]Sebastian Castellio, *De haereticis aut sint persequendi* (Geneva: Droz, 1954), 21–22. Castellio notes that heretics are "avari, scurrae, luxuriosi, ebriosi, persecutores." In other words, they are morally no less than theologically deficient.

[10]The best general introduction is Karen Kupperman, *American Consciousness, 1493–1750* (Chapel Hill: University of North Carolina Press, 1995). In a way, the Amer-

Hans J. Hillerbrand

ican Indians were the sixteenth-century external Other par excellence. They resided outside Europe, possessed a different culture, and were visibly different, so that they demonstrably seemed to stand outside what might be called European consciousness. Moreover, the European determination to take possession of the new lands turned the native Americans into foes. There promptly was an ideological verdict as well. The Spanish conquistadors found that the synthesis of Aristotle's concept of natural slavery and St. Augustine's notion of beneficial coercion provided the ideology to consider the native peoples as inherently inferior. Roger Williams's complaint, in 1654, about the cruel and unnecessary wars against the American Indians of New England was a painful summary of the first century and a half of the encounter between Europeans and native peoples.

Different in appearance, but also language, culture, values, not to mention religion, the Native Americans were declared to be inferior. In a striking manifestation of European hegemonic thinking, even the humanity of the American Indians was called into question. Columbus's cruel (and mindless) diary entries set the tone for what was to become the standard European sentiment, which also found expression in the vocabulary of the Europeans. As Montaigne's musings suggest, the American Indians were savages and beasts, animals and naked people, the last quality denoting not only incompleteness (say, with respect to attire in contrast to the well-dressed Europeans), but moral depravity as well. A papal pronouncement was necessary to settle the theological question of the humanity of the native Americans. The papal bull *Sublimis Deus* of 1537 sided with those who had argued that the native peoples did have souls and were thus fully human. With intriguing irony that very declaration set the stage for stigmatizing the American Indian as the religious Other and put into place a grandiose process of proselytizing that was calculated to do away with their Otherness. The conclusion of the bull: The Indians are truly human and are capable of understanding the Catholic faith, meant that the Native Americans were proper objects for converting to the Christian faith. In striking competition, the priest sought to subject by conversion, while the conquistadors sought to subject by military force.

The missionary command in the Gospels (e.g., Mark 16:15), which had lain dormant in European Christianity for centuries, received a new impetus. A rich literature from the 1490s onward called upon European Christians to rally to the conversion of the American Indians. Early on, the theme was sounded in Thomas More's *Utopia*, and it found steady expression throughout the sixteenth century. Richard Hakluyt's invocation of the Macedonian theme "Come over and help us" later became the seal of the Massachusetts Bay Company, a winsome juxtaposition of religion and precapitalist entrepreneurship.

Missionary effort, no matter how nobly meant and understood, seeks the elimination of the theological Other. Mission is cultural conflict, the colonizations of a native belief system. It presupposes the identification of the objects of missionary zeal as the Other. For the European settlement of North America, however, described by Francisco Lopez de Gomara in 1552 as the greatest event since the creation of the world, apart from the incarnation and death of Christ, the convergence of religion and politics proved productive.

Importantly, the papal bull, with its affirmation of the humanity of the American Indian, had staked out a Catholic claim to power in the Americas. Had the bull denied the American Indians' humanity, it would have meant the forfeiture of Catholic influence. Without the mandate of a missionary impulse the presence of the Catholic Church would have been minimal. The papal pronouncement was thus good politics and good theology. The consequences lasted for centuries.

JEWS: THE PARTIALLY VISIBLE OTHER

The centuries-old story of Christian anti-Semitism is too well known to need to be rehearsed here. The historian must take note of the fact that in the fifteenth century a wave of renewed anti-Semitic agitation had swept through Europe.[11] Once and again, Jews were charged with a variety of perverse practices: usury, blasphemy of the consecrated host, and—above all—the rejection of Jesus as the Messiah. As in earlier times, theological indictment went hand in hand with economic and moral censure, all dramatized by folklore and superstition.

However, by the early sixteenth century, this continuing anti-Semitism was, to a considerable extent, anti-Semitism without Jews. In the course of the fifteenth century Jews had been expelled from most of Europe and from most of the German territories. Alongside the well-known expulsion of the Jews from Spain, expulsion orders were also issued in many German territories and towns: Saxony (1432), Augsburg (1440), Bavaria (1442–50), Württemberg, Salzburg, Nuremberg (1498), Mainz (1470), Brandenburg (1510), Ansbach-Bayreuth (1515), Regensburg (1519).[12] These encompassed just about the majority of the German territories and only left Hesse and a number of free imperial cities open to Jews. This virtual absence of Jews in central Europe notwithstanding, the anti-Semitic agitation against them as the Other continued.

As we have already noted, the societal identification of the Other always includes not only the declaration of a social norm but also the concomitant effort to make the Other visible. Jews shared with other internal outsiders the reality that they were "different," but this difference was what might be called a theological one, namely a lengthy set of beliefs and practices that set them apart from their Christian environment. There was, however, no visible difference. Or, to say it differently, Jews became visible in a manner of speaking only at certain points. Their absence from Christian services of worship or their

---

[11]Helpful general introductions are Jeremy Cohen, *The Friars and the Jews: The Evolution of Medieval Anti-Judaism* (Ithaca: Cornell University Press, 1982), and Alfred Haverkamp, ed., *Zur Geschichte der Juden im Deutschland des späten Mittelalters und der Frühen Neuzeit* (Stuttgart: Hiersemann, 1981). For England, see David S. Katz, *The Jews in the History of England, 1485-1850* (New York: Oxford University Press, 1994).

[12]Markus J. Wenninger, *Man bedarf keiner Juden mehr: Ursachen und Hintergründe ihrer Vertreibung aus den deutschen Reichsstädten im 15. Jahrhundert* (Wien: Böhlau, 1981). For Spain, *The Expulsion of the Jews: 1492 and After*, ed. Raymond G. Waddington and A. H. Williamson (New York: Garland, 1994).

keeping the Sabbath were only two instances of a whole range of behavior that set Jews apart from their respective communities, and thereby made them visible. All this is a (painfully) old story, but what is new in the fifteenth century is the clear effort on the part of society to create visibility. To be the Other, Jews had to be made visible, and the fifteenth century tells of increasing concerted societal efforts to do precisely that. Nicholas of Cusa had Jewish males wear a yellow ring on their clothes, while Jewish women had to affix two blue stripes to their veils. This stipulation was widely imitated.[13] Analogously, the ghetto, the compulsory residence of all Jews in a given part of town, made its appearance. Whatever the societal justification, this was a means to exercise social control; it also was a strategy to make the Other geographically visible.

The coming of the sixteenth century and of the Protestant Reformation changed little of this picture. Protestant reformers echoed the anti-Semitic polemics that Catholic theologians had parlayed since the eleventh century. Indeed, it is one of the ironies of Reformation polemics that the two theological archenemies—Johann Eck and Martin Luther—can vie with one another about who made the most rabid anti-Judaic pronouncements in the sixteenth century: Johann Eck's staunchly anti-Judaic *Ains Judenbuechlins Verlegung* (Ingolstadt, 1541) accomplished the remarkable feat of equaling (if not outdoing) Luther in both invective and content. Later in the century, the Lutheran divine Georg Nigrinus propounded anti-Semitic notions taken straight out of Luther's book, an indication of the striking continuity of Luther's influence beyond the immediate Reformation era.[14]

But it is Martin Luther himself, of course, who is cited as the epitome of sixteenth-century anti-Judaism. Luther reserved some of his most abusive writings for the Jews, notably his *Von den Juden und ihren Lügen* (On the Jews and Their Lies, 1543).[15] Some scholars have

[13]Arno Herzig, "Die Juden in Deutschland zur Zeit Reuchlins," in *Reuchlin und die Juden*, ed. Arno Herzig and Julius Schoeps (Sigmaringen: Thorbecke, 1993), 13. See also Alfred Haverkamp, "Lebensbedingung der Juden im spätmittelalterlichen Deutschland," in *Zerbrochene Geschichte: Leben und Selbstverständnis der Juden in Deutschland*, ed. Dirk Blasis (Frankfurt: Fischer, 1991), 11–31.

[14]Georg Nigrinus, *Juden Feind* (Frankfurt, 1605).

[15]On Luther, see Mark U. Edwards, *Luther's Last Battles: Politics and Polemics, 1531–46* (Ithaca: Cornell, 1983), as well as Hans J. Hillerbrand, "Martin Luther and the Jews," in *Jews and Christians: Exploring the Past, Present, and Future*, ed. James H. Charlesworth (New York: Crossroads, 1990).

argued that as in other respects in this matter, too, Luther became more strident in later years: earlier, in 1523, he had written empathetically "they [the medieval theologians] treated the Jews as if they were dogs and not human," but later he embraced the full range of traditional anti-Semitic notions. His 1543 advisories were that synagogues and Jewish books should be burned, that Jews should be forced to do manual labor, and that they should be expelled from Christian lands.[16] Upon reflection it becomes clear that the underlying momentum is the effort to create visibility so as to get a handle on the matter of social control. In fact, Jews had been expelled from Electoral Saxony in 1536, and when Josel von Rosheim, the spokesman for the German Jewish community, sought Luther's intervention with the Saxon elector to rescind the order, his efforts proved to be in vain.[17] Tellingly, three days before his death early in 1546, Luther in a sermon talked about the Jews one final time by commenting not so much on biblical considerations as on popular superstition: "And if they [the Jews] could kill us altogether, they would gladly do it. In fact, they do it quite often."[18] Luther reiterated notions from earlier writings which are, in their own way, quintessential for the societal identification of the Other: to the denunciation of their faith was added the allegation of moral shortcoming.

There is another telling sentence in the same sermon: "The Jews must convert themselves and if they do not, we will not suffer nor tolerate them in our midst."[19] The fundamental theme of all of Luther's comments on the Jews found succinct expression here: Jews as Jews were unacceptable. The were acceptable only if they surrendered their religious identity—and thus ceased being the religious Other.

Luther's comment offers a revealing insight into the broader topic of society's attitude toward the Other. The Jews' distinctive (albeit invisible) Otherness was identified—their religious otherness—and the verdict was that they were not to be tolerated unless they surrendered that religious Otherness. As Heiko Oberman's *The Roots of Anti-*

---

[16]The tract is found in *Luthers Werke: Weimarer Ausgabe* (WA) 53:526ff. Luther published two additional anti-Jewish tracts that same year: *Vom Schem Hamphoras* and *Von den letzten Worten Davids*.

[17]On him, see Selma Stern, *Josel von Rosheim: Befehlshaber der Judenschaft im Heiligen Römischen Reich Deutscher Nation* (Munich: Gotthold Müller, 1959).

[18]WA 51:195.   [19]WA 51:196.

Semitism aptly points out, Luther's harshness in tone and substance against the Jews had little to do with allegations of crimes and misdemeanors of individual Jews—even though, I would add, he clearly utilized those in his polemic—but much with the collective Jewish reluctance to convert to Christianity. Or to say it differently, Luther's indignation was triggered—and his anti-Judaism activated—by the Jewish unwillingness to surrender their *religious* Otherness.[20] While Luther's reaction of explosive and emotional anger has frequently been cited as excessive, it is, in its essence, paradigmatic of all reactions against the Other. The Other evokes feelings of fear, distrust, apprehension, even anger; the presence of the Other makes for discomfort and easily provides for scapegoats. And the circle closes with the allegation of moral misconduct and shortcomings.

ANABAPTISTS: THE PARTIALLY INVISIBLE OTHER

From their origins in the mid-1520s the Anabaptists of the Reformation were on the receiving end of ubiquitous persecution at the hands of the religious and political establishment. On the face of things, this might be considered surprising in that the Anabaptists' theological deviation (and therefore Otherness) seemed to be about a single theological issue—the timing of baptism. Of course, we do well to keep in mind that theological dissent, major or minor, was unacceptable to sixteenth-century society. The relentless persecution of the Anabaptists took the form of endless interrogations, trials, executions—telling evidence that, as far as society, both Catholic and Protestant, was concerned, they clearly were the Other.[21] The first execution of an Anabaptist occurred in Schwyz in May 1525, barely four months after the first recorded adult baptism in Zollikon outside Zurich.[22] The authorities had moved quickly to enforce religious uniformity. The legal justification cited was the Anabaptists' violation of the Codes of Theodosius, which prescribed capital punishment for the crime of rebaptism.[23] Additional legal statutes against the Anabaptists followed, both in Switzerland and in the empire. In 1529 the diet at

[20]Heiko A. Oberman, *The Roots of Anti-Semitism in the Age of Renaissance and Reformation* (Philadelphia: Fortress, 1984), 162.

[21]On the general topic, see Claus P. Clasen, *Anabaptism: A Social History, 1525–1618* (Ithaca: Cornell, 1972); Gustav Bossert, ed., *Quellen zur Geschichte der Wiedertäufer,* vol. 1: *Herzogtum Württemberg* (Leipzig: Hinrichs, 1930), 161ff.

[22]See Clasen, *Anabaptism,* 371; see also *Corpus Reformatorum,* II:17–18.

[23]*Codex Theodosianus,* XVI:6:1

Speyer declared rebaptism a capital crime punishable by death. The recess of that diet made the religious deviance of the Anabaptists, pure and simple, sufficient ground for their persecution.[24] However, it should be noted that one year earlier an imperial mandate of 4 January 1528 had still argued that the Anabaptists were criminals because they, in addition to disregarding the Christian tradition of infant baptism, also sought to do away with all political authority. This dual charge of religious *and* political deviance was abandoned by the recess of Speyer; now it was the implication.

Theologians and political authorities competed with one another in declaring the Anabaptists the Other for political as well as religious reasons. The two intertwined. On the face of things, the chronological convergence of the rise of Anabaptism and the German Peasants' War of 1524/25 seemed to justify the charge that religious deviance was but a veneer for political insurrection. The charge of political disobedience began to lose credibility, however, as the uprising of the German peasants faded into the past, but it received new impetus when the Anabaptists took control of the city of Münster in the mid-1530s; the specter of Münsterite Anabaptism, dramatized by the Anabaptist introduction of communism and polygamy, was to haunt Anabaptists everywhere for years to come.

The numerous records of Anabaptist interrogations and trials from the sixteenth century show that the charge of insurrection, while constantly made, was never proven, indicating that plotting against civil authority was not on the mind of the Anabaptists. That reality proved to be beside the point, however; the real issue was that society clearly did feel threatened by the Anabaptist dissent and moved to enforce societal uniformity and social control. In order to suppress the movement—scholars are far from agreed if there was in fact a movement—the authorities had to identify Anabaptists and Anabaptist conventicles. That was not easy, for Anabaptism was an underground movement without easily recognizable membership, such as locales or kinship groups. Thus the identification of Anabaptist conventicles had to focus on individuals. To be effective in the exercise of social control, the authorities' challenge was to make the Anabaptists visible, even though on the face of things they did not

[24]Horst Schaepler, *Die rechtliche Behandlung der Täufer in der deutschen Schweiz: Südwestdeutschland und Hessen 1525–1618* (Tübingen: Fabian, 1957), 20ff.

differ from their friends and neighbors. The Anabaptists provided a few clues—their failure to present their infants for baptism or their absence from the common services of worship. But that was hardly sufficient for easy identification.

If—as we know to have been the case—the severe provisions of the numerous anti-Anabaptist statutes issued throughout Europe were not uniformly carried out, this undoubtedly also meant that the policy of suppression did not have universal support among the common people, those, in other words, who would have to be counted on to help the authorities in their pursuit of alleged or suspected Anabaptists. The instances are rare, according to the extant records, that someone reported a neighbor or friend as a suspected Anabaptist to the authorities. Clearly, friends and neighbors must not have felt threatened by the awareness that there were Anabaptists in their midst.

What, then, was the driving force behind the suppression of the Anabaptists? Was it the political milieu because of the authorities' fear of insurrection, or was it the theologians because of their concern for theological purity? Both undoubtedly played a role, but in my judgment the theologians' sentiment was crucial. The theological establishment felt a greater threat. And the theologians not only spoke to the issue of public blasphemy but also argued that insurrection was the (inevitable) by-product of theological deviation. Heretics, in other words, were by definition revolutionaries. They were also something else, namely morally deficient. This surely was the point of the establishment polemic against the Münster Anabaptists.[25]

The systematic suppression of the Anabaptist Other is unthinkable without the active involvement role of the theologians. When in 1530 the Lutheran reformer Friedrich Myconius was perturbed by the execution of six Anabaptists, both Philip Melanchthon and Martin Luther retorted that anyone guilty of blasphemy, which they defined as the public teaching of heretical doctrines, deserved to be executed.[26] Such sentiment was clearly heard by the authorities concerned about law and order and with power to do something about

---

[25]See James M. Stayer, "Vielweiberei als innerweltliche Askese," *Mennonite Geschichte Blätter* 37 (1980): 24–41.

[26]Numerous scholars have pointed to the inconsistency on Luther's part in this regard: from the Catholic perspective this stance had to mean that all Lutheran preachers deserved to be executed!

the matter.[27] Luther's *Exposition of the Eighty-Second Psalm,* also of 1530, sharpened the theological sentiment on the reformers' side by offering a new and intriguing definition of what he called seditious heretics. Luther argued that seditious heretics were those whose heresy pertained to the civic realm—who taught that private property was sinful, that a Christian should forsake both family and private property, and that all property should be held in common. This intriguing definition of heresy, together with the phrase seditious heretics, blurred the distinction between theology and affairs of state and told the political authorities that there was no room for religious dissent.

WITCHES: THE INVISIBLE OTHER

As is well known, beginning in the 1560s and lasting for well over a century, a formidable witch craze swept through European society, arguably the most telling characteristic of the time.[28] The "witch" made her dramatic appearance in Europe. To be sure, witches had been around well before the end of the fifteenth century, but the papal bull *Summis desiderantes* of 1484 and the subsequent publication of the *Malleus Maleficarum (The Witchhammer)* in 1487—a kind of "everything you have ever wanted to know about witches but were afraid to ask," with more than twenty-five reprints—began a profound consciousness-raising throughout Europe. There is no doubt that the *Malleus* was one of those pivotal works that, while lacking originality, prove to be of enormous historical significance. Since it had been published in close chronological proximity to the papal bull, the whole weight of papal authority seemingly stood behind the book. In addition, the *Malleus* offered an encyclopedic treatment of the topic and added, by focusing on women as witches, lurid aspects to the subject matter.

[27]For Melanchthon see *Corpus Reformatorum,* IV:73:7ff. and 111:195. In a second opinion, of 1536, great emphasis is placed on theological deviance. Melanchthon distinguished between insurrectionist and blasphemous teaching of the Anabaptists, with their blasphemy consisting of their rejection of the "ministerium verbi."

[28]The literature is extensive. At the risk of not doing justice to a complex historiography, I note as especially helpful H. C. Erik Midelfort, *Witch Hunting in Southwestern Germany 1662–1684: The Social and Intellectual Foundation* (Palo Alto, Calif.: Stanford, 1972); E. W. Monter, *Witchcraft in France and Switzerland: The Borderlands during the Reformation* (Ithaca: Cornell, 1976), and the useful summary of research, *Hexen und Hexenprozesse,* ed. Walter Behringer (Munich: Deutsche Taschenbuch, 1988).

Hans J. Hillerbrand

In the immediate aftermath of the publication of *The Witchhammer* a wave of witchcraft trials swept across certain parts of Europe (in Germany some twenty trials took place within two decades). There also was a notable increase in artistic appropriations of the witch theme, not to mention a host of faddish imitations of the *Malleus* by plagiarizing authors, theological and other. Since extensive sections of the *Malleus* were nothing but theological pornography, neither notoriety nor penchant for imitation is surprising. Witchology became a growth industry.

But that is not the whole story. There is evidence of popular passivity to, and even resistance against, the incipient witch craze. As has been pointed out, the real wave of persecution of witches and witchcraft did not come until the middle of the sixteenth century. We may conclude that in the late fifteenth century witchcraft (that is, the practice of magic and sorcery) had not yet been defined as social deviance. People saw nothing wrong with magic, particularly since there was "good" magic (such as beguiling a reluctant lover), and notions of nightly flights of women or metamorphoses of animals were not beyond popular imagination and fancy. After all, the stories people had heard from early childhood, the many fables and fairy tales, were full of such magical happenings. Importantly, magic had not been defined solely as malicious. It took until the middle of the sixteenth century for the pleadings of the *Malleus* to become operational and, a few isolated antecedents notwithstanding, for the criminalization of witchcraft to begin in earnest throughout Europe.[29] A change in attitude—and mentality—occurred.

Many suggestions have been made as to the reasons. Emmanuel LeRoy Ladurie's notion of a period of exceptionally disastrous climatic changes—the "short ice age"—is one of the more striking suggestions of recent scholarship.[30] Whatever the cause, a lengthy congery of charges delineated the characteristics of witches and defined witchcraft with increasing precision.

---

[29]See Walter Rummel, *Bauern, Herren und Hexen* (Göttingen: Vandenhoeck & Ruprecht, 1991), 15, as well as Gerhard Schortmann, *Hexenprozesse in Deutschland* (Göttingen: Vandenhoeck & Ruprecht, 1977).

[30]See Hartmut Lehmann, "Frömmigkeitsgeschichtliche Auswirkungen der Kleinen Eiszeit," in *Volksreligiosität in der modernen Sozialgeschichte,* ed. W. Schleder (Göttingen: Vandenhoeck & Ruprecht, 1986), 31–51, as well as Eva Labouvie, *Zauberei und Hexenwerk: Ländlicher Hexenglaube in der frühen Neuzeit* (Frankfurt a.M.: Fischer, 1991).

The papal bull had set the tone with a fairly comprehensive indictment: "With their magic, incantations, and spells witches cause to perish, to suffocate, to die the births of women, the offspring of animals, the fruit of the earth, the grapes and fruit of the trees, as well as men, women, cattle, livestock, and other kinds of animals, together with vineyards, orchards, meadows, corn, wheat, and other fruit of the earth."[31] In short, the sum total of the harm that did (or might) befall creation and humans was now attributed to witches. The theological indictments of the *Witchhammer* against witches cited evil spells, apostasy, weird nocturnal meetings, followed by intercourse with the devil (of an unnatural sort, of course), as the hallmarks of witches. The key charge was the witch's compact with the devil, who as the active party, enticed, tempted, and sealed that compact with sexual intercourse without the intention of procreation. In other words, the witch was the significant Other of the devil. Traditional notions of magic coalesced with the notion of pacts with the devil and of illicit sexuality.

At the root was undoubtedly a fear of female sexuality and a statement about women. Whatever else the attack on witches was in early modern Europe, it also was an attack on women.[32] This is, of course, the significance of the *Malleus,* which included a lengthy section on "the greater susceptibility of women" in its encyclopedic treatment of the topic. Not surprisingly, the descriptions in the *Malleus* of the witches' disturbance of the natural order have to do with sex— witches cause impotence, effect castration and sterilization, infertility, premature births, and in general separate (horror of horrors) the act of sex from the intention of procreation. The charge of sexual intercourse with the devil predestined the witch to be female, which fit harmoniously with the strand of medieval tradition that saw woman as sexually promiscuous.

The European witch craze is an enormously helpful illustration for the place of the Other in society, because the brief summary description just offered indicates that the sundry charges had a common denominator: witches are different, are not like we are; they are the Other. The importance of the dual issues of visibility and moral

---

[31]*Biblioteca sive acta et scriptis magica,* ed. E. D. Hauber (Lemgo, 1738), 1ff.

[32]Note the observation in Jean-Michel Sallmann, "Witches," in *A History of Women,* ed. Natalie Z. Davis and Arlette Farge (Cambridge: Belknap Press, 1993), 445, that women were four times as likely to be charged with witchcraft than were men.

corruption must again be noted. Now the problem was that witches—dramatically more so than either Jews or Anabaptists—were invisible—unless particularly outstanding features of certain suspect women, such as red hair or stunning beauty, were adduced. Since as a rule those suspected as witches were as churchgoing as everyone else in their community and, moreover, unlike the Anabaptists, quite willing to affirm the doctrinal tenets of the prevailing confession, they were truly invisible. Hence, the use of torture to pry confessions out of the victims. Excruciating pain made the victims become verbally visible.

BEGGARS AND PROSTITUTES: THE SOCIALLY
DISRESPECTABLE OTHER

Beggars and begging had increased throughout the fifteenth century. Traditionally, beggars had been placed at a low rung of a hierarchically structured society that had not, however, disowned them. Prior to the fifteenth century, begging was seen as an altogether legitimate way of earning a living in cases where no other means were available, as for example, in the case of a widow, or a blind or a disabled person. Such societal approval was related to the fact that, after all, begging evidently had divine approval, as was daily demonstrated by the begging of the mendicant orders. If the monks were allowed to beg, so surely were the secular beggars. The moral and statutory neutrality, if not benevolence, of society toward begging becomes understandable. Begging constituted no societal threat.

One may argue that this attitude presupposed a fairly stable society in which the number of beggars—that is, their place in a community—did not significantly change. However, as the number of beggars began to swell throughout Europe in the latter part of the fifteenth century, a phenomenon caused by changing economic conditions, begging became an issue. According to one estimate some 10 percent of the population of London lived in poverty by the middle of the sixteenth century.[33] With poverty thus very much a reality, discussion about begging accelerated in the sixteenth century. Distinctions began to be made among types and kinds of beggars—essentially between those whose begging was legitimate and those

---

[33]Steven Rappaport, *Worlds within Worlds: Structures of Life in Sixteenth-Century London* (Cambridge: Cambridge University Press, 1989), 167.

whose was not (shades of the welfare reform discussion of our own day!). More importantly, the sixteenth century is increasingly characterized by governmental efforts at the social control of both begging and beggars.[34]

Beggars were seen as threats to the public order. Harsh penalties were stipulated for unlicensed vagabonds and beggars. Official begging licenses were restricted to disabled men and women, particularly old, widowed ones, or to mothers of young children abandoned by their husbands.[35] In England the connection between begging, vagrancy, and social unrest was made repeatedly and pointedly. In turn, German cities enacted poor laws that distinguished between native and foreign beggars, and English legislation threatened severe measures against the latter, including the use of torture for children under fourteen years of age.[36] The beggar ceased to be simply a poor person; he/she became a social deviant. As an English observer noted, there was as great a difference between a poor man and a beggar, as between a true man and a thief.[37] Literature reflected this changing picture. Typically, begging was characterized as elaborate deviousness, a conspiracy of fraud and corruption, against which severe measures of social control were both necessary and appropriate.[38]

The situation was not too different as regards prostitution.[39] Medieval society had reluctantly embraced Augustine's concession that prostitution was an unavoidable evil that had to be accepted to

[34]Robert Jütte, "Poor Relief and Social Discipline in Sixteenth Century Europe," *European Studies Review* 11 (1981): 25-52; idem, *Abbild und soziale Wirklichkeit des Bettler– und Gaunertums zu Beginn der Neuzeit* (Cologne: Böhlau, 1998), 39; idem, *Poverty and Deviance in Early Modern Europe* (Cambridge: Cambridge University Press, 1994). For the role of the Reformation, see Carter Lindberg, *Beyond Charity: Reformation Initiatives for the Poor* (Minneapolis: Fortress, 1993).

[35]Richard Kagan, *Lucretia's Dreams: Politics and Prophecy in 16th-Century Spain* (Berkeley: University of California Press, 1990), 159.

[36]Thomas Kelly, *Thorns on the Tudor Rose: Monks, Rogues, Vagabonds, and Sturdy Beggars* (Jackson, Miss.: 1977), 55.

[37]As cited in Christopher Thomas Daly, "The Hospitals of London: Administration, Refoundation, and Benefaction, c. 1500–1572" (Ph.D diss., Oxford University, 1993), 127.

[38]For an interesting case study of crime in a major city, see Peter Blastenbrei, *Kriminalität in Rom 1560–1585* (Tübingen: Niemeyer, 1995).

[39]For early modern prostitution generally, see Margaret Rosenthal, *The Honest Courtesan* (Chicago: University of Chicago Press, 1992), and the article "Prostitution," in *The Oxford Encyclopedia of the Reformation* (1996). See also the formidable study of Beate Schuster, *Die freien Frauen: Dirnen und Frauenhäuser im 15. und 16. Jahrhundert* (Frankfurt: Campus, 1995).

prevent yet greater evil. In a way, the structures of medieval society tended to encourage prostitution. Society, aided by Christian senti- ment, affirmed strict canons of monogamy, but not all men had the possibility of marriage, particularly early marriage. The rigid insis- tence on virginity for brides was coupled with a relatively late mar- riage age for males on account of lengthy apprenticeship periods. Social commentators of the time reflected on the matter, as for exam- ple John Marston's *The Dutch Courtesan* (1606), which had in its first act a lengthy praise of prostitution, of course with tongue in cheek, but indicative of a widespread sentiment: "Why is charity grown a sin? Or relieving the poor and impotent an offense? ... They sell their bodies; do not better persons sell their souls?"

In the course of the sixteenth century attitudes toward prostitu- tion became negative and prostitution was increasingly controlled and criminalized.[40] By midcentury most brothels in Germany had been shut down: Augsburg (1532), Basel (1534), Frankfurt (1560), to cite a few examples.[41] Governmental mandates set new parameters of acceptable behavior. Increased social control of prostitutes was accompanied by according them certain privileges (such as rigorous suppression of outside competitors). These privileges were, in fact, as discriminatory as were the means of control. In Cologne, by the mid- dle of the century, the restrictions were particularly harsh. Prostitutes were no longer allowed to receive communion, be buried in church cemeteries, or to have contact with so-called honorable persons except, the historian is inclined to add, contact with those "honor- able" men who, without such strictures and without penalty, joined them in bed. Pope Pius V issued a general prohibition of the burial of prostitutes in church cemeteries.

Why were beggars and prostitutes further outside the parameters of society and more threatening to society in the course of the six- teenth century than they had been earlier? As regards beggars, the answer seems obvious. They were seen as threats to public order. The change in the societal attitude toward prostitutes is more compli-

---

[40]Kathryn Norberg, "Prostitutes," in Davis and Farge, *History of Women,* 458ff. For a fascinating study, see also J. Rossiaud, "Prostitution, jeunesse et societes dans les viles du Sud Est aux XVe siècle," *Annales* 31 (1976): 289–325.

[41]For London, see W. Shugg, "Prostitution in Shakespeare's London," *Shakespeare Studies* 10 (1977): 291–310. For Rome, see Jean Delumeau, *Vie economique et sociale de Rome le seconde moitie du XVIe siècle* (Paris: DeBoccard, 1957).

cated, for certainly on the face of things they were a threat. But as a threat they were taken. The moralistic impulses of both the Protestant and Catholic reformations—Martin Luther had inveighed against the Augustinian principle of reluctant toleration as precisely the kind of moral confusion of medieval Christendom that called for reform, and Calvin's notion of reform, as exemplified in Geneva, sought likewise to do away with moral laxity and compromise. Orderliness and discipline were made part of godliness. And then there was the fear of syphilis, the mysterious "French disease," which had made its appearance late in the fifteenth century, whose containment was seen by the authorities as an important public health issue.[42] In fact, it may well have been the fear of syphilis, seen as a divine scourge, that prompted the intensification of the moral reaction and the measures of tighter social control.

SUMMARY

A. Our summary might well begin with a fairly general observation: At the end of the sixteenth century, Europe was far more repressive of the Other than it had been at the beginning of the century. Rigid enforcement of conformity and exercise of social control were far more common in 1600 than they had been in 1500, even though the beginnings of this development reach back into the fifteenth century. The sixteenth century was vigorous in its continuation of certain trends already established. For example, prostitution, previously accepted by society, was increasingly regimented, with prostitutes assigned the role of marginalized Other. The same held true for Jews and for beggars.

This observation takes us straight to the two most important scholarly discussions pertaining to early modern Europe in recent years. One is Heinz Schilling's provocative notion that a process of confessionalization occurred in European societies—Catholic, Lutheran, and Reformed—in the second half of the sixteenth century. The argument is that all of society, be it education, politics, morality, was conceptualized from the perspective of the particular confession. The other is the notion to reconceptualize European history between roughly 1400 and 1650 as the distinctive period, one of transition

---

[42]Kathryn Norberg, "Prostitutes," in Davis and Farge, *History of women,* 458ff. (see n. 40 above).

between the Middle Ages and Modernity. This notion counters, of course, the traditional perspective that saw the year 1517 not only as the beginning of the Reformation, but also of a new epoch in favor of a much broader development that both precedes and follows the Reformation.[43]

B. This developing regimentation entailed a construction of the new Other. Increasing social control meant that the Other had to be made empirically indentifiable. When the Other is hidden from sight, the exercise of social control is difficult. Sixteenth-century society reacted to invisibility with a determined effort to make the Other visible. Prostitutes had to live (and work) in special quarters, had to wear special clothing, and were made explicitly subject to male supervisors, often the local henchman. Jews had to live in ghettos. Beggars had to wear special badges. Witches were tortured to exact "visible" confessions.

In this regard, an intriguing symbiotic relationship exists between visibility and invisibility. If the strangers are visible, that is, different, as Montaigne tells us with regard to the men brought by sea from a far country, they can easily become the Other. If, however, they are not visible, like the Jews or the Anabaptists, they need to be made visible. In the end, physical distinctiveness becomes a constitutive sign of the Other even though, as we noted at the beginning of this essay, physical distinctiveness also characterizes what we have called the Stranger: in short, a value judgment characterizes the Other. This is brought out tellingly by artistic representations of the Other, in which the caricature, the simplification of style and features, is used to express otherness. Ruth Mellinkoff's two splendid volumes on *Outcasts: Signs of Otherness in Northern European Art of the Late Middle Ages* details the large number of signs that the visual arts used in the late Middle Ages to depict the Other.[44] Mellinkoff finds these commonplace signs clustering around costume, physical features, and gestures. This, of course, reflects the notion that a person's clothing,

---

[43]Heinz Schilling's own key essay is now available in English translation: "Confessionalization in the Empire: Religious and Societal Change in Germany between 1555 and 1620," in *Religion, Political Culture and the Emergence of Early Modern Society* (Leiden: Brill, 1992), 205–46.

[44]Ruth Mellinkoff, *Signs of Otherness in Northern European Art of the Late Middle Ages*, 2 vols. (Berkeley: University of California Press, 1993).

body, and gestures speak as loudly as words.[45] Mellinkoff points out how Africans and Jews are given distinctive physical features (even in the late Middle Ages!) such as enlarged eyes, hooked noses, large lips.[46]

C. The identification of the Other was undertaken by the political authorities. Whether we talk about Anabaptists or witches, the agency of suppression was secular authority. This involvement of secular authority was obvious, of course. There was no other meaningful judicial persecution, which explains why the *Malleus Maleficarum* demanded that the prosecution of witches be handled by the secular authorities. Even the church's demand for social control needed the hand of government.

D. The theologians provided the rationale for the definition of social control. When, for example, in Württemberg in October 1557 Duke Christoph pursued a lenient policy toward the Anabaptists, the most severe expression of which was expulsion, the Lutheran divine Jacob Andreae led a group of Lutheran theologians to argue that stubborn Anabaptist leaders should be executed.[47] In other words, the definition of the Other in the sixteenth century was impossible unless theology served as handmaiden. No matter whether Jews, Anabaptists, even beggars and prostitutes, not to mention American Indians, the theologians provided the ideology of identification of the Other and thereby set the ideological parameters of social control. No matter where we look, theological discourse provided the ideology that defined the Other. Moreover, if regnant ideology bombards society with a constant barrage of arguments that the divine order of things mandates the judgment that there is an Other—who will not, therefore, enter into the kingdom of God—other censures and condemnations will surely follow.

[45]Mellinkoff, *Signs of Otherness*, iii.
[46]Mellinkoff, *Signs of Otherness* 128–29. She cites an early-eighteenth-century author who epitomizes this approach: "Among several hundred of them he has not encountered one without a blemish or some repulsive feature.... They have in general big heads and mouths, pouting lips, protruding eyes, and eyelashes like fistles ... large ears, crooked feet, hands that hang below their knees." Quoted in Joshua Trachtenberg, *The Devil and the Jews: The Medieval Conception of the Jew and Its Relation to Modern Anti-Semitism* (Philadelphia: Jewish Publication Society, 1983), 228.
[47]Still highly useful is John S. Oyer, *Lutheran Reformers Against Anabaptists* (The Hague: Nijhoff, 1964).

E. The theological rationale for the identification of the Other always included a moral indictment. The exercise of social control was uniformly accompanied by the charge of moral shortcoming, in which the charges of promiscuity or sexual deviance were particularly important. And there was always the charge, variously expressed, of the disturbance of the public order.[48] We may presume that the charge was made sincerely, arising out of insecurity concerning the stability of society. Thus, the historian will well tire quickly of the incessant references to the insurrectionist schemes of the Anabaptists. After all, revolutionary Anabaptists were few and very far between in the sixteenth century. But the secular authorities had been persuaded by the theologians that the causality existed, and sensitive as the issue was they made it an important element in their policies. Clearly, the authorities believed the charges; they had no reason to be deceptive or to go to such extraordinary lengths to stress the accusation.

F. We must be careful not to equate the voices that defined the Other with the sentiment of the common people, if for no other reason than that the exercise of control, no matter with what prefix, presupposes power. As regards the Anabaptists, for example, the common people were rather far removed from any ability of identifying them as the Other, something that, by the way, could also be said about the Native Americans. The Native Americans were far, far away, and only the elites were in a position to produce opinion for the common people. The Anabaptists generally were fine neighbors.

In short, when the Other is constructed, we primarily hear the voices of the elite. Accordingly, we are well apprised of official notions concerning the Anabaptists, for example, or concerning the Jews. We know far less, however, about the sentiment of the common people, the burghers of the cities or the peasants in the rural areas. However, it is necessary to distinguish between the two and not take the establishment's sentiment for popular opinion. The time lag between the publication of *The Witchhammer* and the actual onset of the European witch craze is surely one of the many illustrations for the fact that the tightening of social control by the authorities met with a measure of popular resistance. In some cases, the Other did not even have a voice of her own. The victimized witches of the European

---

[48]Leonard Verduin, *The Reformers and Their Stepchildren* (Grand Rapids: Eerdmans, 1964), 221 ff.

witch craze did not leave testimonies of self-declaration. Their confessions, generally made under torture, must be considered dubious at best. Robert Mandrou's widely cited study of the magistracy and witches in seventeenth-century France showed persuasively that the judges imposed their own image onto the defendants.[49] The voice of the Other is generally silent.

G. This takes us to a related point. The polemic, literary as well as artistic, against the Other reflected the strategy of persuasion and pedagogy. Martin Luther's or Johann Brenz's diatribes against the Anabaptists, their insistence on the appropriateness of capital punishment for them, or Thomas Cranmer's *Good Friday* liturgy, must be read as an indication that a case had to be made for the redefinition of social control. These polemics should be seen, not as indicators of popular sentiment, but as the exact opposite. They were written for a pedagogical purpose.

H. Kai Erikson has argued that deviance does not occur when behavior transgresses an established moral rule, but rather the moral rule shifts to define activities as deviant that originally had not been themselves a threat to moral boundaries. The emergence of deviance is not dependent on the action of a transgressor. Rather, the moral rule is modified to include behavior that had existed all along.[50] This happens when society experiences a threat, a crisis, to its collective existence.

Clearly, the Others in the sixteenth century were seen, in one way or another, as threats to the established order.[51] Whether or not the observer will agree that there existed a threat is another question that well illustrates George Duby's notions of the "images mentales," the interrelationship between social reality and the perceptions thereof.[52]

---

[49]Robert Mandrou, *Magistrats et sorciers en France an XVIIe siècle* (Paris: Ploss, 1968).

[50]See Kai T. Erikson, "Notes on the Sociology of Deviance," *Social Problems* 9 (1962): 307–14; also his extensive historical study *Wayward Puritans: A Study in Sociology of Deviance* (New York: Macmillan, 1966). See also Albert Bergesen, "Social Control and Corporate Organization," in *Toward a General Theory of Social Control*, 2:148 (see n. 8 above).

[51]Bergesen, "Social Control and Corporate Organization," 149.

[52]George Duby, "Histoire sociale et ideologies des societies," in *Faire de l'histoire,* ed. Jacques Le Goff and Pierre Nova (Paris: Gallimard, 1974), 147–48.

Erikson's boundary theory of social control and deviance suggests that church and state acted in response to a perceived challenge—the challenge to unquestioned hegemony. The involvement of the church and theologians in this meant that the Other was easily seen as demonic.[53] The argument was that the order of society had been established by God and that any deviation from this order constituted a demonic violation. The Other transgressed against the divine order of things. Understandably, the Anabaptists were a threat to both political and religious authorities.

These comments should not be understood as an effort to flatten the sense of the Other by asserting that, in the final analysis, they were all alike. Michel de Certeau's essay, "The Institution of Rot,"[54] does precisely that with his poststructuralist confrontation with mystical speech. Thereby the most disparate forms of Otherness (e.g., that represented by the torturer or that represented by an overwhelming deity) are folded into a single category.

There are clear differences among the Others. While this paper proposed some common denominators, the differences are real. By embracing the boundary theory of social control, this paper means to call attention not to the stranger, but to the Other, arguing that this Other is a societal construction. From the perspective of society, however, all Others are identical.

This essay suggests that sixteenth-century society was unanimous in its assertion that there was no room for the Other in the inn. To leave the story at that, however, will not tell the whole story. There were a few isolated individuals—Sebastian Franck, Sebastian Castellio, possibly even Erasmus of Rotterdam[55]—for whom the Other was not a meaningful category.[56] Each in his particular way acknowledged that there were strangers but also advocated understanding and acceptance. Sebastian Franck, for example, argued that while the religion of Jews, Muslims (and Christians, for that matter) was wrong, the elect of God can be found also among them. Franck argued that the religious

---

[53]On the demonic perspective of deviance, see Stephen Pfohl, *Images of Deviance and Social Control: A Sociological History* (New York: McGraw-Hill, 1985), 17ff.

[54]Michel de Certeau, "The Institution of Rot, in *Heterologies: Discourse on the "Other"* (Minneapolis: University of Minneapolis, 1986).

[55]Meinulf Barbers, *Toleranz bei Sebastian Franck* (Bonn: Röhrscheid, 1964).

[56]For example, see Simon Markish, *Erasmus and the Jews* (Chicago: University of Chicago Press, 1986).

Other will disappear as soon as false understanding of religion is abandoned.

This, then, is a good place to end these ruminations. Indeed, to end upon mentioning Castellio and Franck leaves us, all things considered, at a cheery place, for these men may well be seen as harbingers of change and of a new beginning—a good way to end a dreary story. All the same, our judgment as scholar and our values as humans must decide if the course of the past four hundred years has borne this out.

Burning of Margarita Revel (age 45, of La Cartere) and Maria de
Pravillerin (age 90 and blind, of S. Giovanni) in Les Vignes, near
Angrogna. From "In the Valleys of Piemont," in *Cruelties exercised
against the Evangelical Church,* book 2.

"With a morsel of bread"

Delineating Differences in the Jewish and Christian Communities of Regensburg before the Pogrom of 1519

Kristin E. S. Zapalac

This article contrasts the ritual definition of communal boundaries in the city of Regensburg at the end of the medieval period. Both Jews and Christians delineated their communities with rituals that involved bread. The Corpus Christi procession, like the mass celebrated at the altars of the city's churches, defined the Christian community hierarchically: its significance lay in the fact that only a priest could transform bread into the body of Christ, a transformation celebrated in the procession that organized the city's inhabitants as "members of the body of Christ," each with his or her own distinct function in the whole. In contrast, the much older ritual establishment of the *'erub* (fusion of the courtyards) focused attention on the "breadness" of the bread that was used and on the Sabbath as a liminal moment in which the whole Jewish community shared that one bread. The two rituals intersected in Regensburg at the end of the medieval period when the city's pious Christian bakers refused to sell bread to the inhabitants of the *Judengasse*, an intersection that culminated in the infamous pogrom of 1519.

IT HAS BEEN SOME TIME NOW since I began to investigate the annual Corpus Christi procession in the free imperial city of Regensburg and the community whose boundaries the procession defined.[1] In a sense, I was, in that investigation, guilty of reconstructing those boundaries, for in Regensburg that procession with the bread consecrated in the mass circumnavigated and defined as Christian a walled city that contained at its heart another set of walls and a Jewish community. Strug-

[1]Kristin E. S. Zapalac, "The Contested Center: Sacred Rituals and Conflicting Authorities in Sixteenth-Century Regensburg," a paper delivered at the Sixteenth Century Studies Conference in 1988, in which I discussed the meaning, transformation, and elimination of the Corpus Christi procession in Regensburg. I am most grateful to Tom Brady for his comments on that paper.

gling not to repeat the late medieval Christian community's erasure of the Jewish community at its heart, I began to search for information about the ways in which the Jewish community—central to the Christian community in economic as well as geographic terms—might have defined itself and its communal space. At the time I had only a dim recollection of a wire I had seen in Baltimore stretched between poles and attributed by my *Doktorvater* Mack Walker to his Orthodox Jewish neighbors.[2] That dim memory led me to discover that the Jewish community in Regensburg had also ritually defined its boundaries—not with wire like the Baltimore community, but with the walls that set it apart from the Christian community, and—ironically—with a loaf of bread to which the Christians might have traced their own ritual usage. What follows is an examination of the similarities and differences between the self-definitions of the two communities.[3]

It was, in fact, similarity rather than difference that lay at the heart of the role played by bread in "delineating difference in the Jewish and Christian communities of Regensburg before the pogrom of 1519." So let me turn from subtitle to title, and specifically to some texts shared and some not shared by the two communities. It was with a "morsel of bread" that Abraham and Sarah had welcomed the three strangers identified with their god (Gen. 18:1–6); it was with a "morsel of bread" that the "father-in-law" of the tribe of Judah had welcomed his Levite son-in-law to Bethlehem, a town whose very name meant "house of bread" (Judg. 19:1–8); it was with a "morsel of bread" that Boas had welcomed the foreigner Ruth (Ruth 2:14). In contrast to these hospitable, inclusive gestures taken from the Scriptures both communities held to be sacred, the exclusively Christian Scriptures contain only a single appearance of a "morsel of bread" (Ψωμίον): in John's Gospel. According to that account, it was with a "morsel of bread" that Jesus marked Judas as the betrayer within, soon to be the outsider among the disciples (John 13:21–30). Perhaps

[2]Although the practice was unusual in American cities in the 1980s, when I observed the stretched wire in that Baltimore suburb, it is no longer uncommon for American Jewish communities to obtain the right to define their boundaries via markers affixed to utility poles.

[3]The examination that follows is a report of research in progress for two chapters in a much longer examination of the differences in Jewish and Christian conceptions of the "self" and the historical consequences of those differences through the early twentieth century.

more significant is the fact that, just as it is only in John's Gospel that the "morsel of bread" rather than the simple (dipping) action of the hand without a specified direct object is the marker of difference, so it is only John who does not place in Jesus' mouth the more familiar and liturgically troublesome reference to a loaf of bread: "hoc est corpus meum."

However the writers of the synoptic Gospels may have understood the words "this is my body" spoken at the Passover eve meal which they describe as Jesus' last, these words had by the late medieval period become a declaration that the bread consecrated in the mass was no longer characterized by "breadness." Given the development of what would become the defining Christian ritual out of the simpler meals eaten in Jewish homes before the dispersion, it is scarcely surprising to discover an egalitarian emphasis on community embedded between two references to the "breaking of bread" in the Acts of the Apostles:

> And they [who were baptized by Peter on Pentecost] devoted themselves to the apostles' teaching and fellowship, to the breaking of bread and the prayers.... And all who believed were together and had all things in common; and they sold their possessions and goods and distributed them to all, as any had need. And day by day, attending the temple together and breaking bread in their homes, they partook of food with glad and generous hearts (Acts 2:42, 44–46).[4]

It was first and foremost Paul, that most zealous of converts, who added to the communal implications of sharing bread a Christological significance. In his first letter to the Christians at Corinth (10:16–17) he wrote: "The bread we break, is it not a participation in the body of Christ? Because there is one bread, we who are many are one body, for we all partake of one bread." Despite the communal focus of his answer, in the same letter Paul himself famously stressed the differences between the members of the body of Christ, their "varieties of service" and "varieties of working." The late medieval mass, the meal at which the laity remained far from the table and were likely to consume the bread (host) only at Easter—and at which only the priest

---

[4]Pointed out by David Stanley, S.J., "Ecumenically Significant Aspects of New Testament Eucharistic Doctrine," in *The Sacraments: An Ecumenical Dilemma* (New York: Paulist Press, 1966), 43–50, here 44–46. Here and in what follows I have quoted from the Revised Standard Version of the Bible: *The New Oxford Annotated Bible with the Apocrypha* (New York: Oxford, 1977).

might sip the wine—might be described as the ultimate representation of the differences between the members of the body of Christ. Altarpiece and woodcut alike taught the alert observer to see in the bread elevated by the priest after his repetition of the words "hoc est corpus meum," not the "accident" of bread but the "reality" of the bleeding body of Christ. The ordinary bread broken at the simple meals at which Luke and John had reported that Jesus had suddenly appeared had been transformed.[5] Now that Christ himself was "seated at the right hand of the Father," bread had become the vehicle for Christ's incarnation, had become the "body of Christ" to which access must be restricted; told "noli me tangere" (John 20:17), the laity reenacted not the role of the doubting disciple Thomas but the role of Mary.

Like the roles of those at the mass, the roles of those involved in the Corpus Christi procession were carefully delineated. Although Charles Zika has recently shown that major Corpus Christi processions in other German cities ordered the cities' churches in the routes they followed,[6] in Regensburg this function was performed by the shorter Corpus Christi processions organized by individual churches. These smaller Corpus Christi processions at individual parish churches displayed the ordered unity and piety of individual guilds and demonstrated the connections and dependencies between the city's Christian as well as secular corporations. For example, the church of St. Cassian, first mentioned in an imperial document of 885 as a possession of the collegiate foundation of the Alte Kapelle and formally incorporated into the foundation in 1224, annually acknowledged its dependent status in a procession in which the monstranced host was carried—accompanied by tailors, locksmiths, and pewterers—from St. Cassian's where their guild altars stood, to the Alte Kapelle. Linear and unidirectional, the shorter processions

---

[5]Luke 24:30; John 21:13. Cf. Jerome's reference in *On Illustrious Men* to Jesus' breaking of bread for James in "the Gospel according to the Hebrews," quoted in *Gospel Parallels: A Synopsis of the First Three Gospels*, ed. Burton H. Throckmorton, Jr. (New York: Nelson, 1957), 190n.

[6]Charles Zika, "Hosts, Processions and Pilgrimages: Controlling the Sacred in Fifteenth-Century Germany," *Past and Present* 118 (1988), 25–64. For further discussion of Corpus Christi processions, see Peter Browe, *Die Verehrung der Eucharistie im Mittelalter* (1933; reprint Sinzig: Sankt Meinrad Reprintverlag, C.M. Esser, 1990); Mervyn James, "Ritual, Drama and Social Body in the Late Medieval English Town," *Past and Present* 98 (1983), 3–29; and Miri Rubin, *Corpus Christi: The Eucharist in Late Medieval Culture* (Cambridge: Cambridge University Press, 1991).

pointed to a single source of protection or of allegiance owed.[7] In contrast, Regensburg's municipal Corpus Christi procession circumscribed the city.[8] Despite this, the theme of the procession was anything but egalitarian.[9]

The foundation of the procession in the first decade of the fifteenth century was attributed to a city councillor, Matthäus Runtinger, the magistrate who had begun the paving of the streets the procession would traverse and who had given a local monastery a gilded silver box topped with a crucifix "in order eternally to hold our Lord's body."[10] The procession established by Runtinger in 1408 focused attention on the plaza before the cathedral, one of the plazas enlarged by Runtinger that same year at municipal expense.[11]

Begun by Runtinger and thereafter organized by the city council, Regensburg's Corpus Christi procession defined community hierarchically as well as geographically.[12] It claimed literally to embody the

[7]Leonhard Widmann, *Chronik von Regensburg*, ed. E. V. Oefele, Die Chroniken der deutschen Städte vom 14. bis in das 16. Jahrhundert, 15 (Leipzig: S. Hirzel, 1878), 204, 206; *Die Kunstdenkmäler von Bayern*, vol. 22: *Stadt Regensburg*, pt. 2: *Die Kirchen der Stadt*, ed. Felix Bader (1933; reprint, Munich: R. Oldenbourg, 1981), 167; *Regensburg: Geschichte in Bilddokumenten*, ed. Andreas Kraus and Wolfgang Pfeiffer (Munich: Beck, 1979), 33; Guido Hable and Raimund Sterl, *Geschichte Regensburgs: Eine Übersicht nach Sachgebieten* (Regensburg: Mittelbayerische Druckerei- und Verlagsgesellschaft, 1970), 113.

[8]On this functional aspect of processions in German cities in general, see Bob Scribner, "Cosmic Order and Daily Life: Sacred and Secular in Pre-Industrial German Society," in *Religion and Society in Early Modern Europe, 1500–1800*, ed. Kaspar von Greyerz (London: German Historical Institute, 1984), 17–32.

[9] Consider, e.g., the papal indulgence (1487), quoted in Carl Theodor Gemeiner, *Reichsstadt Regensburgische Chronik*, 2d ed., 4 vols., ed. Heinz Angermeier (Munich: C. H. Beck, 1971), 3:375n; letters of indulgence from two cardinals (1462, 1471): ibid., 376n, 497n. All three documents refer explicitly to the "general procession" that circumnavigated the city. Cf. the memorandum concerning a special procession with the Corpus Christi and saints' relics to be made to petition God's aid during the Hussite war: "It is the earnest will of the councillors that everyone process reverently and chastely, and that the women in particular go at the end [of the procession] and that they soberly not mix with the men, and whoever transgresses this will be severely punished." Ibid., 2:463n. The procession took place in 1427, not during the octave of Corpus Christi, but in July. (All translations mine, unless otherwise noted.)

[10]Ibid., 2:271n, 384.   [11]Ibid., 220n, 357, 383–84.

[12]The classic work on the medieval Christian conception of the German city as *corpus christianum* is Heinrich Schmidt, *Die deutschen Städtechroniken als Spiegel des bürgerlichen Selbstverständnisses im Spätmittelalter*, Schriftenreihe der historischen Kommission bei der Bayerischen Akademie der Wissenschaften, 3 (Ph.D. diss., University of Göttingen, 1958), esp. 89–97. Cf. Bernd Moeller, *Reichsstadt und Reformation*, Schriften des Vereins für Reformationsgeschichte, 180 (Gütersloh, 1962), available in English as

city, but the *corpus christianum* it embodied was a Pauline body of discrete and ranked members. Even the invitations to participate were extended hierarchically: written invitations to the bishop and chapter were extended formally by the council as a body, those to the abbots and abbesses of orders within the walls by council members personally, and those to the prior of St. Mang across the river and to the abbot of Prüfening by courier. The religious orders themselves and the city's guilds were invited by municipal bailiffs.[13] Honored citizens carrying candles provided by the city council were followed by a hierarchy of guildsmen—from butchers through candlestickmakers and, in the place of prestige just before the Corpus Christi, the bakers. The bakers' particular reputation for piety, the source of their precedence in the Corpus Christi procession, may also account for their refusal to sell bread to the Jews of Regensburg, a refusal that would result in several complaints against them.[14] It was of course not the bread baked by the bakers' guild, but the consecrated bread—the Corpus Christi itself—that was borne in the procession by the bishop in a container like the one Runtinger had donated, under a baldachin provided by the city council and carried by members of the city council accompanied by the city's clerics.[15]

The tension between this hierarchical celebration of the "real presence" of Christ in the elements consecrated by the priest—a celebration and "real presence" to which access was restricted (even the bishop did not touch the monstrance in which the host was displayed, but shielded it from his hands with a humeral veil)—and the celebration of community in a communal meal was made explicit in two ritual actions in 1431, the year of the Hussite War. Before the militiamen of Catholic Regensburg went off to their "holy war" they

---

Imperial Cities and the Reformation, trans. H. C. Erik Midelfort and Mark U. Edwards, Jr. (Philadelphia: Fortress Press, 1972).

[13]Gemeiner, *Chronik*, 3:373–74 (see n. 9 above).

[14]Ibid., 3:373–75 (1463). The guild order was: farmers, bath attendants, carters, cutlers, cooks, wagonwrights and smiths, potters, dyers, locksmiths and cabinetmakers, clothworkers, taverners, tailors, shoemakers and leatherworkers, furriers, woolworkers, fishermen, shopkeepers and beltmakers, goldsmiths and stonecutters, butchers, municipal employees, and, finally, bakers.

[15]Ibid., 202 (1452). It should be noted in this connection that the host, although generally borne in the Corpus Christi procession by the highest ecclesiastic present, was unique in its character as a holy object that was as fully and really present in the humblest chapel as in the cathedral itself.

attended a special mass at St. Emmerams in which, as usual, only the priest consumed the consecrated wine. That mass was followed by a ceremonial sharing of wine supplied by the city council and blessed in the name of St. John the Evangelist, a ritual sharing normally associated with the new year, when it was held to bring luck to the drinkers, but extended also to pilgrims.[16] The mass stood in stark contrast to the communal sharing of wine blessed in the name of the disciple told by Jesus that he would "drink of my cup" (Matt. 20:23; Mark 10:39), the disciple depicted "leaning on Jesus' bosom" at the meal at which Jesus had issued his *mandatum* concerning the bread and wine.[17] It was in fact this contrast that defined the difference between the Catholics of Regensburg and their heterodox Hussite opponents. Curiously, this boundary was portable: following the captain, cavalry, archers, and musketeers as they processed to the battlefield was a wagon carrying the chaplain of the Ahakirche, the chapel next to the *Rathaus* (city hall) recently transferred from St. Emmeram's control to that of the city.[18] He carried the silver chalice reserved for the priest's reception of the wine consecrated in the mass—an explicit rejection of the Utraquist Hussite position on communion in both kinds by the laity. Despite this display of military and spiritual might, the forces of Catholicism were met on the battlefield on the vigil of the Assumption of Mary not by a Constantinian sign but by the Hussite battle hymn "God's Soldiers" and the rumble of Hussite battle wagons. According to one account this competing display of God's support combined with the defeats already suffered to cause the imperial Christians to scatter in disarray. Those Regensburgers who survived returned home without weapons, sacramental objects, or food.[19]

Regensburg's annual Corpus Christi procession circumscribed less contested turf. Or did it? In 1486–87, while Herzog Albrecht IV of Bayern-München, the city's newly contracted lord, was working to

[16]On the *Johannisminnetrunk*, see Adolph Franz, *Die kirchlichen Benediktionen im Mittelalter* (Freiburg i. Br. : Herder, 1909), 1:328–92. Franz notes that the Johannisminne was extended also to soldiers, giving as his sole example this Regensburg event without noting the particular importance of the cup(s) in 1431 (329, n. 5).

[17]The description of the "beloved" disciple at Christ's breast occurs only in the Gospel of John (13:23), the only Gospel in which the *mandatum* is not issued, the bread and wine not prayed over by the god-man. Despite this, medieval depictions of the *mandatum*, like depictions of the betrayal, depict John the Evangelist at Jesus' side.

[18]Mader, *Die Kunstdenkmäler von Bayern*, 22, part 3:86 (see n. 7 above).

[19]I take this account from Gemeiner, *Chronik*, 3:22–23 (see n. 9 above), and Romuald Bauerreiss, *Kirchengeschichte Bayerns* (St. Ottilien: EOS Verlag, 1958), 5:13–14.

improve his own financial situation by obtaining control over Regensburg's Jewish community and to improve the city's financial situation by obtaining a papal bull establishing indulgences for those who attended the Corpus Christi procession, Regensburg's clerics were suggesting that the procession be curtailed until the citizens' anger over clerical immunity from taxation for beer brewing had cooled.[20] In 1504–5, a decade after Albrecht had been forced to abandon his claim to Regensburg, the continued existence of Bavarian partisans in the officially imperial city made it inadvisable to hold the Corpus Christi procession outside the walls while imperial and ducal forces fought nearby over the Bavarian succession.[21] The procession was again omitted during 1512–14, a period of civil strife finally "resolved" by an imperial commission that executed wrongdoers and required the formal submission of the citizenry to an imperial captain. In Regensburg as elsewhere, the Corpus Christi procession or its cancellation was often a marker of the tension that lay at the political heart of the very *corpus christianum* it proclaimed.

Paradoxically, it is the presence of the Jewish community at the geographical heart of medieval Regensburg's *corpus christianum* that may explain the unusual route taken by its municipal procession around the walls, rather than from church to church within the walls.[22] Strikingly, the route taken failed to acknowledge the chapel

---

[20]Gemeiner, *Chronik*, 3:747.

[21]In place of a Corpus Christi procession celebrating the city as harmonious universe, the Regensburg city council that year requested each of the city's parishes to hold individual processions on all feast days, and it organized a municipal procession with the three shrines ("den dreien sergen") containing the relics of SS. Emmeram, Erhard, and Wolfgang, the most important relics in the ecclesiastical foundations within the walls. Gemeiner, *Chronik*, 4:89, 92–93. The city did, however, pay for a curtailed procession; "Ainitz Ausgebn" (1505), fol. 5, Munich, Bayerisches Hauptstaatsarchiv (hereafter BHStA), Gemeiners Nachlaß 16.

[22]I can find no reference to "stations" (whether of the cross or otherwise) at which the procession might have halted. In contrast to the description given by Zika of the Würzburg procession of 1381, the published letters of indulgence refer consistently to a procession "around" the city, and the route itself avoids the major ecclesiastical foundations with the exception of the cathedral itself. Zika, "Hosts, Processions and Pilgrimages," 38–40 (see n. 6 above). The cleric Widmann specifically says of the reading from the four Evangelists that was a part of the curtailed procession of 1532: "all of which is not done when one goes around the city." Widmann, *Chronik von Regensburg*, 114 (see n. 7 above). On the readings and hymns generally used during Corpus Christi processions: Valentin Thalhofer and Ludwig Eisenhofer, *Handbuch der katholischen Liturgik*, 2d ed. (Freiburg i. Br.: Herder, 1912), 1:667. The readings from the four Evangelists are here described as borrowings from penitential processions, such as those associated with Rogation Day.

built within the city's walls to mark the site at which the host, the Corpus Christi itself, had been miraculously preserved from desecration.[23] According to the chroniclers, in 1255 on Maundy Thursday, the very day on which the city's Christians, following the synoptic Gospels, paid solemn homage to Jesus' transformation of what they saw as the Passover meal with the words "hoc est corpus meum," the cathedral priest Ulrich von Dornberg had stumbled while carrying the consecrated bread to the sick. The hosts fell from their container toward the sewer that ran along the street just outside the Jewish quarter. Since it was Holy Week, the gates of the quarter were closed; since the bread spilt was the body of Christ, angels immediately appeared and gathered the bread before it could be desecrated. In order to consecrate the miraculous site, Regensburg's Christian citizens built a wooden chapel to the Savior in three days. Over time the chapel was enlarged and the miraculous proof of the power of the consecrated bread commemorated in a wool tapestry—just as Runtinger was establishing the city's Corpus Christi procession. Clearly, the omission of the chapel from the processional route requires explanation. The route taken by the municipal Corpus Christi procession did more than simply mark the paving of some of the city's streets and plazas. It avoided more than the ranking of the city's various churches. It avoided the only church dedicated to the very sacrament it celebrated, a church located just outside the walls of the *Judengasse*. In so doing, it avoided—attempted to elide—Regensburg's Jewish community. This was all the easier since on the Sunday following Corpus Christi, as on that Maundy Thursday in 1255 and on any occasion on which the consecrated host was carried through the city's

---

[23]The Salvatorkapelle in the church attached to the Augustinian monastery in the center of Regensburg at the southwest corner of the city's Jewish ghetto [= Neupfarrplatz] was founded in 1255 on the site at which a priest had dropped a ciborium only to have the hosts it contained miraculously caught by angels. The foundation myth was preserved in the fifteenth century by a tapestry (ca. 1420), which is now in the Bayerisches Nationalmuseum, Munich. The chapel was referred to in the declaration of indulgence issued by several cardinals for the Regensburg Corpus Christi procession in 1462, but did not lie on the processional route. Gemeiner, *Chronik*, 3:376n (see n. 9 above). A second Salvatorkapelle, built in 1476 to commemorate the preservation of hosts tossed away by a young thief who had stolen another ciborium, did lie on the route of the Corpus Christi procession, but was not mentioned in the papal bull of 1487. The chapel was sold by the Lutheran city council to a tavernkeeper in 1542, but an altar panel depicting the discovery of the discarded hosts survives in the Germanisches Nationalmuseum, Nuremberg. Ibid., 3:375n.

Kristin E. S. Zapalac

streets, no Jew was allowed to leave the ghetto: the gates of the enclave were locked, any windows in its walls shuttered.[24] The walls, however, remained as highly visible reminders of the tensions between the two communities.

It was of course not the walls but their permeability, the interdependence of the two communities as well as their common heritage in Hebrew Scriptures, that was the source of tension. This permeability was emphasized in the lawsuits and stories of conversions from Judaism to Christianity and from Christianity to Judaism.[25] And in the simplest transactions of everyday life. Among complaints lodged in 1499 by the Jewish community with their overlord Herzog Georg of Bayern-Landshut and with the Regensburg city council and its imperial overseer was one concerning daily bread. "No baker will sell us any bread, a situation we with our small children have long had to endure."[26] The issue was critical to a community without its own bakers. Herzog Georg formally reminded the city council that he had a financial stake in the presence of the Jews within its walls and warned the citizens against "this or any other injury that might drive out the Jews."[27] Kaiser Maximilian I, who was in the process of wresting control of Regensburg's Jews from the Bavarian line, also responded to the complaint of 1499; in 1500 he issued a mandate forbidding Regensburg's bakers to refuse to sell bread to the Jews.[28]

Despite such interventions the tensions within the city continued to rise, fed by the popular religious zealotry encouraged by the city's bishop and preachers, as well as by the divisions between the city government and the craftworkers suffering as a result of the city's

[24][Dated before 9 June 1463] "In den Anordnungen der Stadt R. für den Aufzug der Bürger bei der Fronleichnamsfeier wird bestimmt: 'Item Juden sitzen gar still.'" *Urkunden und Aktenstücke zur Geschichte der Juden in Regensburg, 1453–1738*, ed. Raphael Straus, Quellen und Erörterungen zur Bayerischen Geschichte, N.F. 18 (Munich: Beck, 1960), no. 67, quoting the copy of that ordinance in BHStA Munich, Gemeiners Nachlaß 7. Cf. the order issued at the meeting of the German bishops in Vienna in 1267, summarized in Gemeiner, *Chronik*, 3:395 (see n. 9 above).

[25]For stories of conversions to Judaism, see particularly the Judeo-German *Ma'aseh Book: Book of Jewish Tales and Legends,* trans. Moses Gaster (Philadelphia: Jewish Publication Society, 1934).

[26]*Urkunden und Aktenstücke*, no. 693 (see n. 24 above).
[27]Ibid., no. 695.
[28]Ibid., no. 708.

poor economic climate.[29] In a letter dated 1506, the Franciscan Conrad Hermann complained to the Bavarian dukes that a Jew who had lent a baker six Gulden was forcing the baker to supply the Jew's family with bread once a week for an entire year in repayment of the loan.[30] The tension between the craftworker's need to borrow money in a depressed economy and the pawnbroker's efforts to supply his family with bread was reenacted twelve years later when a similar incident became part of the formal complaint of the city's craftworkers against the Jews; a complaint submitted in 1518 petitioned the emperor to allow the city government to exile or at least reduce to fifteen families the Jewish minority under imperial protection.[31] The Jews responded to these charges by complaining once again that the city's bakers would not sell to them, thereby forcing them to appeal to Herzog Georg and to buy their bread across the river from the bakers in his territory.[32]

These complaints, charges, and countercharges provide a window on the religious, economic, and political tensions between the communities on either side of the walls that ringed the *Judengasse* at the center of Regensburg at the beginning of the sixteenth century, and between those communities and the larger entities of Bavaria and the empire itself. The bread eaten daily by Regensburg's Christians and sought by Regensburg's Jews was far removed from the consecrated bread of the medieval mass and of the Corpus Christi procession with which the Christian community of Regensburg defined itself. Yet it was poignantly near to the bread with which the Jews defined themselves and their understanding of community.

The antiquity of Regensburg's Jewish community was demonstrated by its location on the main thoroughfare within the walls that had surrounded the former Roman barracks. It appears that Italian traders had been the first to occupy the post after the Roman troops had left, but that Jewish traders, whose first recorded settlement in Regensburg dates from 981, arrived before the German-Christian arti-

---

[29]On the ritual murder and other accusations: ibid. See also Ronnie Po-chia Hsia, *The Myth of Ritual Murder: Jews and Magic in Reformation Germany* (New Haven: Yale University Press, 1988), esp. 54–56; and idem, *Trent 1475: Stories of a Ritual Murder Trial* (New Haven: Yale University Press, in cooperation with Yeshiva University Library, 1992).

[30]*Urkunden und Aktenstücke*, nos. 762, 833 (see n. 24 above).

[31]Ibid., no. 979.

[32]Ibid., no. 988.

sans.[33] The settlement's location on the major trade routes continued to attract Jews as well as Christians. With commercial development came the need for a *Schul* or synagogue: from the twelfth through the fourteenth centuries Regensburg's *Judengasse* was a vibrant center of Ashkenazic learning in the tradition of the Rheinland. In the first quarter of the thirteenth century a *Schul* was built on land acquired in 1210 from Regensburg's St. Emmeram's monastery as a burial plot.[34] The adjacent cemetery was the sole burial site for the Jews of the entire region. As was also the case in other cities, the tension that arose in the late medieval period between Christians and Jews over loans to ecclesiastical foundations and small loans to craftsmen was a result of the restrictions imposed on Jewish participation in other occupations; in Regensburg that problem was exacerbated by a contemporaneous shift in the trade routes that all but eliminated Regensburg's role as a commercial center. From the end of the thirteenth century on, Jews from Regensburg were involved in financial arrangements with ecclesiastical foundations—with a monastery in Rohr, with the archbishop of Salzburg, with Regensburg's own Obermünster convent, and with the bishops of Freising and of Regensburg itself. Such transactions, sometimes undertaken in partnership with Christians, could result in the pawning of religious objects—even, at one point, a cross said to contain a portion of the true cross—to Jews "to the ignominy of the Lord."[35] According to Raphael Straus, to whom a greater debt is owed by all who would research the Jewish communities of late medieval Germany, it was "not until the 15th century [that] the Jews in Regensburg [came to be] identified as the provider of credit to the little man, the artisan, the shopkeeper, the priest, the scrivener, the midwife."[36] And, as we have seen above, to the baker.

In contrast to the bread significant for its very lack of "breadness" that defined the Christian community, the bread of the *'erub* that defined the Jewish community signified because of its status as ordinary food. In contrast to the annual Christian procession that had had its roots in recent liturgical developments, the weekly or, more probably, annual recreation of the Jewish community's boundary, the *'erub* (the "amalgamation" of all its dwellings, courtyards, and narrow

[33]Raphael Straus, *Regensburg and Augsburg* (Philadelphia: Jewish Publications Society, 1939), 10–11.
[34]Ibid., 90–91.   [35]Ibid., 99–102.   [36]Ibid., 40.

streets into a single space open to all through which objects could be carried on the Sabbath) had ancient roots.

According to the rabbis, Solomon and his council had been responsible for the halakhic ruling that permitted the carrying of objects outside the home on the Sabbath, a decision that made movement possible at the same time that it reenforced the Sabbath boundaries held to have been delineated in the account of the provision of manna in the wilderness given in Exodus (16:5, 29b) by God's injunction to gather a double portion of manna on the sixth day and to remain in one's own place on the seventh.[37] Although the injunction was apparently strictly observed by the communities of the Dead Sea scrolls and the book of Jubilees, as well as by the Karaites, the ritual creation of an *'erub* had by 200 C.E. eased halakhic observance and ritually marked communal space for most Jews.[38] A Midrash on Genesis even insists that Abraham had known the laws of the *'erub* of courtyards.[39] In the Jerusalem Targum the Aramaic paraphrase of Scripture, the fifth verse of Exodus 16 was expanded to read: "And on the sixth day, when they shall prepare what they will have brought in *for themselves to eat on the day of the Sabbath, they shall lay an 'Erub in their houses and they shall form a Shittuf* (partnership) *in their dwellings because of those carrying things about, and they shall have twice as much as they daily gather.*"[40]

The formation of an *'erub* or *shittuf* required two things: that the geographic area involved be enclosed by a wall or other boundary (hence the wire or string I saw in Baltimore) and that those whose dwellings were included "break bread together." The story of the manna from heaven would be interpreted by the Christian community as a symbolic foreshadowing of their god's self-sacrifice in the death of the son Jesus, but it was physical rather than spiritual nour-

[37]Cf. Maimonides, *Treatise II: Laws Concerning the 'Erub*, in *The Book of the Seasons*, trans. Solomon Gandz and Hayman Klein, vol. 3 of *The Code of Maimonides (Mishnah Torah)* (New Haven: Yale University Press, 1961), chap. 1, ¶2, 5.200–1.

[38]Bruce J. Malina, *The Palestinian Manna Tradition: The Manna Tradition in the Palestinian Targums and Its Relationship to the New Testament Writings* (Leiden: E. J. Brill, 1968), 51, nn. 3–4. E. P. Sanders argues that the Sadducees also insisted on the strict observance of the Sabbath and that the *'erub* was a creation of the Pharisees; *Jewish Law from Jesus to the Mishnah: Five Studies* (London: SCM Press, 1990), 6, 8–9, 106–7, 109.

[39]*Midrash Rabbah*, trans. and ed. H. Freedman and M. Simon (London: Soncino Press, 1939), 1:422.

[40]Malina, *Palestinian Manna Tradition*, 44 (see n. 38 above). Italics denote material not in the Hebrew book of Exodus.

ishment that the rabbis stressed in the creation of the *'eruḇ*. The Mishnah, the compendium of the oral law compiled at the beginning of the third century c.e., recorded the opinion of R. Eliezar ben Hyrcanus, the head of a house of study in the early second century, that any foodstuff except water or salt could be used to mark the *'eruḇ* or *shittuf*—water and salt were excluded because neither in itself could constitute a meal. In the next line, however, the Mishnah recorded a stricter ruling: according to R. Joshua ben Hananiah only bread might be used in the creation of the *'eruḇ* (*chatzerot* = of the courtyard).[41] Although the debate was continued in the Gemara, the commentary on the Mishnah that completes the Talmud, all participants agreed that the critical factor in the creation of an *'eruḇ* was the designation of a common space for the consumption of food by all participants.[42] Both the Targum and the Mishnah took the halakhic interpretations of Exodus 16 for granted—a fact indicating that the provisions for the creation of Sabbath boundaries were in place when the authors of the Gospels, the Epistles, and the Acts of the Apostles wrote, that is, that they date from the time of the Temple, if not of Solomon himself.[43]

The centuries of dispersion had not reduced the need for *'eruḇim*; the details of their creation had been discussed, most notably in a treatise on the *'eruḇ* contained in the Mishnah Torah composed ca. 1180 by Maimonides, the physician and scholar whose writings were authoritative far beyond his North African base. Like Rabbi Eliezar, Maimonides held that any foodstuff not forbidden could be used, but only in the creation of the *shittuf*, the token partnership of those residing in the same alley or walled city.[44] Concerning the *'eruḇ chatzerot* (fusion of courtyards), he followed R. Joshua's lead, concluding that only a whole loaf of bread might be used in its preparation. In what may have been a response to the temptations of assimilation, Maimonides insisted that the *'eruḇ chazerot* was necessary even for those who had already created a partnership with other foodstuff, "in order," he wrote, "that their children should not forget the law con

[41]'Erubin 7, 10 in *The Mishnah*, ed. and trans. Herbert Danby (London: Oxford University Press, 1933), 131.

[42] For the Mishnaic passages and their Gemara (commentary, in this case by the Jewish authorities in Babylonia), i.e., the Babylonian Talmud, see *'Erubin*, trans. Israel Slotki (London: Soncino Press, 1938), chap. 3, 26b; chap. 7, 80b–81a, 183, 564.

[43]Malina, *Palestinian Manna Tradition*, 51–52 (see n. 38 above).

[44]Maimonides, *Treatise II: Laws Concerning the 'Erub*, chap. 1, ¶7–8, 202 (see n. 37 above).

cerning the *'eruḇ*."[45] The creation of a separate *'eruḇ* of the courtyards was unnecessary only if the foodstuff used in the creation of the token partnership of the city was a loaf of bread, since, according to Maimonides, "the children would notice the use of the loaves of bread."[46]

Accessibility and visibility were important. If it "is deposited in a courtyard, it should be raised," he wrote, "to a height of not less than a handsbreadth from the ground, in order to make it noticeable."[47] The benediction: "Blessed are you, O Lord our God, King of the universe, who has sanctified [literally 'separated,' 'set apart'] us with His commandments and has given us the commandment concerning the *'eruḇ*" should be followed with the announcement: "By virtue of this token partnership, it shall be permissible for all residents ... to carry articles between the courtyards and the alley[s] on the Sabbath."[48]

Another approach was taken by the lesser-known author of the *Mahzor Vitry*, Rashi's student and colleague Simhah ben Samuel of Vitry, France. Although dated to around 1100 and therefore earlier than Maimonides' work, the *Mahzor Vitry*, reflecting as it does the views of the Ashkenazic school of Rashi, is more apt to reflect the practices in use in Regensburg. According to Simhah's *Mahzor* it was possible to construct an *'eruḇ* on an annual rather than a weekly basis: "If he wants to make an *'eruḇ* on the eve of Pesach for the entire year, the wise man should take flour from each and every house and knead and bake one or two cakes. And he should make them hard so that they won't mold and will be preserved. As long as the cakes are preserved the *'eruḇ* shall be valid and carrying is permitted within [the boundaries of] the *'eruḇ* chazerot." Since the cake prescribed in this section of the *Mahzor Vitry* was unleavened, it was not only less likely to mold but also did not need to be removed or destroyed during Pesach. As would be the case in Maimonides' prescription, the bread of the *'eruḇ* prescribed in the *Mahzor* must be at least fictively accessible to all; as in Maimonides' work, this raised the issue of communal trust, for "if the cakes are eaten or lost, carrying is forbidden unless a [new] *'eruḇ* is made for each and every Sabbath." The annual *'eruḇ* could only be made on the eve of Pesach, the feast marking (as Easter often did for medieval Christians) the start of the new year.

[45]Ibid., chap. 1 ¶8, ¶19, 204, 205.   [46]Ibid., chap. 1 ¶19, 205.
[47]Ibid., chap. 1, ¶8, ¶202, 205.   [48]Ibid., chap. 1, ¶16, ¶17, 204, 205.

Neither the opinion of Maimonides nor that of Simhah precluded the creation of an *'erub* by an individual on behalf of the whole community.[49] According to Simhah, "The wise man may make a valid *'erub* for everyone out of his own flour, but he must announce 'Come and rely on the *'erub* I have made for you.'" The blessing was the same as that reported by Maimonides, but it was followed by these words: "And with this *'erub* let it be permissible for all the residents in these courtyards to carry in and out from house to house and courtyard to courtyard throughout the entire year and on all the Sabbaths that are in it.'"[50]

Although I have yet to find any *responsa* (legal opinions) relating to the construction of an *'erub* in late medieval Regensburg, halakhic compendia dating from both before and after the pogrom of 1519 appear to confirm the annual creation of an *'erub* in that city's *Judengasse*.[51] "It is customary," insists the *Tashbez*, a collection of R. Meir of Rothenburg's halakhic decisions popular in Ashkenazic communities long after his death in 1310, that "on the day preceding Pesach, after midnight, a little flour is collected from all households, and from all this flour one *matzah* is made as an *'erub*, so that everyone may benefit."[52] That sentence appeared, together with instructions like those

---

[49]Although the presumption was that "all the tenants [would] join in providing an article of food," Maimonides provided for the transfer of ownership in the food without notification. Ibid., chap. 1, ¶6, ¶15, ¶17; chap. 5, ¶23, 201, 204, 205, 236. Rather than gather contributions from each household, one needed only to take a loaf of bread or food enough for two meals for one person—an amount deemed by Maimonides to be sufficient "even if the number of persons forming the token partnership runs into thousands and tens of thousands"—and to announce that that food was the property of all, replacing the contribution from each tenant. Because the transfer and the *'erub* or partnership created were held to be advantageous to the putative "recipients," their knowledge of or consent to the transaction was held to be unnecessary. Ibid., chap. 1, ¶9, ¶20, 202, 206.

[50]Simhah ben Samuel of Vitry, *Mahazor Vitry*, ed. Simeon Hurwitz (Jerusalem: "Alef"Makhon le-hotsaat sefarim, 1963), 249. I am deeply indebted to my colleague Brian Weiser for the translation of this text into English. I owe its citation to Eliyahu Ki Tov, *The Book of Our Heritage: The Jewish Year and Its Days of Significance*, trans. N. Bulman and R. Royde (Jerusalem: "A" Publishers, 1968), 2:240–42.

[51]I have been unable to find references to the Regensburg *'erubin* in the *responsa* literature but have by no means exhausted the *responsa* of Meir of Rothenburg, Israel Isserlein, Joseph Karo, Moses Isserles, and Joseph Colon.

[52]*Rothschild Miscellany*, folio 123b. Jerusalem, Israel Museum: ms. 180/51. I am grateful to Marc E. Saperstein and Brian Weiser for their translation of the Hebrew/Aramaic text from a slide and wretched xerox of a page from the facsimile edition with commentary: *The Rothschild Miscellany: A Scholarly Commentary* (London: Facsimile Editions for the Israel Museum, 1989), vol. 1: fol. 123b.

---

given in the *Mahzor Vitry,* in the version of the *Tashbez* included in the so-called *Rothschild Miscellany,* a fascinating illuminated collection copied during the second half of the fifteenth century in North Italy for "a member of the Ashkenazi community" recently immigrated from Germany.[53]

A century later, the *Shulhan 'Arukh* ("Well-Laid Table," 1564–65) of Joseph ben Ephraim Karo was published together with its *Mappa* ("Tablecloth"), the commentary of Karo's contemporary R. Moses Isserles that made it acceptable to Ashkenazic communities. It too emphasized the new relations established by the *'erub* of the court-yards, ruling that "since all the tenants have aquired a share in this loaf and since at the beginning of the Sabbath the loaf is in the house of the one who has made the *'erub,* his dwelling is considered as the dwelling of all tenants." It is this that makes carrying objects between the houses and the court permissible. Ideally, according to the *Shulhan 'Arukh,* "the *'erub* should be established every Friday, and the loaf of bread used for it may be cut up and eaten on the Sabbath," a provision that highlights the very "breadness" of the loaf. Nevertheless, "if one is afraid that he might in the future forget to make an *'erub,* one may make the *'erub* with one loaf of bread for all the Sabbaths until Pesach." In this case, of course, "it is necessary that the loaf be thin and well baked so that it will not become spoiled before Pesach. For the Sabbath during Pesach, the *'erub* should be made with *matzah* prepared according to the law."[54]

The communitarian or even familial character of the bonds created by the Sabbath *'erub* has much in common with the character of the Pesach celebration itself. Even in the period before 70 C.E., when the temple in Jerusalem was the focus of Pesach activities, it had been seen by Philo as creating a "general haven and safe refuge" where the Jews might "enjoy a brief breathing-space in scenes of genial cheerfulness." Both Philo and Josephus had stressed the role the temple celebration of Pesach played in the creation of communal ties; the activities were "the occasion of reciprocity of feeling and constitute[d]

---

[53]*Rothschild Miscellany,* 2:59.

[54]I have used a translation of the abridged version compiled in the nineteenth century by Rabbi Solomon Ganzfried: *Kitzur Shulhan 'Arukh,* chap. 94, sect. 6, ¶11, *Code of Jewish Law,* trans. Hyman E. Goldin (New York: Hebrew Publishing Company, 1991), 138–39.

the surest sign that all are of one mind."[55] Baruch Bokser has addressed the constant renewal of this sense of community in the seders celebrated in Jewish homes of the dispersion that followed the destruction of the temple in 70 C.E. in anthropological terms:

> The rite takes place at a meal which gives the participants a special opportunity to strengthen their bonds of friendship. In Victor Turner's terminology, the setting permits *communitas*, an atmosphere that liberates individuals from social structures that normally separate them.... The Mishnah relaxes social structures in very specific ways. The rite is not exclusive: not just for the intellectuals, the wealthy or the priests; not contingent on the presence of expert singers; not limited to the adults in the household.[56]

The symbolic intent of the *leitourgia* (public action) of *'erub* construction was equally clear to medieval Kabbalists. Neither is its liminality a recent discovery: according to the kabbalist author of the late-thirteenth-century *Tiqqunei ha-Zohar*, "The *'erub* delineates the Middle Column and within it, one may carry from home to home, between the supernal *Shekhinah* [*Binah*] and the lower one [*Malkhut*]."[57] In his *Tola{c}at Ya{c}aquov* (1507), the Spanish-Turkish mystic Meir ibn Gabbai would express the liminal character of the *'erub* in the bridal imagery that would be the Kabbalists' gift to the Sabbath table: "The *'erub* is the symbol of the crowned Bride, the locus at which the [sacred and profane] domains meet."[58] Still more accessible, however, was the familial language of Maimonides' ruling that, "If all the residents of a courtyard eat at the same table, they require no *'erub*, even though each one has his own house, because they are regarded as residents of the same house."[59] In the much more frequent cases in which the construction of an *'erub* was necessary the action of setting food apart as communal was, according to Maimonides, "as if to say: 'We are all associated together and possess one and the same food, and none of us holds a domain distinct from the domain of the other; just as we have equal rights in the area which remains a common domain, so have we all equal rights in each of the

---

[55]Philo, *Special Laws* 1.69–70; quoted from Baruch M. Bokser, *The Origins of the Seder: The Passover Rite and Early Rabbinic Judaism* (Berkeley: University of California Press, 1984), 82; on Josephus, see 83.

[56]Ibid., 80.

[57]Quoted from Elliot K. Ginsburg, *The Sabbath in the Classical Kabbalah* (Albany: State University of New York Press, 1989), 222–23.

[58]*Sod ha-Shabbat* 4; quoted in ibid., 222.

[59]Ibid., chap. 1, ¶6, 201.

places held by each individual tenant as his own share, and all of us together constitute a single domain'."[60] More explicitly, he insisted that "the residents of a courtyard who have prepared an *'erub* become like a single household."[61] Elsewhere, Maimonides hopes that the Sabbath will have an egalitarian impact: that it will "enable people to feel for one-seventh of their lives that they are equals, in order to prepare for the Messianic, complete and universal Sabbath."[62]

As the history of the *'erub* and its roots before the destruction of the second temple in 70 C.E. make clear, the egalitarian impact of its performance is no epiphenomenon of the socioeconomic and political situation in which the Jews found themselves in late medieval northern Europe. The contrast with the rituals of the Christian community and the bread associated with them is equally clear. The significance of the bread of the *'erub* in Regensburg as elsewhere was what one might call its "breadness": it bound the community bounded by the wall together as a single household, a household that literally shared the same bread in a society in which bread was literally the stuff of life. Seen in this light, the Regensburg bakers' refusal to sell bread to the city's Jews—a refusal no doubt linked in the minds of Regensburg's Christians to the guild's reputation for particular devotion to Mary and to the body of Christ embodied in bread as well as to the economic relations between Christians and Jews—must have born a similar double meaning within the Jewish community as well. Not only the stuff of life, but a double-edged marker of community denied. For the Christians the bread denied replaced the morsel of bread that the Jesus of John's Gospel had extended to the "outsider" within—at least until the troubled and troubling discursive and ritual attempts to fix boundaries between the two communities of Regensburg were ended in 1519, when the city council achieved with an infamous pogrom, controversial even in its own day, the elision its processional route had implied.

---

[60]Ibid.

[61]Maimonides, *Treatise II: Laws Concerning the 'Erub*, chap. 1, ¶1, ¶3, 221–22.

[62]Quoted in Alexandre Safran, *Israel in Time and Space: Essays on Basic Themes in Jewish Spiritual Thought*, trans. M. Pater and E. M. Sandle (Jerusalem: Feldheim, 1987), 154. The reference is to Maimonides, *Moreh Nevukhim* 3:43.

The Entrance Hall of the
Regensburg Synagogue,
etching by Altdorfer

The Synagogue of Regensburg,
etching by Altdorfer

Unification and the Chemistry of the Reformation

Jole Shackelford

The writings and historical circumstances of Kort Aslakssøn, a student assistant of Tycho Brahe and later a member of the theology faculty at the University of Copenhagen, illustrate the affinities between certain philosophical and religious doctrines that may account for why Paracelsians were drawn to heterodox religion and, conversely, why some religious sects adopted elements of Paracelsian medical philosophy. Aslakssøn's approach, a product of the intellectual atmosphere of late-sixteenth-century Denmark, resulted from a strong desire for a rationalist worldview that unified scientific and religious principles. His Paracelsian conceptions of matter and the structure of the cosmos were compatible with Calvinist views that were tolerated by the Philippists (a denominational position between strict Lutheranism and Calvinism) but rejected by the more orthodox Lutherans who came to dominate Danish theology in the second decade of the seventeenth century.

DURING RESEARCH into the history of Paracelsian medicine in early modern Scandinavia, I have been struck by the frequent coincidence of interest in Paracelsian ideas and heterodox religion. By Paracelsian medicine I mean the expression of a chemical philosophy and iatrochemical practice that had historical roots in a body of doctrine stemming from treatises attributed to Paracelsus, an early-sixteenth-century Swiss-German reformer. This is by no means a new observation, as it has been long established that the running public debate between the Paracelsians and the medical establishment in France divided rather consistently along confessional lines, Paracelsians being generally Huguenots and their opponents usually Catholics.

Hugh Trevor-Roper, in one of his Renaissance essays, followed the development of the Paracelsian movement in France, England, and the German lands and determined that Paracelsians were associated with religious opposition, be it Huguenot, Puritan, Rosicrucian, or Pietist, in large part because they were defined into these dissenting groups by the dominant orthodoxies as the latter narrowed and codified acceptable doctrine and established a policy of excluding opposing views.[1] This analysis accords well with my own observations, but I have also wondered if there were not ideological commonalities between Paracelsian doctrines and certain heterodoxies that might attract the proponents of one to the content of the other. That is, I wonder if the Paracelsians were drawn to religious dissent as well as being driven there by the demands of orthodoxy. The problem can also be looked at the other way around. Why were members of dissenting communities attracted to Paracelsian ideas? Probably *not* because they were driven to them by medical orthodoxy. In this study I shall explore some of the doctrinal affinities that may have facilitated the joining of Paracelsian cosmology and heterodox religion in late-sixteenth-century Denmark, with the expectation that the results will serve as a heuristic for a wider investigation of the resonances between Paracelsian philosophy and religious concerns in early modern Europe.

The problem of identifying these affinities is both illuminated and complicated by the existence of a textual and doctrinal tradition stemming from religious and theological treatises written by Paracelsus himself. One can speak of a *religio Paracelsica*, as Sten Lindroth did in his landmark study of Paracelsianism in Sweden, a Paracelsian form of religion that drew on Paracelsian religious and cosmological ideas and was invariably associated with groups and viewpoints that ran counter to the established church authority. One might call these people "outsider Protestants," because they were usually "outside"

---

[1]Hugh Trevor-Roper, "The Paracelsian Movement," in *Renaissance Essays* (London: Secker & Warburg, 1985), 149–99, notes that there was no necessary connection between Paracelsianism and Protestants, although most Paracelsians were Protestants. He argues that Paracelsianism, like the Neoplatonism upon which it was based, was still nondenominational in the 1570s but was driven to Protestantism by the Counter-Reformation and then driven to radical Protestantism by the growth of the Protestant orthodoxies (165, 177). This view describes a trajectory for Paracelsian medical philosophy that differs somewhat from that given to Paracelsian religion by George Huntston Williams and other Reformation historians, who identify Paracelsus' views on man, the church, and theology as belonging to the Radical Reformation from the outset.

whatever was regarded by the political leadership as orthodox religion.[2]

To the extent that Paracelsian ideas found an expression in religious writings, the authors of these tracts and their religious tone were generally considered heterodox at best, and often heretical. Such was the case with Caspar Schwenckfeld, Sebastian Franck, Valentin Weigel, and Jacob Boehme, to cite some well-known examples. It might therefore be possible to treat Paracelsian religion on its own merits, as a separate phenomenon that was independent of the medical debates. To this end historians of religion have begun to regard Paracelsus as one of the earlier leaders of the Radical Reformation, as is evident by his inclusion in a German collection of biographical sketches of leading radical reformers, and to associate the Weigelian and pseudo-Weigelian corpus as a legacy of these radical beginnings.[3] George Williams and Steven Ozment have ranked those who followed Paracelsus among the "spiritual" reformers, one of three groups of religious writers who were dissatisfied with the course the Reformation was taking in the sixteenth century. According to Ozment, these reformers professed pacifism, anticlerical impulses, irenicism, and a spiritual interpretation of Christianity. There is a textual continuity, and I believe also a social continuity, between these people and the early Pietist groups of the middle and late seventeenth century, as I have argued elsewhere.[4]

[2]Sten Lindroth, *Paracelsismen i Sverige till 1600-tallets mitt*, Lychnos Bibliotek, no. 7 (Uppsala: Almqvist & Wiksell, 1943). Russell H. Hvolbek used the term "outsider Lutheran" in "Seventeenth Century Dialogues: Jacob Boehme and the New Sciences" (Ph.D. diss., University of Chicago, 1984) to describe Protestants of nominally Lutheran regions who may have considered themselves to be good Lutherans but were defined as heterodox by the Lutheran authorities. For this reason it is debatable whether they should be called Lutherans, and I am now persuaded to use the term "outsider Protestant" instead.

[3]Walter Klaassen, ed., *Profiles of Radical Reformers: Biographical Sketches from Thomas Müntzer to Paracelsus* (Kitchener, Ontario: Herald Press, 1982). This is an English edition of *Radikale Reformatoren*, ed. Hans-Jürgen Goertz (Munich: Beck, 1978). On Weigelian treatises and their importance as vehicles of Paracelsian religion, see Siegfried Wollgast, "Zur Wirkungsgeschichte des Paracelsus im 16. und 17. Jahrhundert," in *Resultate und Desiderate der Paracelsus-Forschung*, ed. Peter Dilg and Hartmut Rudolph, Sudhoffs Archiv Beihefte, no. 31 (Stuttgart: Franz Steiner, 1993), 113–44.

[4]George H. Williams' analysis of the radical reformers is summarized in Steven Ozment, *The Age of Reform 1250–1550: An Intellectual and Religious History of Late Medieval and Reformation Europe* (New Haven: Yale University Press, 1980), esp. 344–46. Paracelsus himself opposed the doctrinal rigidity of the ecclesiastical establishment, which he referred to as the "brick church" (*Mauerkirche*). My study of a Paracelsian phy-

However, tracing the development of Paracelsian religion and the incorporation of Paracelsian philosophical ideas into religious literature does not in itself indicate what sort of commonalities may have existed between the natural philosophy and the religion of these groups. But if these commonalities can be identified, they might illuminate the coincidence of Paracelsianism and heterodoxy more generally, such as we observe in Paris from the 1560s, in the struggles between the Lutherans and Calvinists for control of the Protestant mainstream, and in the rift between Anglicans and Puritans in seventeenth-century England.[5] All these cases are complicated by a variety of social, political, and intellectual factors, which make them difficult to understand.

There may be many reasons for an alignment between Paracelsian medicine and opposition to authority. Social division can arise from purely professional considerations; the conflict between chemical physicians and Galenists can be accounted for as a struggle for dominance of limited professional resources, that is, control of the market.[6] Certainly there is a general sociological dimension, too. Paracelsians, drawn together into a group because of common medical interests and identifying themselves as practicing a particular kind of medicine in order to attract patients and patrons, can easily have been identified as "the other" by a group seeking markers by which to define itself and its opponents. Such a social schism, perhaps originally arising for professional reasons, say, control of the medical market in Paris, could easily escalate in a distressed society to forge ideological links between unrelated markers, say, Paracelsian and Huguenot, even if there were no essential connections between the

---

sician and a probable Paracelsian apothecary in seventeenth-century Norway shows that they each owned a substantial number of books in the "outsider Protestant" spiritualist and separatist genre. See Jole Shackelford, "A Reappraisal of Anna Rhodius: Religious Enthusiasm and Social Unrest in Seventeenth-Century Christiania, Norway," *Scandinavian Studies* 65 (1993): 349–89; also idem, "Hans Jochum Scharff: A Paracelsian Apothecary in 17th-Century Norway," *Norges Apotekerforenings Tidsskrift* 95, no. 9 (15 May 1987): 212–17; and idem, *Paracelsianism in Denmark and Norway in the 16th and 17th Centuries* (Ann Arbor, Mich.: University Microfilms International, 1989), chap. 7.

[5]Frances A. Yates, *The Rosicrucian Enlightenment* (London: Routledge & Kegan Paul, 1972), takes up these issues in a distinctly Anglocentric way.

[6]Harold J. Cook, *The Decline of the Old Medical Regime in Stuart London* (Ithaca, N.Y.: Cornell University Press, 1986), has drawn attention to the importance of the medical marketplace in supporting chemical medicine in England against attempts by the Galenist elite to suppress or subordinate it.

two. Indeed, the struggle between the Paracelsians and Galenists in France had religious and political as well as medical dimensions, suggesting such an interplay of factors.[7] Once a religious orthodoxy is defined and allied with a political authority, it is easy to see how members of the opposition are defined into heterodoxy on account of their political dissent.

One can also perceive a moral angle to the controversy between the Paracelsians and their critics.[8] Using the writings of Oswald Croll, a Paracelsian physician, and Andreas Libavius, a vociferous critic of Paracelsianism, to illuminate the ideological context of late-sixteenth-century chemistry, Owen Hannaway revealed how Croll's Paracelsianism was part and parcel of his Calvinist religious politics, which were associated with the ambitions of Prince Christian of Anhalt. Hannaway seized on Libavius' sharp criticism of Croll as an indicator of the profound ideological rift between Croll and Libavius, who found Paracelsian ideas to be antithetical to his Christian-Aristotelian humanism and his schoolmaster's view of the world.[9] In Hannaway's analysis the epistemological and pedagogical issues with which Libavius was concerned are paramount, and the difference between the Paracelsian Croll and the Aristotelian Libavius is analyzed in terms of a dichotomy of light and dark. Libavius' pedagogy aimed to define philosophical issues clearly and to present them openly, whereas the Paracelsians wrote in mysterious metaphors that cloaked their meanings and protected them from those who were not adepts. However, in a footnote to this, Hannaway observed that Libavius was motivated to write against the Paracelsians by his

[7]On Paracelsianism in France, see Allen Debus, *The French Paracelsians: The Chemical Challenge to Medical and Scientific Tradition in Early Modern France* (Cambridge: Cambridge University Press, 1991), 59–62. Trevor-Roper, "The Paracelsian Movement," 168, notes that the medical and theological faculties at the University of Paris were supported against Paracelsian medicine by the Parlement (see n. 1 above).

[8]It may be that many concerns about religious doctrine boil down to moral concerns, if one can make the distinction. Regardless of what the Athenians thought about Socrates' philosophy and faith, it was his danger as a teacher, as a moral guide to Athenian youth, that occasioned his censure.

[9]Owen Hannaway, *The Chemists and the Word: The Didactic Origins of Chemistry* (Baltimore: Johns Hopkins University Press, 1975). Libavius was a Lutheran humanist and Croll was a Calvinist. However, Hannaway distinguishes between Calvin's humanist Calvinism and Croll's Hermetic-Paracelsian Calvinism (53–54), making the controversy between Libavius and Croll a matter of humanist vs. Paracelsian rather than Lutheran vs. Calvinist. Nevertheless, it is worth noting that Croll was not the only Calvinist whose philosophy was fundamentally Neoplatonist.

perception of an "unholy alliance" between the Paracelsians and the Calvinists.[10] This insight again raises the question of why Paracelsians should be drawn to heterodoxy, in this case Calvinist ideas.[11]

This brings me to consider religious explanations for the association of Paracelsians and heterodox sects. There are at least three overlapping but discernible aspects of religion that might be considered here: prophecy, anticlericalism (separatism), and doctrine. The first of these has received considerable attention from Charles Webster, Bruce Moran, and others, and has been recognized recently by Siegfried Wollgast as a subject worthy of greater in-depth study.[12] Separatism is fundamental to the Reformation mentality, so it is no wonder that opposition to the hegemony of an established orthodoxy seems to have appealed to Paracelsian physicians and sectarian writers alike as a response to the suppression of dissent. Certainly many of the Paracelsians opposed what they perceived as the rigidity and tyranny of organized churches —the "brick church" as Paracelsus called it—as readily as they objected to the scholastic Aristotelianism of the established universities. Both prophecy and separatism can be connected with the early Reformation matrix that produced Paracelsus and other radical reformers and do not by themselves explain the attractiveness of Paracelsian ideas to more mainstream Protestant thinkers. Therefore, I wish to distinguish a third category, doctrine, which encompasses specific theological, anthropological, and liturgical issues that divided denominations in early modern Europe.

[10]Ibid., 94, n. 7.

[11]This nexus between Paracelsian cosmology and religion and Calvinism was associated with the birth of Rosicrucianism and the political aspirations of what has been called the "Calvinist International" by Hugh Trevor-Roper, *From Counter-Reformation to Glorious Revolution* (London: Secker & Warburg, 1992), 41.

[12]Charles Webster, *From Paracelsus to Newton: Magic and the Making of Modern Science* (Cambridge: Cambridge University Press, 1982), notes that reconciliation of cosmology and eschatology was a "delicate problem" for early modern scholars (16). Recently, Bruce T. Moran, "Alchemy, Prophecy, and the Rosicrucians: Raphael Eglinus and Mystical Currents of the Early Seventeenth Century," in *Alchemy and Chemistry in the 16th and 17th Centuries*, ed. Piyo Rattansi and Antonio Clericuzio, International Archives of the History of Ideas, vol. 140 (Dordrecht: Kluwer, 1994), 103–19, has discussed the interpenetration of prophecy and Paracelsianism. Wollgast, "Zur Wirkungsgeschichte des Paracelsus im 16. und 17. Jahrhundert" (see n. 3 above) analyzes Paracelsus' millenarianism and identifies it as a major influence on the religious thought of his contemporaries. Wollgast points to the importance of a widespread apocalyptic and prophetic literature in the seventeenth century that has not been republished or studied by modern scholars. The extent of its dependence on Paracelsian precedents remains unassessed.

The problem I have encountered in attempting to understand and demonstrate the theoretical or doctrinal connections linking some Paracelsians to religious heterodoxies is that it is difficult to find sources that illuminate them and enable the historian to generate plausible explanations for why the defining characteristics of religious heterodoxy—namely specific doctrinal positions on the sacraments, human will, Christology, the reconciliation of divine will and natural law, and so on—should appeal to Paracelsians. Or, to look at the problem from the other side, how can one find evidence that explains why the exceedingly esoteric chemical theory and associated pathology, pharmacology, and praxis of the Paracelsians would be attractive to religious radicals? Certainly there are ample instances that suggest connections of this sort.[13] The physician Oswald Croll, for example, framed his version of Paracelsian doctrine in a Calvinist theology.[14] On the other hand, the shoemaker and lay religious guru Jacob Boehme shaped his version of Lutheran mysticism in ways that were influenced by Paracelsian conceptions.[15]

Critics were also aware of the compatibility of chemical philosophy and sectarian religion. Libavius had to argue that chemistry could exist independently of Paracelsian philosophy in order to separate it from specific religious contexts; in this way he could defend it against wholesale attack by the Parisian medical faculty.[16] Likewise, Robert Boyle was careful to avoid public use of terminology that might associate him and his chemistry with sectarian religion in the minds of his contemporaries. His adaptation of Pierre Gassendi's atomism as a new metaphysical basis for iatrochemistry can be viewed as an attempt to sever these very connections between chemistry and heterodox religion, which had been well established by the

[13]There are important authors who can shed light on this connection, e.g., Paracelsus, Thomas Erastus, Oswald Croll, and Robert Fludd. Scholarship specific to the doctrinal positions and religious postures of such prominent writers will deepen our understanding of the interplay between religious and philosophical ideas among chemical philosophers in this period.

[14]Hannaway, *Chemists and the Word*, 47–57 (see n. 9 above).

[15]On Boehme's Paracelsianism, see Russell H. Hvolbek, "Seventeenth Century Dialogues" (see n. 2 above); Jan-Erik Ebbestad Hansen, *Jacob Bøhme: Liv, tenkning, idehistoriske forutsetninger* (Oslo: Solum, 1985), 223–32; and Andrew Weeks, *Boehme: An Intellectual Biography of the Seventeenth-Century Philosopher and Mystic* (Albany, N.Y.: State University of New York, 1991). I have discussed some of the connections between the work of Boehme and "outsider Protestant" views in *Paracelsianism in Denmark and Norway*, 253–61 (see n. 4 above).

[16]Debus, *The French Paracelsians*, 59–62 (see n. 7 above).

middle of the seventeenth century.[17] Both Libavius and Boyle seem
to have taken for granted that chemistry and chemical theory were by
their day traditionally embedded in a religious framework that they
defined as heterodox and that special persuasion was needed to free
the one from the other.[18]

I thought to use the present occasion to explore these connections in terms of their unity and disunity, that is, if the coincidence
between heterodox religion and Paracelsian cosmology might not
result from a strong desire to formulate a unified doctrine—a broad,
general worldview that is akin to the universal religion sought by the
irenicists. This is a working hypothesis, since a wide body of evidence
in various instances will need to be assessed to make it a reliable heuristic. The specific context I examine here is Paracelsian cosmology in
late-sixteenth- and early-seventeenth-century Denmark, a period that
begins with the introduction of Paracelsian medicine to the Danish
world and culminates in the early years of the Thirty Years' War, by
which time Paracelsian philosophy and religion were associated with
sects that were considered unacceptable to the strengthened Lutheran
orthodoxy. During this same period the religious climate changed
considerably, from a somewhat tolerant Philippism, named after
Philip Melanchthon, to a stricter Lutheranism that gave ideological
sanction to a more centrally controlled state church. This transition
provides an opportunity to investigate the relationship between
Paracelsian doctrines and religious matters before and during the
onset of orthodoxy.[19]

[17]Boyle, e.g., was careful to distance his chemistry from that of the Paracelsians
and Helmontians, in large part because he did not want to be associated with their sec-
tarianism. See Barbara Beigun Kaplan, *"Divulging of Useful Truths in Physick": The Medical Agenda of Robert Boyle* (Baltimore: Johns Hopkins University Press, 1993), 29, 155.

[18]Bruce T. Moran has shown that even though it was possible to separate theory
from praxis in Johannes Hartmann's laboratory instruction, the historical context of
this praxis was still Paracelsian: *Chemical Pharmacy Enters the University: Johannes Hartmann and the Didactic Care of Chymiatria in the Early Seventeenth Century* (Madison, Wis.:
American Institute of the History of Pharmacy, 1991). The Danish physician Ole
Worm, who had tried out Hartmann as a teacher, later advised his student, Niels Chris-
tensen Foss, to study chemistry with an apothecary, suggesting that Hartmann's teaching was unnecessarily theory-laden as well as expensive. See Worm's letter to Foss dated
26 February 1616 in H. D. Schepelern, *Breve fra og til Ole Worm*, vol. 1 (Copenhagen:
Det danske sprog- og litteraturselskab, 1965), 9. In 1623 Worm again advised a student
not to pay much for chemical enlightenment, citing his "own bitter experience" with
Hartmann (letter to Hans Andersen Skovgaard, ibid., 77).

[19]Danish church historians reckon the first period of Lutheran orthodoxy to begin
in 1615. See Bjørn Kornerup, *Den danske Kirkes Historie*, 8 vols., ed. Bjørn Kornerup and
Hal Koch (Copenhagen: Gyldendal, 1959), 4:220–21.

KORT ASLAKSSØN AND PARACELSIAN THOUGHT
IN DENMARK

In late-sixteenth-century Denmark there were several natural philosophers who were interested in Paracelsian physical and metaphysical
constructions. Certainly the Paracelsian physicians Petrus Severinus
and Johannes Pratensis were prominent in the group, as was Tycho
Brahe. But there were probably others, particularly among the students and assistants working under Tycho's tutelage at Uraniborg.
Pratensis died only five years after finishing his education and assum-
ing a chair in medicine at the University of Copenhagen. A close
friend and confidant of Tycho and Severinus, he left almost no written record from which we can learn the details of his philosophical or
religious views. Severinus attained international reputation by publishing a lengthy exposition of Paracelsian metaphysics that is a
detailed, Neoplatonized account of how chemical philosophy provides a suitable foundation for all change in the universe, especially
those changes associated with human physiology and pathology. But
he did not touch on matters of religion in this work.[20]

Tycho Brahe was also acquainted with Paracelsian ideas and
devoted considerable time and money to what he called "terrestrial
astronomy," that is, investigating the chemical nature of the lower
world in order to gain knowledge of how it is knit to the upper world.
Tycho did not overtly discuss theology and religion, but we know
that he was well-read in these matters and considered scriptural
accounts to be worthy of serious consideration in cosmological matters. He was reported to have possessed Paracelsian religious writings,
but nothing further is known about his possible interest in Paracelsian religion. He was probably a Philippist, that is, an adherent to the
teachings of Luther and Philipp Melanchthon, as were most Danish

---

[20]Pratensis composed a lengthy poem that was appended to Severinus' *Idea medicinae* (Basel: Henric Petri, 1571). The two had traveled and studied abroad together for
several years and seem to have been close friends. On Severinus and Pratensis and their
relationship to Tycho Brahe, see Jole Shackelford, "Paracelsianism and Patronage in
Early Modern Denmark," in *Patronage and Institutions: Science, Technology and Medicine
at the European Court 1500–1750*, ed. Bruce T. Moran (Woodbridge, Suffolk: Boydell,
1991), 85–109; also Schackelford, *Paracelsianism in Denmark and Norway*, esp. 27–49,
210–22 (see n. 4 above). On Severinus and his theory, see also Eyvind Bastholm and
Hans Skov, trans., *Petrus Severinus og hans Idea medicinae philosophicae* (Odense: Odense
Universitetsforlag, 1979), and Walter Pagel, *The Smiling Spleen: Paracelsianism in Storm
and Stress* (Basel: Karger, 1984), 17–27.

Jole Shackelford

university theologians, bishops, and some of the leading parish priests, particularly those in Copenhagen.[21]

The Danish Church had been reformed under Johannes Bugenhagen on the basis of Luther's teachings, Melanchthon's *Loci communes*, and the Augsburg Confession. But it was under the powerful leadership of the Danish theologian Niels Hemmingsen that the teachings of Melanchthon—occasionally with somewhat Calvinist interpretations—came to dominate Denmark's ecclesiastical elite in the last quarter of the century. Tycho Brahe and his assistants were of this generation of professors and students who shared Philippist ideas. One of these, a Norwegian named Kort Aslakssøn, ventured into print with a synthesis of chemical cosmology and Philippist doctrine that may shed some light on the intellectual milieu of Tycho Brahe's Uraniborg.

Kort Aslakssøn was a Norwegian by birth but spent his adult life in Denmark. He studied philosophy and theology at the University of Copenhagen for six years before becoming Tycho's assistant in 1590. He lived at Uraniborg with the famous astronomer for the next three years, during which he assisted him with astronomical and also, perhaps, chemical work. When Aslakssøn returned to the University in 1593 he took his master's degree under Anders Krag, a chemical physician and colleague of the well-known Paracelsian Petrus Severinus. Then he turned south. After short stays in Rostock and Wittenberg, where doctrinal intolerance was growing, Aslakssøn gravitated to centers of Calvinist teaching: Herborn, Heidelberg, Basel, and Geneva. There he learned the biblical languages and theology that he would teach after his return to Copenhagen at the turn of the century.

Aslakssøn's early interest in developing a coherent worldview that was both scientifically and theologically sound is evident in his 1597 *On the Nature of the Threefold Heaven*, which he dedicated to Tycho.[22]

---

[21]On Tycho's Paracelsianism and Philippism, see Victor Thoren, *The Lord of Uraniborg: A Biography of Tycho Brahe* (Cambridge: Cambridge University Press, 1990), 11, 14, 59, 80, 82, 100, 118. According to Joachim Morsius, a Rosicrucian, Kort Aslakssøn once told him he had seen Paracelsus' biblical commentaries in Tycho's possession. Quoted by Johan Nordström, "Lejonet från Norden," *Samlaran* 15 (1934): 36: "Vtinam aliquis felici dextra nobis ab interitu vindicaret, eiusdem magni Paracelsi commentationes in integra Biblia, quas ante aliquot annos in itinere meo Danico Hafniae, se vidisse olim apud summe peritum Uraniae coelestis & terrestris Tychonem Braheum, vir Clarissimus & multiplicis eruditionis Conradus Aslacus, Professor Regius, mihi retulit."

[22]Kort Aslakssøn, *De natura caeli triplicis* (Siegen, 1597).

In that treatise he drew on a wide variety of authorities, both ancient and recent, to defend his interpretation of various scriptural references to the "heaven" or "heavens," which he took to refer to three distinct regions: the aer, the *caelestium*, and the supernal heaven. A threefold division of the world was commonplace in Renaissance Platonism, but aspects of Aslakssøn's account reflect distinctly Paracelsian conceptualizations. For one thing, Alsakssøn's scheme implicitly associated the *caelestium* with the firmament and fire as the region above the aer, in the Paracelsian tradition.

Like all Platonists, he believed in a World Soul but conceived of it as a psychophysical spirit like that which chemists draw out of matter. This spirit or energetic faculty was implanted into the cosmos by God at the creation and gives all things life, a view he legitimized by citing Severinus.[23] Aslakssøn's basic theory of generation and corruption is clearly Paracelsian: all things are created from prime matter through the operation of the Archeus, an inner workman who separates and elaborates all things to various degrees—some more perfectly and others abandoned at intermediate stages of development, just as is the case with the generation of metals. Aslakssøn applied this idea to the celestial region as well as to the generation of things on and in the earth, supposing that different celestial bodies were created from one and the same mass but digested and exalted differently.[24]

It is evident from this that Aslakssøn shared Severinus' view of the world as arising from a primal chaos that was sown with *rationes seminales* or seedlike reasons, which were predestined to grow, flower, and decay at specific times. The processes by which these seeds grow and decay are the chemical operations of the Archeus: digestion, separation, elaboration, and exaltation. This is not too surprising. Tycho himself had considered that the "new star" of 1572 was potentially

[23]Aslakssøn might have been citing Severinus, who was the senior royal physician, in hopes of gaining an influential ally, but he was also signaling his familiarity and agreement with Severinus' Paracelsian metaphysics, which was laid out in great detail in Severinus' 1571 *Ideal of Philosophical Medicine*. For more on Aslakssøn's cosmology, see Oskar Garstein, *Cort Aslakssøn: studier over dansk-norsk universitets- og lærdomshistorie omkring aar 1600* (Oslo: Lutherstiftelse, 1953), 173–98; Shackelford, *Paracelsianism in Denmark and Norway*, 239–46 (see n. 4 above), and idem, "Rosicrucianism, Lutheran Orthodoxy, and the Rejection of Paracelsianism in Early Seventeenth-Century Denmark," *Bulletin of the History of Medicine* 70 (1996): 181–204.

[24]Aslakssøn, *De natura caeli triplicis*, 150–51 (see n. 22 above).

(seminally) present in the celestial sphere, awaiting its predestined time to appear. The seventeenth-century Danish astronomer, Christian Sørensen Longomontanus—like Aslakssøn a student of Tycho Brahe—held a similar view of the seminal generation of new stars and comets.

There is no hint that Aslakssøn departed from this cosmology as he became more and more occupied with theology. In his 1605 oration at the University of Copenhagen he again spoke of the world soul (*anima mundi*) that sustains the cosmos, and he cited a series of Renaissance Platonists in support of this assertion, including Paracelsus, Patrizi, and Fernel.[25] During the next several years Aslakssøn further developed his interpretation of Genesis, which he had begun in *On the Nature of the Threefold Heaven*, in a series of theological disputations. This effort culminated in his 1613 work, *Mosaic Physics and Ethics*, in which he sought to fuse his Renaissance Platonist natural philosophy with the account of creation in Genesis, a cosmological synthesis wholly in the spirit of many Paracelsians.[26]

Aslakssøn's use of chemical terminology and concepts to explain the working of the cosmos should come as no surprise, given his educational context. After all, he studied at the University of Copenhagen under a chemist and also at Uraniborg, where the Paracelsian views of Tycho Brahe and his circle, which included Severinus, prevailed. More unexpected, perhaps, and much more interesting, is that he should seek to fuse these ideas with scriptural theology. I believe that this desire to present a unified view of God and nature based on religious scholarship and natural philosophy was also representative of the intellectual goals and values of his peers and that part of the explanation for it lies in the affinities between Paracelsian and Philippist doctrines. Furthermore, these affinities sometimes depended on doctrines that were rejected by more conservative Lutherans, adding a confessional dimension to the debates over Paracelsian philosophical ideas in Denmark.

---

[25]Garstein, *Cort Aslakssøn*, 179 (see n. 23 above).
[26]Ibid., 197. *Physica et ethica Mosaica* (Hannover, 1613). Aslakssøn's annual disputations include three *De mundo*, published in Copenhagen in 1605–7, and three *De creatione*, published there in 1609–11.

PARACELSIANISM AND PHILIPPISM

Danish Philippism may have been more amenable to the Paracelsian blend that characterized Tycho Brahe's circle of friends and assistants than was the stricter Lutheranism that was being codified to the south, precisely because of Melanchthon's legacy. Melanchthon had valued natural philosophy and encouraged an Aristotelian, Christian humanism for the university curriculum. Compared with the more fideistic views of Luther, Melanchthon's willingness to tolerate a greater intellectual diversity favored the development of rationalist theology. But this does not explain why Philippism would be congenial to the Paracelsians, who as a rule found Aristotelian metaphysics wanting; certainly Severinus and others of Tycho Brahe's circle strongly preferred the Neoplatonism of Plotinus and Proclus to the established scholastic Aristotelian theory, which failed to agree with their medical and astronomical observations. It is possible that this Platonizing tendency in late-sixteenth-century Denmark is linked with the contemporary, gradual shift in Danish Philippism toward more Calvinistic interpretations, which precipitated an orthodox reaction.

Melanchthon himself had responded to the Lutheran opposition to reformed Protestants by adopting a "spiritualizing" concept of the Eucharist that did not insist on the strict Lutheran demand for the real presence of Christ's body and blood, a doctrine that defied scientific explanation.[27] Neils Hemmingsen and other Danes who had studied with him at Wittenberg took home to Denmark Melanchthon's willingness to tolerate differing views on doctrinal matters, especially those points considered to be not essential to the faith, the *adiaphora*. When it came to Christ's presence in the Eucharist, for

---

[27]Although Melanchthon never explicitly abandoned the idea that Christ was substantially present in the Eucharist, his pronouncements left ample room for the Cryptocalvinist Philippists to interpret him as permitting a spiritual interpretation. He preferred to think of Christ's body as "with" rather than "in" the bread when he was preparing the *variata* version of the Augsburg Confession. However, by the end of his life he rejected transubstantiation as well as the strict identification of Christ with the bread that was propounded by the Bremen Lutherans. See Michael Rogness, *Philip Melanchthon: Reformer Without Honor* (Minneapolis: Augsburg Publishing House, 1969), 133–35, and James William Richard, *Philip Melanchthon: The Protestant Preceptor of Germany 1497–1560* (1898; reprint, New York: Burt Franklin Reprints, 1974), 245 and 376.

example, Hemmingsen favored the Calvinist view that the sacrament is spiritual and symbolic and that Christ's body remains in heaven.[28]

Niels Hemmingsen soon became Denmark's leading theologian, and under his leadership the Philippists one by one filled the top positions in the Danish church. But the growing power of the strict Lutherans in Saxony, called Gnesiolutherans or Flacians, was not without effect in Denmark, where adherence to the Augsburg Confession of 1530 was the official policy of the realm. The German Lutherans repeatedly complained of Hemmingsen's Calvinist views until King Frederik II was forced to seek his removal from the university in 1579 on the grounds that Hemmingsen had failed to accept the Lutheran teaching on ubiquity and its consequence for the real presence. However, despite Hemmingsen's dismissal and the reaffirmation of the Lutheran basis of the Danish church, the king refused to go all the way and accept the Formula of Concord and the rigid dogmatism pressed by the Gnesiolutherans. Hemmingsen quietly continued to lead Danish theology from retirement, and his Philippist colleagues and students quietly continued to steer the Danish church along a path of doctrinal tolerance.

Now and then, open challenges to Lutheran conceptions led to enforcement of the articles of the Augsburg Confession and conformity to the Lutheran Church Ordinance, but even here the overriding desire among ecclesiastical and university authorities was to maintain unity and harmony within the Danish Church rather than force a rigid Lutheranism on the land. For example, when the priest Iver Bertelsen openly left the ritualized exorcism out of a baptism in 1567 and the case was brought before the university's consistory court, the professors judging the case avoided confronting the doctrinal legitimacy of an omission that Melanchthon had regarded as an *adiaphoron* and ruled merely that the priest could not alter accepted liturgy on his own initiative. In other words, this was to be viewed as a matter of ecclesiastical discipline and not doctrine per se.

Clearly, there was significant sympathy with Bertelsen's action among Denmark's elite. In 1588 Jon Jacobsen Venusinus, the parish priest of a major church in Copenhagen (Helligånds) left out the bap-

---

[28]For Danish church history, I rely heavily on Bjørn Kornerup and Hal Koch, eds., *Den Danske Kirkes Historie*, 4 (see n. 19 above); R. Tonder Nissen, *De nordiske kirkers historie* (Christiania [Oslo]: Steen, 1884); and Oskar Garstein, *Cort Aslakssøn* (see n. 23 above).

tismal exorcism and was suspended until he swore to uphold the traditional liturgy. More to the point here, the parish priest on the island of Hven—Tycho Brahe's fiefdom and the location of Uraniborg—was also punished for omitting, presumably at Tycho's direction, the ritual exorcism. Officially, Frederik II's Denmark held to the traditional Lutheran teaching, which was formulated in the Church Ordinance. Unofficially, church leadership tolerated a multiplicity of views that reflected Danish reality.

We see this clearly in an account left by Erasmus Laetus of the birth and baptism of the king's son in 1577.[29] Laetus, himself a staunch advocate of royal power and Frederik II's enforcement of the Lutheran Reformation in Denmark, grumbled in one of his digressions about dissent from the true Lutheran sacramental views. However, when he came to the description of the baptism itself, he failed to record the exorcism, but merely noted that the king had ordered the baptism to follow the time-honored Danish liturgy. Why did this royal propagandist, who otherwise carefully recorded the details of the baptismal celebration, including the names and ranks of influential persons who were present, quickly pass over the baptism itself? The likely answer is that the issue was too volatile to take sides on officially. In 1577 the king and the university professors were in the middle of deciding how to respond to the Saxon charges against Niels Hemmingsen and, therefore, how to position the Danish church in the doctrinal controversies that were dividing the Protestant world to their south.

But what does baptismal exorcism and Philippism have to do with Paracelsianism? Paracelsian religion and philosophy seem to have prospered where there was a degree of toleration for doctrinal diversity, which accords well with Trevor-Roper's contention that Paracelsians were driven to heterodoxy. However, it is also true that Paracelsianism, despite its reputation today for embracing superstition and folklore, was basically rational, inasmuch as the Paracelsians sought natural explanations for phenomena. This bears on the theological debate in sixteenth-century Denmark in two ways.

First, Philippism was, generally speaking, a more rationalist theology than was strict Lutheranism, which stressed the supremacy of

[29]Rasmus Glad, *Erasmus Laetus' Skrift om Christian IVs Fødsel og Dåb (1577)*, ed. Karen Skovgaard-Petersen and Peter Zeeberg (Copenhagen: Det danske Sprog- og Litteraturselskab, 1992).

faith over reason and saw no need to accommodate rational explanations for unusual phenomena described in Scripture. For Lutherans,
transubstantiation or consubstantiation was to be taken on faith
alone, as were other Christian mysteries.[30] Although Melanchthon
adhered to a humanist Aristotelianism rather than the Renaissance-
Platonist ideas that underlay Paracelsian cosmology, he recognized
the desirability of a coherence between philosophy and theology,
except where key elements that were essential to Protestant faith
might overrule reason. The Philippists followed him inasmuch as
they also valued both reason and faith, and indeed, in the case of
Tycho Brahe, Petrus Severinus, and Kort Aslakssøn, they sought a unified world picture that was both philosophically and scripturally
sound. This does not mean that they sought to subordinate natural
philosophy to biblical literalism. Rather, in keeping with Calvinist
views, they were open to accommodating a figurative reading of
Scripture to what scientific research revealed about the cosmos.[31] It is
true that Tycho Brahe denied the mobility of the earth, which was
required by the Copernican hypothesis, on both scriptural and astronomical grounds; but had there been evidence of stellar parallax,
Tycho would likely have interpreted biblical accounts of the earth's
immobility as figurative. In other words, Tycho did not always subordinate philosophy to the letter of Scripture but demanded that religion and natural philosophy not be in irreconcilable conflict.
Similarly, a consistent feature of Severinus' *semina* theory is that it fits
with Paracelsian and Augustinian readings of Genesis as a chemical
creation of the world into which God sowed the predestined *semina*
(*rationes seminales*), which ripen and bear fruit at appropriate times.
Compatibility between religion and natural philosophy under a unified cosmology demanded that scriptural phenomena be open to
rational explanation in terms of natural processes, which in turn
must be based on a suitable metaphysics able to support scriptural
accounts.

Second, the Paracelsians' philosophy raised questions about the
relationship of spirit to matter, of man's body to the world's body,

[30]On Lutheran transubstantiation, see *The Encyclopedia of the Lutheran Church*
(1965), 2:1338.
[31]On Calvin's principle of accommodation and its importance for the development of science, see G. B. Deason, "The Protestant Reformation and the Rise of Modern
Science," *Scottish Journal of Theology* 38 (1985): 223.

and of man to God. For the Paracelsian physician, healing was a matter of piety and spiritual awareness and not just the handling of the flesh. In at least some cases these questions suggested metaphysical answers that supported a spiritual or symbolic presence of Christ in the Lord's Supper, opposed the doctrine of ubiquity on philosophical and scriptural grounds, and even called into question such fundamental notions as the eternal human nature of Christ. At worst these were heretical pwsitions for all orthodoxies. In their less extreme formulations, Paracelsian Christology and sacramental metaphysics agreed better with Calvinist interpretations than with those of the strict orthodox Lutherans. The latitude of interpretation permitted in Denmark under the Philippists, many of whom had studied at Calvinist universities, did not sharply define Paracelsian ideas as essentially heterodox in the same way as the Lutherans came to do.

Kort Aslakssøn's argument about the nature and location of the heaven to which Christians look forward, the uppermost of the three discussed in his *On the Nature of the Threefold Heaven*, provides a good illustration of how cosmology and theology intersected in his worldview. He claims that this heaven must be "corporeal," by which he means dimensioned, because Christ's human nature and the natures of the elect are to remain there until the end of time (*in aeternum*), as corporeal natures. Therefore, since a body must be in some dimensioned place, this heaven must be such a corporeal space. That is why Acts 3 says that heaven contains the body of Christ. Aslakssøn forestalls the reader's objection that Christ's body and the bodies of the resurrected elect are spiritual, as taught by the apostle Paul, by arguing that the body when glorified does not cease to be physical and natural, but merely ceases being mortal and corruptible. It retains its natural and essential properties. Glorification does not destroy nature but rather perfects it.[32] All of this agrees well with the perceptions of a Paracelsian chemist: exaltation, which I assume to be analogous or even identical to glorification, strips off the accidents that chain a being to imperfection, permitting it to attain its ultimate state as a perfect, spiritual essence. That such spirits are not purely form but are subtly corporeal fits well with the gradations of existence proposed by

---

[32]Aslakssøn, *De natura caeli triplicis*, 193 (see n. 22 above). The author does not cite a verse reference to Acts, but states only "ideoque Act. 3. Caelum dicitur complecti seu continere corpus Christi" [And for that reason, heaven is said in Acts 3 to embrace or contain the body of Christ]. Perhaps this is his reading of verse 21.

Severinus, when he speaks of corporeal-incorporeals and incorporeal-corporeals.

Following this kind of metaphysics, Aslakssøn interprets the apostle Paul to have meant that Christ has two natures, not two distinct bodies. Christ has one body with both corporeal and spiritual natures, with qualities that differ accordingly. Aslakssøn supports this interpretation with the claim that glorified bodies (*corpora gloriosa*) do not differ from natural ones in substance, that is, in essential form and matter, but only qualitatively. Therefore, the resurrected are not pure spirits (forms) but spiritual bodies, and accordingly require a corporeal (i.e., dimensional) heaven. To strengthen this position he quotes from several authorities, including the Calvinists Zanchius and Danaeus.[33] Aslakssøn then notes that Aristotle had denied the possibility of any place beyond the stellar sphere, but counters the Philosopher's authority with a higher one, namely Christ. He paraphrases John 14:2–3, where Christ says, "I leave for a place prepared for you; and when I have gone and prepared a place for you, I will come back and I will take you to me, that you might be where I will be."[34] This, combined with other references to Christ's ascending to a more exalted place, beyond the celestial heaven, led Aslakssøn to the opinion that "heaven" is a physical, dimensioned place beyond the sphere of the fixed stars, in which the spiritual body of Christ and the resurrected elect reside.

The fifth and final proposition of Aslakssøn's discussion of the uppermost heaven is directed against those who would identify God with heaven or those who think that heaven is everywhere. Aslakssøn's argument follows from the previous proposition: the supernal heaven is corporeal, finite, and spatially defined, but God is infinite and not dimensionally limited. This heaven is God's house,

---

[33]Ibid., 194–95. Aslakssøn's use of the concept of a glorified body indicates his Calvinist departure from Melanchthon's theology, which did not use this formulation. See Richard, *Philip Melanchthon*, 365 (see n. 27 above).

[34]Aslakssøn, *De natura caeli triplicis*, 195: "Proficiscor paratum vobis locum; & cum profectus fuero, & paravero vobis locum, rursum veniam, & adsumam vos ad meipsum, ut ubi ego ero, vos sitis." According to the Latin Vulgate: "quia vado parare vobis locum et si abiero et praeparavero vobis locum iterum venio et accipiam vos ad me ipsum ut ubi sum ego et vos sitis"; and the King James Version: "I go to prepare a place for you. And if I go and prepare a place for you, I will come again, and receive you unto myself; that where I am, there ye may be also";

seat, and throne. It is where the angels and the elect reside. It cannot be everywhere.[35]

Although Aslakssøn's opinion about the nature of the supernal or holy heaven is grounded in Calvinist and scriptural authority, not in the work of Paracelsian authors, his arguments follow logically from the physics that he brought to bear on his discussion of the aerial and celestial heavens. His concept of spirit and spiritual body as a subtle, yet dimensioned essence, and his idea that glorification is a kind of exaltation—a process that had a defined physical meaning in Paracelsian chemistry—are in agreement with the ideas found in Severinus' *Ideal of Philosophical Medicine* (*Idea medicinae*) and other Paracelsian tracts. It follows from these arguments about the dimensional nature of heaven and the status of the resurrected as spiritual bodies dwelling there that Christ's human body cannot be present in the Lord's Supper by any rational account. There is, therefore, at least a compatibility, and possibly a causal connection, between Aslakssøn's Paracelsian cosmology and his rejection of Lutheran ubiquity and consubstantiation.

THE REACTION AGAINST PHILIPPISM

The affinity between Paracelsian ideas and the Calvinist-leaning doctrines of the Danish Philippists—labeled Cryptocalvinists by their strict Lutheran detractors—goes a long way toward explaining why religious and cosmological ideas connected with the Paracelsians, especially under the Rosicrucian rubric, became increasingly sharply defined as undesirable and even dangerously heretical as Lutheran orthodoxy tightened its grip on the Danish Church. This happened in the first two decades of the seventeenth century, during which Kort Aslakssøn was near the center of Danish theological debate.

Despite the de facto hegemony of Philippism in the leadership of the Danish church, there were also influential conservative Lutherans in the realm, and after Hemmingsen died in 1600 they began to assert themselves. In 1597, the same year that Kort Aslakssøn published *On the Nature of the Threefold Heaven*, a man named Hans Poulsen Resen was appointed to a chair in theology at Copenhagen. Resen was ambitious, and over a period of several years he gained the support of the king, his chancellor, and the influential conservative Lutheran noble-

[35]Ibid., 201–3.

man, Holger Rosenkrantz. Through a series of confrontations with Philippist bishops and theologians, Resen succeeded in consolidating his position and enforcing an increasingly strict Lutheran orthodoxy on Denmark and Norway. The first of these confrontations was precipitated when Christian IV, probably with the support of Calvinist-leaning Philippists at the university—among them Kort Aslakssøn—sought to leave the exorcism out of the baptism of his daughter in 1606. This was not an isolated event, since at that time a new church ordinance was being drafted for Norway, and the baptismal exorcism had been left out of it, probably reflecting the Philippists' effort to codify their doctrines. Resen objected strenuously, and when the ordinance was approved in 1607, exorcism was once again part of the official liturgy. That same year Resen contrived the dismissal of the senior theologian—a Philippist—and moved up in rank. The resulting vacancy below was filled by Kort Aslakssøn. Aslakssøn was not the first in line for the position, which should have gone to the professor of dialectic, Johannes Stephanius. But Stephanius, like his friend Aslakssøn a former assistant to Tycho Brahe on Hven, was strongly Cryptocalvinist and therefore unacceptable to Resen. Oskar Garstein viewed Aslakssøn as a compromise candidate who was more acceptable to Resen than was Stephanius.[36]

What is the significance of exorcism? Besides being a test case for enforcing the church's ability to suppress local liturgical innovations, the controversy over baptismal exorcism embodied fundamental issues of original sin and the place of "magical" rituals in the church. These are issues on which the strict Lutherans and Calvinist-leaning Paracelsians strongly differed. That they were not merely a matter of concern to theologians is apparent when one considers Tycho Brahe's apparent opposition to the exorcism, and perhaps also his long-term refusal to partake of the Lord's Supper on Hven.

For the seven years following the exorcism controversy, Aslakssøn quietly opposed Resen's increasing power. The gradually escalating struggle between Resen's well-organized and powerful orthodox minority and the unorganized Philippist majority of bishops, priests, and junior faculty, came to a head when a priest in Copenhagen, Olaf Jensen Koch, preached against ubiquity and Christ's eternal human

---

[36]Garstein, *Cort Aslakssøn*, 232–34 (see n. 23 above). Johannes Stephanius (1561–1625) worked as Tycho's student assistant 1582–84. See *Dansk Biografisk Leksikon*, 3d ed., vol. 14 (Copenhagen: Gyldendal, 1983), 95–96.

nature. Resen pressed for his removal from the pulpit on grounds of insubordination. A special court, at which King Christian personally supported Resen, was convened in 1614 to decide the matter. Against the Philippists' charges that he was a Gnesiolutheran and Concordist, that is, a proponent of the Formula of Concord, which had been rejected by the Danish Church, Resen had to ameliorate his Lutheranism to coincide with the Danish confession. Nevertheless, with the king's support, Resen prevailed. Next he moved to defeat Koch's supporters, which included his colleague Kort Aslakssøn. Aslakssøn chose to back down and save his career, marking the beginning of the end of Philippist power in Denmark. After 1614 he avoided all hints of Calvinism. Furthermore, he reversed his former opposition to exorcism, ubiquity, Lutheran consubstantiation, and the real presence of Christ in the Lord's Supper. From then on he cited only strict Lutherans in support of his doctrinal positions, which now conformed to Luther's Catechism, Melanchthon's *Loci communi*, and the Augsburg Confession.

Hans Poulsen Resen became the bishop primate in 1615, ushering in what Danish church historians call the first period of Lutheran orthodoxy. New legislation gave the new orthodoxy legal force. Frederik II's Alien Articles of 1569, which were designed to counter the influence of foreign religion, were reissued in 1615 and again in 1619, making it clear that spiritualist interpretations of the Eucharist were not to be tolerated. In 1617 a strong regulation against witchcraft was promulgated, encouraging priests to scrutinize the beliefs of their parishioners. A rule enacted in 1625 required professors at Copenhagen to take a special oath binding them to the articles of the Augsburg Confession. In 1629 parish priests were given the authority to excommunicate those who had abstained from the Eucharist for more than three months. Another provision of that regulation prohibited anyone from preaching from the pulpit unless he had a *testimonium* from the University of Copenhagen. All these measures aimed to limit dissent and concentrate social power in the hands of the orthodox priests, in what one historian has called a "spiritual police system."

CONCLUSION

I argue elsewhere that the triumph of Lutheran orthodoxy in Denmark created an intellectual climate in which Paracelsian ideas and beliefs could not prosper, at least publicly.[37] In accordance with the model of Paracelsian development given by Trevor-Roper, Paracelsian medical philosophy was driven underground by the sharpening doctrinal distinctions of orthodoxy and the authorities' acquisition of the legal means of enforcing conformity to them. But I think it is also true that the Paracelsian worldview, besides being incompatible with orthodox Lutheranism, also appealed to people who for one reason or another dissented from strict Lutheran dogma. This can explain how seemingly well adjusted, socially accepted people with an interest in Paracelsian medicine could end up associated with religious heterodoxy—and conversely, why heterodox Weigelians and Boehmites and adherents to other manifestations of Paracelsian religion might be attracted to chemical medicine, which had a long association with Paracelsus. The sources I have worked with do not offer decisive indication of when a person became attracted to Paracelsian ideas and when he or she began to follow heterodox religious teachings, but several cases suggest that followers of Paracelsian philosophy sometimes defended heterodox theological and ecclesiastical views and that religious dissenters sometimes adopted Paracelsian chemical and medical ideas.

However, these cases lie beyond the scope of the present study.[38] In the case of Kort Aslakssøn and others associated with Petrus Severinus and Tycho Brahe, the overriding intellectual concern would appear to be a unified cosmology—a single vision of creator and creation that was both Christian and rational. Such agreement implied compatibility or at least complementarity between key points of doctrine, with consequences for chemistry as well as Christology. Ironically, their efforts were defeated by a competing search for unity—not a chemical unity but rather the unity of the oligarchic state and the brick church that Paracelsus abhorred. In the end, the politics of power and control triumphed.

[37]Shackelford, "Rosicrucianism, Lutheran Orthodoxy, and the Rejection of Paracelsianism" (see n. 23 above).

[38]Danish and Norwegian court records permit occasional glimpses of individuals with both Paracelsian and heterodox, "outsider" Protestant connections. I would rank Nicolaus Teting and Hartvig Lohmann in Denmark and Ambrosius Rhodius and Hans Joachim Scharff in Norway among such individuals. On Teting and Lohmann, see Shackelford, *Paracelsianism in Denmark and Norway*, 293–94; on Rhodius and Scharff, 297–336; also idem, "Hans Jochum Scharff" and "A reappraisal of Anna Rhodius" (see n. 4 above).

Anabaptist Women— Radical Women?

Sigrun Haude

Anabaptist women, as part of the Radical Reformation, have to be considered radical in their religious choice. How radical their position as women within the Anabaptist community was presents a much more complex issue. We have to assume that their majority lived a traditional, if expanded female role. But a minority of Anabaptist females found ways to transgress and transform their prescribed part. Through an examination of Anabaptist inquisitorial records, this article concludes that, first, the tendency to divide Anabaptist women's history into two phases—an early one, which allowed women greater freedom, and a later, more restricted one—is contradicted by a considerable number of sources. Moreover, this model accepts male prescripts at face value without inquiring into the responses of women to them. Second, the greatest freedom enjoyed by women can be found in spirit-oriented Anabaptist groups. And third, various Anabaptist women used male perceptions of female simplemindedness to negotiate advantages for themselves and their families.

THE QUESTION WHETHER ANABAPTIST WOMEN WERE RADICAL has a confusing double entendre. Anabaptists were part of the "Radical Reformation"—an umbrella term that most historians have come to apply to the wide variety of heterodox people in the sixteenth century who accepted neither the Catholic nor the so-called mainstream Protestant confessions. Women, as an integral part of these movements, were consequently radical reformers as well. But can the label "radical" also be applied to their womanhood, to their role within the Anabaptist community, and to their position vis-à-vis society as a whole? Did these heterodox women go further in claiming rights than sixteenth-century women in other religious movements?

The study of Anabaptist women is only about fifteen years old and has stirred little general interest. It began, tellingly, with the publication of documents written by male radical reformers on the role of

313

Sigrun Haude

women and was followed by mostly unpublished master's theses.[1] But attention has grown significantly in the last few years, and in 1995 the first conference dedicated to Anabaptist women took place.[2] Historical assessments of women's roles among Anabaptists vary greatly. The views of Claus-Peter Clasen and Joyce Irwin represent one side of the spectrum, namely, that female Anabaptists enjoyed no greater societal role than other women in the sixteenth century.[3] On the other side, George Huntston Williams and Jennifer Reed claim virtual equality between Anabaptist men and women.[4] The one position maintains that Anabaptist women were equal to men in martyr-

[1]Joyce Irwin, *Womanhood in Radical Protestantism 1525–1675* (New York: Edwin Mellen Press, 1979); Leona Stucky Abbott, "Anabaptist Women of the Sixteenth Century" (M.A. thesis, Eden Theological Seminary, 1979); Jenifer Hiett Umble, "Women and Choice: An Examination of the *Martyrs' Mirror*" (M.A. thesis, Southern Methodist University, 1987); Linda Huebert Hecht, "Faith and Action: The Role of Women in the Anabaptist Movement of the Tirol, 1527–1529" (M.A. thesis, University of Waterloo, 1990); Jennifer H. Reed, "Dutch Anabaptist Female Martyrs and Their Response to the Reformation" (M.A. thesis, University of South Florida, 1991); Lois Yvonne Barrett, "Wreath of Glory: Ursula's Prophetic Visions in the Context of Reformation and Revolt in Southwestern Germany, 1524–1530" (Ph.D. diss., Union Institute, 1992).

[2]Keith L. Sprunger, "God's Powerful Army of the Weak: Anabaptist Women of the Radical Reformation," in *Triumph over Silence: Women in Protestant History*, ed. Richard L. Greaves (Westport, Conn.: Greenwood Press, 1985), 45–74; Ellen Macek, "The Emergence of a Feminine Spirituality in *The Book of Martyrs*," *Sixteenth Century Journal* 19, no. 1 (1988): 63–80; Wes Harrison, "The Role of Women in Anabaptist Thought and Practice: The Hutterite Experience of the Sixteenth and Seventeenth Centuries," *Sixteenth Century Journal* 23, no. 1 (1992): 49–69; Marion Kobelt-Groch, *Aufsässige Töchter Gottes: Frauen im Bauernkrieg und in den Täuferbewegungen* (Frankfurt a.M,: Campus Verlag, 1993); C. Arnold Snyder and Linda A. Huebert Hecht, *Profiles of Anabaptist Women: Sixteenth-Century Reforming Pioneers* (Waterloo, Ont.: Wilfried Laurier University Press, 1996); "The Quiet in the Land? Women of Anabaptist Traditions in Historical Perspective," conference at Millersville University, Millersville, Pa., 8–11 June 1995.

[3]Claus-Peter Clasen, *Anabaptism: A Social History, 1525–1618* (Ithaca: Cornell University Press, 1972), 207–8; Joyce Irwin, "Society and the Sexes," *Reformation Europe: A Guide to Research*, ed. Steven Ozment (St. Louis: Center for Reformation Research, 1982), 343–59, here 351.

[4]"The Anabaptist insistence on the covenantal principle of the freedom of conscience for all adult believers, and thereby the implicit extension of the priesthood of the Christophorous laity of women, made women, in at least the role of confessors, the spiritual equals of men. Nowhere else in the Reformation era were women conceived as so nearly companions in the faith, mates in missionary enterprise, and mutual exhorters in readiness for martyrdom as among those for whom believers' baptism was theologically a gender-equalizing covenant." George Huntston Williams, *The Radical Reformation*, 3d ed., Sixteenth Century Essays & Studies, 15 (Kirksville, Mo.: Sixteenth Century Journal Publishers, 1992), 763. Reed, "Dutch Anabaptist Female Martyrs," 33 (see n. 1 above), also argues that Anabaptist women achieved "a level of relative equality with men within the movement."

dom only, the other that, in the face of religious equality, societal limitations on women's roles became all but meaningless.[5] All historians agree, however, that there was a marked difference between the early and the later phases of Anabaptism: what female preaching and teaching we do find occurred during the unstructured beginnings of the movement, not during the later, more institutionalized phase.[6]

The conflicting views about Anabaptist women can be explained in part by the narrow and disparate documentary bases supporting most historical studies. Many of them rely on the *Martyrs Mirror*, a collection of documents that focuses on Dutch Anabaptist martyrs.[7] Linda Hecht's study, on the other hand, hinges on Anabaptist inquisitorial records for only one territory, Tirol, and covers the narrow interval of 1527 to 1529. In addition, ideological differences about emancipation and feminism have contributed to the confusion about the status of women: for some historians, the fact that Anabaptists never changed the hierarchical societal structure of their new communities is a mere trifle in the face of increased religious equality for women.[8] To other scholars, the same standards of equality must be applied to every sector of life. Finally, a foggy understanding of women's roles in Roman Catholicism, Lutheranism, and Calvinism is often responsible for greatly differing views of women's achievements in the Anabaptist movement.

Hoping to gain a clearer picture of Anabaptist women in the sixteenth century, I examined a range of inquisitorial records on Anabaptists, the *Quellen zur Geschichte der Täufer*. The one distinct image that emerges is the complexity of their situation. The records men-

---

[5]For the former position, see Abbott, "Anabaptist Women," 47 (see no. 1 above); Reed, "Dutch Anabaptist Female Martyrs," 123 (see n. 1 above), represents the latter position and argues that, for Anabaptist women, the "limitations of societal roles became virtually meaningless."

[6]Max Weber, *The Sociology of Religion* (Boston: Beacon Press, 1922), 104–5, argued that equality granted to women among the disprivileged rarely continued "beyond the first stage of a religious community's formation.... As routinization and regimentation of community relationships set in, a reaction takes place...." Hecht, "Faith and Action," 9 and 11 (see n. 1 above), agrees with Weber's assessment. She sees the cutoff point for the early period in Tirol in 1529.

[7]*The Bloody Theater or Martyrs Mirror*, comp. Thieleman J. van Braght, 10th ed. (Scottdale, Pa.: Herald Press, 1975).

[8]Even in Münster, where kingship and the community of goods replaced the traditional government and economy and where the introduction of polygyny revolutionized familial structures, the social hierarchy between men and women remained intact.

tion women who were arrested and interrogated and who either recanted or refused to do so. Edicts and ordinances against Anabaptists were explicitly directed against both men and women. More intriguingly, Anabaptist women preached, taught, interpreted Scripture, baptized, evangelized, engaged in theological debates, and led Anabaptist circles.[9] They were secret messengers who organized meetings and carried letters; they authored consolatory writings, provided food for their brothers and sisters in hiding, and were particularly active in proselytizing among other women.[10] They traveled away from home, refused to go to church on Sundays, and were willing to endure the consequences of their actions.[11]

Anabaptist women were certainly active, but the more customarily "male" the activity, the scarcer the evidence of female participation. The women who taught, preached, and baptized were the exception, constituting at best a minority of Anabaptist women and at worst some lone individuals. Admittedly, this is an argument from silence by and large, but because of the thin and patchy records for women's history, we are left with few alternatives. It is easy to imagine that there were more nontraditional Anabaptist women than were

[9]*Urkundliche Quellen zur Hessischen Reformationsgeschichte* (hereafter *UQH*), vol. 4, *Wiedertäuferakten 1527–1626*, ed. Günther Franz (Marburg: Elwert'sche Verlagsbuchhandlung, 1951), 53, no. 21 (31 Aug. 1532); *Quellen zur Geschichte der Wiedertäufer[Täufer]* (hereafter *QGT*), vol. 2, *Markgrafentum Brandenburg, Bayern I. Abteilung*, ed. Karl Schornbaum (Leipzig: Heinsius Nachfolger, 1934), 17, lines 27–32 (1527); *QGT*, vol. 5, *Bayern, II. Abteilung*, ed. Karl Schornbaum (Gütersloh: Bertelsmann, 1951), 144 (6 Aug. 1545; the reported baptism occurred in ca. 1537); *QGT*, vol. 15, *Elsaß III, Stadt Straßburg 1536–1542*, ed. M. Lienhard, S. F. Nelson, and H. G. Rott (Gütersloh: Gerd Mohn, 1986), 179, lines 22, 34–36; *QGT Bayern II*, 154, lines 2–4 (13 Aug. 1545).

[10]*UQH*, 304–5, no. 125 (1544); 188, no. 65 (after 9 Aug. 1538); see also the many examples of consolatory letters written by Anabaptist women in the *Martyrs Mirror* and the comforting letter of one Anabaptist woman to another in *QGT Bayern II*, 157–58 (1545). Note the commentary of the editor, who seems no less surprised than his sixteenth-century predecessors about this document of faith, love, and passion, written by a lay woman, most certainly of a lower societal stratum (ibid., 158, lines 23–27). *QGT Bayern II*, 149, lines 38–42 (12 Aug. 1545); 156, lines 9–10 (1545). That women as carriers of writings and letters must have been a common practice can be gathered from *QGT Bayern II*. The senior members of Nuremberg's council set down that wives and children of Anabaptists who had not been "infected" by the heretical belief may stay in the city, "es erfunde sich dann, das si iren mennern oder eltern irs irrtumbs mit schriften, brief hin und wider zutragen und zubringen verholfen weren" (unless one should learn that they [the women] had helped their husbands and parents in spreading their errors by carrying writings and letters to and fro); (ibid., 90, lines 31–33; this and the following translations of documents are mine).

[11]*UQH*, 70, no. 28 (2 Aug. 1533); 74–75, no. 30 (28 Oct. 1533).

actually reported: First, not every female Anabaptist was apprehended; second, authorities saw what they expected to see, namely, simpleminded women submissive to their spouses—until overwhelming evidence to the contrary forced the authorities to consider other possibilities. Even allowing for a generous degree of inertia by officials, it is difficult to conceive that a majority of Anabaptist women could have assumed nontraditional, "male" roles and that it would not have been noted. Such a charge against Anabaptism would have been too appealing to pass up. "Male" women (*Mannsweiber*) trying to usurp male power would have discredited the movement even further.[12]

So far, I have largely summarized what we already know or suspect about Anabaptist women. The purpose of this study is to test existing assumptions, to describe and analyze illuminating vignettes about women's activities, to explore their commonality with and differences from other sixteenth-century women, and finally, to examine whether Anabaptist women were able to transgress the boundaries, set mostly by men, for women.

The sources reveal that the traditional way of dividing the history of Anabaptist women into two phases—an early, unorganized one and a later, more institutionalized period—is neither helpful nor generally applicable. For a movement that did not start at a clearly defined point but had multiple origins both in time and place and comprised diverse religious groups, this is an exceedingly vague concept. When did the early phase end and the later one begin? That question has to be answered differently for almost every geographical region. Moreover, many documents confound early-late constructs, even when regional differences are taken into consideration. Incidents of preaching and teaching by women occurred during all periods, and women could always be found as central figures in congregations.[13] Were these exceptions? Certainly! Yet, the same

---

[12]Natalie Zemon Davis records such a concern for Calvinists in France. When Renée de France tried to "meddle" in the affairs of the Consistory, a pastor wrote to Calvin: "She is turning everything upside-down in our ecclesiastical assembly.... Our Consistory will be the laughing-stock of papists and Anabaptists. They'll say we're being ruled by women." Cited from the *Calvini Opera* in Davis, "City Women and Religious Change," *Society and Culture in Early Modern France* (Stanford: Stanford University Press, 1975), 65–95, here 84.

[13]In 1545 a young woman reported Magdalena Rayserin, an old woman in Augsburg, as having received Anabaptists frequently; *QGT Bayern II*, 154, lines 2–3. In 1544

might be true for most of our evidence. Why is it, then, that this two-phase model, so successfully applied to the situation of women during other revolutions, does not fit well for the Anabaptist case? I would suggest that it was due to Anabaptism's continued persecution: women remained essential and much needed as sisters in perseverance and survival.[14] This does not necessarily mean that, therefore, Anabaptist women enjoyed more equality, but rather that the picture is more intricate. Anabaptist men never intended to grant women exceptional roles in their communities, and yet men could not afford to do without extraordinary support from women.

What is perhaps most disconcerting about this early-late model is its sole reliance on male prescripts. It ignores the female perspective and women's response to male efforts to put them back in "their place." If men like David Joris and Menno Simons forbade women to preach and teach, does that mean that women obeyed? We have evidence that women prophesied, taught, and preached throughout the sixteenth century—isolated cases perhaps, but nonetheless a sign that some women developed their own ways of dealing with societal realities and responding to male rule.

Women's roles did, however, differ according to the nature of the Anabaptist group. Within Anabaptism, as within the Radical Reformation in general, there was a wide variety of religious and political expressions. Females experienced the greatest equality with men

---

ministers of Hesse filed a complaint against women who did not come to church but held conventicles in their houses; *UQH*, 291, no. 2. In 1564 Georg Hailmann and his wife were reported as teaching the Anabaptist heresy; *QGT*, vol. 4, *Baden und Pfalz*, ed. Manfred Krebs (Gütersloh: Bertelsmann, 1971), 165, lines 14–15. The twentieth-century editor refers in his heading only to the husband as teacher—not much has changed in the last 450 years! In 1566 a bailiff (*Amtmann*) in the county Fürstenberg reported about a stubborn and impertinent woman: "Sie spricht dem neuen pfarherr so frech zu, dass ich mich iren verwunder" (She speaks with such impertinence to the minister that I have to wonder about her); ibid., 368, lines 20–21. In the territory of Strasbourg on the right side of the Rhine, two widows had great success in converting several people of the community in 1560; ibid., 441–42.

[14]In the eighteenth century, the Methodist movement opened the office of preaching and teaching to women as well. This decision was made not just on theological but also on practical grounds: the expansion of Methodism led to a demand for preachers that could not be met by male preachers alone. Cf. Richard L. Greaves, "Introduction," in *Triumph over Silence: Women in Protestant History*, ed. Greaves (Westport, Conn.: Greenwood Press, 1985), 9.

when congregations emphasized the Spirit over Scripture.[15] This is not an entirely new insight among historians, but the exceptional position of visionaries has typically been explained on the basis of scriptural texts. Supposedly, women's prophesying was tolerated because, according to Joel 2:28–29, in the last days, God will pour out his Spirit on men *and* women.[16] In contrast, those Anabaptists emphasizing the written word could not skirt Paul's command that women keep silent in church. Yet, why should a religious group that rejected the "frozen word" feel bound by a scriptural text? Furthermore, why did biblically oriented communities choose to follow the restrictive Pauline statement rather than his liberating vision that there is neither man nor woman? It seems that male Anabaptists selectively chose their biblical proof texts: It was not the Bible but preexisting biases that shaped men's attitude toward women.

Therefore, the reasons for female visionaries' greater equality and freedom to speak must lie elsewhere. Let us look at the evidence. In Strasbourg, Saxony, and Franconia, Anabaptist prophetesses held eminent places in their communities. The list of prophets compiled by the Strasbourg authorities includes eleven men and seven women. Anabaptist leader Melchior Hoffman recorded the visions of Ursula Jost and Barbara Rebstock, Strasbourg's most important female visionaries.[17] Ursula's visions were published and widely distributed, thus influencing a large segment of the Anabaptist movement.[18] After Ursula died, Barbara Rebstock replaced her in the inner sanctum of Strasbourg prophets. When in 1537/38 the Anabaptist leader David Joris tried to persuade the Melchiorites to join his movement, Barbara Rebstock spoke up. "Led by the Spirit," she accused David Joris of trying to pick the fruit from the trees before it was ripe.[19] Perturbed and deflated, Joris warned the Strasbourg Anabaptists to beware of women.[20] His complaint was not against women in general, for Joris referred positively to a letter he had received from Anneken Jans of

---

[15]The case of the kingdom of Münster demonstrates that visionary communities did not always allow women a greater role. Cf. R. Po-chia Hsia, "Münster and the Anabaptists," in *The German People and the Reformation*, ed. Po-chia Hsia (Ithaca: Cornell University Press, 1988), 51–69, esp. 55–60.

[16]Cf. particularly Barrett, "Wreath of Glory" (see n. 1 above).

[17]*QGT Elsaß III*, 163, no. 6.

[18]Cf. Barrett, "Wreath of Glory" (see n. 1 above).

[19]*QGT Elsaß III*, 179, lines 22, 34–36. Earlier she had objected to the content of a letter that Joris had sent to the Melchiorites in Strasbourg; ibid., 163, lines 14–20.

[20]"Hoet v voir die wiuen"; *QGT Elsaß III*, 180, line 29.

Rotterdam.[21] Instead, he objected to a certain type of woman. Barbara Rebstock represented the outspoken troublemaker while Anneken Jans stood for the obedient, quietly suffering woman, tolerated and appreciated by Joris as the inconspicuous backbone of the movement. Likewise, the followers of Niclas Storch, active in Luther's home territory,[22] and the so-called Uttenreuter Dreamers in Franconia paid attention to visions and prophecies. Both men and women prophesied on the basis of dreams and exchanged visions.[23]

Some historians have argued that Anabaptist women created a better environment for male-female equality because they accepted God as their only authority. And indeed, many statements by women bear out this conclusion.[24] However, those Anabaptist communities that emphasized Scripture rather than the Spirit were still led by one or two teachers who held the power to interpret the Bible and to baptize. Therefore, Scripture-oriented Anabaptists retained a hierarchy within their congregations. For visionaries, however, the whole intermediary layer of teachers and missionaries did not exist. Women were called directly by God to speak up or to keep silent; God was the only teacher they recognized; it was God's voice that led them into the new community of believers.[25]

---

[21]*QGT Elsaß III*, 182, lines 17–18.

[22]For women followers of Storch, see Susan C. Karant-Nunn, "Continuity and Change: Some Effects of the Reformation on the Women of Zwickau," *Sixteenth Century Journal* 13 (1982): 17–42, esp. 37–41, and Siegfried Hoyer, "Die Zwickauer Storchianer— Vorläufer der Täufer?" *Sächsische Heimatblätter*, suppl. 13 (1986): 60–78, esp. 69–70.

[23]"Und solches war bei gedachtem Storchen und seiner rott, beides mans und weibs personen, gar gemein, dass sie im traum, auch wol wachend, bei lichtem, hellem tag aus des teufels vorbilden gesicht sahen, heimliche verborgen ding eröffneten und zukunftige sachen verkundigten" (It was common among the lot of said Storch, that both men and women, whether they were dreaming or awake during bright daylight, saw visions of the devil's creation, revealed secret, hidden things, and foretold matters in the future); *QGT Brandenburg, Bayern I*, 7, lines 7–11 (1525); ibid., 289, lines 1–7 (1531). On a more mundane level, one woman even held the key to the common chest; ibid., 222, lines 20–21 (1531).

[24]"Item si [Barbara Würzelburger] kund nit bei ir erfinden von dem zu steen und wider got iren hern zu tun. Si hab sich got irem hern ergeben, dabei well si besteen..."; *QGT Bayern II*, 29, lines 24–26 (1528); "Des hab sie sich gegen gott und kainen menschen verpflicht und verpunden nach der lere gottes: das si woll alle trubseligkait und widerwertigkait mit gedult leiden und tragen.... Sie hab sich mit niemand verpunden dann mit gott"; ibid., 171, lines 21–24, 29–30 (1529).

[25]"Der her hab zu ir [Anna des Schmids von Uttenreut hausfrau] gesagt, sie sol keinem menschen vertrauen allein gott.... Und hab zu ir gesagt, wen ir geben sei zu reden, so soll sie reden, sei ir aber geben zu schweigen, so soll sie schweigen.... Sie hab nichts

The most unsettling fact about these heretics was their marriage practice. They freely dissolved and reentered marriage with whomever the Spirit allegedly suggested. The Uttenreuter Dreamers differed from the Münster Anabaptists and their polygynous practice in that marrying among the former proved a two-way street: relying on their visions, women, too, could choose their own spouses.[26] Thus, Anabaptist groups led by the Spirit, with no one else to direct minds and activities or to claim authority of any kind, proved the most fertile ground for a new vision and a new role for women.

Finally, this study focuses on the persistent conviction among men that women were simpleminded, and on women's response to this attitude. The evidence suggests that a considerable number of women (we will never know the real figure) exploited their lot as supposedly ignorant simpletons to their advantage and thus took charge of their own and their families' lives. The belief that women were dense, demure, and domestic died hard among the always male authorities. The inquisitors of Hesse went furthest in drawing the concomitant conclusion that, therefore, women did not play an active role in the Anabaptist movement—despite considerable evidence to the contrary.[27] Anabaptist women were registered only as wives who followed their husbands into heresy without making a

---

mit der schrift zu schicken, sie gleub allein an die lebendige stim gottes.... Sie leren von keinem prediger nichts, allein von gott"; *QGT Bayern II*, 230, lines 24–33, 35–36 (1531); Margret Striglin: "Der her sei ir lerer"; ibid., line 39; Else Kern: "Es hab sie niemand gelert on allein, was sie der geist lerte und ir eingebe.... Sie wiss kein obersten, sie sind alle also durcheinander gangen, und was eim furkomen ist, demselben hat es nachgevolgt" (She was taught by no one except by what the Spirit instructed and revealed to her.... She knows no superior, they all mingled, and followed whatever vision was revealed to someone); ibid., 301, lines 30–31; 302, lines 7–8 (1531). Muel Jecklas: "Gottes stimb hab sie in dise bruderschaft pracht"; *QGT Brandenburg, Bayern I*, 231, line 3 (1531). The arrested Uttenreuter women, despite being sick and frail from their imprisonment, refused to be advised by the authorities and mocked their interrogator; ibid., 240, no. 262.

[26]Else Kern: "Da sie ungeverlich sechs wochen bei dem Schmid gewest, da wer ir zenachts furkomen, sie solt den Schmid zu der ee nemen"; *QGT Brandenburg, Bayern I*, 302, lines 32–34.

[27]Other territories, like the county Zweibrücken-Bitsch, showed an awareness that women became Anabaptists without their husbands and vice versa; see *QGT Baden und Pfalz*, 292–93.

decision of their own.[28] The councilors did not lack testimony that women could think for themselves. Margret Gompel, when interrogated regarding her beliefs and why she did not attend church on Sundays, replied that the minister's sermons had not led to any improvement in the community. And since she herself could read, she simply stayed home.[29] Margarete Koch, pressured to recant her Anabaptist beliefs, asked for one or two days to think it over, but then persisted in her faith. She had heard about three different preachers—a papist, a Protestant, but then also Melchior Rinck (an Anabaptist leader), whom she considered a true preacher and whose message she deemed sincere. Thus, she would stand by it.[30] None of these witnesses prompted the authorities to alter their perception of women.[31]

---

[28]In a draft to an ordinance against Anabaptists of 1536, "wives of Anabaptists" is the only designated category for women. The authorities were convinced that women joined the Anabaptist movements only as ignorant wives of their already heretical husbands; *UQH*, 138, no. 47 (summer 1536). The same ambiguity or inability on the part of the magistracies to gauge the position of Anabaptist women surfaces in other inquisitorial records for Hesse. Most mandates, ordinances, or reports regarding Anabaptists speak of "manns- und weibspersonen" as being involved in the heresy. However, frequently the reader encounters in the same or subsequent documents the question whether one should send wife and children after the expelled. The assumption is again that those who were responsible, were male; see, e.g., *QGT Bayern II*, 88, lines 24–25. When single women are mentioned, they are said to have come from "foreign countries": apart from the fact that authorities had found many Anabaptist couples, there had also been "weiber allein us frembden landen, Frangken, dem stift von Fulda..." (single women from foreign lands, Franconia, the bishopric of Fulda...); *UQH*, 70, no. 28 (2 Aug. 1533).

[29]"Margret, Stoffel Gompels eliche hausfrau, sagt, sie veracht gots wort nicht, auch den predicanten nicht, sie wol auch den predicanten irethalben entschuldiget haben, sie sehe aber kein besserung nicht, so kunde sie selbs lesen, darumb blieb sie doheime"; *UQH*, 74, no. 30 (28 Oct. 1533). Margret's husband had also been interrogated; ibid.

[30]*UQH*, 153, no. 54 (22 May 1537).

[31]Around 1543 several Hessian ministers filed complaints against Anabaptists. They began with a list of married women who had failed to come to Sunday sermons and were holding gatherings at their own homes: "Volgkern Beiders weib geht nit in die kirchen. Jost Ysslebens weib gehe nit zur kirchen. Die Huffin geht nit in die kirchen, ist dem pfarhern gesagt, die widerteufer versamblen sich im selben hause. Pfarher zu Herde zeigt an ... der widerteufer halben: Fridschen weib zu Herde geht nit in die kirchen, auch ir kinder. Was hin und wider steubt, versamblet sich in irem hause"; *UQH*, 291, no. 121. The subsequent order by the Landgrave regarding appropriate punishment shows that there were many more women involved than men; ibid., 293, no. 121 (1544). In 1555 Duke Wilhelm of Henneberg notified Philip of Hesse that the Landgrave's sister (Countess Elizabeth of Saxony) was providing shelter and food for an Anabaptist; ibid., 332, no. 143. Even so, the authorities held fast to their cherished conviction that it was not women but rather their husbands who were responsible for

In 1538 a secretary uncovered books and consolatory writings in the prison cells of Anabaptists "written by male and female hands."[32] Women as authors and sustainers of heresy—how did this discovery agree with the image of ignorant and silent wives who were all but forced to follow husbands into heresy? One can sense the great surprise that prompted this detail to be recorded.

It is clear how authorities arrived at such views of Anabaptist women. They categorized Anabaptists into groups of leaders and ignorant followers. Women, as the intellectual inferiors of men, naturally belonged to the latter category, together with the majority of ignorant men. And indeed, during many recantations, Anabaptist women took recourse to their simplicity of mind, and more often than not, they might have meant this excuse sincerely.[33] But women also took advantage of the authorities' readiness to consider them as simpletons and thus were able to turn the tables. By pleading weakness of mind and by appealing to the magistrates' sense of responsibility toward them, women could negotiate their way out of trouble and back into their home communities after they had been expelled. The skill with which some of these documents have been constructed makes us wonder how simpleminded these women really were.[34]

---

the decision to join the Anabaptists, as is clear from a questionnaire of June 1544 to be directed to the Anabaptists; no. 12 reads: "Item ob sie auch ire weibe und kinder zu solcher ler und handel verursacht oder gezwungen, und ob sie dieselben auch mit zur predig gefurt haben oder nit"; ibid., 303, no. 125. The same conviction resounds in an accusation from Brandenburg against male Anabaptists belonging to the sect of "dreamers" (*Träumer*) who had broken their marriages: they had "die heiligen ee von got eingesetzt zerrissen, andere weiber genomen, auch iren weibern andere menner zu nemen erlaubt, dadurch sie nit allein den eebruch begangen, sonder auch ire weiber zu solchen streflichen laster bewegt und ursach geben"; *QGT Bayern II*, 282, lines 28–31 (1531).

[32]"Seind auch etliche beschribene bucher doselbs [in prison] gefunden und etliche trostschrifte von mann- und weibshenden geschriben..."; *UQH*, 188, no. 65 (after 9 Aug. 1538).

[33]E.g., *QGT Bayern II*, 17, lines 7–9 (1528): "So hat unsers burgers des Zwickls hausfrau uns nachmals zum hochsten anzaigen lassen, das si allain aus irem ainfalt und unverstand durch dieienen pueben zu der widertauf bered worden."

[34]Pleading for her return to Regensburg, Brigitta Baumeister described herself as "ein junges, unverstendiges und der ding unerfarnes weipspild durch etlicher unrechtmessige ler leider verfuert und zum widertauf bewegt..." (a young, ignorant and inexperienced woman who unfortunately had been led astray by several false teachings and had been induced to be rebaptized...); *QGT Bayern II*, 113, lines 28–30 (26 June 1540?). Brigitta, who had joined the Anabaptists without her husband (114, line 11), chal-

Sigrun Haude

Several records strike us almost as buffoonery. Consider, for example, the shocking discovery of female writings in prison. How did the secretary discover the books in the first place? In a long series of interrogations, the secretary called for the next Anabaptist but was told by the officer that the summoned person was not in his cell. The secretary himself immediately went to the prison and discovered that Jorg Schnabel had left eight days earlier to be with his wife and children. Another Anabaptist had done the same. Suspicious that the warden (*Vogt*) and his officers were accomplices in the escape, the secretary inquired further. But the Anabaptists were quick to exonerate the warden and his men. The incarcerated claimed that the Lord had provided them with means to enter and leave prison freely. Not quite convinced, the secretary pressed on and learned that yet another Anabaptist prisoner had instructed his wife to send their son along with a small saw. Confronted with this evidence, the warden admitted that he had given in to the Anabaptists' wives, on account of his good opinion of them, and had allowed them in front of the prison. The women had told him that they wanted to hear whether their husbands would finally recant and return home. The Anabaptists had been going in and out freely for about a year and, as the secretary feared, had been holding many gatherings around the country. What is more, this seemingly miraculous arrangement had probably won the Anabaptists many fascinated followers among the simple-minded.[35] It was women who had capitalized on the guards' benevolence toward ignorant females and who took advantage of the situation to benefit themselves and their families.

How different, then, were Anabaptist women from their sixteenth-century sisters in Protestant and Catholic churches?[36] The

---

lenged the Council of Regensburg to imagine what might become of her if "ich anfeltiges weip von meinem veterland verstossen, daselbst keinen trost süechen, gar und ganz verlassen sein und aus armut und plodigkeit weiblichs geschlechts zu noch grosserm ubel zu komen besorgen muss…" (I, a simpleminded woman, cast out of my homeland so that I cannot look for any comfort there, and entirely abandoned, have to fear to come to even greater harm because of poverty and the stupidity of the female gender); lines 13–16. It is difficult to imagine the author of this skillfully crafted plea as a representative of female simplemindedness. It seems more likely that women such as Brigitta used male arguments to their own benefit.

[35]*UQH*, 190, no. 65 (10 Aug. 1538).

[36]For the most recent extensive bibliography on women in early modern Europe, see Merry E. Wiesner, *Women and Gender in Early Modern Europe: New Approaches to European History* (Cambridge: Cambridge University Press, 1993).

answer to this question needs to be explored in greater depth than possible here. But we are struck already by the great commonality in the roles women had in different religious movements. Lutheran and Calvinist women defended their faith, preached, and taught.[37] Catholic women, whether married or nuns, missionized and stood up for their faith against the encroachment by Protestants.[38]

Some scholars have argued that among Anabaptist women there was a greater impetus to read, in keeping with the strong emphasis on the Bible. But *sola scriptura* was a Reformation principle that encouraged reading among the Evangelicals as well.[39] Similarly, the idea of the "priesthood of all believers" led to the conviction of an immediacy to God that was not reserved for Anabaptism. Protestant women, too, claimed God as their sole authority, defying any other judge of their faith. And this new religious freedom coexisted with wifely obedience to husbands in *all* religious movements.

Still, there were some differences. Only Anabaptist women were allowed to leave their nonbelieving husbands; but then again, most females were expected to marry soon after entering the Anabaptist community. While class distinctions were retained in Protestant and Catholic churches, they did not play a role in most Anabaptist groups.[40] Furthermore, constant persecution of Anabaptists led to a notable expansion of women's roles; however, women were overwhelmingly denied leadership positions. Nevertheless, because Anabaptists had to avoid any public displays of religious devotion and could only meet in secret, private homes—the very domain of women—advanced to center stage and provided rich opportunities for women's involvement.

Some historians have claimed that women joined the Anabaptists in particular, and heretical movements in general, to gain greater freedom and more rights.[41] Shannon McSheffrey has problematized this

[37]Ibid., 186–88; for Calvinist city women, see Davis, "City Women and Religious Change," 82–83; for women in general, 92 (see n. 12 above).

[38]Wiesner, *Women and Gender*, 193, 195–96 (see n. 36 above).

[39]Calvinists defended women's right to read the Bible in the vernacular; similarly, popular Calvinist literature favored the "new woman" who refuted the stupid priest by citing Scripture; see Davis, "City Women and Religious Change," 77–78 (see n. 12 above). In the English church, however, women were prohibited from reading; see Wiesner, *Women and Gender*, 188–89.

[40]See Wiesner, *Women and Gender*, 189, on the situation among Protestant and Catholic women.

[41]Hecht, "Faith and Action," 16, 59–60 (see n. 1 above).

conclusion for Lollard women,[42] and I would urge the same caution here. As my study and others have shown, Anabaptists offered women few choices that were not available in other religious groups. Women may not always have joined the Anabaptists for purely religious reasons,[43] but how many benefits, other than spiritual, could one gain by joining a movement in which the almost assured fate was persecution, if not execution? We should, however, not underestimate the spirit of companionship that emerges in a movement under persecution and adds an attractive feature to its profile.[44]

In summary, I have argued that the greatest freedom enjoyed by women can be found in those Anabaptist groups that emphasized visions, prophecies, and the Spirit. These women based their activities on their direct empowerment by God and thus denied any worldly authority to curtail them. Second, a certain number of Anabaptist women used the male perception of women's simplemindedness to negotiate advantages for themselves and their families. In an ironic twist, male bias toward women became instrumental for contriving greater freedom. And third, the general distinction between an earlier unstructured phase in which Anabaptist women had the greatest freedom, and a later more institutionalized period during which women were forced back into their traditional societal roles, is neither a useful device for enhancing our understanding of Anabaptist women, nor does it find general corroboration in the documents. This is not to say that we cannot find such developments at all, but that this phenomenon cannot be generalized for Anabaptist women. A fundamental problem evident in this two-phase model is that Anabaptist women's history is still written primarily from the point of view of male-defined boundaries and concepts. These structures are commonly taken at face value without investigating how women received them and how they responded to them. Some of the cases I have examined reveal the discrepancies between the part ascribed to women and how women through their actions defined their roles.

[42]McSheffrey, *Gender and Heresy: Women and Men in Lollard Communities, 1420–1530* (Philadelphia: University of Pennsylvania Press, 1995), 2–4, 138–39. Davis, in "City Women and Religious Change," 81, argues that those French city women who joined the Calvinist movement did so not to gain greater independence but to complement their already more independent selves (see n. 12 above).

[43]See Hecht, "Faith and Action," 19, for the Tirol (see n. 1 above).

[44]For examples of the spirit of companionship, see the Anabaptist correspondence in the *Martyrs Mirror* (see n. 7 above).

Furthermore, it is crucial to apply the same standards of interpretation to the sources prior to and after the supposed shift. Otherwise, we are in danger of interpreting, on one hand, the scarce documentation of female leadership for the later phase as evidence of women's curtailed equality and, on the other, the almost equally sparse records for the earlier period as signs of women's greater freedom to act.

In the final analysis, there is no easy answer to the question whether Anabaptist women were radical. With regard to their religious choices and the consequences they suffered we have to answer in the affirmative. In terms of their societal position, the answer is much more complex. Anabaptist women as a whole did not break from the traditional role ascribed to women. On the other hand, some of them did resist their societal limitations. Due to the thin documentation and its still rudimentary investigation, we would be wise to allow for a certain latitude in interpretation. Our evidence that certain Anabaptist females transformed women's traditional roles may reflect just a few scattered individuals,[45] or it may point to a considerable minority among Anabaptist women. There is reason to see the available testimonies in the more optimistic light: after all, with its center in private homes rather than in churches and public buildings, Anabaptism provided an excellent opening for women to subvert established male patterns.

[45]Merry Wiesner and Susan Karant-Nunn contend that one of the most striking features of early modern women is the individual nature of their action. See Wiesner, "Women's Response to the Reformation," in *The German People and the Reformation*, ed. R. Po-chia Hsia (Ithaca: Cornell University Press, 1988), 148–71, here 170, and Karant-Nunn, "Continuity and Change," 38 (see n. 22 above). Davis, in "City Women and Religious Change," 92–93, argues that organized group action can be found only among Catholic women (see n. 12 above).

Wife of John Beukels (John of Leiden)
by Aldegrever

The Regulation of Hebrew Printing in Germany, 1555–1630

Confessional Politics and the Limits of Jewish Toleration

Stephen G. Burnett

In the contentious religious and political climate of the German empire between 1555 and 1630, rulers of Lutheran, Reformed, and Catholic cities and territories all agreed that "Jewish blasphemies" were intolerable in a Christian state, yet Jewish printing came to be both legally and politically feasible during these years. This essay examines the German imperial laws that governed the book trade, the religious and political factors that rulers were obliged to weigh when considering whether to allow Jewish printing in their domains, and the policies and safeguards that they could adopt to attenuate these potential risks. In the end, Jewish printing became more acceptable because of two intellectual developments: the emergence of a broadly accepted standard for censorship of Jewish books and the professional Christian Hebraists, who could evaluate Jewish book manuscripts for blasphemous or seditious content.

IN EARLY OCTOBER 1559, Mark Sittich, suffragan bishop of Constance, received a disturbing report from Bernard Segisser, an episcopal vogt in Kaiserstuhl: The Count of Sulz had allowed Jews who lived in the town of Tiengen, on the German side of the Rhine, to open a Jewish press. The burghers of the town were worried, fearing that they would suffer "ruinous damage" (*verderplichen Schaden*) because of the press. Since Tiengen was located in the bishopric of Constance, what were the bishop's instructions?[1] Lacking any clear legal precedents, Bishop

---

[1]Bernhard Segisser to Mark Sittich, Kaiserstuhl, 30 September 1559, in J. Bader, "Urkunden und Regeste aus dem ehemaligen Klettgauer Archive," *Zeitschrift für die Geschichte des Oberrheins* 13 (1861): 476.

Sittich gave Segisser a rather vague response: Since the Jews of the empire enjoyed the favor of Emperor Ferdinand I, they should be allowed to continue printing so long as they did so in Hebrew rather than in a language that Christians could read.[2] Sittich had apparently forgotten that the county of Sulz was not under imperial jurisdiction but was subject to the Swiss Confederation.[3] When the existence of the Jewish press was revealed at the 24 June 1560 meeting of confederation leaders, the representatives of both Catholic and Protestant cantons, in an unusual display of ecumenical unity, demanded that it be closed immediately.[4] What particularly upset them was that the Talmud, a work they considered injurious to the Christian faith, was to be printed in Tiengen.[5]

The religious tensions of the decades preceding the Thirty Years' War, along with the consensus among Reformed, Catholic, and Lutheran theologians that Judaism was a false religion, might suggest that any attempt to print Jewish books in Germany would have suffered the same fate as the Tiengen press. Yet between the Tiengen incident of 1560 and the approval of a Jewish press in the principality of Hanau in 1609, a legal framework did emerge in Germany that made it far easier to print and market Jewish books there. In this essay I analyze this development by posing three questions: First, what were the laws that governed the book trade within the German empire, and how were these laws applied to Jewish printers? Second, what unwritten political and religious factors did civic and territorial rulers have to weigh when deciding whether to allow Jewish printing?

[2]Sittich to Segisser, 31 October 1559, in Bader, "Urkunden und Regeste," 477. Sittich may have been thinking about the generous decree issued by Ferdinand on 30 April 1548 concerning the rights of Jews in Lower Austria. See Selma Stern, *Josel of Rosheim: Commander of Jewry in the Holy Roman Empire of the German Nation*, trans. Gertrude Hirschler (Philadelphia: Jewish Publication Society, 1965), 245 and 314, n. 12.

[3]*Handbuch der Historischen Stätten Deutschlands*, vol. 6: *Baden-Württemberg*, ed. Max Miller and Gerhard Taddey, 2d ed. (Stuttgart: Kröner, 1980), 410.

[4]Minutes of the Swiss Confederation meeting in Baden, 24 June 1560, Aargau Staatsarchiv, Gemein eidgenössische Abschiede 2, no. 2476, 104r; summary in *Der amtliche Abschiedesammlung*, vol. 4, pt. 2 (Bern: G. Rätzer, 1861), 131; cf. their letter of complaint: Cities and Territories of the Swiss Confederation to the Count of Sulz, Baden, 4 July 1560, Karlsruhe, Generallandesarchiv, Abt. 224, Akten Tiengen, fasc. 62.

[5]The issue was raised after a representative from Lucerne complained about finding defamatory books (*Schmähschriften*) for sale in the Zurich market. A Zurich representative countered this accusation by revealing the existence of a Jewish press in Tiengen, which was to print the Talmud. *Der amtliche Abschiedesammlung*, vol. 4, pt. 2, p. 131.

Third, what policies and safeguards could a Christian magistrate adopt to reduce the political and religious risks inherent in allowing a Jewish press to operate? By addressing these questions, we will discover not only how German lawyers, theologians, and Christian Hebraists created a narrow but viable legal niche for Jewish printing but also how this consensus reflected the status of Judaism and Jews within the multiconfessional German empire.

To illustrate how Jewish presses were regulated, I use archival materials relating to the activities of three different firms: Ambrosius Froben's printing firm in Basel, whose brief venture in Jewish printing produced the heavily censored Basel Talmud (1578–80); the Jewish firm in Thannhausen in Burgau (1592–94), which was subject to the Hapsburgs; and the most successful one, the Hebrew printing firm in Hanau (1609–30), located in the county of Hanau-Münzenberg, a reformed principality that shared borders with the archbishopric of Mainz and the Lutheran imperial city of Frankfurt am Main.[6] I focus especially on these firms since they were all active after the imperial system of press oversight was fully implemented.

While there is evidence of censorship by ecclesiastical and secular authorities in Germany before the Reformation, it was Martin Luther with his overly active pen who encouraged imperial authorities to create a legal framework for controlling what was printed and sold within Germany. A series of laws beginning with Charles V's edict at the Diet of Worms in 1521 that condemned Luther's writings, and augmented by *Reichsabschiede* passed by the imperial diets of Nuremberg in 1524, Speyer in 1529, and Augsburg in 1530, made it clear that territorial princes and city magistrates were responsible for ensur-

---

[6]On the presses of Tiengen and Thannhausen, see Moshe N. Rosenfeld, "The Development of Hebrew Printing in the Sixteenth and Seventeenth Centuries," in *A Sign and a Witness: 2,000 Years of Hebrew Books and Illustrated Manuscripts*, ed. Leonard Singer Gold (New York: New York Public Library; Oxford: Oxford University Press, 1988), 96–97, and Heinrich Sinz, *Beiträge zur Geschichte des Marktes und Landkapitals Ichenhausen im 16. und 17. Jahrhundert* (Ichenhausen: Josef Wagner, 1930), 69–71 (Thannhausen only); on the Basel Talmud, see Ernst Staehelin, "Des Basler Buchdruckers Ambrosius Froben Talmudausgabe und Handel mit Rom," *Basler Zeitschrift für Geschichte und Altertumskunde* 30 (1931): 7–37, and Joseph Prijs, *Die Basler Hebräische Drucke (1492–1866)*, ed. Bernhard Prijs (Olten: Urs Graf, 1964), 171–210; on the Hanau Hebrew press, see Stephen G. Burnett, "Hebrew Censorship in Hanau: A Mirror of Jewish-Christian Coexistence in Seventeenth Century Germany," in *The Expulsion of the Jews: 1492 and After*, ed. Raymond B. Waddington and Arthur H. Williamson, Garland Studies in the Renaissance, vol. 2 (New York: Garland, 1994), 199–222.

ing that all books produced under their jurisdiction be properly censored prior to printing and that all offenders, whether authors, printers, or booksellers, be punished.[7] These early censorship ordinances were expanded, at least in theory, into a system of empirewide press controls through decisions made by the Diet of Speyer (1570) and further elaborated in the *Reichspolizeiordnung* of 1577.[8] According to these statutes, all presses thenceforth should be located in imperial cities, university towns, or in the residence towns of princes. Presses in any other location would thenceforth be considered clandestine presses (*Winckeldruckereien*); the operators of such presses would be subject to arrest and the seizure both of their presses and any books that had already been produced. Moreover, each and every book had to bear the name of its author, the city where it was produced, and the year it was printed in order to identify who was responsible for its creation and censorship.[9] By confining presses to larger towns, the authorities hoped to ensure that proper censorship of books would take place.

The formation of the Imperial Book Commission in the imperial city of Frankfurt in 1579 served as the final link in the chain of imperial press regulations. Since Frankfurt, the site of the most important book fair in the empire, was technically under imperial jurisdiction, the emperor was within his rights to appoint a committee of experts to monitor what books were available for sale in the city, both those produced domestically and those imported from other lands.[10] By

---

[7]Ulrich Eisenhardt, *Die kaiserliche Aufsicht über Buchdruck, Buchhandel und Presse im Heiligen Römischen Reich Deutscher Nation (1496–1806): Ein Beitrag zur Geschichte der Bücher und Pressezensur*, Studien und Quellen zur Geschichte des Deutschen Verfassungsrechts, Reihe A: Studien, vol. 3 (Karlsruhe: C. F. Müller, 1970), 6.

[8]Ulrich Eisenhardt, "Staatliche und kirchliche Einflussnahmen auf den deutschen Buchhandel im 16. Jahrhundert," in *Beiträge zur Geschichte des Buchwesens im konfessionellen Zeitalter,* ed. Herbert G. Göpfert, et al., Wolfenbütteler Schriften zur Geschichte des Buchwesens, vol. 11 (Wiesbaden: Harrassowitz, 1985), 301–3. For a discussion of how imperial decisions and ordinances were enacted during this period, see *Handwörterbuch zur Deutschen Rechtsgeschichte*, ed. Adalbert Erler, Ekkehard Kaufmann, and Wolfgang Stammler (Berlin: Erich Schmidt, 1990), s.v. "Reichsgesetzgebung."

[9]*Neue und vollständigere Sammlung der Reichsabschiede welche von den Zeiten Kayser Conrads des II. bis jetzo, auf den Teutschen Reichstagen abgesfasset worden ...* (1747; reprint, Osnabrück: Otto Zeller, 1967), 3:308, par. 154–59 (Reichsabschied von Speyer 1570); 3:395–97, Titul xxxv (Reichspolizeiordnung von 1577).

[10]Wolfgang Brückner, "Die Gegenreformation im politischen Kampf um die Frankfurter Buchmessen: Die Kaiserliche Zensur zwischen 1567 und 1619," *Archiv für Frankfurts Geschichte und Kunst* 48 (1962): 68–69.

mandating where printing could occur, requiring stringent prepubli-cation censorship, and appointing an oversight commission to report on what books were available for sale at the Frankfurt book fair, the emperor had created, at least in theory, an effective oversight system for books produced within the empire and to some extent those pro-duced outside. In addition, the laws and the commission served to regulate Jewish printing, which both Catholics and Protestants agreed needed careful oversight.[11]

When considering Jewish printing, German princely and munici-pal authorities were obliged to address two questions: Was it legal to print Jewish books? If so, under what conditions? Dr. Wilhelm Sturio, councillor to Count Philipp Ludwig of Hanau, prepared a legal opin-ion in early 1609 that illustrates just how little guidance law and pre-cedent gave to answer these questions. He noted that in the past Jewish printing had been permitted by many rulers in many places: The pope had allowed Jewish printing in Venice, the emperor had done so in Prague, the king of Spain permitted it in Cremona (Italy), as had the magistrates of Basel and Augsburg in their cities.[12] There-fore it was permissible to allow Jewish printing. Sturio went on to link the question with a related issue that Johannes Reuchlin had addressed in his famous opinion on Jewish books: whether the Jews should be allowed to keep their own books, especially the Talmud. Although Emperor Maximilian I had ruled technically against Reuch-lin, Sturio stressed that the latter had won the battle for learned and

---

[11]In its first response to Emperor Rudolf II the Basel city council stressed that the Talmud edition then being printed by Froben would be satisfactorily censored "so that all Christians, whatever their confession, would admit its validity and be in agreement with it" (domit allen Christen, welcher Confession die weren, Rechnung zugeben sich erbotten und gesynnet siye); all translations mine unless otherwise noted. Basel Bürger-meister and city council to Emperor Rudolf II, Basel, 2 February 1579, Basel Staatsar-chiv, Handel und Gewebe JJJ 13, fol. 36 r. My discussion of Froben's Talmud edition is based primarily upon the file assembled by the Basel city government to keep a record of events and rulings connected with the affair.

[12]Wilhelm Sturio, [Opinion], 21 February 1609, Marburg Staatsarchiv, Best. 81 BI 81, no. 23, fol. 3v. Fra Felice de Prato petitioned the pope on behalf of Daniel Bomberg for permission to print Hebrew titles in 1515. Marvin J. Heller, *Printing the Talmud: A History of the Earliest Printed Editions of the Talmud* (Brooklyn: Im Hasefer, 1992), 136. On the Augsburg press, see Mosche N. Rosenfeld, *Der Jüdische Buchdruck in Augsburg in der ersten Hälfte des 16. Jahrhunderts* (London: Rosenfeld, 1985).

public opinion.[13] If Jews could own and sell their own books, then presumably their books could also legally be printed. The only restrictions upon Jewish printing suggested by Sturio were that each book be censored and approved before it was printed and that the compositor be obliged to take an oath to use only the text approved by the authorities and make no unauthorized changes.[14] In Sturio's opinion there were no legal obstacles to Hanau's hosting a Jewish press.

Two of the three presses under consideration were located in towns that fit the legal requirements of the *Reichspolizeiordnung* of 1577. Both Basel and Hanau were university towns and had learned personnel available who could ensure that books were censored properly.[15] Thannhausen, however, did not fit this description. It was a small jurisdiction ruled by a *Marktherr*, Philipp von Bicken, and located within the *Markgrafshaft* of Burgau, which was subject to the Hapsburg archducal court of Innsbruck.[16] The town of Thannhausen itself was fairly small and had no institution of higher learning. The Jewish press was also small, employing two Jewish printers, R. Isaac

[13]"Reuchlin's opinion was victorious in this battle and was approved by the most learned people throughout Germany" (Reuchlins meinung hat in diesen Streit gesiget welche die furnembste gelehrteste leute in Deutschlandt beigefallen). Ibid., fols. 3r–v. For a discussion of Reuchlin's opinion and its legal basis, see Friedrich Lotter, "Der Rechtstatus der Juden in den Schriften Reuchlins zum Pfefferkornstreit," in *Reuchlin und die Juden*, ed. Arno Herzig and Julius H. Schoeps, Pforzheimer Reuchlinschriften, no. 3 (Sigmaringen: Thorbecke, 1993), 65–88. On Emperor Maximilian's prohibition of Reuchlin's works, see Eisenhardt, "Staatliche und kirchliche Einflussnahmen," 300 (see n. 8 above).

[14]Wilhelm Sturio, [Opinion], 21 February 1609, Marburg Staatsarchiv, Best. 81 BI 81, no. 23, fol. 4r.

[15]Whereas Basel University was well established by this time, the Hanau Hohe Landesschule was a relatively recent development; Gerhard Menk, *Die Hohe Schule Herborn in ihrer Frühzeit (1584–1660): Ein Beitrag zum Hochschulwesen des deutschen Kalvinismus im Zeitalter der Gegenreformation*, Veröffentlichungen der Historischen Kommission für Nassau, no. 30 (Wiesbaden: Historische Kommiss. für Nassau, 1981), 187–91.

[16]Thannhausen had been pawned by the duke of Bavaria to the von Bicken family and was apparently administered by Philipp von Bicken. When the Innsbruck chancery ordered the seizure of the Thannhausen press, the cover letter was addressed to Philipp von Bicken or "in his absense to his administrator." A later *Schutzbrief* for the Jews of Thannhausen and its near vicinity, dated 22 February 1600, bore the names Johann Adam, Jost Philipp, and Hans Hartmann von Bicken, suggesting that all three brothers were in fact responsible for governing the area. Leutkirch, Germany, Fürstlich Waldburg Zeil'sches Gesamtarchiv, Ms. ZAKi 1284, reported by the archivist, Rudolf Beck, letter to the author, 13 March 1991. See also Joseph Hahn, *Krumbach*, Historischer Atlas von Bayern, Teil Schwaben, Heft 12 (Munich: Kommission für Bayerische Landesgeschichte, 1982), 121–23.

Mazia and Simon Levi Günzburg, and two non-Jewish printers, Stefan Schormann and Peter Grässel.[17] They were able to print only two prayer books before the press came to the attention of the Burgau authorities.[18] The Burgau administrator's report to Innsbruck of their activities elicited an unequivocal response from the archducal government: the press was to be closed down, the printers arrested, and every book produced by them seized.[19] The authorities arrested R. Mazia (Simon Levi Gunzburg and the two gentile printers were able to evade capture), and they impounded the press and every available copy of the books produced there.[20] Although the authorities agreed with the Jewish printers that their books had been approved for publication elsewhere, including the imperial capital of Prague, the printers had not sought the permission of the Burgau authorities to print them in Thannhausen and yet planned to export them to other countries, giving the impression that their activities had been approved.[21]

The attitude of the Innsbruck government toward the prosecution of what they clearly considered a clandestine press contrasts markedly with the openness with which the Jewish printers conducted their business. The two books produced in Thannhausen carried on the title page the name of the place of production and even the names of

[17]On R. Isaac Mazia, see Stefan Rohrbacher, "Medinat Schwaben: Jüdisches Leben in einer süddeutschen Landschaft in der Frühneuzeit," in *Judengemeinden in Schwaben Kontext des Alten Reiches*, ed. Rolf Kiessling, Colloquia Augustana, vol. 2 (Berlin: Akademie, 1995), 102–3, and Eric Zimmer's biographical introduction to R. Isaac Mazia, *Sheelot u-teshuvot Yefe Nof*, ed. Avigdor Berger (Jerusalem: Makhon Yerushalaim, 1985) [Hebrew].

[18]Rosenfeld, "The Development of Hebrew Printing," 97 (see n. 6 above).

[19]Innsbruck chancery to the Burgau administrator, 27 June 1594, Augsburg Staatsarchiv, Vorderösterreich Lit. 650, fols. 416v–417v; and ibid., 1 August 1594, fols. 423r–424v. My discussion of the Thannhausen press is based upon several letter collections (*Kopialbücher*) of the Innsbruck government's dealing with affairs in Burgau. Previously kept in the Neuburg a. d. Donau Staatsarchiv collection (and so noted in Sinz, see n. 6 above), it is now preserved in the Augsburg Staatsarchiv.

[20]Innsbruck chancery to the administrator of Burgau, 3 September 1594, Augsburg Staatsarchiv, Vorderösterreich Lit. 650, fols. 431r–v. Rohrbacher argued that the Burgau authorities were only partially successful in their prosecution of the printers because of the complicated semiautonomous legal status of Thannhausen itself. The press corrector was able to evade capture by remaining within *Markt* Thannhausen, where he was not subject to arrest; Stefan Rohrbacher, letter to the author, 29 January 1996, and "Medinat Schwaben," 104 (see n. 17 above).

[21]Innsbruck chancery to Melchior Zangen, 1 September 1594, Augsburg Staatsarchiv, Vorderösterreich Lit. 650, fol. 429r; ibid., to the administrator of Burgau, 1 December 1594, Augsburg Staatsarchiv, fols. 443r–v; cf. Sinz, *Beiträge*, 71 (see n. 6 above).

Stephen G. Burnett

the two Jewish workers who produced them, although admittedly only in Hebrew type.[22] The printers openly planned to export their wares to Poland and to Siebenbürgen, in what is today Romania.[23] While there is no indication that he made provision to censor the books produced there, Philipp von Bicken clearly thought that he was within his rights to allow a Jewish print shop to operate in Thannhausen.[24] The Burgau authorities, however, strictly applied the provisions of the *Polizeiordnung*: The books were impounded and copies were sent for censorship review to Melchior Zangen, provost of Ehingen, and to Johannes Faber, rector of the Jesuit college of Innsbruck.[25] The printing equipment, which had been purchased by Schormann and Grässel from Adam Berg of Munich, was confiscated and later sold by the authorities.[26] R. Mazia remained under arrest from August until October 1594, after which he was released on bail; his case was finally resolved on 4 June 1597, when he was obliged to pay a fine of 200 florins to settle the matter.[27]

If locating in an appropriate town was important for a commercially viable Jewish press, making provision for adequate censorship was absolutely essential. The presses in Basel and Hanau both pro-

[22]I consulted a photograph of the title page for the *Mahzor* prayer book, printed in Hans Bronnenmaier, *Thannhauser Heimatbuch* (Augsburg: n. p., [1960]), 58, and a transcription of the title page for *Zulatot* in David Wallersteiner, "Die jüdische Druckerei in Thannhausen," *Bayerische Israelitische Gemeindezeitung* 12 (1926): 321.

[23]Innsbruck chancery to the administrator of Burgau, 1 August 1594, Augsburg Staatsarchiv, Vorderösterreich Lit. 650, fol. 423 r.

[24]Philipp von Bicken may also have counted on the political influence of his brother Johann Adam to protect him. Seven years later Johann Adam was appointed archbishop of Mainz. See Anton P. Brück, "Johann Adam von Bicken: Erzbischof und Kurfürst von Mainz 1601–1604," *Archiv für Mittelrheinische Kirchengeschichte* 23 (1971): 147–87.

[25]Innsbruck chancery to Melchior Zangen, 1 September 1594, and Innsbruck chancery to Johann Faber, 1 September 1594, Augsburg Staatsarchiv, Vorderösterreich Lit. 650, fols. 429 r–431 r. Faber's task was to send copies of each book to his colleagues in Augsburg, or at the academies of Dillingen or Ingolstadt for further study. Sinz, *Beiträge,* 70 (see note 6 above).

[26]Berg complained three times to the Burgau authorities between 1599 and 1604 that the Thannhausen printers, now out of business, had not finished paying for the presses he sold them for their venture; Augsburg Staatsarchiv, Vorderösterreich Lit. 651, fols. 467 r–v (23 June 1599), and Vorderösterreich Lit. 652, fols. 242 r–v (4 May 1602) and Lit. 652, fols. 462 v–463 r (21 July 1604).

[27]Innsbruck chancery to the provincial governor of Burgau, 30 January 1597, Augsburg Staatsarchiv, Vorderösterreich Lit. 651, fols. 93 r–v and also fols. 146 v–147 r. The records I have found do not indicate whether Philipp von Bicken was punished in any way for allowing the press to operate.

duced tractates of the Talmud, and the elaborate precautions that the authorities and printers took in both places to ensure that they could be sold legally demonstrate how important an issue censorship could be in an era of confessional conflict. On 2 April 1578, Ambrosius Froben of Basel signed an agreement with Simon von Günzburg of Frankfurt, stipulating that Günzburg would pay him to print the Talmud in Basel; Günzburg would be responsible for selling it.[28] Froben knew that he would have to ensure that the work was censored well enough to satisfy both Protestants and Catholics, and he made provision for adequate censorship of the work long before signing the contract. The contract itself stated that Marco Marino, the papal inquisitor of Venice, who was also a competent Hebraist, would serve as censor for the work. Froben had also arranged almost a year earlier for Pierre Chevallier of Geneva to serve as his on-site censor.[29] Froben felt that a Catholic censor was necessary, because twenty-five years earlier, in 1553, the papacy had ordered the destruction of Talmuds throughout Italy.[30] Nine years later the Tridentine Index (1564) specified that if the text of the Talmud were produced "without the title 'Talmud' and without calumnies and insults to the Christian religion," it would be permissible. Under the circumstances, only a learned Catholic censor of high standing within the Church could

---

[28]Heinrich Pallmann, "Ambrosius Froben von Basel als Drucker des Talmud," *Archiv des Deutschen Buchhandels* 7 (1882): 46–47. On Simon von Günzburg, see Alexander Dietz, *Stammbuch der Frankfurter Juden: Geschichtliche Mitteilungen über die Frankfurter jüdischen Familien von 1349–1849* (Frankfurt a.M.: J. St. Goar, 1907), 132–33.

[29]Bonaventura Vulcanius mentioned Chevallier's role in a letter to Jean Baptiste Heintzel, Basel, between 20 June and 14 July 1577, *Correspondance de Bonaventura Vulcanius pendant son séjour à Cologne, Genève et Bale (1573–1577)*, ed. H. De Vries de Heekelingen (La Haye: Martinus Nijhoff, 1923), 263. On 20 January 1578 the Geneva city council ordered Chevallier not to return to Basel, in an attempt to hinder his participation in preparing the Talmud for publication; *Registres de la Compagnie des Pasteurs de Genève*, vol. 4, *1575–1582*, ed. Olivier Labarthe and Bernard Lescaze (Geneva: Librairie Droz, 1974), 104, n. 3. In addition to censoring the Talmud, Chevallier also worked for Froben as a corrector; see the certificate of good conduct issued by Ulrich Schultheiss and the Basel city council for Chevallier, Basel, September 1581, Basel Staatsarchiv, Missiven A 43, fol. 380a.

[30]See Kenneth R. Stow, "The Burning of the Talmud in 1553, in Light of Sixteenth-Century Catholic Attitudes Toward the Talmud," *Bibliothèque d'Humanisme et Renaissance* 34 (1972): 435–59; also idem, *Catholic Thought and Papal Jewry Policy 1555–1593*, Moreshet Series, vol. 5 (New York: Jewish Theological Seminary, 1977), 49–50, 54–59.

Stephen G. Burnett

certify Froben's Talmud text as meeting these standards.[31] A Reformed censor was, however, just as necessary for the city of Basel since the magistrate was responsible for ensuring proper censorship of books.[32] The two censors between them produced a thoroughly butchered Talmud edition, which was not well received by Jewish customers but could be produced legally and sold within the German empire.[33]

After the Herculean efforts of Froben to produce a properly censored Talmud, the Hebrew printers of Hanau had relatively little difficulty in arranging for reprints of some of the Basel tractates between 1617 and 1622.[34] As with all Hebrew books, each tractate had to be vetted beforehand by Walter Keuchen, the rector of the Hohe Landesschule in Hanau. Keuchen submitted a written report on each tractate, with a recommendation to print; but the magistrate reserved for itself the final decision, which was usually scrawled at the bottom of Keuchen's report.[35] As with every book he reviewed, Keuchen looked for statements that were either patently anti-Christian or unambiguously offensive to a Christian magistrate.[36] The only additional precaution that Keuchen took was to review the final form of each gathering to make sure that no unauthorized changes had been introduced by the printers to the text approved by the censor, and thus by the magistrate.[37] Only a book whose text had been approved by the magistrate, through the latter's agent the censor, could bear the

---

[31]"si tamen prodierint sine nomine Thalmud et sine iniuriis et calumniis in religionem christianam tolerabuntur"; cf. Staehelin, "Des Basler Buchdruckers Ambrosius Froben Talmudausgabe," 9 (see n. 6 above). On the fate of the Talmud at the Council of Trent, see Salo Baron, "The Council of Trent and Rabbinic Literature," in *Ancient and Medieval Jewish History: Essays by Salo Wittmayer Baron*, ed. Leon A. Feldman (New Brunswick: Rutgers University Press, 1972), 353–71.

[32]Carl Roth, "Die Bücherzensur im Alten Basel," *Zentralblatt für Bibliothekswesen* 31 (1914): 49–50.

[33]Heller, *Printing the Talmud*, 255–61, 420–21 (see n. 12 above).

[34]BT *Nidda* (1617), *Tehorot* (1621), and *Hulin* (1622) were produced in Hanau; cf. Walter Keuchen's censorship reports: Marburg Staatsarchiv, Best 81 B81 3/4, no. 5, fols. 68 (9 May 1617), 77 (15 June 1620), and 79 (3 May 1622). Ultimately a Hebrew press in Lublin bought the remaining copies of these tractates and incorporated them into a Talmud printing then under way; Heller, *Printing the Talmud*, 357 (see n.12 above).

[35]Burnett, "Hebrew Censorship," 206 (see n. 6 above).

[36]Keuchen and his predecessor H. Heidfeld rejected only two out of forty-three books submitted for censorship; Burnett, "Hebrew Censorship," 207, and n. 59.

[37]Ibid., 207, and n. 58.

legend *Cum licentia superiorum,* printed in Latin characters so that officials of all stripes could read it.[38]

Such expensive, time-consuming censorship was crucially important for printers and magistrates alike since Hebrew books were necessarily an export commodity and therefore had to satisfy imperial as well as local authorities. Despite all of his efforts, Ambrosius Froben ran afoul of imperial authorities in his efforts to sell the Talmud within the German empire. Froben's troubles began when a letter arrived from the imperial chancery in Prague on 29 November 1578, which ordered him to stop producing the Talmud.[39] The letter branded the Talmud as a work that contained both statements attacking the triune God and Christ as well as blasphemous teaching and "Jewish fables."[40] Before responding to the imperial order, the Basel city council requested that both Froben and the theological faculty give their opinion.[41] The theologians addressed the problem of blasphemy by assuring the city council that any blasphemous statements would certainly be removed from the book; it was their duty to remove them. They stressed the potential utility of the Talmud to Christians, citing Peter Galatinus and Reuchlin as examples of earlier scholars who considered the Talmud worth Christian study.[42] They also rather mischievously noted that if all works containing the least

---

[38]Ibid., 206.

[39]The letter, which has not been preserved, was dated 30 October 1578. How the imperial government received notice that Froben was producing the Talmud has not been recorded; perhaps a report was sent by someone attending the Frankfurt book fair during the fall of 1578, since at that time Froben made the first delivery of printed Talmud tractates.

[40]Opinion of Basel theology faculty, n. d. [written between 29 November 1578 and 2 February 1579], quoting from the Prague chancery letter of 30 October 1578. Basel Staatsarchiv, Handel und Gewebe, JJJ 13, fol. 46r.

[41]Basel's diplomatic response to the emperor was given in a measured tone, in part because the empire still considered Basel to be an imperial estate; while the Swiss Confederation had been recognized by the emperors since 1499, Basel had joined only in 1501. On several occasions during the sixteenth and early seventeenth century emperors had tried to press claims against Basel; the city's status was not resolved until 1648 through a provision of the treaty of Westphalia. Peter Stadler, "Das Zeitalter der Gegenreformation," in *Handbuch der Schweizer Geschichte* (Zurich: Berichthaus, 1972), 1:640–42.

[42]On Reuchlin's opinion of the Talmud, see Hans-Martin Kirn, *Das Bild vom Juden im Deutschland des frühen 16. Jahrhunderts dargestellt an den Schriften Johannes Pfefferkorns,* Texts and Studies in Medieval and Early Modern Judaism, vol. 3 (Tübingen: J. C. B. Mohr, 1989), 131–40; on Galatinus' views, see Stow, "Burning of the Talmud," 445, 449–51 (see n. 30 above).

bit of blasphemy were to be banned, the list would include the works of pagan philosophers, poets, and even scientists that were presently used in schools. Galen, for example, had referred slightingly to Christ.[43] Even the writings of Church fathers such as Tertullian and Augustine contained doctrinal errors.[44] Froben's letter contained a discussion of the printing history of the Talmud and its possible usefulness to Christians as a source of historical and medical information.[45] The city council drafted a long letter, dated 2 February 1579, which incorporated arguments drawn from both Froben and the theologians. Emperor Rudolf II, as yet unconvinced, responded with another letter, dated 25 June 1579, demanding that Froben cease printing the Talmud and that he supply a copy of what he had printed to imperial authorities for their judgment. The city council responded on 25 July with a much shorter letter restating that the Basel Talmud was being properly censored and, indeed, that the chief censor was the Catholic inquisitor of Venice.[46] In the end Froben was apparently able to satisfy imperial authorities that he had taken adequate precautions to ensure that his Talmud edition was properly censored.

[43]"[T]he ancient philosophers, poets, and other books written in Greek and Latin which are commonly used at present in Christian schools contain defamatory remarks. These include remarks against Moses in Quintilian and others, against the holy David in Simplicio, against Christ in the renowned Galen, and other [such remarks] are on this account also tolerated. In Christendom so many wonderful, useful things can be learned [from these authors] and the blasphemies are so easily detected" (den alten Phiosophen, poeten und andere buecher in griechischen und lateinischen sprach geschrieben jeden zeit in den Christen schulen gemeinlich gebraucht in welchen doch ettlich schmachen sich heitten funden. Alls wider den Mosen in Quintiliano und anderen. Vider den heiligen Davidt in Simplicio. Vider Christum den hochberumbten Galenum und anderer seind darum geduldet. In den Christenheit das sovil herrlichen nutzlichen dingen daraus erlernet mögen werden. Und die lesterungen sar leicht zumerckhen). Opinion of Basel theology faculty, n. d. [written between 29 November 1578 and 2 February 1579], quoting from the Prague chancery letter of 30 October 1578. Basel Staatsarchiv, Handel und Gewebe, JJJ 13, fol. 48r.

[44]Ibid.

[45]Froben's Opinion for the Basel city council, n.d. [written between 29 November 1578 and 2 February 1579]; Basel Staatsarchiv, Handel und Gewebe JJJ 13, fol. 40v.

[46]Emperor Rudolf II to the Basel Bürgermeister and city council, Prague, 25 June 1579; Basel Staatsarchiv, Handel und Gewebe JJJ 13, fols. 52r–v, in Achilles Nordmann, "Geschichte der Juden in Basel seit dem Ende der zweiten Gemeinde bis zur Einführung der Glaubens- und Gewissensfreiheit, 1397–1875," *Basler Zeitschrift für Geschichte und Altertumskunde* 13 (1914): 166–67; Basel Bürgermeister and city council to Emperor Rudolf II, Basel, 25 July 1579; Basel Staatsarchiv, Handel und Gewebe JJJ 13, fols. 23r–24v, in Nordmann, "Geschichte," 167–68.

If Froben's argument with the imperial government, carried out through the good offices of the Basel magistrate, was not unnerving enough for him, shortly afterwards he encountered another arm of the imperial system of press oversight: the newly energized Imperial Book Commission at Frankfurt. Between 10 and 16 September 1579, Froben, along with other booksellers, was interviewed by Dr. Johann Vest of the commission. Dr. Vest reported Froben's statement that Basel was in communication with the imperial court in Prague, but that he had not yet received a response.[47] With inspectors actively monitoring booksellers' wares at Frankfurt, imperial authorities were conceivably in a position to suppress books like the Basel Talmud. While I have not found any record of a Hebrew book that was in fact suppressed by imperial fiat, this does not mean that it did not or could not happen, particularly given the climate of religious conflict that existed in Germany between the Peace of Augsburg and the Thirty Years' War.

Apart from strictly legal concerns, there were other political and religious factors that affected the regulation of Hebrew printing during this period. By allowing Jewish printing, a Christian magistrate courted danger in three ways, as the Hanau and Basel authorities discovered. Some theologians questioned the propriety of a Christian state's support of the practice of Judaism by allowing Jewish printing. Others feared that confessional opponents would be able to use the policy as ammunition in a polemical campaign of defamation. Toleration of Jewish printing might also disturb confessional allies and result in a form of religious or political ostracism. If Wilhelm Sturio was sanguine about the legality of Jewish printing in the German empire when he wrote his legal opinion on 21 February 1609, he may have had second thoughts after attending what must have been a raucous meeting of the Hanau princely council the next day. Three of the four councillors were utterly opposed to Jewish printing in Hanau. Pastor Heinrich Heidfeld argued that, for theological reasons, a Christian state should not be involved with Jewish printing since printing should be used above all for God's glory. The Jewish printers sought to make money and to propagate their blasphemies, perpetu-

---

[47]Vest's report was printed by Brückner, "Die Gegenreformation," 71 (see no. 10 above).

ating their blindness and stubbornness to the truth of the gospel.[48] councillor Pötter suggested that even properly censored Jewish books consisted of "their superstitions, deliria, fables, false comments, and blasphemies."[49] In the earlier dispute over the Basel Talmud, Jean Heinzelius, a Genevan pastor, stated that he did not see how it was possible for any Talmud edition, however thoroughly censored, to contain anything but blasphemies, frightful things, and monstrosities.[50] One of Froben's own employees, Bonaventura Vulcanius, compared the censoring of the Talmud of all blasphemies to "cleansing the Augean stable of pigs,"[51] implying that a Herculean task of cleansing yet remained to be done. Clearly within Reformed as well as Lutheran and Catholic circles, theologians had deep misgivings even about censored Jewish books. Such books served only to confirm the Jews in their pernicious unbelief.[52]

---

[48]"[T]he Jews seek through use of the press only their own corruption, financial gain and blasphemy, and will also be encouraged in their blindness and stiff-necked obstinance" (die Truckerejen furnemlich zu gottes Ehren verordnet welcher die Juden nicht, sondern nur alhie ihren Corruptelos, finanz, und lästerey hierdurch suchen, werden auch dadurch in ihrer verblendung und halsstarrigkeit je mehr und mehr gesteiffet); *Extract Protocols vom 22. Febr. Ao 609*, Marburg Staatsarchiv, Best 81 BI 81, no. 23, fol. 6v. Heidfeld expressed much the same sentiment in his first and only Hebrew censorship report. Marburg Staatsarchiv, Best. 81 B81 3/4 no. 5, fol. 18 (23 May 1609). Heidfeld was pastor of the German reformed church in Hanau. See Heinrich Bott, *Gründung und Anfänge der Neustadt Hanau 1596–1620*, Veröffentlichungen der Historischen Kommission für Hessen und Waldeck, no. 30 (Marburg: N. G. Elwert, 1970–71), 2:481.

[49]"Auch gedancken gebehren, alss ob man hiedruch ihre superstitiones, deliria, fabulas, falsa commenta, et blasphemias in Christem ... helttenn." *Extract*, Marburg Staatsarchiv, Best 81 BI 81, no. 23, fol. 5v. The speaker was probably Peter Pötter, director of the Hanau princely chancery. Bott, *Hanau*, 2: 504.

[50]"Satis mirari nequeo academiam vestram Talmudi permittere editionem cum nihil aliud quam diras et immanes contineat blasphemias." Quoted by Vulcanius in a letter to Rudolf Gualther, Basel, 14 July 1577, in *Correspondance de Bonaventura Vulcanius*, 266 (see no. 29 above).

[51]"Sed ne haec quidem ratio mihi satisfacit, nihilo profecto magis quam si quis dicat, Augiae stabulum a porcis repurgatum esse." Vulcanius to Jean Baptiste Heintzel, Basel, between 20 June and 14 July 1577, in *Correspondance de Bonaventura Vulcanius*, 263.

[52]There were both Catholic and Lutheran theologians who argued that Jews should be allowed to use only the Bible; see Stow, "Burning the Talmud," 443 (see no. 30 above); Martin Friedrich, *Zwischen Abwehr und Bekehrung: Die Stellung der deutschen evangelischen Theologie zum Judentum im 17. Jahrhundert*, Beiträge zur Historischen Theologie, no. 72 (Tübingen: Mohr, 1988), 20–21. Luther himself was outspokenly in favor of confiscating Jewish books; see *Von den Juden und ihren Lügen*, in *D. Martin Luthers Werke: Kritische Ausgabe, Abteilung Schriften* (Weimar: Böhlau, 1883–1983), 53:536, lines 29–33.

By allowing Jewish printing, Hanau also might have to pay a political and religious price. As mentioned, councillor Pötter asserted that Hanau's reputation could be damaged badly by printing Jewish books.[53] Lutheran polemicists such as Aegidius Hunnius routinely condemned Calvinists as "judaizers." Dr. Philip Bott warned his colleagues that to take the Jew's part by permitting Jewish printing was to provoke a wave of calumnies from Hanau's confessional enemies.[54]

Bott's fears that Jewish printing in Hanau might provoke interconfessional polemics were not unrealistic. In addition to freelance Lutheran and Catholic polemicists, there was also papal policy to consider. Papal diplomats after 1553 had been active in trying to discourage printing of the Talmud in Italy and Poland.[55] Papal legate Feliciano Ninguarda attempted to pressure Basel into withdrawing their permission for Froben to print the Talmud. Working behind the scenes, Ninguarda and the representatives of Catholic cantons orchestrated a diplomatic showdown with Basel at the annual meeting of the Swiss Confederation in July of 1579.[56] Lucerne and Fribourg agreed to demand that Basel suppress the publication of the Talmud without mentioning the nuncio or the pope as the inspiration for their complaint.[57] To allow Jewish printing, especially of the Talmud, was to take a political risk.

[53]See n. 49 above.
[54]"If we give the Jews permission to open a press, the Ubiquitarians [i.e., Lutherans], Jesuits and others will say now we see what we are dealing with, and what Hunnius wrote in *Calvin Judaizer* (Marburg, 1589, etc.) was true, indeed [our decision] will provoke criticism, disputations, and hatred from every side"(Solte man nun den Juden itzo die Truckereÿ zulassen, worden die Ubiquitarÿ, Jesuiter und anderer sagen, Itzo sege man wo mit man umbginge, und das es doch whar wehre was Hunnius de *Calvino-Judaizans* geschrieben, ja es werd allerhand disput. calumnien und veracht hierdurch erregt werd); ibid., fol. 7r. Dr. Philipp Bott was princely court secretary and a councillor of Hanau. Bott, *Hanau*, 2:445 (see n. 48 above).
[55]Caligari to the Cardinal of Como [Ptolomeo Galli of Como], Krakow, 21 December 1578, in *Monumenta Poloniae Vaticana*, vol. 4, *I. A. Caligarii Nuntii Apost. in Polonia Epistolas et Acta, 1578–1581*, Editionum Collegii Historici Academiae Litterarum Cracoviensis, no. 74 (Krakow: Academiae Litterarum Cracoviensis, 1915), 95–98 (document 62).
[56]Staehelin, "Des Basler Buchdruckers Ambrosius Frobens Talmudausgabe," 15–17 (see n. 6 above). See *Die Nuntiatur Giovanni Francesco Bonhomini, 1579–1581*, ed. Franz Steffens and Heinrich Reinhardt, Nuntiaturberichte aus der Schweiz seit dem Concil von Trient nebst ergänzenden Aktenstücken (Solothurn: Druck und Commissionsverlag der Union, 1906), I: 347–48 (6 June 1579), 369 (29 June 1579), 376 (3 [?] July 1579), 392–93 (15 July 1579); documents 308, 309, 329, 332, 345.
[57]*Die Nuntiatur*, 1:348, 369

None of the Hanau councillors mentioned that allowing Jewish printing might serve to alienate confessional allies, but the city of Basel experienced a measure of this alienation when it permitted Froben to print the Talmud there. News of the Basel city council's decision caused a great stir among theologians in both Zurich and Geneva. Beginning in mid-1577 Vulcanius sent letters to Rudolf Gualther and Ludwig Lavater in Zurich and to members of the Company of Pastors in Geneva decrying Froben's plans. Since the church leaders of Zurich and Geneva were no longer on speaking terms with Simon Sulzer, the Antistes of the Basel church, they directed their letters of protest to Johann Jacob Grynaeus, a young member of the theology faculty, who, although he was Reformed in his theology, had also approved the printing of the Talmud.[58] Theodore Beza in particular opposed Froben's Talmud printing and led an effort to prevent Froben's censor, Chevallier, from leaving Geneva at all.[59] Whether the decision to print the Talmud could have worsened Basel's already dismal ecclesiastical relations with other Swiss evangelical churches is open to question, but it was a matter of concern, at least among other Swiss Protestant leaders.

In a deeply theological age, particularly at a time when religion served as an important pillar of state and society and when theological quarrels could serve as a pretext for political brinksmanship between confessional alliances, the concerns of theologians about the religious and political dangers of Jewish printing could not simply be brushed off.[60] The civic authorities of Basel and Hanau were obliged

[58]See Ludwig Lavater to Johann Jacob Grynaeus, Zurich, 24 June 1577, Basel Universitätsbibliothek Ms G2 II, 2, fols. 68–69, Rudolf Gualther to Johann Jacob Grynaeus, Zurich, 1 August 1577, Basel Universitätsbibliothek Ms G II 5, pp. 656–57, and Vulcanius to Gualther, Basel, 14 July 1577, in *Correspondance de Bonaventura Vulcanius*, 266 (see n. 29 above). On the sources of Basel's confessional isolation, see Amy Nelson Burnett, "Simon Sulzer and the Consequences of the 1563 Strasbourg Consensus in Switzerland," *Archiv für Reformationsgeschichte* 83 (1992): 154–79.

[59]Theodore Beza to Johann Jacob Grynaeus, 12 October 1579 and also 13 October 1579, Basel Universitätsbibliothek MS Ki Ar 18b, fols. 62–63, and Grynaeus to Beza, Basel, 24 October [1579]; Gotha: Forschungsbibliothek Ms. A 405, fol. 424. See also [Immanuel Tremellius] to Beza, n. p. [before 6 October 1579]; Geneva: Musée historique de la Réformation, Ms. Tronchin 5, fols. 34–35, and Jean Hortin to Beza, Bern, 3 November 1579; Geneva: Musée historique de la Réformation, Ms. Tronchin 5, fols. 51–52. On Beza's efforts directed against Chevallier, see *Registres*, 4:104 and n. 3 (see n. 29 above).

[60]Heinz Schilling, "Confessionalization in the Empire: Religious and Societal Change in Germany between 1555 and 1620," in his *Religion, Political Culture and the*

to formulate appropriate policies in order to convince detractors, both from among their confessional allies and their confessional opponents that their Hebrew presses published no Jewish blasphemies. Three approaches to the problem are evident in the Hanau and Basel records. The first precaution involved limiting the types of books that could be produced. The Hanau authorities believed that any Jewish book that had been published elsewhere could safely be reprinted. The press license granted by the count stipulated that only works printed elsewhere might be produced at Hanau.[61] Another policy that was used to fend off possible criticism involved careful evaluation of Hebrew books in light of Christian dogma. When Walter Keuchen, the Hanau censor, sought to evaluate books for blasphemous or seditious passages, he focused upon exactly what was written instead of interpreting it within the conceptual framework of Judaism. For example, in reviewing a prayer book in 1610, Keuchen noted that most of the prayers were derived from the Psalms or other parts of the Hebrew Bible. When the prayers mentioned the gentiles it was to ask God to be gracious to them. Even prayers for deliverance from the yoke of captivity and restoration to the land of their fathers were derived from the prophets. Presumably, Keuchen and his superiors understood that when German Jews prayed these prayers they had their Christian overlords in mind; but so long as the Jews did not explicitly say so the censors were satisfied.[62]

Emergence of Early Modern Society: Essays in German and Dutch History, trans. Stephen G. Burnett, Studies in Medieval and Early Modern Thought, 50 (Leiden: Brill, 1992), 205–45, esp. 235–40.

[61]According to the privilege, the Hebrew printers were to produce "the books of Moses, Kings, and the Prophets and other parts of the Old Testament, as well as other Hebrew books previously approved and printed elsewhere" (die bucher Mosis, der Königen und Propheten und andere dess alten Testaments, auch sonsten püchern anderswo gedruckte und erlaubte hebraische bucher). Printing privilege for Jacob Bassler, Seligmann Jud and their Frankfurt financial supporters, granted by Count Philipp Ludwig, Hanau, 1 May 1609, Marburg Staatsarchiv, Best. 81 BI, no. 23, fol. 20r. Ultimately this restriction was relaxed, and at least ten original works (out of forty-two books known either to have been submitted for pre-publication censorship or printed) were produced in Hanau. Cf. Burnett, "Hebrew Censorship," 205–7, 219, n. 63 (see n. 6. above).

[62]Marburg Staatsarchiv, Best. 81 B81 3/4 no. 5, fol. 22 (21 November 1610), quoted in Burnett, "Hebrew Censorship," 207–8, 219–20, n. 64. Reuchlin, when considering this problem, noted that God alone knew the hearts of those who prayed prayers such as the *Birkat ha-Minim*; William Horbury, "The Benediction of the Minim and Early Jewish-Christian Controversy," *Journal of Theological Studies* 33 (1982): 21.

The most unusual defense of Jewish printing, however, came not from Hanau, but from Basel. Whereas both Ambrosius Froben and the Basel theologians mentioned that Christian scholars might find part of the Talmud "useful" for their work, it was Froben, in his response to the first letter from the imperial chancery, who presented the most complete case for it. Once all of the blasphemies were removed from the Talmud, what was left? To be sure, the remaining text contained Jewish "fables," but nothing that would offend Christians. It also contained information on Jewish customs, political thought, civil law, and even medicine.[63] What the theologians had stated implicitly when referring to the blasphemies present in classical works, Froben stated explicitly: The Talmud was a potentially valuable source of information for Christians to study and exploit. Its claims to religious truth were irrelevant to its academic value, just as the writings of pagan Greek and Latin writers could be studied without accepting their views on religion. Although this argument clearly did not convince many other Reformed Swiss, it was accepted by the leaders of the Basel church, making it possible for them to justify Jewish printing as a possible benefit to Christians as well as Jews.[64]

At the very heart of German imperial press regulation during the early modern period was the question of censorship. The most important legal issue to be resolved before a Jewish press could be licensed or a single Jewish book printed was the nature of "Jewish blasphemy."[65] In the end, two important developments made it possible for confessionally divided Germany to tolerate not only the Jewish book trade but also Jewish printing. One was the existence of a substantial number of Jewish books, mainly produced in Italy and

[63]Ambrosius Froben to the Basel city council, n. d. [written between 29 November 1578 and 2 February 1579], Basel Staatsarchiv, Handel und Gewebe JJJ 13, fol. 40v.

[64]Sebastian Beck and Johannes Buxtorf stressed the potential usefulness of a rabbinical Bible edition for Christians when they appealed to the Basel city council for permission to print one there. See *Bericht über das Biblisch Truck, so man jetzt und zu trucken begehret*, 5 September 1617, Basel Staatsarchiv, Handel und Gewebe JJJ 1.

[65]Blasphemy was considered an offense against God by the individual blasphemer and was also dangerous to society as a whole. If the authorities did not act to punish blasphemy, the *Königliche Satzung von den Goteslästerern* (1495) states, they could expect "famine, earthquakes, pestilence," and other catastrophes. The idea that the earth itself would rise up against a society that tolerated blasphemy dates back to the *Corpus iuris civilis*, novelle 77, and ultimately derives from biblical law (e.g., Deut. 28:15–46, etc.). See J. Segall, "Geschichte und Strafrechte: Strafbare Handlungen gegen unkörperliche Rechtgüter, par. 19: Verbrechen wider die Glaubenslehre," *Strafrechtliche Abhandlungen* [Breslau] 183 (1914): 144–45.

Poland, which had presumably been properly censored. These books, together with the censorial guidelines that had been hammered out, mainly by Italian Catholic authorities, made it feasible for German states to tolerate reprints of them.[66] Basel and Hanau ran somewhat less of a risk of printing material that was potentially offensive to confessional opponents since both Protestant and Catholic states had agreed upon a definition of Jewish blasphemy.

The other factor was the growth and spread of Hebrew learning among adherents of all three major Christian confessions in Germany. I have alluded to five censors, none of whom were Jewish converts to Christianity; two were Catholic, three Reformed.[67] By the time that the Thannhausen press was shut down in 1594, the archducal government could pass on copies of books printed there to theological experts and confidently expect timely reports as to their content. The magistrate of Hanau received a long series of reports from Walter Keuchen between 1610 and 1622, some of which are excellent pieces of analysis. Keuchen's superiors and the Catholic authorities in Innsbruck were both confident that their subordinates had the linguistic and conceptual knowledge to read these Jewish books and to judge whether or not they contained blasphemy or sedition. In the end, the imperial system of press oversight of Jewish printing rested entirely upon the abilities of individual Hebrew censors. Ordinary imperial officials, border guards, merchants, lawyers, and others could not tell a licit Hebrew book from an illegal one; all they could read were the words *Cum licentia superiorum* and whatever other parts of the title page were printed in Latin.

How do these developments in the regulation of Jewish printing reflect the social and religious boundaries that divided Christian from Jew in early modern Germany? While many princes and town magis-

---

[66]Some of the best evidence for what Catholic censors sought to suppress may be found in expurgation lists used by authorities to "correct" books already in the hands of private owners; see Gustave Sacerdote, "Deux Index Expurgatoires de Livres Hébreux," *Revue des études juives* 30 (1895): 257–83, and Isaiah Sonne, *Expurgation of Jewish Books, the Work of Jewish Scholars: A Contribution to the History of Censorship of Hebrew Books in Italy during the Sixteenth Century* (New York: New York Public Library, 1943). The publication of many "Jewish ethnographies" also played a role in publicizing unacceptable prayers; see Burnett, "Hebrew Censorship in Hanau," 204 (see n. 6 above).

[67]Thannhausen: Melchior Zangen; Basel: Pierre Chevallier, Marco Marino; Hanau: Walter Keuchen and Heinrich Heidfeld. Sturio mentioned Buxtorf as a possible censor in his opinion, 21 February 1609, Marburg Staatsarchiv, Best. 81 BI 81, no. 23, fol. 3v.

trates continued to have grave misgivings about Jewish residence, Judaism, and Jewish printing, some rulers, theologians, and scholars had come to believe that the practice of Judaism, as reflected in the Jewish books produced in Basel and Hanau, was not harmful to Christian society, only to the Jews themselves. The authorities could be confident that the Jews were not indulging in blasphemy or sedition, because they could call upon Christian Hebraists to verify that this was the case. There was a place for Jewish religious and intellectual expression within Germany, but such expression could take place only in the languages of the Jews, Hebrew and Yiddish. Jews did have a more secure place within German law and society than they had had since the mid-fifteenth century, but they remained a closely regulated, foreign presence. Because German Jews rejected the state religion of the lands where they lived and wrote books in languages that only they and learned Christians could read, they would always remain outsiders in their native land.

ACKNOWLEDGMENTS

Research for this article was supported in part by a Research Grant from the American Philosophical Society (1995). I am grateful to Dr. Uta Löwenstein of the Hessisches Staatsarchiv–Marburg, Dr. P. R. Máthé of the Aarau Staatsarchiv, Dr. Reinhard Bodenmann of the Musée Historique de la Réformation in Geneva, and Dr. Reinhard H. Seitz, Director of the Augsburg Staatsarchiv for their efforts in searching out the previously unknown manuscript sources that appear in this paper. Dr. Stefan Rohrbacher read a draft of this article and made a number of helpful suggestions concerning Thannhausen.

The Executioner's Healing Touch

Health and Honor in Early Modern German Medical Practice

Kathy Stuart

Executioners carried on an active medical practice in early modern Germany, deriving medical raw materials from the bodies of executed criminals, a practice undisputed in learned and popular medicine. Executioners were labeled as dishonorable; their dishonor was so contagious that even the most casual social contact with an executioner could taint an honorable citizen's honor. However, within the medical context, the executioner's dishonor was latent and posed no threat to his patients. Executioners attracted patients from all social strata, commoners and aristocrats alike. Executioners' popular appeal as healers derived from the religious setting of the ritual of public execution: The condemned criminal was transformed into the repentant "poor sinner" and launched into eternity cleansed of sin. The criminal's body acquired a sacral healing power, much like a saint's relics, in the course of the execution. The executioner was able to manipulate this power as he processed the criminal's body in his medical practice.

"IT IS ONE THING TO LET YOURSELF BE CURED BY THE HANGMAN, it is another thing entirely to be tortured under his hand."[1] Thus a journeyman embroiderer commented on a virulent conflict over honor that had erupted in his guild in the free imperial city of Augsburg in 1668. A fellow journeyman, Augustin Gerstecker, had been arrested for witchcraft and tortured by the executioner, only to be found innocent and released. The authorities declared that he had purged himself of suspicion through torture. Nonetheless, the embroiderers

---

[1]"Vom Henker sich curieren lassen, und unter seiner Hand bei der scharfen Frag sein, ist ein anders." (All translations by the author.) Stadtarchiv Augsburg (StadtAA), Handwerkerakten (HWA), Bortenmacher 4, 1664–1672, report from 29 Nov. 1668.

excluded him from their guild: while he might have been innocent of the crime, the executioner's touch had left a permanent taint on his honor. The embroiderers explained, "If you get a stain on your clothing, you can wash it out. Nonetheless, you cannot say that the stain was never there."[2]

This case is typical of ritual pollution conflicts involving *Unehrlichkeit* (dishonor), which frequently convulsed early modern German guilds. Executioners were the central figures in a complex of trades labeled as *unehrlich* (dishonorable) in early modern Germany. Dishonor was a hereditary social and legal distinction, and in the case of the executioner, dishonor could be highly contagious. Eating, drinking, riding in a carriage with an executioner, or accompanying his corpse to the grave—these were all potentially polluting actions that might leave a taint on a guildsman's honor, putting his social and economic existence in jeopardy. To come under the executioner's hands during an honor punishment or during judicial torture left a mark of infamy on one's reputation.[3]

"To let yourself be cured by the hangman," however, did not pose a threat to an artisan's honor. Early modern German executioners carried on an active medical practice and were regularly consulted by honorable guildsmen and by members of all other social estates. Executioner medicine presents us with a number of incongruities. First, we are surprised to learn that the executioner's symbolic role as one who was licensed to kill was offset by his role as a healer. The very man whose official function was to kill and maim spent much of his time "off duty" practicing medicine. Second, the phenomenon of executioner medicine demonstrates the complexity and fluidity of the social boundary separating honorable estates from "dishonorable people" and the fundamental ambivalence of artisans as they negotiated this boundary. Executioners were not polluting all the time. It

---

[2]"Wann einer ein Flecken in ein Kleid bekomme, so kenne zwar der Flecken wider ausgewaschen werden, gleichwol aber kenne nicht gesagt werden, daß kein Flecken darin gewesen." Ibid.

[3]On *unehrliche Leute* (dishonorable people), see Kathy Stuart, "The Boundaries of Honor: 'Dishonorable People' in Augsburg, 1500–1800" (Ph.D. diss., Yale University, 1993), and idem, "Unehrlichkeitskonflikte in Augsburg in der frühen Neuzeit," *Zeitschrift des historischen Vereins für Schwaben* 83 (1990): 113–29. See also Karl-Sigismund Kramer, "Ehrliche/Unehrliche Gewerbe," in *Handwörterbuch zur deutschen Rechtsgeschichte*, ed. Adalbert Erler and Ekkehardt Kaufmann, vol. 1 (Berlin: Erich Schmidt Verlag, 1971), 855–58.

was completely unproblematic to consult them in medical matters. A patient could leave the executioner's home after close personal and often physical contact with the executioner with his or her honor intact. The executioner's healing touch left no mark on his patients' honor.

Depending on the context, then, the executioner's touch could be a source either of death, mutilation, and infamy or of healing and health. Artisans—and executioners' patients of much higher estate— never explained according to what criteria they distinguished between, on the one hand, social contexts in which contact with the executioner could be polluting and, on the other, unpolluting medical contacts. Nor did they explain why they considered the executioner to be so gifted in medical matters in the first place. What is so incongruous or paradoxical to the modern observer seems to have corresponded for early modern Germans to a particular logic, a particular way of making associations; for them the executioner's healing power and its unproblematic nature was self-evident. Since it is not self-evident to us, we will attempt to unravel such symbolic associations by asking the following questions: What exactly were the interconnections between executioners' functions in criminal justice and their medical practice? Why did early modern Germans consider executioners to be gifted healers? And what happened to executioners' dishonor in the context of their medical practice?

To answer these questions we will approach the phenomenon of executioner medicine from a number of perspectives. We will begin by reconstructing executioner medical practice in the greatest possible detail: What ailments did executioners treat, and how? Who were their patients, and how did executioners and their patients interact? What kind of social relationships did they establish? How does the interaction of executioners with their patients compare with other early modern patient-healer relationships? Next, we will consider how executioners chose to style themselves in their competition with authorized "professional" medical practitioners, the medical doctors and barber-surgeons. Both executioners and official practitioners developed particular rhetorical strategies as they maneuvered for position in the medical marketplace.

This paper will demonstrate that executioners were very successful in such medical competition. Executioners drew patients from all social classes, and their medical talents allowed them to come in contact with people of the highest social estate. We find executioners—defined in contemporary legal literature as "repulsive" and "contemptible"[4]—practicing medicine in the homes of patricians, aristocrats, and territorial lords. In these contexts, executioners' infamy was latent or in some sense became inverted into its opposite: executioners as healers were accorded a particular social recognition, prestige, and fame.

We will find that there were some obvious connections between executioner medicine and executioners' functions in criminal justice, which are clearly expressed in the sources, and some more deep-seated, underlying assumptions that led early modern Germans to associate executions and medicine. There was a disjunction, a clash, between executioners' self-presentation as sober, rational, qualified, hardworking medical professionals and the symbolic, in some sense magical associations that ultimately explained their popular appeal as healers. Contemporaries did not articulate these associations explicitly, but we can discern them by placing executioner medicine in the context of the execution ritual itself. I will suggest that the fundamentally Christian idiom of the early modern execution ritual presents the key to unlocking the symbolic logic of executioner medicine and to resolving the apparent paradox of the executioner's dual role as healer and killer.

This essay is based on two groups of sources. First, there are sources from Augsburg that allow me to reconstruct executioner medical practice in one city from the sixteenth through the eighteenth centuries: the records of the barber-surgeons' guild and of the Collegium Medicum, the corporate organization of medical doctors.[5] These records contain lengthy petitions by the executioners themselves, in which they exchanged recriminations with official medical practitioners. The second group of sources allows me to place the detailed picture of executioner medicine in Augsburg in an imperial context. These are the collection of imperial "legitimations" located in the imperial archive in Vienna.[6] This collection contains several

---

[4]See, e.g., Paul Döpler, *Theatrum Poenarum, Supplicorum, et Executionum Criminalium, der Schauplatz der Leib und Lebensstrafen* (Sonderhausen, 1697), 537, 559, 566. Döpler calls them "abscheulich," "garstig," and "verächtlich."

[5]StadtAA, Collegium Medicum (CM), and HWA, Bader und Barbiere.

[6]Haus-, Hof- und Staatsarchiv (HHStA), Vienna, Restitutiones natalium ac legitimationes.

petitions by executioners asking the emperor to cleanse them of their hereditary infamy and to grant them imperial privileges that would allow them free practice of medicine. These petitions are from all over the empire: Basel, Cologne, Danzig, Nuremberg, Silesia, and Hessia, among other places.

EXECUTIONER MEDICINE

Sources on the medical practice of executioners are abundant for the early modern period. Executioners acting as healers were common throughout the empire. In 1443 the executioner of Frankfurt set up a stand within the city to sell medicines. In 1471 the magistrate of Hildesheim in northern Germany instructed the executioner to treat pregnant women. In 1560 the Schaffhausen city government paid the executioner to treat several citizens who were suffering from venereal disease. In 1618 the Hamburg city government ordered its executioner to treat two mentally ill girls in the city orphanage. In some instances, the executioner's medical skills—with animals and humans—were even considered a professional requirement. In 1590 Frankfurt chose one candidate for the executioner's post over others because he presented certificates proving "he was a good horse doctor." In 1648 the city of Eger hired an executioner under the condition that he could heal broken legs. Examples of the executioner's medical practice continue through the eighteenth century.[7]

---

[7]On Hildesheim, see Wolfgang Oppelt, *Über die Unehrlichkeit des Scharfrichters: Unter bevorzugter Verwendung von Ansbacher Quellen* (Langfeld: Gottschalk, 1976), 377. On Schaffhausen, see Hans von Hentig, "Zur Genealogie des Scharfrichters," *Schweizerische Zeitschrift für Strafrecht* 80 (1964): 198–99. On Hamburg, see Otto Beneke, *Von Unehrlichen Leuten: Cultur-Historische Studien und Geschichten* (Hamburg: Perthes, Besser & Mauke, 1863), 149. On medical skills as a professional prerequisite, see Albrecht Keller, *Der Scharfrichter in der deutschen Kulturgeschichte* (1921; reprint, Hildesheim: G. Olms, 1968), 225. On executioner medicine in Prussia, see Christian Otto Mylius, ed., *Corpus Constitutionum Marchicarum, oder Königlich Preussische und Churfürstlich Brandenburgische ... Ordnungen ...*, vol. 5 (Berlin: Buchladen des Waysenhauses, 1740), 278; and Franz Heinemann, "Der Henker als Volks- und Viehärzte seit Ausgang des Mittelalters," *Schweizerisches Archiv für Volkskunde* 4 (1900): 14. On the executioner medical practice in general, see also Johann Glenzdorf and Fritz Treichel, *Henker, Schinder und Arme Sünder* (Bad Münder: W. Rost, 1970), 104–12, with many further examples.

The earliest source for executioner medical practice in Augsburg is a petition from 1533 by the executioner Caspar Behem.[8] He recently had been hired as executioner and had several patients under his care when, prompted by his conscience, he decided to resign his post and henceforth earn his living "piously and honorably" as a medical practitioner. But Behem soon fell on hard times. He saw his "small fortune" diminish and found that he could not make a living on medicine alone. There were many doctors available, he wrote, and "perhaps because the rich do not want to entrust themselves to me" he was consulted only by the poor who could not afford to pay him. He begged the council to give him back his post as executioner. He promised that as executioner he would make "the art of his medicine" available to poor citizens free of charge. But we find no further record of an executioner Behem in Augsburg. The council apparently turned him down, most likely because after his resignation they no longer considered him reliable—not because they disapproved of his medical practice. Behem's offer to treat the poor for free obviously was intended to strengthen his application.

A few years later, in 1540, Wolf Forssdorffer, an executioner from Pfaffenhofen in Bavaria, was whipped, exposed on the pillory, and banished from the city for life. He had posed as a medical doctor and sold medicines in Augsburg. He had also practiced white magic, retrieved lost objects, and told fortunes.[9] Forssdorffer was punished for his magic and the adoption of a false identity, not for his medical practice as such. Forssdorffer's case is atypical in two ways. First, executioners normally did not conceal their identity. Instead they regarded medical practice as a legitimate right of their profession, even advertising the fact that they were executioners in order to draw more patients. Second, as will become clear, executioners usually did not mix medicine and magic. The council, in any case, was ill-disposed towards such transient foreign executioners and magicians, as they were towards all vagrants. In that same year the executioner from the neighboring city of Landsberg was expelled for hawking his

---

[8]The petition is not dated but it is most likely from 1533, since it mentions the firing of an executioner, "Master Peter," in that year. The handwriting appears to be from the early sixteenth century. If there is an error, the petition should be dated earlier rather than later, when all executioners can be identified. StadtAA, Reichsstadtakten, Stadtbed. 1081/46.

[9]StadtAA, Strafamt, Urgicht Wolf Forssdorffer, 1540, VII:6.

medicines in Augsburg.[10] The city government did not object, however, to the medical practice of their own executioner, Veit Stolz. A decree from 1545 allowed Stolz to treat broken bones, though it forbade him to give other types of medical treatments.[11]

Not only the executioner himself, but his entire family shared in his power to heal. In 1567 the municipal midwives complained that the executioner's sister-in-law was treating pregnant women in the suburbs: "She delivers the women ... of their children and carries them to be baptized," as if she were a licensed midwife.[12] In 1573 the barber-surgeons accused "the executioner together with his wife and children" of quackery.[13] In 1611 a woman with a broken hand sought out the executioner's wife for treatment.[14] In 1686 the barber-surgeons complained to the council about the medical practice of Anna Catherina Hartmann, the wife of the executioner Matheus Hartmann.[15] Obviously, it was not at all unusual for the women in executioner households to participate in the executioner's practice.

Why did executioners and their families have such an affinity for medicine? The connection between executioners' medical practice and their criminal functions was quite clear to contemporaries: executioners drew much of their medical expertise directly from their performance of criminal punishments. The executioner's craft required a certain knowledge of human anatomy. Executioners had to judge the physical condition of prisoners when deciding which torture to apply, and they had to nurse them back to health after the interrogation. Thus, for example, in 1694 the executioner Johann Adam Hartmann was ordered to examine the physical constitution of a seventy-nine-year-old female suspect and report "what type of torture she could still endure."[16] Investigations into witchcraft called for particularly detailed inspections. It was regular procedure to shave the

---

[10]StadtAA, GRP 5, 1539–1540, fol. 226r, for 15 June, 1540.

[11]StadtAA, RP 19, 1545, part II, fol. 48v for 10 Nov. 1545.

[12]StadtAA, CM, Hebammen/Obfrauen, 1548–1813, for 14 Oct. 1567.

[13]StadtAA, CM, Pfuscher, 1562–1793, petition from 5 Dec. 1573.

[14]StadtAA, HWA, Bader und Barbiere 3, 1601–1633, petition from 17 Dec. 1611.

[15]The barber-surgeons complained of "allerhand Stimpler ... als Totengräber, Henkerin und Schergen." StadtAA, HWA, Bader und Barbiere 8, 1679–1688, petition from 18 May 1686.

[16]StadtAA, Geheime Ratsprotokoll (GRP) 23, 1693–1696, fols. 459v–460r, for 15 June 1694.

suspect's entire body to search for the devil's mark.[17] The executioner's wife might perform this examination on female suspects, as in 1686, when the executioner Johann Adam Hartmann was ordered to appear in prison with his wife, who was to examine a suspected witch. Their charge was to find the witch's mark "particularly in secret parts."[18] There are, however, no sources to indicate that this was the general procedure for examining female delinquents. Quite likely, female prisoners usually endured the indignity of an examination by the executioner himself.

The executioner's tasks in criminal justice provided him with greater opportunity to study the human body than university-trained doctors. Before the mid-seventeenth century autopsies performed by medical doctors on human bodies were exceptional events. A chronicle reports such an autopsy by a medical doctor in Augsburg in 1643 as an unusual occurrence.[19] For reasons that are not quite clear, the regular practice of human dissections or autopsies by medical doctors or barber-surgeons began much later, remained much less frequent, and seems to have incurred greater cultural resistance in German-speaking lands than in Italy, for example. Whereas dissections and autopsies became common in Italy in the course of the fourteenth century, anatomical dissection for teaching purposes was not introduced at the University of Cologne, for instance, before 1658. The government had to force barber-surgeons and midwives to attend by threatening them with fines.[20]

By contrast, it seems to have been common practice in the empire for executioners to dissect their victims. Master Franz Schmidt, executioner in Nuremberg from 1578 to 1617, who acquired a certain posthumous fame because he kept a diary in which he recorded all criminal punishments he performed, noted on several occasions that

---

[17]For an example of the detail of such examinations, see StadtAA, Strafamt, Urgicht Augustin Gerstecker, 1665, III.20, V.5, Meister Marx's testimony for 16 April 1665.

[18]StadtAA, Ratsprotokoll (RP) 82:612 for 4 May 1686.

[19]StadtAA, Chroniken 27, for 9 May 1643.

[20]For Italy, see Katherine Park, "The Criminal and the Saintly Body: Autopsy and Dissection in Renaissance Italy," *Renaissance Quarterly* 47 (1994): 8. For Cologne, see Robert Jütte, *Ärzte, Heiler, und Patienten: Medizinischer Alltag in der frühen Neuzeit* (Munich: Artemis & Winkler, 1991), 116–17.

he had dissected a delinquent's body.[21] In Munich, on those occasions when medical doctors and barber-surgeons did perform autopsies, the executioner participated in such examinations, as a 1641 decree that condemns the executioner's attendance attests.[22] In Augsburg, autopsies by medical doctors remained infrequent until the mid-eighteenth century. A "List of Malefactors," which recorded executions from 1700 on, did not note an autopsy performed by medical doctors before 1737.[23] Until then, the right of executioners to dissect criminals' bodies appears to have been undisputed. Medical doctors did not encroach on this traditional practice before the mid-eighteenth century. In 1742 the executioner Johann Georg Trenkler was required to deliver the bodies of executed criminals to the hospital to be dissected by the medical doctors, and in 1747 he was explicitly forbidden to perform dissections.[24]

This constituted a blow to the executioner's traditional medical practice, which required a regular supply of cadavers. It is not clear whether executioners performed dissections in order to gain a better understanding of human anatomy; their primary goal, in any case, was to acquire raw materials for their medical treatments. Executioners derived many of the ingredients for their medicines from the bodies of executed criminals. Thus, for example, the executioner's wife who cared for the woman with the broken hand in 1611 used human fat in her treatment.[25] Human fat, specifically *Armsünderfett* (poor sinner's fat) taken from the bodies of executed criminals, was considered a potent medicine and was used to cure a wide variety of ailments, particularly broken bones, sprains, or crippling arthritis. According to a traditional rhyme,

---

[21]For instance, after the beheading of a robber on 21 July 1578, Meister Franz recorded that he "dissected and cut him." Jürgen Carl Jacobs and Heinz Rölleke, eds., *Das Tagebuch des Meister Franz, Scharfrichter zu Nürnberg* (1801; reprint, Dortmund: Harenberg, 1980), 8.

[22]Stadtarchiv München, Bürgermeister und Rat 60 B 3, Scharfrichter Mandat from 20 June 1641.

[23]Stadt- und Staatsbibliothek Augsburg (SStBA), 2 cod Aug 285, "Maleficanten Liste" for 1737.

[24]StadtAA, RP 116, 1742, p. 372, 26 May 1742, and Reichsstadtakten, Stadtbed. 1081/46, decree from 28 March 1747.

[25]StadtAA, HWA, Bader und Barbiere 3, 1601–1633, petition from 17 Dec. 1611.

Kathy Stuart

Zerlassen Menschenfett ist gut für lahme Glieder,
So man sie damit schmiert, sie werden richtig wieder.[26]

[Melted human fat is good for lame limbs.
If one rubs them with it, they become right again.]

Armsünderfett seems to have been a stock remedy in the executioner's medical repertoire. In 1661 medical doctors remarked contemptuously that the executioner should stick to his human fat and dog grease, for "just because he can reset the dislocated joints of tortured delinquents does not mean he understands illnesses and can cure them."[27] This did not mean that the doctors considered human fat inefficacious; they were only trying to exclude the executioner from their preserve of internal medicine. Indeed, there seems to have been a general consensus concerning the healing power of poor sinner's fat. In Munich, for instance, the executioner delivered human fat to the city's apothecaries by the pound until the mid-eighteenth century, a sure sign that the executioner was not alone in prescribing it.[28] As late as 1747 the executioner Johann Georg Trenkler buttressed his petition to be allowed to continue dissecting executed delinquents by pointing out that this was the best source of human fat. "The whole town knows," he wrote, "that by mixing a salve with human fat ... I have cured several patients of their nerve gout."[29] He also treated cramps, goiter, and other bodily pains with this remedy.[30] The council turned Trenkler down, not because they objected to the use of human fat in medicines but because by this time the medical doctors were regularly performing dissections. The doctors, the council decreed, would provide the apothecaries and country doctors with human fat from their anatomical demonstrations, a clear indication that the use of human fat was still an accepted medical practice in the

---

[26]For this rhyme and other uses of *Armsünderfett*, s.v. "Fett," in *Handwörterbuch des deutschen Aberglaubens.*

[27]StadtAA, CM, Apotheker von 1564–1804, Tom II, correspondence Jan.-Feb., 1661.

[28]Jutta Nowosadtko, *Scharfrichter und Abdecker: Der Alltag zweier 'unehrlicher Berufe' in der Frühen Neuzeit* (Paderborn: Ferdinand Schöningh, 1994), 170.

[29]StadtAA, Reichsstadtakten, Stadtbed. 1081/46, petition from 18 March 1747, and decree from 28 March 1747.

[30]In early modern Italy executioners sold human fat as a painkiller. Giovanna Ferrari, "Public Anatomy Lessons and the Carneval: The Anatomy Theatre of Bologna," *Past and Present* 117 (1987): 50–106.

mid-eighteenth century.[31] The use of human fat, then, was not particular to executioner medicine; executioners simply had privileged access to it for most of the early modern period.

Human fat was not the only body part executioners used in their medical treatments. In 1617, a chronicle records, the executioner sold the skull of a young woman to an apothecary for six Gulden. The chronicler did not note how the skull was to be used.[32] Folklorists report that human skull was baked, ground into a powder, and then administered in a drink as a cure for epilepsy.[33] This was also the use recommended in the official London pharmacopoeia of 1617, another indication that the medicinal use of human body parts was not limited to executioner medicine, or for that matter to German medical practice.[34] The Augsburg executioner Trenkler also reported on the beneficial effect of another body part. In a petition from 1747 he wrote that he had "given pregnant women very valuable help by applying human skin," though he did not specify how. Licensed midwives used human skin in their practice as well. In early-seventeenth-century Munich, for example, the executioner Hans Stadler made a special arrangement with a local midwife: he would supply her with human skins in exchange for her free assistance to his wife during pregnancy.[35] According to folklorists, the tanned human skin was cut into straps, which women in labor wore as belts in order to help the birthing process.[36] Goiter was treated by wearing a strip of tanned human skin around the neck.[37] The use of executed criminals' blood as a cure for epilepsy was documented in wide regions of the empire and Europe throughout the early modern period and well into the

[31]See n. 29 above.

[32]StadtAA, Chroniken 27, for 23 Feb. 1617.

[33]Oskar von Hovorka and Adolf Kronfeld, *Vergleichende Volksmedizin: Eine Darstellung volksmedizinischer Sitten und Gebräuche*, vol. 2 (Stuttgart: Strecker & Strecker, 1909), 211.

[34]William Brockbank, "Sovereign Remedies: A Critical Depreciation of the 17th-Century London Pharmacopoeia," *Medical History* 8 (1964): 3. On English popular beliefs in the healing powers of the cadavers of executed criminals, see Peter Linebaugh, "The Tyburn Riot against the Surgeons," in *Albion's Fatal Tree: Crime and Society in Eighteenth-Century England*, ed. Douglas Hay et al. (New York: Pantheon, 1975), 109–11.

[35]Nowosadtko, *Scharfrichter und Abdecker*, 170 (see n. 28 above).

[36]On the medicinal powers of human skin, s.v. "Haut," and "Hingerichteter, Armsünder, Hinrichtung," *Handwörterbuch* (see n. 26 above).

[37]G. Lämmert, *Volksmedizin und Medizinischer Aberglaube in Bayern* (Würzburg: F. A. Julien, 1869), 239.

nineteenth century. Epileptics waited at the scaffold as a beheading took place and drank the "poor sinner's blood" immediately while it was still fresh and warm.[38] At an early-sixteenth-century execution in Swabia a vagrant grabbed the beheaded body "before it had fallen, and drank the blood from him, and they say he was cured of the falling sickness from it."[39]

In 1662 Johann Joachim Becher, personal physician to the elector of Mainz, recommended that apothecaries keep at least twenty-four types of human material in stock at all times.[40] And indeed, apothecary inventories and pharmacopoeias confirm that a ready supply was on hand. The official pharmacopoeia of 1652 of the free imperial city of Nuremberg, which served as model in South Germany, lists whole human skull (*Cranii Humani Integri*) and prepared human skull, human grains (*Granii Humanii*), mummy, human fat (*Pinguedo Hominis*), salt from human grains (*Salis Granii Humani*), and spirit of human bone (*Spiritus Ossium Humanorum*).[41] In 1737 apothecaries in Ulm were required to stock all of these materials, as well as moss that had grown on human skulls, and a Bavarian ordinance from 1755 mandated the regular delivery of human fat to military hospitals.[42]

---

[38]For graphic descriptions of this practice from the sixteenth through the nineteenth centuries, s.v. "Hingerichteter" *Handwörterbuch* (see n. 36 above), and Richard J. Evans, "Öffentlichkeit und Autorität: Zur Geschichte der Hinrichtungen in Deutschland vom Allgemeinen Landrecht bis zum dritten Reich," in *Räuber, Volk, und Obrigkeit: Studien zur Geschichte der Kriminalität in Deutschland seit dem 18. Jahrhundert*, ed. Heinz Reif (Frankfurt a.M.: Suhrkamp, 1984), 197–202. For examples from Sweden, Denmark, and Switzerland from the early modern period and nineteenth century, see Mabel Peacock, "Executed Criminals and Folk-Medicine," *Folk-Lore* 7 (1896): 268–83.

[39]This is recorded in the Zimmern Chronicle, the house chronicle of the Zimmern, a Swabian aristocratic family, written from the sixteenth through the eighteenth centuries. Quoted in "Hingerichteter," 47 (see n. 36 above).

[40]Elfriede Grabner, "Der Mensch als Arzenei: Alpenländische Belege zu einem Kärntner Schauermärlein," in *Festgabe für Oskar Moser: Beiträge zur Volkskunde Kärntens* (Klagenfurt: Verlag des Landesmuseums für Kärnten, 1974), 86.

[41]SStBA, 4 Med 399, *Erneuerte Gesetz, Ordnung und Tax Eines Edlen … Raths des Heil: Reichs Statt Nürnberg, dem Collegio Moedic, den Apothekern … gegeben* (Nuremberg, 1652).

[42]StadtAA, CM, *Medizinal und Apotheker Ordnungen: Des Heiligen Reichs-Stadt Ulm Erneuerter Apotheker Tax* (Ulm, 1737), and CM, Deputation ad Collegium Medicum, Apotheker Ordnungen: *Ordnung über die Militärischen Krankenhäuser … nebst der Apotheker Tax, auf s[eine] … Churfürst in Bayern verfasset* (Augsburg, 1755). For further examples, see SStBA, 4 Med 39, *Neue Apotheker Taxa der Stadt Basel* (Basel, 1701), or Ludwig von Hörnigk, *Politia Medica* (Frankfurt a.M., 1638), 56, 80, 82–84. For nineteenth-century examples, see Grabner, "Der Mensch als Arzenei," 86 (see n. 40 above).

All these examples demonstrate that the medicinal use of human body parts was undisputed in unofficial as well as in licensed medical practice, in popular as well as in learned medicine. Contemporaries did not explain from what principles they deduced the healing powers of the cadaver. On one thing, however, everyone was agreed: there was nothing magical or supernatural about using human raw materials in medicine. The medical efficacy of human body parts derived from the powers that were naturally inherent in them.[43] When the Munich executioner Hans Stadler came under suspicion of practicing white magic in the early seventeenth century, he protested that he only used "natural means" in his medicines, namely, "herbs, roots, and human fat."[44] Obviously, early modern Germans drew the boundary between medicine and magic, between natural and supernatural efficacy, in a different place than we would.

THE EXECUTIONER'S PRACTICE

If executioner medicine was considered natural, nonmagical, what did executioners do with their raw materials? How did they treat their patients? We will reconstruct the medical practice of executioners in the greatest possible detail in order to gain a better understanding of executioner medicine itself and the nature of executioners' interaction with their patients. Here the imperial legitimations provide a valuable supplement to the Augsburg sources, since executioners often included letters of recommendation by patients in order to support their petitions.

Treating broken bones, sprains, dislocated joints, and external injuries seems to have been the executioner's particular specialty. Even when the authorities—under the prodding of licensed barber-surgeons and medical doctors—sought to suppress executioner medicine, executioners were allowed to treat such external ailments. This seems to have fallen within the traditional rights of executioners throughout the empire. In 1661 the city of Nuremberg, answering an inquiry from Augsburg, reported that their executioner was permitted

[43]See, e.g., Philippe Ariès' discussion of the writings of the German physician Christian Friedrich Garmann (1640–1709); in idem, *De Miraculis Mortuorum* (Dresden, 1709), Garmann argues that cadavers provided effective medical remedies of a non-magical character; Philippe Ariès, *The Hour of our Death*, trans. Helen Weaver (New York and Oxford: Oxford University Press, 1991), 357.

[44]Nowosadtko, *Scharfrichter und Abdecker*, 186 (see n. 28 above).

to treat external injuries "about which they have some knowledge." In 1708 and again in 1744 executioners in Prussia were granted the right to treat broken legs.[45] Patients' letters seem to confirm executioners' skill in treating external injuries. The patients tell dramatic stories of suffering for weeks or months at the hands of doctors and barber-surgeons, tales of gangrenous limbs and impending amputations. When all seemed lost, they placed themselves under the care of the executioner who saved their limbs after all. In 1747 Lorentz Seitz, for example, a journeyman brewer in Nuremberg, was rescued from knife-happy barber-surgeons by the ministrations of Johann Michael Schmidt, the local executioner. Schmidt saved Seitz' wounded leg, which the barber-surgeons had threatened to amputate, by visiting him in his home and applying new bandages twice a day: "In this way, with God's help he put me back together again..., so that I can walk and work...."[46] Seitz is frustratingly vague, however, concerning the details of the treatment. Did the executioner apply human fat? Seitz and all other patients remain silent on this point. We cannot know whether we should interpret this silence to mean that the use of human fat on external injuries was so obvious as to need no mention, or whether the medicinal use of human raw materials was perhaps not entirely unproblematic after all.

What outraged official practitioners, in particular the medical doctors, even more than executioners' treatment of external injuries, was that executioners did not limit themselves to broken bones but regularly encroached on what the physicians considered their legal monopoly: internal medicine. In a petition to the Augsburg city council in 1661, the medical doctors complained that the executioner was so impudent that he not only "writes prescriptions, but sometimes mixes the medicines himself, examines urine, gives advice, and distributes purgations and medicines, in private and in public, in and outside of his house."[47] The truth of the doctors' complaint is confirmed both in the letters of patients and in the petitions of execu-

---

[45]StadtAA, CM, Pfuscher, 1562–1793, letter from Nuremberg from 15 May 1661; for Prussia, see Mylius, *Corpus Constitutionum Marchicarum*, 278 (see n. 7 above).

[46]HHStA, Vienna, Restitutiones, Fz. 6/S, Johann Michael Schmidt, 1747.

[47]The doctors claimed that the executioner "sich ... erkühnet ... interna Medicamenta ... nicht alleine zue verschreiben, sondern auch ... selbsten zue praeparieren, die urin zue besichtigen, auch mit Rath, purgationen, und Arzeneyen Ausgebung, haimblich und offentlich, Inner: und Ausser seines Hauses, zue practicieren." StadtAA, CM, Apotheker von 1564–1804, Tom II, correspondence Jan.-Feb. 1661.

tioners themselves. When Augsburg's executioner Johann Adam Hartmann petitioned the emperor for a legitimation in 1708, he wrote that he had been "practicing not only surgery, but internal and external medicine as well."[48] Patients also described executioners' practice of uroscopy. In 1750 an eyeglasses-maker from Fürth brought a urine sample from his wife, who was suffering from "a growth in her body," to the executioner in Nuremberg: "Then, by looking at the urine, he told me so much about what was ailing my wife that I could not have described it better myself."[49] Apparently the eyeglasses-maker gave the executioner the urine to inspect without elaborating on his wife's symptoms—perhaps as a kind of test of the executioner's skill. The executioner passed this test to his satisfaction and began treating his wife. Patient letters give the impression that executioners treated almost any imaginable complaint. In the 1740s and 1750s the Nuremberg executioner Johann Michael Schmidt treated patients for fever, hemorrhaging from the vagina, broken bones, gangrenous limbs, "weakness in the head," and epilepsy.[50] Balthasar Hirschfeld, an executioner in Mainz who practiced in the 1760s, treated rheumatism, consumption, burns, paralysis, cancerous growths, and broken bones.[51]

The letters also make it clear that executioners did indeed *touch* their patients, in some if not in all cases. As we saw, executioners bandaged patients, something hard to do without touching. In 1763 a councillor to the archbishop of Mainz specifically referred to the executioner's healing *touch*: he attested that executioner Hirschfeld had cured his daughter by "taking [her] under his skilled hands."[52] The councillor's wording is remarkable, because the expression to come "under the executioner's hands" was more commonly used to

[48]HHStA, Vienna, Restitutiones, Fz. 3/H, Johann Adam Hartmann, 1708.
[49]HHStA, Vienna, Restitutiones, Fz. 6/S, Johann Michael Schmidt, 1757.
[50]HHStA, Vienna, Restitutiones, Fz. 6/S, Johann Michael Schmidt, 1754.
[51]HHStA, Vienna, Restitutiones, Fz. 3/H, Balthasar Hirschfeld, 1766.
[52]Ibid. It does not go without saying that early modern healers necessarily *touched* their patients. In her painstaking reconstruction of the practice of an eighteenth-century medical doctor, Barbara Duden, *The Woman beneath the Skin: A Doctor's Patients in Eighteenth-Century Germany,* trans. Thomas Dunlap (Cambridge, Mass: Harvard University Press,1991), 83–85, describes how the doctor treated some of his patients for years without ever laying eyes on them, let alone touching them, by means of analyzing urine samples the patients had sent and making long-distance diagnoses. Duden goes so far as to write of a "touch taboo" of physicians in relation to their female patients.

describe being subjected to judicial torture or corporal punishment at the hands of the executioner.

There was one side of the executioner's practice, however, that was not mentioned at all in the patients' letters or the executioners' petitions. This was the one area where official practitioners would most likely have been willing to acknowledge the executioner's expertise, namely, the detection and treatment of supernatural complaints. In 1701 an Augsburg merchant consulted the executioner Johann Adam Hartmann because his small daughter was suffering from cramps and a swollen stomach. After examining the girl's urine, which he found to be healthy, Master Johann Adam concluded that the illness did not derive from natural causes. The child was the victim of witchcraft. Hartmann's treatment consisted of infusions of "witches' powder."[53] As late as 1741 the executioner Johann Georg Trenkler claimed that he had cured the young daughter of a lawyer and syndic to the cathedral chapter of *maleficium*.[54] It is not surprising that people consulted the executioner to identify and ward off the evil effects of harmful magic; after all, if he could identify a witch's mark in the course of a judicial investigation, should he not also be able to discern the symptoms of *maleficium* in daily life? However, the fact that executioners' treatment of supernatural complaints is so rarely mentioned in the sources seems to indicate that this aspect of their practice was considered more problematic than their treatment of "natural" complaints by "natural" means. Why executioners might have chosen to de-emphasize any supernatural competency will become clear later on when we analyze their rhetorical strategies.

Who were the executioners' patients? Our evidence for Augsburg executioners is very fragmentary. We saw that Caspar Behem complained in 1533 that most of his patients were impoverished, "perhaps because the rich do not want to entrust themselves to me."[55] But Behem's experience seems to have been atypical. Other executioners treated patients from various social classes. In 1591 Veit Malsch, a transient foreign executioner who was accused of theft, testified that he had cured a nobleman for 22 Gulden, no mean sum

---

[53]StadtAA, Strafamt, Urgicht Christeiner, 1701, VIII, testimony of Johann Adam Hartmann.

[54]StadtAA, RP 115, 1741, p. 469 for 27 July 1741.

[55]StadtAA, Reichsstadtakten, Stadtbed. 1081/46. On the date of Behem's petition, see n. 8 above.

considering that the annual salary for a municipal midwife was just 8 Gulden.[56] He had also treated a cook for the same amount.[57] Stonemasons and other artisans regularly consulted the executioner for medical advice.[58] In 1679, Marx Philipp Hartmann had a "Duke of Lorraine," a territorial lord, in treatment.[59] We saw that Johann Adam Hartmann treated a merchant's daughter for *maleficium* in 1701.[60] In 1719 Hartmann counted "peasants and local common people" and "Swabian country- and townfolk" among his patients.[61] In 1726 a vagrant weaver was arrested outside the Augsburg city walls. He told his interrogators that he was on his way to the executioner to seek treatment for the open wounds on his feet; he had heard that Augsburg's executioner cured such injuries well and cheaply.[62] We have seen that Johann Georg Trenkler cured the daughter of a lawyer and syndic to the cathedral chapter of witchcraft in 1741.[63] In a petition from 1747 Trenkler wrote that his treatment was helping many people, both Catholics and Protestants.[64] It is clear that Augsburg executioners had quite a mixed clientele. Impoverished residents, country folk, vagrants, middling artisans, Catholics and Protestants, members of the upper classes, a merchant, a lawyer, a nobleman, a territorial lord—all used the executioner's services.

Executioners' petitions for legitimation and their patients' letters afford a more detailed view of the kind of patients particular executioners could attract. In 1624 Nuremberg's executioner Franz Schmidt included a list of patients "of high and exalted estate" with his petition. The list included imperial councillors, cathedral canons, aristocrats, patricians, and members of the city council, forty-one people in all.[65] Johann Michael Schmidt, who served as Nuremberg's execu-

---

[56]Merry Wiesner, *Working Women in Renaissance Germany* (New Brunswick, N.J.: Rutgers University Press, 1986), 56.

[57]StadtAA, Strafamt, Urgicht Veit Malch, 1591c, VIII, 7, 26. I am grateful to Anne Tlusty of Bucknell University for bringing this case to my attention.

[58]StadtAA, Maurer 2, 1651–1687, petition from 4 Dec. 1677.

[59]StadtAA, CM, Schedarum quarum in Actis Collegii medici mentio sit, Fasc. IIdus, ad Prot. Vol. I pertinens ..., 1673–1683.

[60]StadtAA, Strafamt, Urgicht Christeiner, 1701, VIII, testimony of Johann Adam Hartmann.

[61]StadtAA, CM, in genere, 1548–1795, for 29 July 1719.

[62]StadtAA, Buchloe 4, list of vagrants from 29 March 1726.

[63]StadtAA, RP 115, 1741, p. 469 for 27 July 1741.

[64]StadtAA, Reichsstadtakten, Stadtbed. 1081/46, petition from 18 March 1747.

[65]HHStA, Vienna, Restitutiones, Fz. 6/S, Franz Schmidt, 1624.

tioner from 1726 to 1753, served a much humbler clientele. His patients included the wife of an eyeglasses-maker, a journeyman brewer, a goldsmith from a neighboring village, the wife of a comb-maker, a retailer, a peasant, a baker, and a journeyman miller, among others.[66] The patients of Balthasar Hirschfeld, executioner in the archbishopric of Mainz in the 1760s, were of considerably higher status. Four were clearly aristocratic. His patients included a cathedral canon, the choirmaster at the cathedral, a baron, a baroness, a Jesuit, two members of the archbishop's council, and two army officers.[67]

The executioners obviously requested letters from the most illustrious patients they could find, so these lists hardly constitute representative samples of executioners' clientele. The patients' letters do amply demonstrate, however, that medicine enabled executioners to gain access to the highest reaches of society. Furthermore, an executioner's high-class patients seem to have felt some measure of obligation towards him, since they were willing to write letters on his behalf. The letters also show that the social boundary between laity and clergy had no effect on an executioner's drawing power. Rich and poor, clerics and lay people, men and women—all felt no compunction in consulting the executioner in medical matters.

Dishonor never became an issue in the medical contacts between executioners and their patients. No cases exist in which an honorable citizen became contaminated by the executioner's medical treatment. Executioners practiced openly, and their patients consulted them openly. "It is only the imagination of our own time that has the hangman's visitors secretly sneak through the alleyways by night," a legal historian has commented on this phenomenon.[68] If anything, executioner medicine seems to have been particularly public. Executioners, like other medical practitioners, placed great emphasis on their reputation as healers. They boasted of their popularity in their petitions, and even local governments attested to the medical renown of their executioners with apparent pride; in 1663, for instance, the government of Cologne reported that the "fame" of their executioner Johann Georg Hoffmann had spread throughout the region.[69]

---

[66]HHStA, Vienna, Restitutiones, Fz. 6/S, Johann Michael Schmidt, 1754.
[67]HHStA, Vienna, Restitutiones, Fz. 6/S, Balthasar Hirschfeld, 1766.
[68]Joachim Gernhuber, "Strafvollzug und Unehrlichkeit," *Zeitschrift der Savigny-Stiftung für Rechtsgeschichte, Germanische Abteilung* 74 (1957): 141.
[69]HHStA, Vienna, Restitutiones, Fz. 2/3, Johann Georg Hoffmann, 1663.

Barbara Duden has described how a doctor's reputation spread word-of-mouth and how sick people found the healer of their choice by relying on an extensive network of family, friends, and acquaintances from whom they heard about particular practitioners and whose recommendations they followed: "Patients make a practice; in order to survive, one had to be introduced."[70] The same held true for the executioner. Patients found their way to the executioner through a variety of social connections. In 1751 a Nuremberg goldsmith consulted executioner Schmidt on the "insistent recommendation of various people and good friends."[71] In the same year, the woman who suffered from monthly bleedings from her head ended up in the executioner's practice because "good people finally advised me that I should go to our executioner Johann Michael Schmidt. He is supposed to be very learned...."[72]

The public nature of executioner medicine was not exceptional compared with other types of medical practice, by both licensed and unlicensed healers. Indeed, healing relationships and the healing process in general seem to have been quite public in early modern Europe. The medical historian Robert Jütte argues that early modern medical practice constituted a "particular type of public sphere": the physician was called to the sickbed where he interacted with his patient before an audience consisting of the patient's relatives and visiting friends.[73] Barbara Duden comments on the public nature of the therapeutic process and the public context in which communication between doctor and patient took place. Patients did not hesitate to have blood and urine samples delivered to their doctor, publicly and openly, by their friends, neighbors, or messengers. These intermediaries could also report to the doctor about the patient's "flows, bleeding, color of urine, the sliminess of the blood drawn—everything that emanated from the body" in exquisite detail. This communication network linking doctor and patient was characterized by the "publicness of bodily phenomena we today carefully conceal."[74] In her discussion of medical "charlatans" and mountebanks, Alison Lingo argues that the public setting of street healing was an essential

---

[70]Duden, *Woman beneath the Skin*, 55 (see n. 52 above).
[71]HHStA, Vienna, Restitutiones, Fz. 6/S, Johann Michael Schmidt, 1757.
[72]Ibid.
[73]Jütte, *Ärzte, Heiler und Patienten*, 211–12 (see n. 20 above).
[74]Duden, *Woman beneath the Skin*, 85–86 (see n. 52 above).

part of the therapeutic process: "Public healing was a kind of social ritual which contributed to the spiritual, if not the physical health of the sick." The public context of the healing relationship contributed to "the totality of the whole experience."[75] Executioners' public practice and the public nature of the interaction with their patients seem to follow the common pattern of healing relationships in early modern Europe.

RHETORICAL STRATEGIES OF MEDICAL COMPETITION

Interaction between executioners and their patients was unproblematic; no conflicts resulted from the executioner's dishonor in this medical context. The executioner's medical practice was, however, a source of perennial conflict between executioners and licensed medical practitioners, the barber-surgeons and university-trained physicians. The issue in these conflicts was not the executioner's legal infamy or the problem of pollution. These conflicts centered around division of labor in the medical marketplace. Licensed medical practitioners strongly resented executioner medicine, which they considered an encroachment on their legal monopoly. Licensed practitioners rarely made an issue of the executioner's dishonor; instead, they concentrated on questions of competency and medical training. Executioners defended their medical practice by presenting themselves as qualified medical professionals.

In 1573 the medical doctors in Augsburg complained that the executioner and his family members were usurping their prerogatives more than ever, "healing not only broken legs, but old and new injuries, and mixing all kinds of medicines." The executioner could afford to provide the service more cheaply than they, because he also received his executioner's wages. This competition by the executioner caused them "great ridicule, contempt, and humiliation ... as if we had not learned our trade."[76] It is not clear how the government responded to this petition. In 1594, however, the government issued a decree to protect the medical doctors from unlicensed competition. The decree forbade "quacks, such as the local executioner ... and other such cow doctors who do not read Latin" to examine urine or

---

[75]Alison K. Lingo, "Empirics and Charlatans in Early Modern France: The Genesis of the Classification of the 'Other' in Medical Practice," *Journal of Social History* 19 (1986): 587.

[76]StadtAA, CM, Pfuscher, 1562–1793, petition from 5 Dec. 1573.

mix purgatives and other medicines, since their potions were often so strong that their patients died from them.[77] The barber-surgeons' ordinance even included an article intended to protect their legal monopoly on medical practice. Article 39 ordered: "Should the executioner, or women, or other such unqualified persons dare to bandage a wounded person ... or do a bloodletting ... then they should be brought before the Punishment Lords and receive fit punishment."[78] Guild ordinances took the form of governmental decrees, so this article demonstrates at once the barber-surgeons' fear of the executioner's competition and the government's intention to protect the medical monopoly of licensed medical practitioners.

The chronic conflict between executioners and medical professionals took on particular virulence during the tenure of the executioner Master Marx Philipp Hartmann. Hartmann had a remarkable career. He came to Augsburg from the neighboring free imperial city of Ulm in 1652 and moved into the executioner Dietrich Metz's household as his assistant. In that same year he married Metz's daughter Barbara. In 1654 when his father-in-law resigned his post, Marx succeeded him as master executioner.[79] He did not wait long to start up his medical practice. Our first sources for Marx's practice are complaints in 1658 and 1659 by the Collegium Medicum, asking authorities to forbid his practice of internal medicine.[80] It is not clear whether the government acted on these appeals; in 1661 the Collegium Medicum was again involved in a conflict with Master Marx. One medical doctor was outraged to learn that one of his patients had sought the help of the executioner. In order to find out what medicines Marx had prescribed, the doctor went to the apothecary only to find the executioner's servant in the shop collecting various ingredients for his master's potions. Beside himself, the doctor attacked the executioner's servant, throwing all his herbs and oils on the ground.

---

[77]Ibid., decree from 1594.

[78]"Wann der Züchtiger, die Frauenbilder, oder andere dergleichen unbefugte Personen sich understehn sollten, ein verwundete Person zu binden: desgleichen wann solche ... Personen ... sich des Aderlassens, Zungenlösens, und Scherens underfangen wurden, so sollen dieselben ... den Straffherren angezeigt werden damit sie ihre geziehmende straf darum empfangen." StadtAA, HWA, Bader und Barbiere 8, 1679–1688, Barber-surgeon ordinance from 1638.

[79]StadtAA, HAP 1650–1659, fol. 143r, for 29 Sept. 1652; Reichsstadtakten, Stadtbed. 1081/46, employment contract from 9 June 1654.

[80]StadtAA, AHV, CM Prot.1:614–15, 623.

The Collegium Medicum then petitioned the city government: the council should suppress medical quacks, "pure idiots," who were ignorant of Latin and consequently could not know the fundamental principles of medicines. The executioner, they claimed, "among all the idiots knows Latin the least." With his quackery he had destroyed the health of many patients and even killed some. The medical doctors buttressed their case against the executioner by making inquiries into the public health policies of other free imperial cities. Frankfurt reported that its medical ordinances forbade the executioner to practice medicine, and Nuremberg responded that its executioner was allowed to treat only external injuries. If the government allowed such abuses to continue in Augsburg, the doctors argued, it would harm the reputation of this "world-famous republic," undermining the authority of the council and demeaning the Collegium Medicum.

Master Marx's response reveals much about the executioner's self-understanding as a healer. He defended himself vigorously against this attack on his medical competence and expressed pride in his own medical talents and the medical practice of executioners in general. Marx argued that even though he had not studied his medical art at the universities, he had learned medicine from early youth in "long, continual, and daily practice" under the tutelage of his parents and grandparents. He had studied with his father-in-law, Dietrich Metz, his predecessor in office, who had been a famous "doctor." Hartmann was not exaggerating here; a chronicle recorded Metz's death in 1658 with the comment, "He was a good *medicus*. When doctors and barber-surgeons gave up on a patient, he managed to cure them."[81] The medical practice by executioners was certainly nothing new, Hartmann continued, but dated back to the distant past. His treatments were based on long experience and study. He had inherited voluminous manuscripts from which he took the recipes for his medicines. (That Marx truly was serious about his medical studies is illustrated by his last will and testament: he owned twenty-one medical texts.) He obeyed the local apothecary ordinance, Marx continued. He bought the ingredients for his medicines in local apothecary shops and had his prescriptions filled there. His opponents, he claimed, would be unable to find any patients whose health he had ruined. But he could

---

[81]StadtAA, Chroniken 27, for 1 Dec. 1658.

readily produce thirty to forty patients whom the medical doctors had given up on, but whom he had cured.

Marx was obviously trying to present himself as a sober, educated professional. Executioners petitioning for legitimations pursued similar strategies. They consistently emphasized their "learning" (*Wissenschaft*) and the training they had received from their predecessors. Their medical training seemed to be both artisanal and theoretical. Executioners provided their sons with hands-on medical training and at the same time encouraged them in their studies. Several executioners' sons were planning to study medicine at the university, pending the imperial legitimation which was a necessary precondition for matriculation.[82] Executioner medicine appears very "male" in such petitions, since appeal was made to male models of training and education. Executioners never mentioned that the women in their households were practicing medicine as well.

Executioners also presented themselves in such a way as to fend off any suspicion of superstitious practices. This explains why executioners' detection and treatment of *maleficium* never came up in their petitions and why they placed such emphasis on the "natural" efficacy of their medicines. Executioners constantly reiterated that their medicine was based on work. Executioner medicine was no easy, "magical" quick fix; their medical successes depended on continuous diligence and effort. And, of course, whenever executioners cured a patient successfully, this happened with "God's help" and to "God's greater honor."[83]

Augsburg's executioner Marx Philipp Hartmann lost his case against the medical doctors in 1661. The Augsburg city government showed itself unimpressed by their executioner's rhetorical strategy. Previous medical ordinances had forbidden the free practice of medicine by executioners. Indeed, by forbidding the executioner and other "cow doctors who do not read Latin" to practice, the ordinance of 1594 had already focused on the same issue the medical doctors chose to emphasize in their petition. In 1661 the government again agreed with the doctors' argument that since Hartmann did not know Latin—"much less Greek"—he could not know the fundamental prin-

[82]See, e.g., HHStA, Vienna, Restitutiones, Fz. 6/S, Franz Schmidt, 1624, or Fz. 1/B, Johannes Bast, 1701. Bast was trying to get two sons into a medical faculty at the time of his petition in 1701.

[83]See, e.g., HHStA, Vienna, Restitutiones, Fz. 6/S, Christian Strauch, 1677.

ciples of medicine. The mayor sent a beadle to Hartmann with the order that he was to abstain from "internal medicine." However, he was allowed to continue treating external injuries, such as broken bones. "It remains to be seen whether he will obey the order," a medical doctor commented on these proceedings.[84] And Marx did not obey. The magistrates found it necessary to issue new decrees forbidding the executioner's medical practice in 1667, 1668, and 1671.[85] Despite all governmental interdictions, the executioner remained a part of the medical marketplace.

A few years later the Collegium Medicum again challenged Marx's medical practice. In 1678 the neighboring city of Schwäbisch Hall conferred with the Collegium Medicum on its policy toward the executioner's medical practice, and the physicians took this opportunity to direct yet another petition to the city government. Earlier decrees against Master Marx were not being enforced, they claimed, because he had found some support in high places. He could continue his quackery because he benefited from the protection of "one or another gentleman, and we have been forced to suffer it." The city government should finally enforce its statutes, not only to maintain public order and the common good within the republic, but also because these abuses ran "counter to God's commands," who decreed that everyone should remain "within the bounds of a certain estate and office."[86]

Marx did not stay within the bounds of his estate, however. The following year he ended his career as executioner in a spectacular case of upward social mobility. A chronicle recorded the execution of a thief on 17 June 1679 with the comment, "This was the last whom Master Marx Philipp Hartmann beheaded. He then received an imperial privilege allowing him to practice as other doctors, without objection."[87] That summer, after having served as executioner for twenty-eight years, Marx managed to obtain an imperial legitimation. He and his daughter had been legally "placed in the estate of honor by his Imperial Majesty" by this act of legitimation. Marx had also received

[84]StadtAA, CM, Apotheker von 1564–1804, Tom II, correspondence Jan.-Feb., 1661; AHV, CM Prot. I, pp. 666–70; CM, Pfuscher, 1562–1793, correspondence with Frankfurt and Nuremberg from 7 March and 15 May 1661.
[85]StadtAA, HWA, Bader und Barbiere 8, 1679–1688. A petition from 13 July 1686 lists earlier decrees from 17 Sept. 1667, 18 Sept. 1668, and 8 Oct. 1671.
[86]StadtAA, CM, Pfuscher, 1562–1793, from 10 March and 23 June 1678.
[87]SStBA, Aug. 4 cod Aug. HV 250, Maleficantenliste 1409–1757, fol. 17v.

an imperial privilege to practice medicine. He now planned to settle in Augsburg and continue his practice. To that end he applied for citizenship for himself and his daughter, since he was confident that he could "make his living with honor." The city granted him and his daughter citizenship.[88] In official documents Hartmann was now described as *medicinae practicus* (imperially privileged medical practitioner). The label of executioner disappeared, and no mention was made in official records of Marx's past profession.

ARS MORIENDI: EXECUTION, REDEMPTION, AND MEDICINE

Executioners presented themselves as sober, serious, learned, hard-working medical professionals. There was nothing "magical" or miraculous about their medical practice. The issue of their legal infamy did not come up, either in their relations with their patients or in their conflicts with licensed practitioners. Executioners who petitioned for legitimations in order to practice medicine full-time distanced themselves from their duties in criminal justice. They claimed to be too old to perform the physically demanding task of carrying out criminal executions, or they hired someone else to perform executions, while they devoted themselves to medicine. This line of argumentation was part of their strategy for achieving upward social mobility through medicine. Their dishonor, after all, derived from their functions in criminal justice. A legitimation could take effect only if the executioner discontinued performing criminal executions.

But as executioners distanced themselves from criminal justice, they distanced themselves from the original source of their healing powers. In popular perception, the executioner's gift as healer was not simply the result of learning and hard work. Executioners' medical gifts depended on their functions in criminal justice. Ultimately, we can resolve the paradox of executioner medicine only by understanding executioner medical practice in the context of criminal executions.

So far we have established that executioners practiced medicine because it was a required skill in the context of their duties in criminal justice (evaluating what level of torture to apply, mending the tor-

---

[88]StadtAA, Bürgeraufnahme, Fasc. 12a, 1673–1680, no. 10, 7 Sept. and 5 Oct. 1679.

tured delinquent), and because they had privileged access to cadavers of executed criminals, a source of highly efficacious raw materials for the medicines they mixed. But this only means that we have compounded the paradox of the executioner's dual role as killer and healer with yet another paradox: Why did doctors, governmental authorities, executioners, and their patients believe that human cadavers, in particular the cadavers of executed criminals, held such potent healing powers? Why should the body of an executed criminal, who had committed heinous crimes, who had become dishonorable under the executioner's hand during judicial torture, who was subjected to the infamy of public execution, and whose corpse could also become a source of pollution, have healing powers?[89]

Artisans felt profoundly ambivalent toward criminals' corpses. Touching the cadaver seems to have been permissible for medical purposes *only*. All other types of contact with the cadaver bore the risk of infamy. In 1562 the Augsburg tanners guild declared dishonorable a master who had tanned a human skin.[90] For a pregnant woman to wear the tanned skin of an executed criminal posed no threat to her honor; for an artisan to tan the skin in the first place did. Dissecting the criminal's body for the sake of gaining medical raw materials was unproblematic as far as the city government was concerned. However, in 1587 when a journeyman weaver cut the toe off the corpse of a criminal who had been broken on the wheel and whose body now lay exposed at the site of execution, this was another matter. The journeyman believed that carrying the toe in his pocket would bring him better luck at the gaming table. But while using body parts for medicine was natural and permissible, using a toe to influence fortune was not. The government arrested the journeyman under suspicion of witchcraft. After being interrogated under torture, the journeyman got off lightly: he was whipped and banished for "superstitious" practices. In the meantime, his guild had expelled him as dishonorable for touching the infamous cadaver.[91] Apothecaries, medical practitioners of all kinds, and patients handled medical raw materials derived from criminals' cadavers on a regular basis. However, in 1684 when

---

[89]Richard Evans poses this same question in "Öffentlichkeit und Authorität," 199 (see n. 38 above)·

[90]StadtAA, HWA, Gerber 1, 1548–1584, for 23 Nov. 1562.

[91]StadtAA, Strafamt, Urgicht Leonhard Nadler, 1587a, I, 20, 21; Strafbuch 1581–1587, 24 Jan. 1587, fol. 214v.

gravediggers buried the body of an executed criminal, they were labeled as dishonorable for that very reason.[92]

How can this ambivalence be explained? Resolving this problem will take us a long way in understanding the executioner's dual role as healer and killer and in explaining why his dishonor was inactive or indeed inverted into its opposite in the context of his medical practice. We have to understand executioner medicine not in opposition to but as a logical consequence of executioners' function in criminal justice. The underlying logic of executioner medicine derives from the execution ritual itself.

The condemned criminal underwent extensive preparation for the ceremonial role he or she would play in the execution ritual. Once the sentence was announced, the defendant was called the "poor sinner." The execution was set for three days after the trial.[93] These three days were intended as a period of reconciliation for the poor sinner, both with the worldly authorities and with God. It may be no coincidence that the authorities allotted three days for "repentance and reconciliation with God,"[94] the same length of time Christ spent in the tomb between crucifixion and resurrection. During these days the condemned was moved to a cleaner, lighter cell and provided with whatever foods he or she asked for. The sources do not show whether Augsburg's poor sinners partook of a "last meal" with judges and executioner, as was customary in other parts of Germany. By accepting special food, whether during the three days preceding execution or at a ceremonial last meal, the condemned expressed that he or she was at peace with the judges.[95] This was an indication that the execution might run smoothly.

While undergoing such worldly reconciliation, the condemned simultaneously became the object of intense clerical attention. The central focus of these last three days was the poor sinner's spiritual state. Two or three Catholic or Lutheran clergymen were appointed to minister to the condemned, taking turns visiting for hours every day,

[92]StadtAA, Bestand Gottesäcker, "Acta, die Totengrebel betreff," June 1684–April 1685.

[93]StadtAA, Schätze 194a, Eidbuch, fols. 40–41; Strafamt, Modus Procedendi in Malefizsachen (2 uncatalogued booklets); SStBA, 2 Aug Cod 268. The execution ritual remained essentially the same from the sixteenth through the eighteenth centuries.

[94]StadtAA, RP 127, 8 June 1747, pp. 376–77.

[95]On the various forms of the last meal and the functions of this ritual, see Hans von Hentig, *Vom Ursprung der Henkersmahlzeit* (Tübingen: J.C.B. Mohr, 1958).

instructing the poor sinner in the basics of the faith, inducing remorse and repentance, and explaining Christ's sacrifice. Finally, the clergyman would hear the poor sinner's confession, grant absolution, and offer the Eucharist. This procedure did not vary significantly according to confession. A Protestant received the Eucharist under both kinds; clergymen of both confessions granted absolution. The clerics exhorted the poor sinners to meditate on the agonies of Christ and, if the prisoner was Catholic, on the martyrdom of the saints, encouraging them to see their own impending deaths as a reenactment of such holy deaths. Broadsheets established parallels between the sufferings of the condemned criminal and the agonies of Christ or the martyrdom of the saints by styling the poor sinner, regardless of gender, as the "bride of Christ," and the clergymen as the best men who would lead the bride to the bridegroom, Christ.[96] Pamphlets also described the condemned as nursing in the "Five Holy Wounds" of Christ.[97] These pamphlets described the last days and hours of condemned criminals using the same imagery as late medieval female saints used to describe their ecstatic religious experiences.[98] Broadsheets described the march out to the scaffold as the poor sinner's rush toward salvation and compared the infamy of death by execution to the glory of resurrection. On the day of execution, the clergymen accompanied the condemned in the procession, mounted the scaffold, and held a cross close to the poor sinner's face at the very moment of execution, so that the last thing he or she beheld in this world was the cross.[99]

There was a tension between honor and grace in the execution ritual. While death by execution was infamous in the eyes of the world, the poor sinner's death was a good death, even a blessed death in Christian cosmology. The condemned died, as one execution ser-

---

[96]SStBA, 4 Aug. 744, *Des auf dem Rad ligenden Samuel Keckens Erzehlung seines Mords, Bekehrung, und Todes, nebenst aufrichtigen von ihm, in dem Gefengnus, aufgesetzten Buss-Gedanken* ... (Augsburg: Caspar Brechenmacher, 1711).

[97]SStBA, 4 Aug. 2408: *Trauergeschichte und schröckliches Lebensende des nebst vier anderen Malefikanten sub 20sten May 1786 zu Augsburg durch das Schwert vom Leben zum Tod gebrachten Missethaters, Johann Woelfle* (Augsburg: Johann Bernhard Stadlberger, n.d.)

[98]Caroline Walker Bynum, *Fragmentation and Redemption: Essays on Gender and the Human Body in Medieval Religion* (New York: Zone Books, 1991), 205.

[99]This is seen in numerous seventeenth- and eighteenth-century broadsheets that depict executions. See SStBA, Graphik 29/112–137, Verbrecher, etc.

mon put it, "with all possible help and means of salvation."[100] Since the poor sinner knew the moment of death ahead of time, he or she could confess, receive absolution and the Eucharist, and thus enter eternity cleansed of sin, unlike other Christians, who had to fear a hasty and untimely death.

Public executions took the form of religious ceremonies, of sacrificial ritual. The white dress sometimes worn by the condemned criminal expressed the purity of the poor sinner during this last trial. In the execution ritual the criminal was transformed from an infamous villain into a saint.[101] A chronicle entry recording a botched execution in Munich in 1438 refers to this transformation explicitly. A hanged delinquent was taken down from the gallows, only to be found still breathing. The chronicler comments, "Since he became holy on the gallows, they let him go."[102]

This analogy between poor sinner and saint is substantiated by some distinct parallels between the medicinal use of criminals' bodies and the healing power of relics. We saw that ground human skull was an efficacious treatment for epilepsy. Sufferers of epilepsy also drank wine from hanged men's skulls, a practice similar to drinking hallowed wine from the skulls of saints officially recognized by the church.[103] "Poor sinner's fat" can be compared to the holy healing oils that exuded from the bodies of saints.[104] When women in labor wore a belt of tanned human skin, this was similar to a Swabian religious ceremony involving St. Margaret: pregnant women worshipped St. Margaret, who had the power of the "loosening belt"; tying a string or cloth around their waists in the name of St. Margaret guar-

---

[100]SStBA, 4 Aug 1478: *Zweyfache Glückseligkeit aus der von Rechts wegen vollzogenen Todesstrafe, in einer Sittenrede auf dem katholischen Gottesacker ... von P. Bonaventura Lueger..., als einige Maleficanten, den 20 May des 1786 Jahres zu Augsburg vom Leben zum Tode hingerichtet worden* (Augsburg: Johann Nernhardt Stadlberger, n.d.).

[101]For a similar discussion of the execution ritual, see Gustav Radbruch, "Ars Moriendi: Scharfrichter—Seelsorger—Armersünder—Volk," in, idem, *Elegantiae Juris Criminalis: Vierzehn Studien zur Geschichte des Strafrechts* (Basel: Verlag für Recht und Gesellschaft AG., 1950), 141–73; Evans, "Öffentlichkeit und Authorität," 200 (see n. 38 above); and Park, "The Criminal and the Saintly Body," 23 (see n. 20 above).

[102]Louis Morsak, "Aus dem Rechtsleben bayerischer Wallfahrten," in *Forschungen zur Rechtsarchäologie und rechtlichen Volkskunde*, ed. Louis Carlen (Zurich: Schulthess Polygraphischer Verlag, 1978), 115.

[103]Peacock, "Executed Criminals and Folk-Medicine," 276 (see n. 38 above); Morsak, 114–15.

[104]Bynum, *Fragmentation and Redemption*, 18 (see n. 98 above); Lämmert, *Volksmedizin*, 26 (see n. 37 above).

anteed easy labor. The belt of human leather also resembled the popular belief in the curative powers of belts "the true length of Jesus." Pregnant women wore a belt thought to be equal in length to Jesus' actual height, again to ease labor pains.[105] I have not been able to discover whether belts of poor sinner's leather were supposed to be of any specified length.

Like a saint's body, the body of the poor sinner acquired a kind of sacral power in the course of the execution ritual. It was from this sacral power that the healing efficacy of the criminal's body derived.[106] The executioner was able to tap into the sacral power of the poor sinner's body as he handled and processed the cadaver in his medical practice. It is this symbolic association that turned the executioner into a gifted healer in popular imagination.

The belief in the executioner's healing powers and in the medical efficacy of his human raw materials was common to elite and popular culture, as well as to learned and popular medicine. We saw that executioners drew patients from all social classes and that learned doctors included human body parts in their official pharmacopoeias. Executioner medicine in many ways resembled the medical practice of other healers, both licensed and unlicensed. The healing process was essentially public, and executioners established social relations with their patients much as other practitioners did. Executioners sought to distance themselves from any kind of superstition or magic and presented their practice and their medicines as based on natural principles. By presenting themselves as learned, rational, and hardworking, executioners imitated university-trained physicians. Some sons of executioners hoped to become medical doctors themselves by trying to gain access to medical faculties. The deep-seated assumptions that, as I have argued, connected executioner medicine with execution ritual in popular imagination were never articulated by contemporaries.

Government authorities adopted an ambivalent position toward executioner medicine. On paper, governments supported the legal monopoly of licensed medical professionals, the barber-surgeons and medical doctors. From the sixteenth century on, the authorities regularly published decrees forbidding or limiting the medical practice of

[105]Lämmert, *Volksmedizin*, 165–66.
[106]Evans, "Öffentlichkeit und Authorität," 200 (see n. 38 above).

executioners. These edicts echoed the arguments of the medical doctors, which attacked the lack of professional credentials: the executioner was a "cow doctor" who knew neither Latin nor Greek. But these decrees were never enforced. That the government allowed executioner medical practice to continue, despite all edicts to the contrary, is indicative of its tacit recognition of the executioner's medical competence. We saw that the Augsburg Collegium Medicum complained in 1678 that Master Marx's practice continued to flourish in spite of all decrees issued against him, because he had support in high places. Patients' letters demonstrate that when patricians, imperial councillors, and territorial officials became ill, they ignored local medical ordinances and consulted the executioner. Another indication that elites throughout the empire shared the common belief in executioners' medical talents is the fact that local governments supported their petitions for legitimations; most importantly, emperors were willing to grant them, thus legalizing executioner medicine.

The Execution of the Condemned (anon.), showing three different
methods of torture in use in the 16th century.

Sovereignty and Heresy

Constantin Fasolt

Sovereignty is normally thought to be a principle of secular truth that is diametrically opposed to religious faith. More rarely it is itself thought to be a religious principle. But given its early modern origins it is perhaps best regarded as a peculiar kind of heresy that opposes only the reach of religious dogma, not its content. That may help to understand three things: first, why religion was successfully expelled from the realm of politics (neutralization of religion); second, why it was reintroduced in the realm of nature (naturalization of religion); and third, why the political consequences of the naturalization of religion have been largely invisible (blinding of the faithful). The chief article of the modern faith defines the boundary between nature and culture. A modern heretic is someone who doubts or violates that boundary against the wishes of the sovereign. If the invention of sovereignty thus put an end to wars of religion, it also made wars of nature conceivable.

HERESY CAN BE DEFINED as "adherence to a religious opinion that is contrary to an established dogma of a church" or, more technically, as "a deliberate and obstinate denial of a revealed truth by a baptized member of the Roman Catholic Church." Sovereignty, on the other hand, can be defined as "supreme power, especially over a body politic."[1]

Heresy and sovereignty thus seem to belong to mutually exclusive spheres. Heresy is a matter of religion. Sovereignty is a matter of state. Heresy exists where people believe that religious truths can be grasped with enough certainty to make it worth their while to suppress whoever denies those truths. People like that do not have much use for the concept of sovereignty because they are not normally inclined to consider anyone as holding supreme power over anything, unless it is God's holding supreme power over the world. Sovereignty, on the other hand, exists where people believe that positive laws and standing armies make a better foundation for a body politic than do reli-

---

[1]See *Webster's Third New International Dictionary of the English Language* (1961).

gious truths. People like that do not have much use for the concept of heresy because they are not normally inclined to include religious truths among the proper business of a sovereign ruler. At first sight, there does not appear to be much of a relationship between heresy and sovereignty at all.

That is one of the reasons why historians like to divide the history of Europe into a medieval and a modern part. In the medieval part, they say, people did include religious truths among the proper business of rulers and preferred the rule of God over the rule of man. Hence the Middle Ages were dominated by the church and full of heretics as well as their persecutors. But in the early modern period people began to have differences of opinion about religious truths that they found impossible to settle by violent or peaceful means. Hence faith in the rule of God collapsed and heresy disappeared along with the persecution of heresy. Instead, there emerged sovereignty. That is to say, there emerged a kind of public authority that refrained from all attempts to read the mind of God and devoted itself all the more effectively to stopping individuals who believed that they had read the mind of God from knocking their differently minded neighbors over the head. As a result the modern period has been dominated by the state, reason, and a gratifying tolerance for diversity of opinion, combined with an equally gratifying ability to suppress wrongdoing, which all right-thinking people realize deserves to be suppressed, as opposed to mere wrong thinking, which all right-thinking people will leave the wrong thinkers to practice as they please. That, in a nutshell, is the standard account of the history of European political thought.[2]

There is, as far as I can see, only one real alternative to the standard account. It is held by a minority of historians, but the minority is rapidly gaining ground.[3] It seems to be inspired by suspicion of a

[2]More precisely, it is the underlying assumption that frames standard accounts of the history of political thought. As such, it is present in works like George H. Sabine, *A History of Political Theory*, 4th ed. (Hinsdale, Ill.: Dryden Press, 1973), or Leo Strauss and Joseph Cropsey, eds., *History of Political Philosophy*, 3d ed. (Chicago: University of Chicago Press, 1987). It is similarly present in classics with a sharper focus, like John William Allen, *A History of Political Thought in the Sixteenth Century* (London: Methuen, 1928), and Pierre Mesnard, *L'Essor de la philosophie politique au XVIe siècle* (Paris: Boivin & Cie, 1936). But most commonly historians of political thought holding such views act on them by paying little or no attention to the Middle Ages.

[3]Good examples are Ernest Gellner, *Nations and Nationalism* (Ithaca: Cornell University Press, 1983), R. I. Moore, *The Formation of a Persecuting Society: Power and Devi-*

historical narrative that makes us moderns look so much better than our medieval forebears, and perhaps by a certain respect for the principle that no one ought to be a judge in his own cause. According to the nonstandard account, the disjunction between the spheres of sovereignty and heresy is an illusion. We may call ourselves tolerant and enlightened, but in reality we are just as intolerant and superstitious as our medieval ancestors—if not more so. We no longer persecute heretics, but that is only because we persecute them without calling them heretics. Anyone with eyes to see and ears to hear ought to be able to tell that modern people have practiced persecutions no less, and recently much more, horrible than any practiced by medieval people. What is the nation state if not a church? What does that church aspire to, if not universal dominion? And what are the rights of man if not the articles of a modern faith on whose authority modern inquisitors have sought out, tried, convicted, sentenced, and killed thousands and millions of innocent victims both at home and abroad? In the light of such views the boundary between the Middle Ages and modernity is nothing but a semantic veil by which we try to hide our shame over having made no progress at all from medieval barbarism.[4]

---

ance in Western Europe, 950–1250 (Oxford: Blackwell, 1987), and perhaps Edward W. Said, *Orientalism* (New York: Vintage Books, 1979), though I am not at all sure that any of these authors would agree with my characterization. Michel Foucault, *Discipline and Punish: The Birth of the Prison*, trans. Alan Sheridan (New York: Pantheon Books, 1977), also deserves mention. Farther back there are Carl L. Becker, *The Heavenly City of the Eighteenth Century Philosophers* (New Haven: Yale University Press, 1932), and Carl Schmitt, *Political Theology: Four Chapters on the Concept of Sovereignty*, trans. George Schwab (Cambridge, Mass.: MIT Press, 1985; German original published in 1922). Still farther back lurks Friedrich Nietzsche, *On the Genealogy of Morals*, trans. Walter Kaufmann and R. J. Hollingdale (New York: Random House, 1967).

[4]There is yet another possibility that was popular among Catholic and romantically inspired historians during the nineteenth century, then fell out of fashion, but has recently had a revival: instead of blaming modern people for being just as barbaric as medieval people, you can praise medieval people for being just as enlightened as modern people. Look, for example, at Kenneth Pennington, *The Prince and the Law, 1200–1600: Sovereignty and Rights in the Western Legal Tradition* (Berkeley: University of California Press, 1993), and Pennington's teacher Brian Tierney, "Origins of Natural Rights Language: Texts and Contexts, 1150–1250," *History of Political Thought*, 10 (1989): 615–46. This is an interesting reversal of what I have just called the nonstandard account. Conceptually, however, the problems it poses are very similar to those of the nonstandard account itself. Like the nonstandard account, it erases the boundary between the middle and the modern period of history that is so crucial to the standard account.

There is something badly wrong with both of these views. On the surface, they may look very different from each other. But in fact they are not. They are diametrically opposed to each other, and as is often the case with things that are diametrically opposed, the similarities are greater than the differences. Both accounts reduce the range of possible relationships between heresy and sovereignty to two: either the spheres of heresy and sovereignty are mutually exclusive, or they overlap. Either there is a real boundary between medieval religious thinking and modern secular thinking, or there is not. In the first case, sovereignty is seen to be a principle of secular truth that is diametrically opposed to religious faith. Hence there can be no heresies in the modern world. In the second case, sovereignty is seen to be identical with a religious principle. Hence there are heresies in the modern world. The difference is that the standard account says "yes" where the nonstandard one says "no." But the conceptual instrument on which they rely is the same. And because it is a blunt instrument, it produces the same kind of misjudgments and the same kind of inability to account for the difference between medieval and modern political thought.

If you should object that this is a caricature of existing views of the relationship between heresy and sovereignty, I would agree. Of course it is a caricature. Every sensible person I know has doubts about the simple story of progress from the barbaric persecutions practiced by the medieval church in the name of faith to the enlightened forbearance of the modern state. And no sensible person I know maintains that heresies in the modern world cannot be distinguished from heresies in the Middle Ages.

Nonetheless, the caricature is justified. We may all know that it is a caricature. But I am not at all sure that we know how to replace it. One could add many finer points to the picture. One could soften the contrasts, expand the size of this essay to that of a book—or even many books—and transform it into something that could be called a history with more justice than the sketch I have just offered. But I doubt that any of that would replace the contrast between religious faith and secular truth as the chief means at our disposal for explaining what happened to political thought in the transition from the Middle Ages to modernity—and if it did, it would produce confusion. That seems to be our quandary: either we are stuck with caricature, or we reap confusion.

How to get out of that quandary? Consider the possibility that the spheres marked by heresy and sovereignty are neither mutually exclusive nor identical. Consider the possibility that sovereignty ought to be regarded neither as a principle of secular truth nor as a principle of religious faith, but as a kind of heresy. And then consider the implications.

That there is something heretical about sovereignty is not difficult to show. Let me give you two examples. One comes from Bartolus of Sassoferrato (1313/14–1357), perhaps the greatest medieval interpreter of Roman law. Bartolus is especially interesting because he is well known to have been in the vanguard of those who were trying to conceptualize something like sovereignty for the Italian city states and the kings of France and England as early as the first half of the fourteenth century. But there comes a moment when he confronts the question whether anyone may deny the right of the Roman emperor to rule the entire world. And his answer is that whoever did so "would be a heretic, for he speaks against the determination of the church and the text of the Holy Gospel, where it says that 'there went out a decree from Caesar Augustus that all the world should be surveyed,' as you can read in Luke, chapter 2. Christ himself thus recognized the emperor as lord."[5]

The other example comes from Pope Innocent X. In 1648 Innocent X had to decide whether he could approve the treaty of West-

---

[5]"Et forte si quis diceret dominum Imperatorem non esse dominum et monarcham totius orbis, esset haereticus, quia diceret contra determinationem ecclesiae, contra textum S. Evangelii, dum dicit, 'Exivit edictum a Caesare Augusto ut describeretur universus orbis,' ut habes Luc. ii. c. Ita etiam recognovit Christus Imperatorem ut dominum." Bartolus on Digesta 49.15.24, s.v. *hostes*, no. 7, in *Opera* (Venetiis: Apud Iuntas, 1570–71) 6:228r, col. a. I am taking the "forte" to go with "si quis diceret." If it is taken to go with "esset haereticus," Bartolus' claim would be more mildly put, but no less telling. I should add that interpreters of Bartolus are deeply divided over the question how to interpret his statements in favor of the emperor's right to rule the world, given his declarations that the Italian city states are free to publish statutes on their own and that the king of France recognizes no superior. Compare, for example, Marcel David, "Le Contenu de l'hégémonie impériale dans la doctrine de Bartole" in *Bartolo da Sassoferrato: Studi e documenti per il VI centenario* (Milan: Giuffrè, 1962), 2:199–216, and Maurice H. Keen, "The Political Thought of the Fourteenth-Century Civilians," in *Trends in Medieval Political Thought*, ed. Beryl Smalley (Oxford: Blackwell, 1965), 105–26, esp. 115–16, with Quentin Skinner, *The Foundations of Modern Political Thought* (Cambridge: Cambridge University Press, 1978), 1:10, or Kenneth Pennington, *The Prince and the Law, 1200–1600: Sovereignty and Rights in the Western Legal Tradition* (Berkeley: University of California Press, 1993), 197.

Constantin Fasolt

phalia. That treaty gave German princes as much sovereignty as they were ever going to enjoy, and it extended the same courtesy to Protestant and Catholic princes alike. Could the pope go along with that? Pope Innocent thought not. Why not? Because Protestants were heretics. Acknowledging the sovereignty of heretics was not among the courses of action he considered safe or sound. Hence he annulled the pertinent articles, explicitly on grounds of heresy—and in so doing effectively removed the papacy from participation in the European state system for a long time to come.[6]

In two important cases, one at the beginning of the early modern period and one towards its end, sovereignty was thus condemned as heretical. That, it seems to me, is a decent enough reason to regard it as a kind of heresy. But not, I hasten to add, unless we immediately go on to point out that it was a very peculiar kind of heresy indeed. It was heretical in that the will of the sovereign was obstinately and deliberately opposed to the dogma of the church. But it was peculiar in that it opposed only the reach of dogma, not its content, and that it ended up by confining dogma to the sphere of what we nowadays call "the church" in contradistinction to "the state," not at all by replacing it with an alternative dogma. Sovereignty is rather like heresy never brought to completion.

Seen in this light, the relationship between sovereignty and heresy is ambiguous. But I think the ambiguity can be resolved by distinguishing three consequences that followed from the invention of the peculiar kind of heresy that we call sovereignty.

The first is familiar. I would like to call it the neutralization of religion. The medieval church had been well equipped to deal with heretics who claimed to have a grasp on some alternative religious truth. Sovereigns, however, made no such claims. They simply refused to stand for battle on the grounds of religion. They stood for battle on

[6]Innocent X, "Zelo Domus Dei," in *Magnum Bullarium Romanum* (Rome: Typis et sumptibus Hieronymi Mainardi, 1733–62), 6/3 (1760): 173–75. For details see Konrad Repgen, "Der päpstliche Protest gegen den Westfälischen Frieden und die Friedenspolitik Urbans VIII.," *Historisches Jahrbuch* 75 (1956): 94–122. Repgen notes that the only major European powers not to sign the treaty of Westphalia were the two that were the fondest of universal government: the papacy and the Ottomans. He also shows in marvelous detail that Innocent X's annulment was not at all inevitable. But even though popes more like Urban VIII could very well have postponed the day of reckoning indefinitely, I am not sure that they could have avoided it altogether. Innocent X's action may not have been inevitable, but it was temptingly plausible.

the grounds of the particular territory they happened to control and the particular laws by which they aspired to control that territory— positive temporal laws, not eternal religious laws.[7] That was an enemy the church was not equipped to combat. From their point of view Bartolus and Innocent X were perfectly correct in their assessment of sovereignty. But the experience of a hundred years of religious war condemned their point of view to irrelevance. By the middle of the seventeenth century the choice seemed to be between continued support for religious truth as a foundation for politics, which meant war, and the replacement of religious truth with sovereignty, which meant peace. That choice was clear. As a result, religion was expelled from the realm of politics, and the very concept of heresy as an ingredient in the makings of political communities was effectively destroyed. By the eighteenth century, religion had been neutralized.

No one, I think, explained that kind of reasoning more succinctly than Jean-Jacques Rousseau in his *Social Contract*:

> All justice comes from God, who alone is its source; and if only we knew how to receive it from that exalted fountain, we should need neither government nor laws. There is undoubtedly a universal justice which springs from reason alone, but if that justice is to be acknowledged as such it must be reciprocal. Humanly speaking, the laws of natural justice, lacking any natural sanction, are unavailing among men.... So there must be covenants and positive laws to unite rights with duties and to direct justice to its object.[8]

The second consequence of the invention of sovereignty is not so familiar. But I think it is more important. I would like to call it the naturalization of religion. For it seems to me that the same people who expelled religion from the sphere of politics reintroduced it in the realm of nature.

---

[7]Jean Bodin was therefore only consistent in abolishing the distinction between moral and immoral governments as meaningless for political theory and asserting that sovereigns might very well be tyrants: "Yet the tyrant is nonetheless a sovereign, just as the violent possession of a robber is true and natural possession even if against the law, and those who had it previously are dispossessed"; Jean Bodin, *On Sovereignty: Four Chapters from Six Books of the Commonwealth*, ed. and trans. Julian H. Franklin (Cambridge: Cambridge University Press, 1992), 6.

[8]Jean-Jacques Rousseau, *The Social Contract*, bk. 2, chap. 6, trans. Maurice Cranston (Harmondsworth: Penguin, 1968), 80–81.

For evidence, let me refer you back to the quotation from Rousseau that I just gave you. Rousseau asserts that "the laws of natural justice, lacking any natural sanction, are unavailing among men." That assertion is an article of faith if ever I saw one. To be sure, I know of no rational proof for the proposition that the laws of natural justice do enjoy a natural sanction. But neither do I know of any rational proof for the proposition that they do not. I am not even sure what the laws of natural justice say. I am sure that Rousseau does not prove his assertion. Instead of offering proof, he offers an assumption. And the assumption is that the realm of nature and the realm of human affairs are separated from each other in such a way that the laws that obtain in the one do not carry over into the other.

That assumption, it seems to me, is the religious foundation of politics in the modern world. Perhaps it is better called a revelation than an assumption.[9] It underlies any number of other basic distinctions that we are accustomed to take for granted, like those between mind and body, subject and object, faith and works, morals and politics, science and history, nature and culture, male and female, public and private, self and other. It is also constitutive of sovereignty. For it is only on the assumption that the laws of nature have no effect on human society that it becomes intelligible why we might need sovereigns who make purely positive laws in order to preserve human society.[10] Sovereignty thus rests on foundations different from but no less religious than those of the medieval church.

[9]Rousseau was hardly the first or the most important recipient of this revelation. There is a famous statement in the fifteenth chapter of Machiavelli's *Prince* to rather similar effect. The categorical distinction that Luther drew between the kingdom of God and the kingdom of man belongs in the same context. And one could very well make a case for adding Marsiglio of Padua to this list. Rousseau is useful because he lived towards the end of the historical developments that transformed this assumption from the outrageous heresy that it appeared to be, to at least some of the more orthodox contemporaries of Marsiglio, into a self-evident truth. Hence he was in a better position to state it succinctly.

[10]It is telling, I think, that we use the same word to refer to the subject of the Cartesian *cogito*, the subject of scientific study, and the subject of a sovereign state. These are, respectively, the subject that practices science, the subject on which science is practiced, and the subject that allows itself to be kept in line by a sovereign ruler legislating rules of conduct that are, at bottom, arbitrary because science has not so far managed (and is now no longer expected) to accomplish what Descartes seems to have hoped it eventually would, namely, extend the success it enjoys in the study of nature by producing a scientifically grounded morality. Languages other than English make it more difficult to establish this point, but not at all impossible.

The third consequence follows directly from the first and the second. I would like to call it the blinding of the faithful. It is that the religious foundations of sovereignty are virtually impossible to recognize for modern people. Our historical experience has given us an example of what it means to have religion. The example is the religion we have neutralized. If you believe that you must be subject to the pope in order to go to heaven, that is religion. Or if you believe that the fundamental distinction in the world is between Christians and infidels, that is also religion. But if you believe that good citizens are subject to a sovereign state, that is not religion; that is common sense. And if you believe that the fundamental distinction in the world is between mind and body, that is also not religion; that is reason.

We remember all too well the religion we have neutralized. Therefore we have no eyes for the religion we have naturalized.[11] We have accepted the boundaries of nature as a matter of faith. We have not subjected them to examination, except in the narrow circles of professionals officially privileged to perform just such examinations and, of course, the not-much-wider circles of radicals, kooks, spiritualists, sectarians, anarchists, and other types of modern unbelievers whom we lack even the words to designate as anything other than dwelling beyond the limits of legitimate discourse.

Under modern circumstances it would therefore be a mistake to look for heretics in the area of religion. Religion is what we persist in calling the religion we have neutralized. But the religion that is in

---

[11]That may explain why there seems to be no good history of religion in the modern world—unless you take histories chronicling the multiplication of the several modern confessions or the history of secularization to be histories of religion. Expecting a good history of the modern religion from a modern historian is about as fair as expecting a good history of medieval Christianity from a medieval theologian. How can you write a history of "the truth"? Here we may be imitating our medieval forebears. Having neutralized paganism, they, too, were convinced that the religion to which they subscribed was actually a rational truth of nature, though they were less confident than we are about the ability of human beings to identify that rational truth without divine assistance. Thomas Aquinas, *Summa Theologiae*, I–II, q. 91, is quite clear about this. To be sure, he distinguishes divine law from eternal law. Divine law is what you find in the Bible. Eternal law is the law in the mind of God. But there is no substantial difference between them, and both are equally rational. The difference is merely that God has chosen to reveal one part of the eternal law to human beings—what he calls the divine law—but not the other part. See St. Thomas Aquinas, *The Treatise on Law [Being "Summa Theologiae", I-II, QQ. 90 through 97]*, ed. with introd., trans., and commentary by R. J. Henle, S.J. (Notre Dame and London: University of Notre Dame Press, 1993), 148–84.

effect today is the one that was naturalized in the early modern period, and we do not call it religion. Modern heretics are therefore far more likely to be found among the ranks of those who doubt or violate the boundary between nature and culture that is the chief article of faith in the modern religion. Witches were the first and may well remain the most telling example. There are good reasons why the persecution of witches overlapped with the age of religious wars; why intolerance of "unnatural" practices hardened as tolerance for religious nonconformity grew; and why persecutions of people perceived to be endangering the various manifestations of sovereignty can still be called "witch-hunts." These are related aspects of a single process. The same Jean Bodin who invented sovereignty and redefined the relationship between history, law, and nature published one of the most astonishing attacks on witchcraft to appear in the sixteenth century.[12] Interpreters have commonly regarded it as puzzling that a thinker of such stature should in this instance have proved himself so sadly superstitious.[13] I think he merely proved himself consistent. Which may help to explain why today's debates about homosexuality, abortion, and the relationship between race and intelligence are proving to be so peculiarly recalcitrant to any rational resolution.

We are slowly beginning to become conscious of these matters. That is a cause of some delight for an early modern historian like myself, who believes that a better understanding of early modern history cannot but increase that consciousness. But the delight is not altogether unqualified. It is worth remembering that there once were narrow circles of medieval professionals who enjoyed a privilege of examining the boundaries of the faith precisely analogous to the privilege enjoyed by their modern successors of examining the boundaries of nature. The age of religious wars began when one of those examinations (intended to deal with indulgences, announced in Wittenberg, composed in Latin) unexpectedly caught the popular imagination. The result was the violent disintegration of a social and

[12]Jean Bodin, *De la démonomanie des sorciers* (Paris: Jacques du Puys, 1580).
[13]See Stefan Janson, *Jean Bodin, Johann Fischart: De la démonomanie des sorciers (1580), vom ausgelassnen wütigen Teuffelsheer (1581) und ihre Fallberichte* (Frankfurt: Lang, 1980), and Ursula Lange, *Untersuchungen zu Bodins Demonomanie* (Frankfurt: Klostermann, 1970). Cf. Lucien Febvre, "Witchcraft: Nonsense or a Mental Revolution?" in *A New Kind of History and Other Essays*, ed. Peter Burke, trans. K. Folca (New York: Harper & Row, 1973), 185–92.

political order. It is a sobering thought that something like that could happen to us. Perhaps Francis Fukuyama has a point after all.[14] Perhaps we are facing the end of history. Not the one he had in mind, but the one that would follow from the disintegration of the modern social and political order in wars, not of religion, but of nature.

[14]Francis Fukuyama, *The End of History and the Last Man* (New York: Free Press, 1992). Briefly stated, Fukuyama argues that the modern, western, liberal state is the best form of social and political organization known to man that can actually be put into effect, and that the collapse of communism has proved it to be just that. It can therefore be expected to rule indefinitely. That would indeed put an end to history, except in the sense of working out the details. It is therefore worth pointing out that a similar position could just as plausibly have been defended by a prophet living towards the end of the fifteenth century. As Bernd Moeller, "Piety in Germany Around 1500," trans. Steven E. Ozmentw, *The Reformation in Medieval Perspective*, ed. Steven E. Ozment (Chicago: Quadrangle Books, 1971), 50–75, has been at pains to impress upon historians, the period just before the Reformation was not only a time when popular identification with the established church ran, by all reliable measures, at an all-time high, but also the first time in medieval history when not a single major heretical movement was threatening the established church. At that moment it could very well have seemed as though the steam had gone out of heresy and that the Roman Catholic Church had won for good. At the very same moment, however, witch trials were beginning to replace trials for heresy, and a generation later the Reformation was on the scene. There is no inherent reason to be sure that what looks to some like the decisive conquest of the world by the modern nation state could not similarly turn out to be the prelude to the distintegration of the faith by which that state is inspired.

IMP·CAES·MAXIMIL·AVG

1518

· H · BVRCKMAIR

About the Contributors

STEPHEN G. BURNETT is assistant professor of history, classics, and Judaic studies at the University of Nebraska–Lincoln. He is the author of *From Christian Hebraism to Jewish Studies: Johannes Buxtorf (1564–1629) and Hebrew Learning in the Seventeenth Century* (1996) as well as articles on Hebrew printing and anti-Semitism in Reformation-era Europe.

PAUL F. CASEY is professor of German at the University of Missouri in Columbia. He has held teaching positions at universities in Bonn, Germany, and Galway, Ireland. His research specialty is German literature and social history of the sixteenth century, in which areas he has published several monographs. His collected edition of the works of the sixteenth-century Saxon dramatist Paul Rebhun is in press.

PIA F. CUNEO is is assistant professor of art history at the University of Arizona. She has published articles on the art production of Renaissance Augsburg. Her book *Art and Politics in Early Modern Germany: Joerg Breu the Elder and the Fashioning of Political Identity* is forthcoming.

CONSTANTIN FASOLT is associate professor of medieval and early modern European history at the University of Chicago. His research focuses on the history of social, legal, and political thought. He is the author of *Council and Hierarchy: The Political Thought of William Durant the Younger* (1991) and is completing a book on Hermann Conring's (1606–1681) *New Discourse on the Roman-German Emperor*. In 1996–1997 he was a Guggenheim Fellow and a Fellow of the National Humanities Center.

MARC R. FORSTER is associate professor of history at Connecticut College. He is the author of *The Counter-Reformation in the Villages: Religion and Reform in the Bishopric of Speyer* (1992) as well as a number of articles on popular Catholicism in early modern Germany. He is currently completing a study of the development of Catholic identity in Southwest Germany in the seventeenth and eighteenth centuries

SIGRUN HAUDE is assistant professor of history at the University of Cincinnati. She has published and read papers on reactions to the Anabaptist reign of Münster (1534–1535), on Cologne during the Reformation era, and on confessionalization and political collaboration during the 1530s.

393

About the Contributors

HANS J. HILLERBRAND is professor of religion and history at Duke University. He previously taught at the City University of New York and at Southern Methodist University. He has published a number of studies on Anabaptism and broader topics pertaining to the Reformation. Most recently he served as editor of the four-volume *Oxford Encyclopedia of the Reformation* (1996).

EDMUND M. KERN received his Ph.D. from the University of Minnesota before becoming an assistant professor of history at Lawrence University in Appleton, Wisconsin. His essays on witchcraft and religious culture have appeared in *The Sixteenth Century Journal* and *The Journal of Ecclesiastical History;* his article on skepticism and social discipline during the end of the Austrian witch trials will appear in *The Austrian History Yearbook.* Currently he is completing a book manuscript based upon his dissertation, tentatively titled "Witchcraft and the Confessional State: Religion and Politics in the Styrian Witch Trials, 1546–1746."

DAVID MARTIN LUEBKE is assistant professor in the Department of History at the University of Oregon. His most recent work is *His Majesty's Rebels: Communities, Factions, and Rural Revolt in the Black Forest 1725–1745* (1997) and "'Naïve Monarchism' and Marian Veneration in Early Modern Germany," in *Past and Present* 154 (1997). He is currently at work on a study of confessionalism, popular culture, and the politics of princes and Estates in eighteenth-century East Frisia.

FRIEDRICH POLLEROß is professor of art at the Institut für Kunstgeschichte, University of Vienna. His areas of research are in portraiture, iconography, and artistic representation of rulers in early modern Europe. He is a member of the international research group "Lieux de pouvoir." He is one of the editors of the journal *Frühneuzeit-info* (Vienna) and a frequent contributor to lexica and other collections on early modern art and architecture. He is the author of *Das sakrale Identifikationsporträt: Ein höfischer Bildtypus vom 13. bis zum 20. Jahrhundert,* 2 vols. (1988).

MAX REINHART is associate professor of German at the University of Georgia. He is the author of *Johann Hellwig: A Descriptive Bibliography* (1993), *Johann Hellwig's "Die Nymphe Noris" (1650): A Critical Edition* (1994); co-editor of *Cultural Contentions in Early Modern Germany,* special double issue of *Colloquia Germanica* (1995), and co-editor of *German Writers of the Renaissance and Reformation, 1280–1580,* vol. 179 of *Dictionary of Literary Biography* (1997). His articles on fifteenth-, sixteenth-, and seventeenth-century German literature have appeared in international journals, collections, and lexica, and he is presently finishing an edition of the four political pamphlets of the younger Georg Philipp Harsdörffer and a study of the reception of Claudian in early modern Germany. He is the founder and past president of Frühe Neuzeit Interdisziplinär and was co-director of FNI's first international conference at Duke University in 1995.

About the Contributors

STEVEN SAUNDERS is associate professor of music at Colby College. His research interests include sacred music of the early seventeenth century and nineteenth-century popular song. His recent work has centered on music at the Hapsburg court in Vienna, and includes *Cross, Sword, and Lyre: Sacred Music at the Imperial Court of Ferdinand II of Habsburg* (1995) and *Fourteen Motets from the Court of Ferdinand II* (1995). He has received fellowships and awards for his teaching and research, including grants from the Fulbright Commission, American Musicological Society, National Endowment for the Humanities, and American Council of Learned Societies.

JOLE SHACKELFORD's recent publications include "Rosicrucianism, Lutheran Orthodoxy, and the Rejection of Paracelsianism in Early Seventeenth-Century Denmark," *Bulletin of the History of Medicine* 70 (1996); "Early Reception of Paracelsian Theory: Severinus and Erastus," *Sixteenth Century Journal* 26 (1995); and a chapter entitled "Seeds with a Mechanical Purpose: Severinus' Semina and Seventeenth-Century Matter Theory," in *Reading the Book of Nature: The Other Side of the Scientific Revolution*, edited by Allen Debus and Michael Walton (1998). He is currently assistant professor at the University of Minnesota, teaching in the history of science and technology program.

JEFFREY CHIPPS SMITH is a professor of art history at the University of Texas at Austin, where he has taught Northern Renaissance and Baroque art since 1979. His is the author of about 100 books, articles, and reviews including *Nuremberg, A Renaissance City, 1500–1618* (1983), editor of *New Perspectives on the Art of Renaissance Nuremberg: Five Essays* (1985), and *German Sculpture of the Later Renaissance, c. 1520–1580: Art in an Age of Uncertainty* (1994). The latter received the Phyllis Goodhart Gordan Book Prize (1996) from the Renaissance Society of America, the Vasari Book Prize from the Dallas Museum of Art, and was a finalist for the Charles Rufus Morey Book Prize of the College Art Association. Smith is currently a member of the board of directors of the College Art Association.

MICHAEL STOLLEIS is professor for public law and legal history, University of Frankfurt am Main, director of the Max-Planck-Institut for European Legal History. His main interests, centered in the early modern period, are in the history of the science of public law. Among the numerous titles to his credit are *Geschichte des öffentlichen Rechts in Deutschland*, 2 vols. (1988–92), *Recht im Unrecht: Studien zur Rechtsgeschichte des Nationalsozialismus* (1994), *Junges Deutschland: Jüdische Emanzipation und liberale Staatsrechtslehre in Deutschland* (1994), and *The Law Under the Swastika: Studies on Legal History in Nazi Germany* (1998).

KATHY STUART assistant professor of history at the University of California, Davis. She is the author of "Unehrlichkeitskonflikte in Augsburg in der frühen Neuzeit," in *Zeitschrift des historischen Vereins fUur Schwaben* (1990).

PAUL WALKER holds a Master of Music in organ performance from the University of Kansas and a Ph.D. in historical musicology from the University of Buffalo. He directs the Early Music Ensemble at the University of Virginia, is organist/choirmaster at Christ Episcopal Church, Charlottesville, and directs the Charlottesville-based ensemble *Zephyrus,* which has just released its first CD. His book *Theories of Fugue from the Age of Josquin to the Age of Bach* is forthcoming, and he is contributing the articles on fugue and related topics to the next edition of *The New Grove Dictionary of Music and Musicians.*

CHRISTOPHER S. WOOD is associate professor of the history of art at Yale University. He is the author of *Albrecht Altdorfer and the Origins of Landscape* (1993) and the editor of *Vienna School Reader: Politics and Art Historical Method in the 1930s* (1998). He is currently working on art and antiquarianism in Germany around 1500.

KRISTIN E. S. ZAPALAC is a faculty member at Washington University in Saint Louis, where she teaches students the intricacies of HTML and the Internet as well as those of the Renaissance and Reformation. Her first book *"In His Image and Likeness": Political Iconography and Religious Change in Regensburg, 1500–1600* appeared in 1990. Her second book focuses on the differing conceptions of self-identity and gender in the Jewish and Christian communities of western Europe and the Americas in the centuries between the first century C.E. and the lynching of Leo Frank in Atlanta in 1915 as seen through the lens of differing receptions of the story of Judith and Holofernes.

Index

Index

Index

Gantert, Moritz, 87-89, 99
Gardner, Howard, 217
Garstein, Oskar, 310
Gassendi, Pierre, 297
Geneva Company of Pastors, and Jewish printing, 344
geography, and history, 39, 44-46
Georg (Herzog of Bayern-Landshut), 280-81
Gerhard, Hubert
 Apocalyptic Woman, 163, 169
 St. *Michael Vanquishing Lucifer*, 154, 155, 157-58
Germany
 Reformation historiography, 40-43
 wars with France (1672-97), 24
Gerstecker, Augustin, 349
Gerster, Conrad, 86
Gerster, Georg, 89
Glarean, Heinrich, 212
Gleim, Johann Wilhelm Ludwig, 28
Gnesiolutherans, 304
Göckingk, Leopold, 29
Goethe, Johann Wolfgang von, 27, 29
Gompel, Margarete, 322
Gössingen village, 73
Gottlob von Justi, Johann Heinrich, 27-28
Grässel, Peter, 334-36
Graz, 48, 50, 122, 136, 145
Gretser, Jakob, *Triumph of St. Michael*, 163-64
Grotnitz von Grodnow, Carl Melchior, 23
Grynaeus, Johann Jacob, 344
Gryphius, Andreas, 23
Gualther, Rudolf, 344
Guernerio, Giovanni Francesco, 130-31
Günzburg, Eberlin von, *Mich wundert das kein gelt…*, 180-81
Günzburg, Simon Levi, 334, 337
Günzburg, Simon von, 180-81
Gurtweil village, 81

Häberlin, Carl Friedrich, 31
Hagenauer, Friedrich, 242, 243
Hailtingen village, 73
Hananiah, Joshua ben (rabbi), 284
Hanau-Münzenberg, Jewish press, 330-31, 334, 341-43
Hannas, Marc Anton, 169
Hannaway, Owen, 295

Hapsburgs
 and Peace of Prague, 22
 politicization of sacred music, 187-208
 rhetorical and emblematic depictions of, 126-27, 136-38
 rise and decline of, 25-26
Harr, James, 214
Harsdörffer, Georg Philipp, 23
Hartmann, Anna Catharina, 355
Hartmann, August, 104
Hartmann, Johann Adam, 355-56, 363, 364, 366
Hartmann, Johannes, 298n18
Hartmann, Marx Philipp, 365, 369-73
Hartmann, Mattheus, 355
Harvey, David, 44
Haude, Sigrun, 9, 313-27
Hauenstein county
 clans: Bächle, 82-89, 95, 97; Binkert, 86, 97; Brutschi, 89, 99; Dietschi, 89, 95; Dogern, 86; Dörflinger, 86, 98; Ebner, 89, 97, 98; Eckert, 88-89; Eisele, 92, 98, Fink, 89, 95; Gamp, 89, 99; Gärtner, 89; Gerster, 86-89, 100; Hüpfer, 89, 99; Jordan, 89, 99; Kaiser, 89, 100; Keppeler, 89, 97; Leber, 98; Mattner, 100; Schäffer, 87-89, 99; Schaller, 83-89, 92, 95, 100; Stigler, 98; Thoma, 89, 95, 97; Villinger, 89, 99; Vogelbacher, 89, 100
 factionalism in, 77-100
 health, 263, 349-79 (*See also* medicine)
Hebenstreit, Hans and Georg, 159
Hecht, Linda, 315
Heckel, Martin, 17
Heidfeld, Heinrich, 341
Heinse, Wilhelm, 30
Heinzelius, Jean, 342
Hemmingson, Neils, 300-5
Heraeus, Carl Gustav, 126-28, 131, 138, 143, 145
heresy, and sovereignty, 381-91
Hermann, Conrad (Franciscan), 281
Hermann the Cherusker, 15, 28
Heumann von Teutschenbrunn, Johann, 28
Heydenreich, Erhard, 237
Hildebrandt, Johann Lukas von, 127, 143
Hillerbrand, Hans J., 8, 245-69
Hirschfeld, Balthasar, 363, 366

Index

Karo, Joseph ben Ephraim, 287
Kerll, Johann Kaspar, 192
Kern, Edmund M., 6, 9, 35-54
Keuchen, Walter, 338, 345, 347
Kilian, Lukas (engraver), 158
kinship, and factionalism, 77-100
Kircher, Athanasius, 126, 140, 141, 199
Kißlegg village, 63
Klaj, Johann, 23
Klein, Julie Thompson, 3
Klinger, Friedrich, 29
Kleiner, Salomon, engraving by, 136
Kleist, Heinrich von, 32
Klopstock, Friedrich Gottlieb, 28
Koch, Margarete, 322
Koch, Olaf Jensen, 310-11
Koerner, Joseph Leo, 229
Krafftenfels, Jacob, 72
Krag, Anders, 300
Kristeller, Paul Oskar, 211
Krumper, Hans, 166

Ladurie, Emmanuel Le Roy, 258
Laetus, Erasmus, 305
Langenschemmern commune, 55-75
language, German purity movement,
    21, 23
Lapide, Hippolithus à, 20
Lavater, Ludwig, 344
law
    abbatical, 90-91
    constitutional, 19, 30-32
    courts, 17, 18, 27
    divine and eternal (Aquinas),
        389n11
    inheritance, in Austria, 92
    on Jewish printing, 333-34, 341-42
    public, and patriotism, 11-33
Lecler, Joseph, 246
Lencker, Christoph (goldsmith), 161
Lenz, Johann Michael Reinhold, 29
Leopold I, 25, 128, 188
Leopold Wilhelm (archduke), 192
Le Roy Ladurie, Emmanuel, 258
Libavius, Andreas, 295-97
Lichtenberg, Georg Christoph, 28
Limnaeus, Johannes, 19, 20
Lindroth, Sten, 292
Lingo, Alison K. 367-68
literature
    and architecture, 122
    Baroque, and imperial patriotism, 23
    Enlightenment, in Germany, 28-29

literature *continued*
    myth, 102
    patriotic, 22-23
    of Reformation history, 39-47
    Sturm und Drang poetry, 29
liturgy, and music, 219
Logau, Friedrich von, 23, 25
Lohenstein, Daniel Casper von, 23
Lollards, 326
Longomontanus, Christian Sørensen
    (astronomer), 302
Louis XIV, wars of, 32
Löwenstein, Uta, 348
Luebke, David Martin, 6, 77-100
Luther, Martin
    Ain Sermon von dem Wucher (1520),
        180
    on blasphemy, 256
    An den christlichen Adel, 180
    Exposition of the 82nd Psalm, 257
    on Judas, 108-9
    on prostitution, 263
    *Sermon von Kaufhandlung und
        Wucher,* 180
    Von den Juden und ihren Lügen, 252-53
Lutheranism, 342-43
    in broadsheet propaganda, 177
    in Denmark, 303-4
    and the Eucharist, 304
    and German drama, 117
    and German patriotism, 17-18
    and Jewish printing, 331, 342-43
    and music, 219
    and Paracelsianism, 297, 298, 309

McSheffrey, Shannon, 325
magic/magicians
    criminalization of, 258-59, 354
    remedies against, 364
Maimonides, on *erub* tradition, 284-86,
    288-89
Maldiney, Henri, 231
Mallet, Paul Henri, *Edda*, 28
Malleus Maleficarum (The Witchhammer),
    257-59
Malsch, Veit, 364
Mandrou, Robert, 267
Marc, Franz, 230
Margaret (saint), 377-78
Mariazell, 122
Marino, Marco, 337
marriage, Anabaptist practices, 321, 325
Marsilius of Padua, 18

Index

Index

Smissek, Johann (engraver), <u>149</u>
Smith, Jeffrey Chipps, 7, 8. 147-69
Smith, Jonathan Z., 248
social control, and deviance, 245-69
Society for 17th-Century Music, 220
Soja, Edward W., 44
sovereignty, and heresy, 381-91
Stadler, Hans, 359
Stange, Alfred, 229
Stephanius, Johannes, 310
Stolberg, Christian and Friedrich, 29
Stolleis, Michael, 5, 11-33
Stolz, Veit, 355
Storch, Niclas, 320
Strankhaar, Giselbertus (priest), 64-65
Straus, Raphael, 232, 282
Strauss, Gerald, 36-41
Stuart, Kathy, 10, 349-79
Sturio, Wilhelm (councillor), 333-34, 341
Styria duchy, 36, 47-53
Sulzer, Simon, 344
Sustris, Friedrich, 152
Sweden, Paracelsianism in, 292
Switzerland, persecution of Anabaptists, 254-55

Tacitus, 15
Tackett, Timothy, 59
Tafertsweiler commune, 72
Talmud, 330, 331, 333n11, 337, 339, 341-42
Targum, and *erub* tradition, 283-84
Tashbez, and *erub* tradition, 286, 287
Thannhausen, Burgau, Jewish press, 331, 334, 334n16, 335
theater
    Alsfelder Passionsspiel, 106
    Naogeorgus, Thomas, *Judas Iscariotes tragoedia ...*, 101-19
    Oberammergau passion play, 104
    Triumph of St. Michael play, 163-64
Theodosius, Codes of, 254
theology. *See also* religion
    adiaphora, of Melanchthon, 303-4
    and female independence, 325, 326
    and music, 219
    and the Other, 256-57
    Philippism, and Paracelsianism, 303-9
    and social control, 265
Thoma, Georg (headman), 85-86, 89, 91
Tiengen, Germany, 329-30

torture, 349, 354, 355
trade deficits, critique of, 176, 178
Trenkler, Johann Georg, 357, 358-59, 364, 365
Trevor-Roper, Hugh, 291, 292n1, 305, 312
Tridentine reforms. *See also* Counter-Reformation
    and local religion, 64, 66, 151-52
Trier, war with France, 24
Trog, Hans, 211-12
Tröndle, Joseph (miller), 79-80, 92
Trost, A., <u>134</u>
Truchsess von Waldburg, Gebhard, 151
trumpets, in religiopolitical music, 194-95, 201
Turks
    Türkenmode, 25
    war of (1593-1609), 19, 24

Union of Princes (*Fürstenbund*), 26
University at Altdorf, 19
University of Basel, 209
University of Cologne, 356
University of Copenhagen, 300, 302, 311
University of Virginia, 213, 218
Unteralpfen village, 80

Valentini, Giovanni, 190, 194, 195, 197-99
Venusinus, Jon Jacobsen, 304
Vest, Johann (doctor), 341
Vienna
    sacred music, 187-208
    public patriotism, 25
Virgin Mary. *See* Mary (Virgin)
visibility
    in *erub* tradition, 285
    and "Otherness," 248, 251-52, 254-55, 257-59, 264
Voltaire, François Marie Arouet, 30
Voss, Johann Heinrich, 29
Vulcanius, Bonaventura, 342, 344
Vultejus, Hermann, 20

Wagner, Karl, S.J., 168
Wagner, Richard, 209
Waldkirch parish, 82
Waldmössingen village, 61
Walker, Mack, 272